RICHARD HAKLUYT AND THE ENGLISH VOYAGES

PRINCIPAL NAVI-
GATIONS, VOIAGES,
TRAFFIQVES AND DISCO-
ueries of the English Nation, made by Sea
or ouer-land, to the remote and farthest distant quarters of the Earth, at any time within
the compasse of these 1500. yeeres: Deuided
into three seuerall Volumes, according to the
positions of the Regions, whereunto
they were directed.

This first Volume containing the woorthy Discoueries,
&c. of the English toward the North and Northeast by sea,
as of *Lapland, Scrikfinia, Corelia*, the Baie of S. *Nicolas*, the Isles of *Col-
goieue, Vaigatz*, and *Noua Zembla*, toward the great riuer *Ob*,
with the mighty Empire of *Russia*, the *Caspian* sea, *Geor-
gia, Armenia, Media, Persia, Boghar* in *Bactria*,
and diuers kingdoms of *Tartaria*:

Together with many notable monuments and testimonies of the ancient forren trades, and of the warrelike and
other shipping of this realme of *England* in former ages.

VVhereunto is annexed also a briefe Commentarie of the true
state of *Island*, and of the Northren Seas and
lands situate that way.

*And lastly, the memorable defeate of the Spanish huge
Armada, Anno 1588.* and the famous victorie
atchieued at the citie of *Cadiz, 1596.*
are described.

By RICHARD HAKLVYT *Master of*
Artes, and sometime Student of Christ-
Church in Oxford.

Imprinted at London by GEORGE
BISHOP, RALPH NEWBERIE
and ROBERT BARKER.
1598.

FIG. 1—Title page of the first volume of Hakluyt's *Voyages*, 1598 edition.

RICHARD HAKLUYT AND THE ENGLISH VOYAGES

GEORGE BRUNER PARKS

Edited, with an Introduction, by
JAMES A. WILLIAMSON, D. Lit.

Second Edition

FREDERICK UNGAR PUBLISHING CO.
NEW YORK

Printed in the United States of America

Library of Congress Catalog Card No. 61-13628

PREFACE TO THE SECOND EDITION

This book was first published in 1928 as Special Publication 10 of the American Geographical Society of New York. The volume had three objectives. The first was biographical, to assemble for the first time the record of the events of the life of Richard Hakluyt, whose collection of the *English Voyages* is a classic of the Elizabethan age. His life as an active scholar, government consultant, and man of letters makes a story of intellectual achievement and a measure of worldly success.

My second objective was to relate the life of Hakluyt to the oversea enterprises of trade and discovery which resulted in the expansion of England. His activity as geographical adviser to these enterprises and as persistent publicist for them is seen to be the key of his career. With his older cousin Richard, who set the example, he presented geographical or economic memoranda of advice or policy to Drake, Gilbert, Ralegh, and the Queen, as well as to the Muscovy Company, the Levant Company, and the East India Company. In developing this theme, the book adds confirmation to the historical thesis that Elizabethan enterprises overseas were not rash and headlong, but were undertaken after careful inquiry.

My third aim was to present Hakluyt's literary history, the record of his publications, their *raisons d'être,* their sequence, their importance.

By a not unusual coincidence, another scholar was at work at the same time, but unknown to me, on much the same material. Dr. E. G. R. Taylor, Professor of Geography in the University of London, published in 1930 a history of *Tudor Geography,* and in 1934 its sequel, *Late Tudor and Early Stuart Geography,* in which the Hakluyts naturally bulked large. In 1935 she edited for the Hakluyt Society *The Original Writings & Correspondence of the Two Richard Hakluyts* (series 2, vols. 76, 77). This work contains the basic documents of the lives and writings of both men. It finally clarifies the family connections—and I have made corrections accordingly in my Appendices I and II—and it casts further light on the personal relations of the Hakluyts with officials and merchants.

For Hakluyt's writings, I add one book, which I had overlooked, to those which he sponsored for publication, as I list them in Appendix III; in the same Appendix, I have brought down to date the list of studies of Hakluyt. For the great collection of the *Voyages,* I am aware that a more elaborate study should be made. We need a straight bibliographical record of the narratives it contains, item by item, with an indication of source and author, of extant manuscript versions, if any, and of later editions by the Hakluyt Society or elsewhere. This bibliography *raisonnée* would become more than voluminous in adding, as it must, a like record of the numerous voyage narratives which Hakluyt's successor Purchas inherited from him and published in *Purchas his Pilgrimes*.

Hakluyt's *Voyages* is still only a part of the travel writing of the Elizabethans, and the whole body of that writing needs its own history. Appendix IV of this book, a list of Tudor books of travel and geography, was meant to supply the basis for such a history. Further study, supported by a Guggenheim fellowship and a Huntington Library fellowship, has enabled me among other things to expand and reorganize this bibliography in my "Books of Travel" and geographical description to 1660 contributed to the *Cambridge Bibliography of English Literature* (vol. I, 1941, pp. 763-798; vol. V, Supplement, 1957, pp. 330-333). Other scholars have published significant works of bibliography. Professor Taylor has included in her books of Tudor geography an authoritative list of books on mathematical geography and navigation. Professor Edward G. Cox has published a massive record of all travel narratives before 1800 which have appeared in English. It has still seemed desirable to redesign Appendix IV here by including in it the Tudor works of travel which were germane to Hakluyt's interest as historian of travel overseas. Consequently I have omitted the works in mathematical geography and navigation, and those also on travel in England, and present as a new Appendix IV a new list of Tudor books of travel and geographical description overseas, noting also relevant maps done by or for the explorers.

In looking back finally over these thirty years, I applaud the continuing scholarly study of the Tudor voyages which has produced the histories of Williamson and Taylor and Quinn and Rowse and Mattingly, to name but a few, as it has produced the steady flow of editions for the Hakluyt Society of the works of travel themselves. Having celebrated its centenary in 1946, the Society still faithfully follows Hakluyt in the "search and discovery of the world" which was his ardent aim.

GEORGE B. PARKS

Queens College of the
City of New York

PREFACE

This book has evolved from a course of lectures delivered at Amherst College in 1919. The terms of the Rufus B. Kellogg Fellowship, which was the excuse for the lectures, require their publication. I am grateful to the Faculty of the College for admitting me to the opportunities of the Fellowship.

Those who knew Columbia University before the war will recognize in this book something of the cast of thought of Professor James Harvey Robinson. He has known nothing of my research, however, and is not to be blamed for the book. I am thankful to Professor Ashley H. Thorndike, of Columbia, for permitting this study to be made under his auspices, and to Professor Harry Morgan Ayres, who was good enough to read it. To Dr. A. J. Barnouw, Queen Wilhelmina Professor, I am grateful for special aid.

It is a pleasure to acknowledge the professional help of my colleague Professor Richard Foster Jones and of Miss Lilian J. Redstone in English libraries, and of the staffs of the John Carter Brown and the New York Public libraries. For the photograph of the Molineux Globe, I wish to acknowledge my indebtedness to the Honourable Society of the Middle Temple. Many friends have at times been caught in the wheels of my research, and many scholars to whom I am unknown have answered my appeals. I thank them here again for their patient help. Finally, I am grateful for the good offices of the American Geographical Society, which have gained for me the authoritative criticism of Professor Edward P. Cheyney and of Dr. James A. Williamson, the editor, and a final editing by Mr. A. A. Brooks, of the staff of the Society.

Tu terras, Haklete, novas meditaris et Indos,
Cataiaeque vias per freta longa doces.

—*William Gager,* 1583.

TABLE OF CONTENTS

ILLUSTRATIONS

INTRODUCTION

The Elizabethan age was not spacious, as we are sometimes told, but narrow and needy. It was a time of industrious study of man and nature as well as of books, and its adventures were undertaken not from swashbuckling zest but because good men found their country in a tight place and staked their lives and fortunes to redeem it. It was a time of more loss than profit, of more misery than glory. Drake's record has deceived many; he was an exception, not a type. He was supremely fortunate, but few of those who followed him came home rich; most of them left their bones in the tropics. Sir Humphrey Gilbert did hard and varied service and made nothing by it. Sir John Hawkins deserves to live less for his slaving than for his prosaic battle with corruption in the Navy Office. Sir Francis Walsingham, a chronic invalid, toiled for the state, lived frugally, and died in debt. And as a type of the merchant-patriot we may take old Michael Lok, who made a modest fortune in European trade, staked every penny on the Arctic passage to Cathay, was bankrupt and imprisoned, spent his declining years in exile, and is last seen at eighty, still writing and scheming for the discovery which would profit his country but hardly himself. If we probe beneath the incidents and seek out the motives we find no absent-minded empire-building but a reasoned, coöperative effort which left no means untried to attain a definite goal. The way of these men was hard, and their reward small. Posterity can see that they were successful beyond their dreams, but they themselves closed their eyes on failure; the success revealed itself slowly after they were dead. Richard Hakluyt's epic is no paean of victory but a tribute to service and suffering; his heroes are not "glorious" but "worthy." That is the best word he can bestow upon them.

The Elizabethan field has still its harvest to be reaped; and the Hakluyts, as their works are revealed in these pages, may point the way to it. That way is not chiefly to retail exciting incidents, although they have their illustrative uses, but to study history and to think.

From it there emerges the truth about Elizabethan efforts, and much more besides. For the sixteenth century is but the first chapter of the modern drama, itself preceded by a medieval prologue. In four centuries European man has attained to world power, power not only over other races of men but also over seas, deserts, jungles, and mountains, the obstacles of nature which have in previous ages circumscribed the actions of the most gifted peoples. He has not done this by superior intelligence, nor is it at all certain that he owes his success very largely to superior ethics. That and other circumstances are debatable; but at least it is clear that an indispensable factor in the process has been the series of reactions set up by the European world travelers of the sixteenth century. Discovery led to trade and to the plunder of helpless peoples possessed of mineral wealth. Stores of gold, silver, and gems became available as currency; great trading operations concentrated much of this wealth in a few hands; and before the close of that first century there were great capitalists on the Continent and smaller ones in England controlling a fund of fluid wealth ready to be directed to enterprise which promised further advance of the same sort. This prominence of the new kind of wealth was the most significant product of the age of discovery. Wealth in the form of landed estates had been real enough but not available for the promotion of mercantile undertakings; wealth represented by a strong room filled with bullion was a dynamic force, a concentration of power capable of being exerted in any direction.

There followed the seventeenth century, of colonization and the oceanic trading monopolies, systematically designed for the acquisition of more fluid capital. England, France, and Holland challenged and surpassed Portugal and Spain, who had been first in the field but had allowed their methods to become stereotyped and lifeless. Collateral developments aided mercantile efficiency. National law in strongly governed states rendered wealth secure. International law began to take shape and acquire validity. Religious inhibitions on the free use of capital grew obsolete. Joint stock, the sale of shares, insurance, paper substitutes for coin, all invented by medieval Italians for their Mediterranean trade, attained a world-wide vogue. Communication became more rapid, and the multiplication of printed books stored and transmitted a fluid capital of experience comparable to that of gold. The energizing force flowed into ever new veins, industry subdivided and specialized, comfort became more general, and untrammelled thought grew more ingenious in ministering to it. Social Europe in the age of Louis XIV was a different world from the Europe of the Emperor Sigismund and the Hundred Years' War—a tract of prosperity compared with a waste of brutish misery; and the story was yet at its beginning.

In the eighteenth century the colonies grew up and became nations; the thirteen English colonies of America at least did so, whilst those of Spain and Portugal developed in the same direction, and the little nucleus of Frenchmen on the St. Lawrence had multiplied to 70,000 when they came under the British flag. The multiplication of the American stock, even more than its political development, was the outstanding world phenomenon of this century. In 1700 the thirteen colonies contained about 200,000 people; every twenty years or so the numbers doubled; and by 1800 the population of the United States was over 5,000,000. These people were still almost exclusively agricultural. They imported nearly all their cloth, ironware, pottery, and luxury manufactures; and the reaction of this great new market upon the industries of Europe was immense. Central and South America added their demands. The West Indies of England, France, and Spain employed great numbers of slaves, enriched planters and traders, and called in their turn for manufactures in exchange for their products. In the East the process was different, but its effects were the same. Where the seventeenth century had witnessed trading posts in India, the eighteenth saw its conquest and the fuller exploitation of its market for manufactured goods. The Dutch extended their hold upon the islands of Asia, and all the sea powers reached farther still to tap the commerce of China. France, in spite of disastrous wars and more disastrous finance, expanded her trade abroad and her industries at home and, if she had reformed instead of destroying her institutions, might have taken the lead in the industrial transformation that has produced the world of today. That, as it fell out, became the destiny of England. Her ocean trade was as great as that of France; and her home population, which had to feed it, was only one-third as numerous. Thus demand necessitated a new kind of supply, mass production for distant markets, scope for the inventions of an alert people, and the application of a now enormous capital to the new organization.

A hundred years ago the world entered an unprecedented phase. "Modern history" began with the Renaissance; but, unless we are to apply the term to two very dissimilar periods, we must reckon that it ended with Napoleon. The age that then commenced awaits a name, and only its tendencies are as yet discernible; its main characteristics have still, perhaps, to show themselves. In one aspect it is but an intensification of the earlier process; more transoceanic settlement of Europeans, more tropical dependencies, more mass manufacture, more raw materials, much more fluid capital. But in another sense it is different. In the seventeenth century, even in the eighteenth, few men were conscious of change. There was a slow beneficent movement, but environment remained substantially unaltered. In the present period a man who lives out his years is born in one world and dies in another. The old, even the middle-aged, are strangers in an unfamiliar scene. The pace has many times multiplied in proportion to the duration of life, and one of its consequences has been the mental and moral unrest of the modern world. This rapid development is agreed to be, in the main, beneficial. Yet it has disquieting features. The question is not whether the advance of scientific organization is in itself desirable, but whether it may not be outrunning the capacity of man to adapt himself to it. With the statement of the question this survey reaches the limits of history and may fitly be brought to a close.

Such has been the working of the forces brought to birth by those old students, speculators, and men of action of the Renaissance. Apart from its intrinsic interest it calls for study, for it is only by knowing the past and realizing how it has produced the present that we can hope to control our own surroundings. Fertile scholarship is working towards a synthesis soundly based upon a multitude of special studies in which history, geography, and economic science bear the leading parts. That is only a statement of what the Elizabethans aimed at in their attempt to solve the problems of their time. And so we come to the special subject of this book.

The history of Elizabethan expansion is to a great extent the work of Richard Hakluyt, to a greater extent perhaps than the record of any other large movement can be ascribed to the labors of any one historian. He preserved a mass of material that would otherwise have perished, and he handled it with an enthusiasm and common sense which have made his work live through the centuries in a manner that its mere content would not have ensured. To appreciate that point we need only compare the collection of Samuel Purchas, similar in topics and greater in bulk, yet dull and repellent to the reader and not exploited even by scholars with the assiduity bestowed upon the *English Voyages*. Purchas arranged a museum; Hakluyt gathered the materials of a history and dealt so cunningly with them that they became a history whilst retaining their guise of raw materials—a double achievement which no modern editor has had the art to imitate.

The value of the *English Voyages* to compilers of narrative has long been known. It has perhaps been overestimated, for the riches of the book seem to excuse one for neglecting to look elsewhere. It is too easy to assume that Hakluyt is complete and that further research is needless. That, however, is not true; Hakluyt is no more complete than any contemporary historian can be. Political hindrances, personal jealousies, the reticence of men about their past, an honorable respect for such scruples, some inevitable falsity of perspective have all led to suppressions. The last of these errors is certainly the least conspicuous; in the main, Hakluyt's perspective from the sixteenth century is that which the twentieth century is rediscovering, and conscious omissions form the chief reason why research has need to dig under and around him. The reality of that need requires emphasis, and we may be sure that Hakluyt himself would today be the first to recommend it.

His work, which will be shown to consist of much more than the *English Voyages,* has another value, which has not been so well understood; it helps to reveal the ideas and outlook of the Elizabethans. The ideas governed the actions and can be understood by reading the textbooks of the time, by studying its propaganda and its personal relationships, and by scrutinizing its deeds before their proper background, the historical and geographical knowledge of their doers. Hakluyt did much to synthetize this knowledge for his own generation; but his contribution and that of others have been too little regarded by later interpreters, with unfortunate results to the presentation of history.

One may in fact be bold to say that the commonly accepted story of Elizabethan expansion is vitiated by false traditions concocted partly by those whose study has been too shallow and still more by those who have viewed too narrow a field. Instead of a reasoned unity we have too often a series of episodes, brilliant but disconnected, annals and not history. The brilliance conceals the defect. The details are so interesting—Drake's plunder, Gilbert's heroism, the flamboyance of Raleigh, the greatest costume actor in any age—that general readers and popular writers have asked for nothing more, have taken for granted that the Elizabethans were romantic and unaccountable, and have forgotten that the actions of large groups of men need a sober explanation and, for the performers, undoubtedly had one. So we have as a usual conception that Drake in his Pacific raid was nothing but a glorious pirate, that Hawkins was a mere slave trader and therefore disreputable, that Raleigh alone begot a colonial empire, that the East India Company was founded because pepper was dear, that the mass of English merchants and seamen were of no importance and need not be mentioned, and that Hakluyt was a literary man fired with romance, whose studies served for delight and nothing more.

Such things, it is true, are not expressly stated in learned works, but they are sometimes implied in them; for the romantic tradition has created such an atmosphere that even those who have read the truth in the records have allowed their vision to be fogged. In more popular writings the error holds full sway, for romance is a better seller than reality; and one-sided books continue to appear, overdrawing first Drake then Raleigh (they are the favorites) and exhibiting the special illusion of biographers, that their hero alone did everything notable in his age.[1] A more general theme is no less constant: that England's greatness was due to persons of poor character, scapegraces and ne'er-do-wells, a reckless, improvident, almost imbecile crew, and that Providence admired their boyish hardihood and brought to nought the subtlety of their rivals. That is a deception arising from an English habit of self-depreciation, first practiced by the Puritans as a pious reaction against the worldly self-confidence of their predecessors and remaining as a permanent strand in the national character. Cromwell, we may remember, going into action at the head of the best-trained army an English field had ever seen, ascribed the victory of "a company of poor ignorant men"—fifty per cent more numerous than their opponents—to divine intervention alone. Modern romanc-

[1] Written before the publication of Mr. Milton Waldman's *Raleigh* (London 1928), to which the remark certainly does not apply.

ers have seized upon the paradox whilst varying its terms. For the modest Puritan they have substituted the legendary younger son with his company of tatterdemalions, and they have obscured the truth that it was by organization and not improvidence that great leaders accomplished great deeds. A war-drilled generation knows better, but literary convention is apt to lag behind experience.

A different approach discovers a truer story. It is symptomatic of the methods so commonly applied in the past to the study of Elizabethan expansion that the life and work of Richard Hakluyt, the clergyman, and of his cousin, Richard Hakluyt, the lawyer, have never before been fully examined. The record of their careers is barren of adventure and almost of incident and offers no attraction to the romantic biographer. Yet, as Professor Parks shows in this book, it is an important record to the historian and one that gives him an established body of contemporary doctrine to which he may relate the diverse undertakings of the time; or, to use a metaphor, provides a backbone to which a dismembered skeleton may be articulated. More than this, it shows the doctrine in course of development, from the medieval ignorance of the age of discovery to the clear-cut aims with which the seventeenth century set forth on its career of oversea construction. In this process the elder Hakluyt (the lawyer) is virtually a newly discovered agent. We have had hitherto a very dim conception of him, but his function as an accumulator and exchanger of information is here established, to the strengthening of the argument that a conscious design inspired the actions of his age. His younger cousin had been more celebrated but always for only a portion of his work, and he too stands forth in a new guise as an unwearied agent in almost all the propaganda of the movement towards expansion. His unselfishness and breadth of mind have hitherto been guessed at rather than fully proved; and the revelation of his often anonymous contributions to the cause, both in labor and in money, places his fame upon a secure foundation.

Dr. Parks rightly makes the work rather than the private life of his subjects the principal theme. But he has not neglected the most trivial details, and those which would spoil the proportion of his exposition are elaborately dealt with in the appendixes.

The work of the Hakluyts can not by its nature stand alone. It must be related to the general advance of the studies in which they excelled. To handle that subject in detail would require several large volumes—Professor C. R. Beazley, it may be recalled, occupied three with his *Dawn of Modern Geography,* covering the introductory period to 1420; and in Hakluyt's century the material and its complexity are enormously magnified. The present book, therefore, can cover the ground only in an allusive fashion. It contrives, nevertheless, to indicate the milestones of advance and to name the foreign authorities in such a way as to furnish a guide to study; whilst an appendix contains a complete bibliography of the English works of the period. This, with the bibliography of Hakluyt's own writings, should prove an invaluable aid to scholarship.

In conclusion, it may be fairly urged that Dr. Parks has handled a difficult theme with unfailing mastery, with a balance and realism that will appeal to those who have read widely in the subject, and that he has made a solid contribution to the growing synthesis of oceanic history.

J. A. WILLIAMSON

CHAPTER I

The New Geography in Tudor England

1485–1553

In the year of the Spanish Armada, Richard Hakluyt, preacher, made ready for the press the book of the voyages of his nation. The stalwart black-letter volume has taken its place with the classics of heroism. Its author has taken his with the epic chroniclers. It is his book that has kindled and, more than any other, has kept alight the glow that illuminates the days of the great Queen.

So much is acknowledged. What is not yet told is the story of the man who made the *English Voyages*. He was not himself a sea ranger. He merely recorded the deeds of Drake and Raleigh, of Willoughby and Davis and Cavendish. Their deeds and their names have been honored with understanding. His epic has been honored, and his example; but he himself has been left in obscurity.

It is to lighten this darkness that I have presumed to write this book. It is the first life of Hakluyt. If only because it is the first, it will bring together a large number of facts about him that have not yet been noticed. His family connections will be established. It will be shown that he was the son of a London merchant, himself a member of a distinguished Hereford family. To explain his education at Westminster School and at Oxford, it will be necessary to speak first of his elder cousin of the same name and interests, Richard Hakluyt lawyer, and to tell his life story as well.

The lawyer came to his maturity at the beginning of the reign of Elizabeth, when English commerce started a new and important movement towards Africa and Asia. The lawyer shared in the movement, we can now observe, as a kind of adviser to merchant companies. At the same time he trained his ward and cousin to a life function. The lawyer found an avocation; the cousin made for himself a career and became the first professional geographer in England's history.

Both the Hakluyts had their special function in a complex society. It is no longer necessary to think of Tudor England as an age of brilliant individuals who improvised empires. Greater Britain was not built up in a fit of absent-mindedness. It was achieved by organized and intelligent action. The political organizing of the expansion is now a matter of common knowledge. The economic organization, the grouping of merchants and money behind the captains, is a matter of record. What I shall add is an account of the organizing of knowledge, the knowledge which summed up for both the merchant and the soldier the world's experience of commerce and colonizing.

The leaders of the expansion needed geography quite as much as they needed vigor and enterprise and personal splendor. They must know where to go, what to buy and sell and consume and produce, what peoples and climates and customs to be ready for. On these matters the Hakluyts became authorities. The elder came up to London for his legal training at about the time when the Russia Company was formed, in 1553, to set the example of remote trading and exploring; but he was later to advise the company on its ventures towards Cathay. He was consulted by the new Turkey Company of 1581, when England resumed the Mediterranean route to the East. He gave advice to Frobisher when, in the fifteen-seventies, Englishmen turned again to exploring and then to settling in America. He advised Gilbert on his Newfoundland colony and wrote propaganda for Raleigh.

The younger Hakluyt began in the fifteen-eighties where his cousin left off. He advised Gilbert and did much for Raleigh. He became a director of Raleigh's Virginia, and he was one of the four who received from King James the charter for the finally successful Virginia. He was equally active in the ventures that reached the East. He aided in the experiments of the eighties and nineties. He was lavish of advice, in the new century, to aid in the firm foundation of the East India Company. He mixed in other ventures, but these were the outstanding ones that carried the English flag to East and West. The history of Hakluyt's career is in large part the intellectual history of the beginnings of the British Empire.

Our clergyman thus stands as one of the heroes, one of the directing minds, of the new age. As one of its spokesmen, he necessarily adds his voice to the expression of the new national spirit. *The Discourse on the Western Planting,* which he wrote for Raleigh's Virginia, is the statement of a commercial policy and a colonial policy. It speaks with the voice of the new nationalism. The same voice resounds more majestically through the plain and noble narratives of the *English Voyages.*

To qualify as an adviser and a spokesman Hakluyt needed training in geographical science. For the frame of his knowledge he inevitably went back to Ptolemy. After the discovery of Ptolemy's book at the beginning of the fifteenth century, the Alexandrian was acknowledged as the great geographer of all time. Neither Columbus nor Vasco da Gama shook his authority. His book was repeatedly republished throughout the sixteenth century, edited and amended but still Ptolemy's

But there was a new geography, or rather a new geography was forming. The earth was redivided into four parts instead of three, and innumerable travelers brought in innumerable corrections of detail. Ptolemy could no longer suffice in the age of the discoveries. A geographer must apply to the records of travel themselves. These records were often printed in small volumes. They were digested into histories. By the middle of the sixteenth century they were already finding their way into great travel collections like that of Ramusio of Venice. But the records were not only in books; they were to be sought also in state papers, in traders' reports, and even in the memories of the illiterate.

Such records the elder Hakluyt studied for his clients. Such records the younger Hakluyt collected and studied all his life and published voluminously. As the story of his labors is pieced together in this book, it will become increasingly clear that he gave himself thoroughly to his science. It is no longer possible to regard him as merely a clergyman with a taste for other people's adventures. His was a professional devotion to learning, the devotion of the scholar of the Renaissance. In tracing his history I shall also be tracing in part the history of the revival of learning in England.

By the same token the *English Voyages* is not the result of a fortuitous inspiration. It now takes its place in Hakluyt's history as the flower of his career, the planned and purposeful career of the geographer. The Elizabethan epic speaks, I have said, with the voice of the new England; but it speaks even more clearly with the voice of that new era of the human mind which is known as the Renaissance.

The man Hakluyt was not, of course, a mere cog in a social machine. He was an honorable and respected clergyman; he led a normal family life. His social function reveals in him a more than normal energy and devotion; he was a personality. Behind the work of science stood the scientist—trained, eager, and unwearying. Behind the scientist stood the patriot, for whom the "love of my country devoured all difficulties."

But the scientist was the apostle of a new learning; the patriot was the spokesman of a new England. To understand Hakluyt, we must begin his story in his grandfather's time, with an account of the new learning in the new England.

2

England took a long time to discover, in the age of discovery, the sudden expansion of the world. That expansion was made, and made known, by the great seafaring nations; and England, despite its island site, was not yet a great seafaring nation. It was an agricultural country that exported wool, though it had begun to make the wool into cloth, and it depended largely on continental merchants for its trade and on continental ships for its journeyings overseas. Englishmen had not, like the Northmen, a tradition of the open sea. Like Chaucer's Shipman in the thirteen-hundreds, they sailed "from Gootland [Baltic] to the Cape of Finisterre" and into "every creek in Bretayne and in Spain." Englishmen had gone on the Crusades and individually had wandered about Europe and into Africa. But as a whole they kept to the adjacent coasts. They exported wool to Flanders. They imported wine and woad from Bordeaux. They had begun, in the fifteenth century, to exchange woolen goods for timber in the Baltic, for luxuries at Lisbon and in the Levant. But a large part of their trade was still carried by Venetians and Germans, and even their supply of fish was shipped in the main by foreigners.

It is not surprising, then, that Englishmen took small part in the discoveries of the fourteenth and fifteenth centuries. Italian merchants and mariners gathered exotic wares from the ends of the Mediterranean and traveled to the heart of Asia and to China. Portuguese, Spaniards, and Frenchmen crept down the fringe of Africa and at last launched out across the Atlantic to reach the wealth of Cathay direct. While other Europeans were approaching the boundaries of their world with the new instrument of the magnetic needle and with the new need of markets, Englishmen remained unmoved at home.[1]

They might have been more active if the latitude of England had been lower. The fishermen who sailed from Bristol north to Iceland were not unmoved. Perhaps as early as 1480 they sailed west instead of north. They went out in the several voyages of the Cabots, from 1497 on, and found some western islands which happened to belong to a new world. But they found little to tempt them farther; and if Columbus had sailed west from England, he would have found no more than the Cabots and would hardly have repeated his voyage. And Henry VII was not unmoved. If he did not favor Columbus,[2] he encouraged the plans of the Cabots, and his son after him listened eagerly to explorers. For a time the merchants of Bristol were as hopeful as those of Seville, and the scouting of the Cabots grew into several voyages of great expectations. But the passage to Asia was not found. North America revealed no treasure, no useful commodity but fish. And the activity of Bristol, instead of founding a New England to balance a New Spain, merely discovered a new fishing ground.

It is not surprising that the remote island which itself took small part in the discoveries should seem hardly aware of the discoveries of other nations. Of the vigorous intellectual activity that stirred Europeans, from Cracow to Seville, to set down the new knowledge of the world, there is hardly any sign in England. Continental presses were from the first set busily to work to print in many languages the epochal letters of Columbus and Vespucci and later the first history of

[1] The most satisfactory account of English maritime and commercial enterprise in the period is given by James A. Williamson, *Maritime Enterprise 1485–1558* (Oxford 1913).

[2] Henry Vignaud, *La grande entreprise de Christophe Colombe*, I 453–479 (Paris 1911).

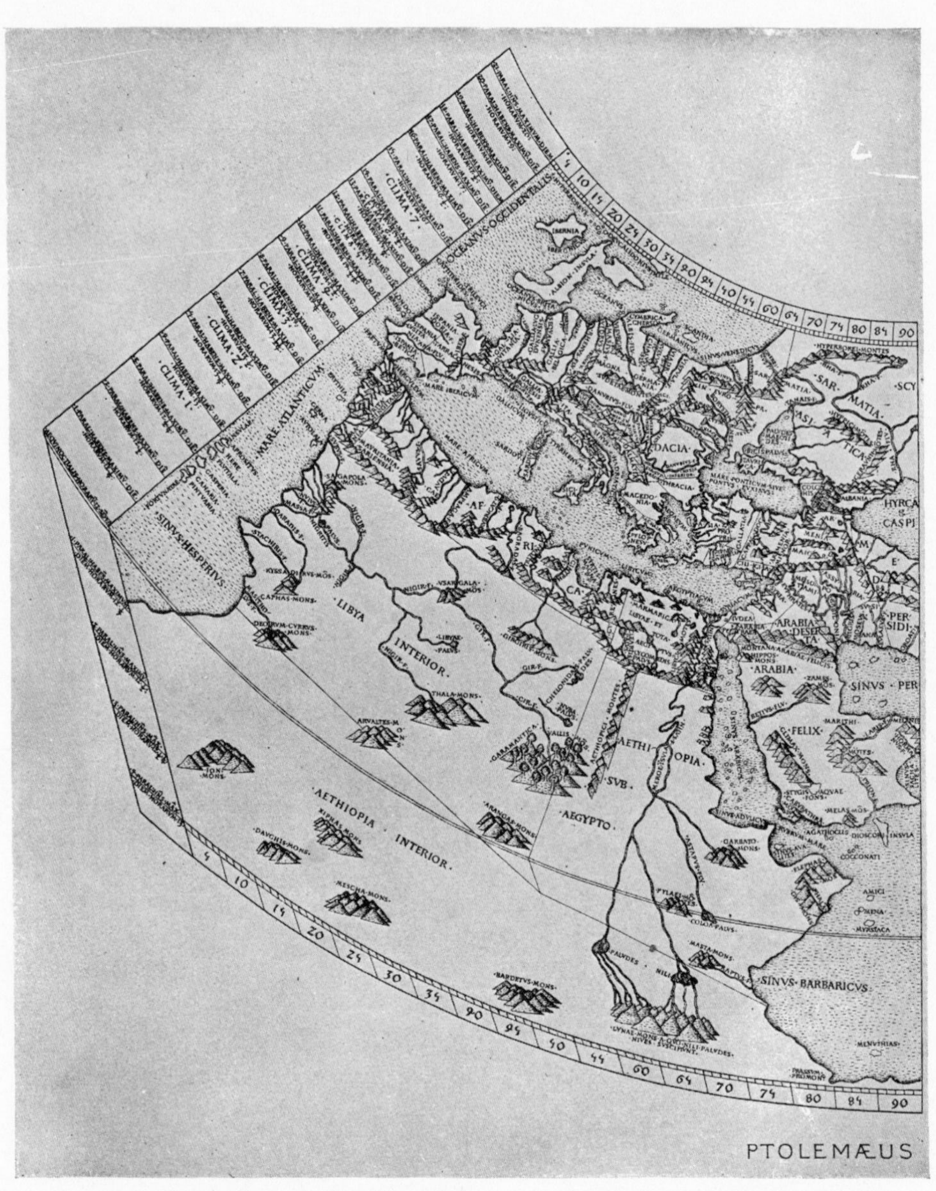

FIG. 2—The World according to Ptolemy. From his *Geographia*, 1490 edition.

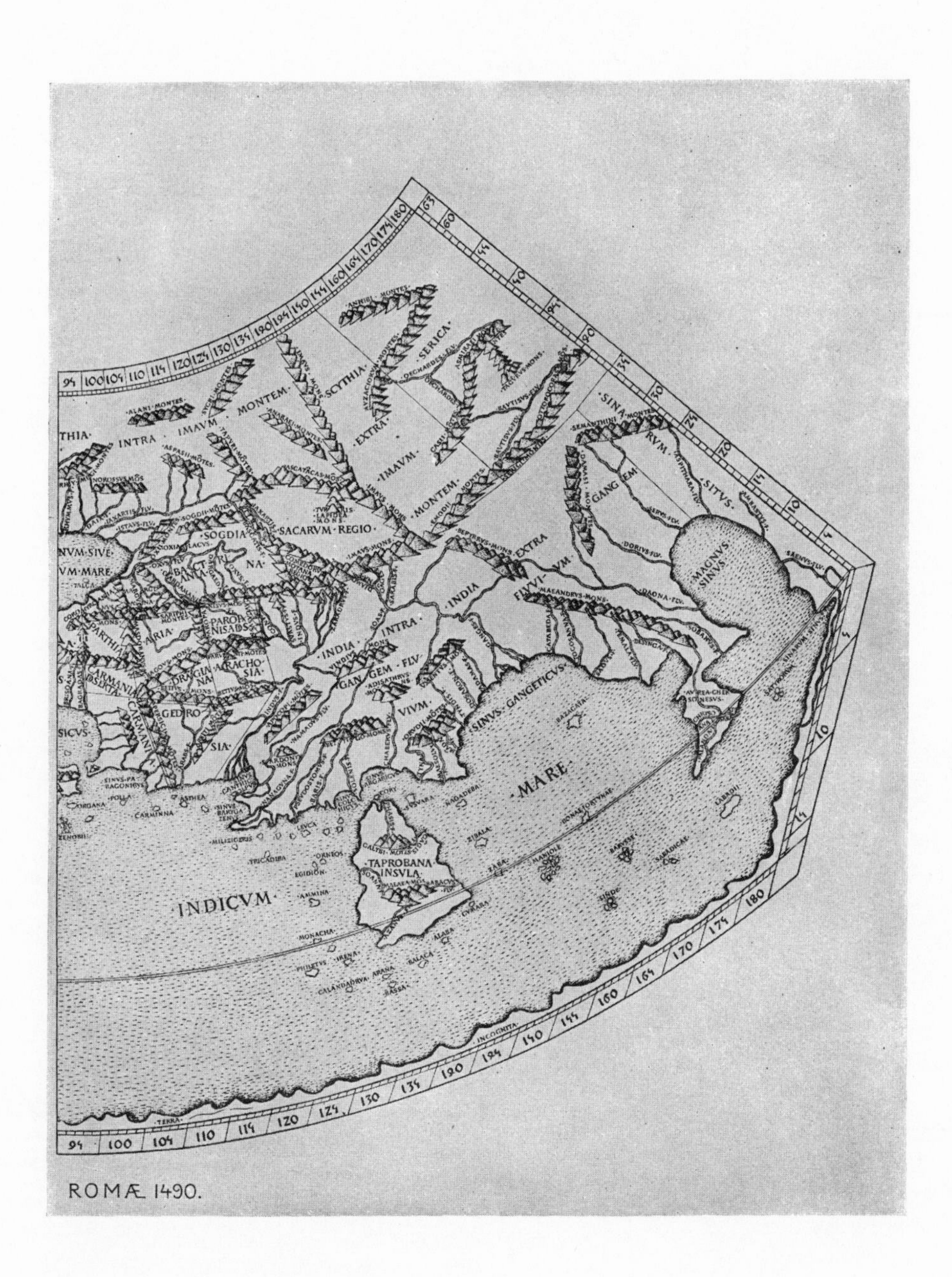

INTRA IMAVM MONTEM
SCYTHIA
EXTRA
IMAVM
MONTEM
SERICA
SINA
RVM
SITVS
SACARVM REGIO
SOGDIA
INDIA
INTRA
EXTRA
GANGEM FLV
SINVS GANGETICVS
MARE
MAGNVS SINVS
TAPROBANA INSVLA
INDICVM
ARIA
ARACHOSIA
GEDRO
SIA
PARTHIA
ALANI MONTES

ROMÆ 1490.

the discoveries as it was told in the chatty letters of Peter Martyr. Ptolemy's geography (Fig. 2) was repeatedly reëdited and revised to include the new knowledge. Maps were drawn and remodeled, alike by professional navigators and by academic scientists. New geographies were steadily compiled by new geographers. Yet for sixty years after 1492 not a single geographical work of any importance was published in England to record an English interest in the new age or in the science that was expanding to account for it.[3]

I do not mean to say that there was no English interest in geography. The history of the science can show honorable names in earlier England. Bede revived and made current in the western world the Greek doctrine that the earth was round. The intelligent layman King Alfred added new geographical records to his translated Orosius. Roger Bacon improved on Ptolemy's estimate of the size of the earth. John Holywood's treatise on the sphere was a standard text in the schools. But at the end of the Middle Ages there were no English investigators to compare with the earlier ones, and even the classical geography hardly reached England until the sixteenth century.[4]

The books that England printed may explain this. Caxton, the pioneer, made an imposing publisher's list, and he did not forget geography. What geography meant to him may be seen in his two early titles. Higden's *Description of Britain,* of the preceding century, he published in 1480. Of more importance was the standard geography of the later Middle Ages, which Caxton twice published. This was the thirteenth-century *Mirror and Description of the World,* ascribed to Vincent of Beauvais. It was hardly a modern work nor a particularly useful one in the new dawn of the revival. Mandeville was rather better. His book was of the fourteenth century. It was an authentic record of travel to Cathay, even if it was not his own travel, and in its time was more popular than Marco Polo. When Pynson and Wynkyn de Worde both published Mandeville at the end of the century, they were clearing the way for the new geography.[5]

But the new geography had first to go to school to the geography of the ancients. Ptolemy was already in print in Europe when Caxton started his presses. Yet neither Caxton nor any other English printer gave attention to him, nor for that matter to Strabo, his observant predecessor, nor even to the encyclopedic Pliny. Those ancients, tow-

[3] The amplest history of American geography in the age of discovery is embodied in the *Narrative and Critical History of America,* edited by Justin Winsor (Boston 1884–89, 8 vols.), and for this chapter I have especially relied on Volume III, "Notes on Chapter VI," which are entitled "The Earliest English Publications on America." Henry Harrisse, *The Discovery of North America* (London 1892), is the later and more compact authority. For the advancing knowledge of the East I know of no authorities so comprehensive.

[4] C. R. Beazley, *The Dawn of Modern Geography 300–1420* (London 1897–1906, 3 vols.) is the main authority for the history of medieval geography, supplemented by J. K. Wright, *The Geographical Lore of the Time of the Crusades* (New York 1925).

[5] See E. Gordon Duff, *Fifteenth Century Books,* in *Bibliographical Society Publications* 18 (London 1917).

ering dimly above the medieval horizon, were to wait until the age of Elizabeth to be clearly seen in England.

They were to be seen, of course, in manuscript and in foreign editions; and it follows that some English humanists must have been aware of "cosmography," which lurked like a poor relation behind the astronomy of the schools. Geography was not mentioned in the Oxford statutes of the fifteenth century. But the lecturer on astronomy, which was mentioned, might happen to hunt out the *Almagest* of Ptolemy in the great new library of Duke Humphrey of Gloucester; and, if he went so far to the source of his science, he might go farther and find in the same collection the *Cosmographia* of the Alexandrian. He might also strike the geographical vein in Pliny, and, if he were a zealous student, he might take down the medieval encyclopedists, Bacon and Albertus Magnus and Vincent of Beauvais, who companioned Ptolemy and Aristotle and Galen in the same magnificent library.[6]

We do not know that he did any of these things. Nor can we infer much more from the studies of the humanists at the end of the fifteenth century. It may be important that Grocyn owned copies of Ptolemy and of Pomponius Mela's late-Roman textbook. In 1520 a copy of the latter work, along with new books on astronomy, was sold by an Oxford bookseller.[7] In 1511 the visiting Erasmus, who was later to publish the first Greek edition of Ptolemy, required of his ideal schoolmaster for the new St. Paul's School a knowledge of the classical geography; and it is possible that both William Lilly and John Rightwise were thus qualified.[8] Sir Thomas Elyot's *Governour,* of 1531, prescribed for noble youths the study of Ptolemy's maps, as well as of the standard classical textbooks of Solinus, Mela, and Dionysius of Alexandria.[9]

The science, therefore, was not forgotten. These chance gleanings among the humanists show an interest in at least the classical geography, an interest begotten of the revival of learning. One suspects that it was hardly a living interest; for both Erasmus and Elyot valued geography only because it illustrated ancient history. For them it was hardly a living subject. It was a discipline, not the instrument of a new age.

Perhaps this is not a fair criticism. Even if it were, there would be some masters and some schoolboys who would not be satisfied with just the amount of geography needed to understand the Peloponnesian War. Some humanists also are clearly out of reach of the same criticism. Sir Thomas More realized the living value of the science. In

[6] See the list of the Duke's volumes in *Munimenta academica* (Rolls Series), II 758–772.

[7] Grocyn's library is listed in *Oxford Historical Society Publications* 16 (1890). John Dorne's sales list is given *ibid.* 5 (1885).

[8] The *De ratione studii* of Erasmus is given in F. Seebohm, *The Oxford Reformers* (London 1896 edit.), p. 217.

[9] *The Governour,* I 80 (H. H. S. Croft edit., London 1880).

fact, he was the first Englishman to reveal in print an apprehension of the geographical revolution. His *Utopia* of 1516 could perhaps have been written exactly as well if there had been no discoveries since Plato. But it is a tribute to More's breadth of interest that his imaginary voyage led to the new worlds. He had read Vespucci's letters, which were printed throughout Europe. He had heard of new continents, although he did not know the name America, now nine years old. For his far traveler he imagined a Hythlodaye who had gone on Vespucci's fourth voyage westward and had then branched off on a course of his own. His Utopia he placed somewhere beyond Mexico. He had discovered the discoveries which were superseding Ptolemy.[10]

Another humanist was seriously interested in the new geography; but he was not English. The Spanish doctor Vives, brought to England for the instruction of Oxford and the Princess Mary, gave a just place to geography in his educational plan of 1531. Vives was a modernist; and, when he came to geography in his curriculum, he was not thinking only of its classical uses. Like Erasmus and Elyot, he recommended Ptolemy. Unlike them, he marked his interest in geography as a living science. He recommended not only the study of Ptolemy but also the study of Ptolemy's maps as now "emendated," or brought up to date. Even more, he went on to recommend the study of "the recent discoveries in the East and West from the navigation of our people," especially in the reports of Peter Martyr, their first historian.[11]

There was growing then, in court and university, an interest in the expansion of the world, an interest fanned by those humanists who looked to present knowledge as well as to past. How far that interest extended one cannot say. Here and there among the upper classes there must have been students of the science; yet they spent no enthusiasm in translating or editing or making treatises. At least there is no enthusiasm recorded, as there was to be after the middle of the century. If Englishmen thought of America at all, and I take America as a symbol of the new science, they must have thought of it as a fishing station near Iceland, or as an obstacle on the road to Cathay; or perhaps as the source of the drug guaiacum, which the new medical works were praising as a remedy for venereal disease.[12] Probably they did not think much of it. Certainly Alexander Barclay did not. His version of the *Ship of Fools,* of 1509, which is probably the first book published in England to mention "the new fonde londe," gave a section of satire to the "folyshe descripcion and inquisicion of dyvers countrees and regions."[13]

[10] The *Utopia* mentions Vespucci on page 14, Book I (Burnet translation, London 1838 edit.), and may have derived certain ideas about the Utopians from the record of Vespucci's first voyage. See G. Dudok, *Sir Thomas More and His Utopia* (Amsterdam 1924).

[11] Vives, *De tradendis disciplinis*, Book IV: quoted, as are other cases of the sort, in Foster Watson, *Beginnings of the Teaching of Modern Subjects in England* (London 1909), Chapter III.

[12] *New English Dictionary*, "guaiacum."

[13] *The Ship of Fools*, II 25 (Edinburgh 1874 edit.).

In fact, the first half of the Tudor century shows only one Englishman with an immediate intellectual interest in the new age. This was More's brother-in-law John Rastell, lawyer, printer, and man of letters; and his *Interlude of the Four Elements* is the only publication under either of the Henrys that reveals a more than casual interest in the new geography.

The *Interlude,* which may be dated about 1517, is essentially a lecture, disguised as a play, on natural science. In the part of it given to cosmography the lecturer is at pains to add to the geography of the schools. After the classic three divisions of the earth's surface he describes the new Quarta Pars, America; and it is important that his fourth part is not the South America which geographers had first set up as a new continent because it was first discovered, but the northern land which had been discovered from England some twenty years since. Some geographers were still describing North America as a group of islands. Others were making it a part of Asia and continued to do so. To call North America a continent was to be definitely aware of a fact known to pilots but as yet hardly admitted into books. Rastell was in touch with the very latest knowledge.

Furthermore, he assumed that the new continent still had attractions for English enterprise. When one finds that timber and fish were the attractions, one is sure that Rastell's knowledge was not merely academic. Bishop Bale was to call him "cosmographus," and he was one for practical reasons. The proof has recently come to light. Rastell was the promoter of a voyage to Cabot's islands, of which the outcome has long been obscure; and the play now appears to have been written in order to vent its author's disappointment. For the expedition had been looted by the mariners under the promoter's very eyes and halted before it had got clear of Ireland; and, whether or not Rastell won his suit for redress, he at least had his revenge in the bitter words of the play. I suspect that he had another motive as well, a motive that was also not academic. He was trying to provoke support for a further American voyage. Such a motive would explain his long lecture on timber and fish; and when it is remembered that, as a relative of More and a member of the Temple, he could command an influential audience, such a motive becomes extremely plausible. It may be, in short, that there is a definite link between the writing of the play and the project of 1521 for a second expedition from London.[14]

It may be judged then that Rastell became "cosmographus" for purely practical reasons—because he was interested in trade with the new world. At any rate, he was interested; he learned some geography; and he published a play which set forth some of his knowledge

[14] Rastell's enterprise has been revealed by Dr. A. W. Reed in the *Mariner's Mirror*, vol. IX, no. 5 (London 1923), where are printed the highly interesting papers filed in Rastell's suit in the Court of Requests.

and tried to turn it to advantage. This adventure in publicity makes him typical of most of the English cosmographers of the century. With but few exceptions, they were not academically interested in the science. As merchants, mariners, or colonizers they were to acquire knowledge for their special purpose and to spread it in print in order to guide their subordinates or to enlist subscribers. Interest in geography was to spread as geography became useful to trade.

It is to be noticed that Rastell did not follow up his first venture, either in enterprise or in publicity. Having started the first transatlantic voyage made from a port other than Bristol and having written the first English statement of the new discoveries as well as the first American prospectus, he seems to have dropped the subject. The reluctance of the City to carry on the plan of 1521 may have been one cause, the failure of the 1527 voyage may have been another—always supposing that he had something to do with those ventures. Being a printer of some initiative he might still have gone on to domesticate in England some of the new geographies or travel records, of which so many were being published abroad in so many editions; but he did not.

Nor did anyone else in his time. An occasional printer, in the twenties and thirties, issued a book or two on astronomy and geography; but when the books are examined, it is found that they do not pretend to any serious enlightenment. They are mere abstracts from Ptolemy or from medieval scientists. Except for the translated *Rutter of the Sea,* a table of sailing distances, they are remote, barely informing, unaware of any additions to the science since antiquity.[15] For its substantial revival in England, geography had to wait until the beginning in earnest of English trade with new countries.

Meantime the spark of humanism burst into unexpected flame. It was not Ptolemy or Columbus who inspired John Leland to his great geographical enterprise. Rather it was the passion for books. Leland set himself first to recover the "monuments of ancient writers" which might be scattered about the kingdom. Like the Italian humanists in search of Greek manuscripts, he found and preserved "many good authors" out of England's past and derived a catalogue of their illustrious names. So the love of books passed into the love of learning, and his work in biography furnished the plan and much of the matter for his friend Bale's *British Writers.*[16]

But Leland had not gone for nothing to St. Paul's School and Cambridge and Paris in the first flush of their humanist enthusiasm. Having rescued England's authors, he would now illustrate their patriotism and his own by drawing from them a description of England as it was. Sixty books, or chapters, he planned to write on An-

[15] See the list in Appendix IV.

[16] Leland's project is explained in his *New Years Gift* of 1545 (published 1549): reprinted in the introduction to the *Itinerary* (Lucy Toulmin Smith edit., London 1907).

cient Britain: one for each shire and for the islands round about, and additional ones on the nobility and on ancient place names.

A bookish humanist would have stopped there, content to revive the national past. For some reason Leland was not a bookish humanist. He was also a poet, and he went mad later on. Now he was seized with "a love to see thoroughly all those parts of this opulent and ample realm that I have read of in the aforesaid writers." So he set out about the shires and for six years or more went up and down the land taking notes.

His journeys over, he was able to say, in 1545, that "there is almost neither cape nor bay, haven, creek, or pier, river or confluence of rivers, . . . woods, cities, burgs, castles, principal manor places, monasteries, and colleges, but I have seen them." A survey of England was Leland's accomplishment. From the knowledge of books he had passed on to the knowledge of things, from the revival to the advancement of learning. Only the plan of his survey was published in his lifetime; but his collections and his notes were handed down and in the next generation formed the base of Camden's elaborate survey which he called the *Britannia*.

Leland's enthusiasm may have worked to further purpose. His printer, Reyner or Reginald Wolfe, had come to England from Strasbourg in 1537. While he was becoming King's printer in the classical languages, while his active presses made him many times Warden of the Stationers' Company, Wolfe's active mind led him to an even more grandiose plan than Leland's.[17]

He meant, wrote one of his assistants, "in his lifetime to publish an universal cosmography of the whole world, therewith also certain particular histories of every known nation." "After five and twenty years travail spent therein," he died, leaving his collections to his son. The labor was too immense for England's printers. It is uncertain how much Wolfe collected during his long travail. Only part of it came to publication, the great *Chronicles* of Holinshed and the descriptions of England and Scotland. But the plan was noble, and it links with Leland's as the great result, in two of the branches of learning, of the new intellectual passion.

The result was still far in the future. Leland's only published record of his work did not appear until 1549, and his *Itinerary* was not published at all until the eighteenth century. Wolfe's labors did not begin until Leland's were over, and they did not see the light until the later seventies. From other directions the new science was summoning its forces.

In the year 1547 a brilliant young humanist, John Dee, fellow of the new Trinity College in Cambridge, went to Louvain to study with

[17] Wolfe's project was explained by Raphael Holinshed in the dedication to Lord Burleigh of the *Chronicles of England* (1577).

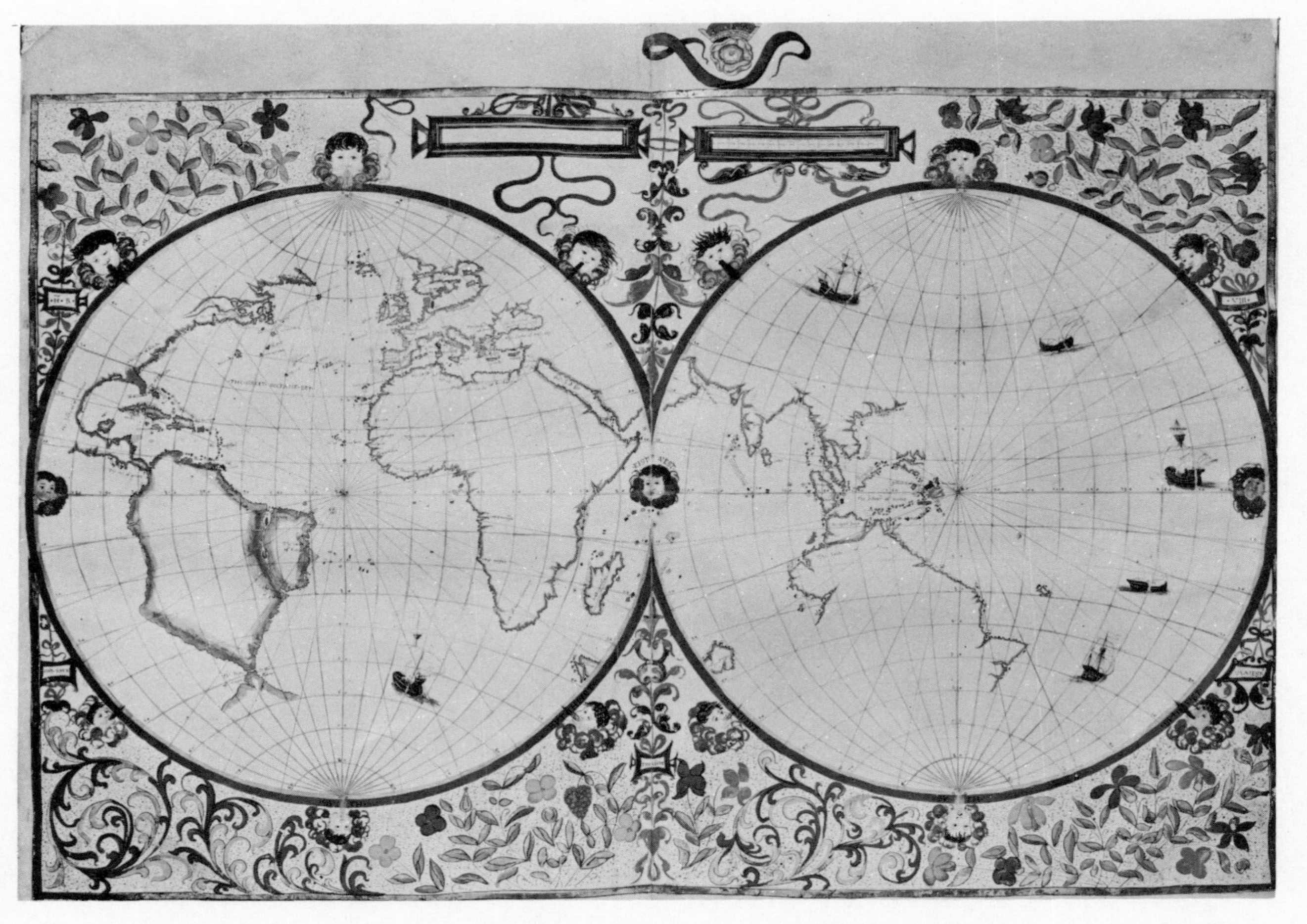

FIG. 3—A Map of the World, from the atlas made by John Rotz for Henry VIII, 1542. Royal MSS 20 E ix, ff. 29b–30. By courtesy of the British Museum.

Gemma Frisius and Mercator, the leading geographers of northern Europe. He returned at the end of a summer with a certain air of triumph and some new instruments. Two years later the new Cambridge statutes installed the study of the classical geographers—Mela, Pliny, Strabo, and Ptolemy—as a branch of mathematics. The two events mark the academic revival of this branch of learning, the climax of the labors of Erasmus, More, Vives, and Leland. The new geography was at last imported into England.[18] In the earlier year a parallel importation brought back to England the aged Sebastian Cabot. Cabot, the new geographer, was imported to direct a new and important English enterprise overseas. Both the new geographer and the new geography were to be useful in the imminent expansion of English trade. Geography was at length to be acclimatized.

3

Until the middle of the century, as the record shows, distant seafaring was a rare accomplishment with Englishmen; and until Englishmen went far afield they had small need of the new knowledge. It is true that Bristol merchants had sent out the Venetian Cabots in the wake of Columbus. Together with Portuguese from the Azores, these merchants had attempted, in the first years after 1500, to follow up the Cabot discoveries. Merchants of London had equipped Rastell's expedition of 1517 as well as the later ones to Newfoundland of 1527 and 1536. But though the first discoverer had been granted ten royal pounds for his "new isle," no other profits were found to justify more going to sea. The Cabot discoveries were at once recognized by the map makers of Europe. Henry VIII showed an intermittent interest in following them up. But they were followed up from England only by the few fishermen who competed with the many foreign fishermen on the Grand Banks.

Having little business in strange waters, the English needed little knowledge of the discoveries. It is recorded that the Cabot ventures were much talked of at the time; but the talk was a nine days' wonder. Whatever knowledge was needed could be imported from abroad to meet the occasion, whether it were the practical knowledge of a Cabot or the academic knowledge of an editor of Ptolemy. Casual voyagers may indeed have added to the national experience. Bristol fishermen may have strayed from Newfoundland into the St. Lawrence or down the Atlantic coast; but, if they did, they left no record sufficient to contest the French claim to that discovery in the twenties and thirties. English ships were to be found in the Levant bound for Aleppo or Rhodes or Candia; but their trade was small and ceased to be appreciable after 1551.[19] A Plymouth mariner like Wil-

[18] J. B. Mullinger, *History of the University of Cambridge*, II 110 (London 1888).

[19] Albert L. Rowland has just studied the Levant trade in *England and Turkey: The Rise of Diplomatic and Commercial Relations*, in University of Pennsylvania *Studies in English Commerce and Exploration in the Reign of Elizabeth* (Philadelphia 1924).

liam Hawkins, who made the first known voyages from England to Africa and Brazil in the thirties, may have brought back much knowledge of foreign lands; but the chances are that he was guided by French pilots when he got beyond Spain.[20] In the fifties the new African voyages to the Gold Coast, where Englishmen had not hitherto adventured, were led by a Portuguese pilot.

So for practical purposes English acquaintance with the new worlds was generally made at second hand. It was the foreign pilot who led the way. Maps were not yet good enough to venture by, and the foreign pilot knew the way. Just as Genoese mariners had been enlisted by Portugal in the fourteenth century to teach the Portuguese to sail down the coast of Africa, so foreign seamen were now to lead Englishmen into the unknown. The first voyage by veteran Bristol mariners to report discovery was led by Venetian John Cabot, who in 1497 found a "new Isle" and originated the English claim to North America. A Portuguese from the Azores led further northwest voyages from Bristol in 1501 and 1502, and Sebastian Cabot's voyage in 1509 to find the Passage may have reached the Arctic Circle. A planned London voyage of 1521 was blocked by objection that Cabot, a foreigner, would lead it. The Northwest expedition of 1527 was led by a Piedmontese. A northern voyage planned for 1541 was dependent upon a Spanish seaman, probably Cabot again, whom the king hoped to seduce from his allegiance. The African voyages of the fifties, I repeat, relied on the maritime lore of the Portuguese. And finally it was Sebastian Cabot who in 1553 launched, although he did not lead, the first voyage to the Northeast, the voyage from which can be dated the beginning of the English expansion.[21]

Nor did the employment of foreign pilots cease with the launching of successful English voyages. In 1563 Elizabeth promised a large reward to the Frenchman Ribaut if he would lead an English colony, instead of a French, to Florida. In 1562 John Hawkins found in the Canary Islands a guide for his first voyage to Africa and the West Indies, and a Frenchman piloted him to Florida in 1565. Drake dragooned Spanish pilots to guide him across both the Atlantic and the Pacific Ocean. A Portuguese, Simon Fernandez, piloted all the Elizabethan colonies to America; and in the eighties Portuguese pilots gave the younger Hakluyt his first direct knowledge of the East.[22]

If knowledge of the ocean routes was thus imported at need in the person of foreign pilots, specific information in geography was also obtained abroad. The instances are few of Englishmen gathering geographical knowledge, since there was little need for it. The first

[20] J. A. Williamson, *Sir John Hawkins*, pp. 7–9, 13–15, citing Plymouth customs records for William Hawkins' Brazil voyage of 1540 led by "John Landye" (Exchequer Records, E. 122, 116/11 and 13).

[21] Williamson's *Maritime Enterprise* is still the authority.

[22] See the narratives themselves in Hakluyt's *Voyages*.

example introduces the earliest, although not the earliest published, English book on the new worlds; and it was written in Seville. The author was Robert Thorne, a merchant there resident, son of one of the Bristol merchants who tried to follow up the Cabot discovery.[23] The book, or letters, of 1527, constituted an appeal to Henry VIII to "set forth" further voyages of exploration. It contained much geographical information, which was necessarily derived, as was the accompanying map, from Spain. It is not known if the *Book of Robert Thorne* had an influence on the king or his subjects; but an exploring voyage set out from London in the same year, and another nine years later.

Thorne's map was crude enough, and it may have been for that reason that the English king obtained the much better Italian map of North America (Fig. 3), drawn by Verrazano.[24] This again was not published; but its acquisition shows that the King, or someone else in power, was sufficiently interested to seek information from abroad. To Thorne's Spanish and Verrazano's Italian information must be added a third document, which was French. This was a manuscript *Book of Hydrography,* written in 1542 by a Norman mariner, Jean Roze, who was then serving in the English navy: a book which included an atlas of beautifully embellished maps, among them the first two maps of America known to have been drawn in England (Fig. 2).[25] Finally there should be added the atlas of marine charts, or portolani, which the Italian Battista Agnese dedicated to Henry VIII in 1536 and which is said to be more interesting as drawing than as cartography.[26]

Verrazano and Roze successively brought down to date the existing knowledge of North America: the one recording the voyage which had first announced in print that the coast was continuous from Florida to Cape Breton, the other recording the St. Lawrence discoveries of Cartier. Their maps show that someone in England was keeping up to date in knowledge of America and that that someone was probably official. In any case the foreign source of the knowledge is important to my thesis, which is again that for more than half a century after Columbus and Cabot geography was for Englishmen an alien product. The academic study of the science, in so far as there was any, was done in foreign books. The practical experience needed in an occasional enterprise was almost always imported in the person of

[23] *The Book of Robert Thorne* was first printed by Hakluyt in the *Divers Voyages* (1582) and was reprinted in *The English Voyages* (1589), II 159. I cite throughout from the Glasgow 1903–05 edition of the latter.

[24] The map in Hakluyt's *Divers Voyages* was modeled on Verrazano's, which Hakluyt there declares to have been obtained by Henry VIII. There was also a Verrazano globe. See Henry Harrisse, *The Discovery of North America*, p. 166.

[25] For Roze, see the *Narrative and Critical History of America*, IV 83; and E.-T. Hamy, in *Bulletin de géographie historique*, no. 2 (1889), issued by the Ministère de l'Instruction Publique, Comité des Travaux Historiques et Scientifiques.

[26] For Agnese, see Harrisse, *op. cit.*, p. 235.

foreign pilots. The specific knowledge needed to support oversea voyages was likewise imported, as is shown by the works of Thorne, Verrazano, Roze, and Agnese.

If the new knowledge was acclimatized in England after 1550, the change was in large part accomplished by the magical movement of trade, which required a corresponding movement of knowledge. The recall of Sebastian Cabot was the climax of the English demand upon European oversea experience. Granted in 1548 an impressive royal pension, the chief navigator of Spain was set to organize the decisive English enterprise. He launched the northeast expedition of 1553, which was expected to reach Cathay but which instead discovered Russia; and, when the results of that discovery were known, it was Cabot who was made in 1555 the first governor of the Russia Company, which may be called the parent of England overseas.

It goes almost without saying that the knowledge and experience required for this enterprise were by no means entirely foreign. English merchant adventurers were used to trading overseas, even if they were not used to trading with Russia or Cathay. English mariners were used to the seas, if not to the remote oceans. English enterprisers were used to the organizing of foreign voyages, to Spain, to Danzig, and even to Syria. But the special contribution of the foreigner was critical. The task of Sebastian Cabot was triple. As seaman and geographer he laid down the nautical and geographical directions for the voyage. As organizer and leader of expeditions he prescribed rules of discipline and trading methods. As entrepreneur even, though he is not known to have engaged in company promoting, he must have contributed to the organizing of the merchant company of which he was made governor. In all the elements of enterprise, in sum, his experience was potent.

A beginning once made, the direction of oversea affairs passed speedily to native hands. The Russia Company grew and prospered. It sent out annual ships to what is now Archangel and later to Narva in the Baltic. It cast its agents as far afield as Bokhara and Persia, to add to Russian timber and furs the luxuries of the East. When it did not prosper, it expanded in other oversea directions. But it remained essentially English. After Cabot's death in or soon after 1557 no foreigners were called to organize merchant companies except those foreign importers living in England who came to share their trade with Englishmen. Except for the abortive Ribaut colony, no foreigners were again asked to organize expeditions. Foreign sailors continued to be employed as pilots; but except in the case of the Virginian voyages, which were led throughout by a Portuguese, and except for some later African experiments, the foreign pilot was not needed after the first voyage. Foreign seamen or geographers were sometimes consulted as experts, as when Gilbert consulted the geographer royal of France on his colony; but no foreign expert was to be given a free hand as Cabot had been. Foreign works on geography continued to be used even when, as in the Frobisher voyages to the Northwest, no foreigner knew the country to be reached; but before the end of the century English geographers were supplying charts and even globes. As the organizing of distant enterprises was rapidly taken up by Englishmen, so the organizing of experience into the science of geography came more and more into English hands and especially into the hands of the two Hakluyts.

CHAPTER II

The New Geographers

1547–1561

The patient reader may well be wondering what has happened in this discussion to the science of geography. Our story began respectably with Duke Humphrey's library; but after some talk of the humanists, it immediately lost itself in an account of pilots and traders. Here is no science, one exclaims; here is only information, casual and unorganized.

The charge is true. There is yet, in our story, no question of science. Geographical science must start with Ptolemy; and even if Sebastian Cabot read the Alexandrian, it is doubtful if Thorne or Roze or even King Henry did. They may not even have read the editors and successors of Ptolemy, from Jacobus Angelus to Mercator. Much less did they edit or supersede him themselves.

I do not thereupon remark that the English are a practical people, who find science left a foundling upon the doorstep. To the rest of Europe science was quite as much a foundling. The chemistry of the sixteenth century was a by-product of the arts of medicine and metallurgy. So with geography. For Cabot was by profession as much a business manager or executive as a geographer. Mercator and Ortelius were engravers, the academic geographers were mathematicians; and in the Middle Ages geography had been kept alive by the sailing charts, or portolani, of the sailor rather than by the exercises of the schools. One does not need the wisdom of Solomon to judge between the academic and the practical claimants of the foundling. The case is decided for the practical. It was practice and not theory that, in England at least, was to bring up the foundling until it was old enough to go to school. Or, to speak in plain terms, it was the practical man who learned his geography as he needed it; and when he had become expert he no longer had time to be a practical man and sooner or later became a scientist.

He became expert very soon in Tudor England. The emerging of the expert is indeed a sign of the complexity speedily assumed by Tudor trade. The Englishman who had been overseas qualified as an authority on commerce and geography. Anthony Jenkinson, for example, who carried the Russia Company trade to Bokhara in the sixties, drew the map of Russia which became the European standard.[1] A man of action like Sir Humphrey Gilbert worked out for his own

[1] Jenkinson's map of Russia was used by Ortelius in his atlas, the *Theatrum orbis terrarum* of 1570.

FIG. 4—Queen Elizabeth. From Henry Holland, *Herωologia anglica*, London 1620.

FIG. 5—John Dee. Portrait in the Ashmolean Museum. Reproduced by courtesy of the Oxford University Press from *Shakespeare's England*, Oxford 1917, vol. I, opp. p. 473.

enterprises a *Discourse of the Northwest Passage,* drawing on the knowledge of books as well as of travelers. Even more surprisingly there appeared the type we may call the closet expert, the man who had not been overseas but who studied the experiences of those who had.

Occasionally there was room for the man of theory, the academically trained. In matters of navigation, which we may first consider, there was room for the mathematician, and first of all for John Dee, whom we have seen traveling to the Low Countries for instruction. He returned with globes and a complicated instrument, the "astronomical rings" of Gemma Frisius; and, it may be, he made some stir with them at Cambridge and elsewhere (Fig. 5). For he presently wrote for the young King Edward VI, and presented, probably through his fellow collegian the King's tutor, two astronomical treatises. One, of 1550, explained the use of the celestial globe; the other, of 1551, the movements of the heavenly bodies. These works are thought to have gained for Dee his royal recognition—at first in the form of a pension, later translated into two church livings—generally in the form of persistent royal claims upon his knowledge, which made him, for the next thirty years, a sort of court scientist. He was frequently desired to cast horoscopes. He fixed the day for Elizabeth's coronation. He journeyed to the continent for medical advice on the Queen's illnesses. He amused the court with his scientific apparatus; and when the court was interested in oversea matters Dee satisfied its curiosity.[2]

He was consulted in this way at the time of the first northeast expedition, that of 1553, which we think of as beginning in earnest the English expansion. For this voyage one might suppose there was least need of academic advice. The leading pilots, Richard Chancellor and Stephen Borough, were trained navigators with Mediterranean experience. The directing spirit of the enterprise, Sebastian Cabot, had spent a long life not only as navigator but as trainer of navigators; and he used not only his own experience but the full experience of the India House at Seville in drawing up the instructions for the voyage. Yet to supplement this, the best experience of England and Spain, Dee was found useful; for he drew out, for Chancellor's own use as he says, the astronomical tables, or ephemerides, on which depended all observations.

These tables may have been extensive enough to serve the Russia Company pilots for many years; but there is no evidence. The episode contains all that we know of Dee's relations with the company and with maritime matters in general for twenty years to come. During those decades the versatile court scientist gave himself to all

[2] The information about John Dee is drawn from the rather sketchy *Life of Dr. John Dee,* by Charlotte Fell-Smith (London 1909), and from the principal source of that book, John Dee's own account of himself which he called *A Compendious Rehearsal* (1592—printed in *Chetham Society Miscellanies,* vol. I, 1851). The task still remains of accounting for Dee's amazing scientific career.

manner of investigations as if he were a Royal Society in one person; and it was not until a second cycle of the expansion, which we may place about 1575, that he again opened his knowledge and his library to the uses of trade.

The reason probably is that, in matters of navigation, the navigators themselves fully realized the need of organizing their experience. That they did so may explain the slight influence of another academic scientist, William Cunningham. This Cambridge physician was amply recognized in his own profession, being summoned to lecture in Surgeons' Hall in London; but I cannot find that his excursus into geography and navigation was fruitful. His *Cosmographical Glasse,* of 1559, was an elementary treatise, mainly on mathematical geography. It was by no means up to date, and it was speedily superseded. None the less, it remains the first substantial English work on the subject, the first book to prove that England had at last taken up geography.[3]

That it was published at all—and it was an expensive volume—is probably the most significant thing about it. The significance is greater because it seems to have been a purely academic work. For its publishing I cannot find any other motive, as I can for most works of the kind. It was dedicated to Sir Robert Dudley, the later Leicester, and may have been the result of the author's study years in Germany and therefore another sign of the importing of the science. Dudley seems to have taken no interest in it. The hint in the preface that the author had other works ready was not taken up, and, except for an almanac or two, these other works remained unpublished. The *Glasse* itself did not satisfy the leaders of enterprise of the time, for they shortly afterward published another treatise of the kind, as I shall show in a moment. A copy was indeed included in the large ship's library that was later taken by Frobisher to the Northwest, but only, I suppose, because the book was unique in English. Hakluyt never mentioned it; the book was not reprinted; and Cunningham the geographer remains but an apparition.

The fact seems to be that the navigators themselves took up the theory of their art. Had they had their way, they would have built up a thoroughgoing school of navigation under state auspices. They had the Spanish model consciously before them. For it is not to be forgotten that, within fifteen years after the return of Columbus, the India House in Seville had founded a school for pilots whose cachet was indispensable to navigators of the Atlantic. Vespucci had been the first pilot major, or lecturer and licenser, and, from 1516 on, Sebastian Cabot. The latter may have attempted to found a similar

[3] What little is known of Cunningham is given in C. H. and Thompson Cooper, *Athenae Cantabrigienses* (Cambridge 1858, etc.).

school in England; but the Spanish example was speedily held up by another for emulation.[4]

The younger Hakluyt was later to hear the story and to record it for his own purposes. It concerned Stephen Borough, chief pilot of the Russia trade after Chancellor's death at sea. After the second attempt to force a Northeast Passage Borough visited Seville, probably in 1558, and was received by the pilots of the India House with the ceremonies due to so distinguished a colleague. From that reception Borough returned to England with an ambitious plan.[5]

The first step was easily taken. Borough persuaded the governors of the Russia Company to have translated and published the official India House treatise on navigation, the *Arte of Navigation* by Martin Cortes. This was not the first geographical book since 1553; it was not the first English work on navigation, since it followed Cunningham by two years. But it was the first work known to have been authorized by the leaders of trade, the first sign of an apprehension that not merely the experience of a Cabot needed importing but the formulated experience of Spain as well. The wisdom of the project is proved by the event. From its first appearance the treatise became standard, if we may judge by its frequent reprints throughout the century. Original works on the subject, such as Cunningham's, were to find their way into print, as were translations of other Continental works on navigation. Some original works were to be compiled later, as English sailors mastered their art, by such eminent seamen as John Davis. None the less, the book of Cortes continued to hold its own until well into the next century.

This feat accomplished, Borough passed to his more important plan of importing not merely Spanish knowledge but Spanish practice —of installing in England a school for pilots. Possibly, as chief pilot of the Russia Company, he kept some such school himself for the younger men in the service. But he wished the state to supervise the training of seamen; and he wrote a paper in 1562 which set down "Three especial causes (why the) office of Pilot Mayor is allowed and esteemed in Spain, Portugal, etc." Had the paper been approved, Borough would have been appointed to the office; but he was several centuries ahead of his time. He was indeed appointed to a post in the navy, perhaps with power to do as he desired; but nothing seems to have come of it. The task was left to others, notably to the younger

[4] The functions of the Spanish India House and Council of the Indies are discussed at length in C. H. Haring, *Trade and Navigation between Spain and the Indies in the Time of the Hapsburgs* (Cambridge, Mass. 1918).

[5] For Stephen Borough there is the *Dictionary of National Biography;* for his reception in Seville, the dedication of Hakluyt's *Divers Voyages* (1582); for his interest in Cortes' *Arte of Navigation*, the dedication of Eden's version of that work, reprinted by Edward Arber, *The First Three English Books on America*, Introduction (Birmingham 1885); for his "Three especial causes," Lansdowne MSS 116. William Borough's account of himself occurs in the dedication of his map of Russia and is to be found in the latest edition of Hakluyt, *Voyages*, III 209–212.

Hakluyt, to appeal for state support and control of mariners' education.

The education of mariners of course went on, as it could not help going on with men of active minds like Borough. An interesting testimony may be gathered from the life of his younger brother William, who may be counted a typical Elizabethan seaman. Dedicating to the Queen his map of Russia, William Borough thus wrote of himself:

"My mind earnestly bent to the knowledge of navigation and hydrography from my youth . . . hath eftsoons been moved by diligent study to search out the chiefest points to them belonging: and not therewith sufficed hath also sought by experience in divers discoveries and other voyages and travails to practice the same. I was in the first voyage for the discovery of the parts of Russia which began in anno 1553 (being then sixteen years of age), also in the year 1556 . . . and in the year 1557. . . . Since which time, by my continual practice in the voyages made yearly to St. Nicholas [Archangel] in Russia, or to the Narve [Baltic Russia], and to some other countries, also by sea: as likewise in passing from St. Nicholas to Moscow and from Moscow to Narve, and from thence back again to St. Nicholas by land, in the years 1574 and 1575 (being then agent in those countries for the company . . .): setting down always with great care and diligence true observations and notes of all those countries, islands, coasts of the sea, and other things requisite to the arts of navigation and hydrography. . . ."

With men of great care and diligence to consider the problems of navigation, the merchant marine may well have looked after itself without state attention; and indeed the results of the Spanish system had not been above reproach. One suspects, however, that English navigators continued to need training. Otherwise Frobisher would not have needed to call in Dee at the time of the northwest expeditions of the seventies. Otherwise it would not have been necessary to employ foreign pilots in the American voyages. Otherwise the younger Hakluyt would not have taken to heart the problem that Stephen Borough sought to solve, nor would his influential friends have tried to solve it as they did.

At any rate, something had been accomplished. As Englishmen made longer voyages they became interested in the art of voyaging. In addition to their necessary empirical training they learned to call upon the academic expert. Profiting by the Spanish model, they took to developing the theory of navigation, first in foreign textbooks, and then, after 1570, in their own. Finally, and perhaps most significantly, they realized the need of knowledge, the need of organizing experience for their ventures; and they built up some sort of mechanism for satisfying the need.

FIG. 6—Map of Russia by Anthony Jenkinson, 1562. From Abraham Ortelius, *Theatrum Orbis Terrarum*, Antwerp 1570, map 46.

FIG. 7—Mounted travelers of the early sixteenth century. From Royal MSS 18 D ii, fol. 148. By courtesy of the British Museum.

2

If commercial enterprise had thus drawn in its wake one form of intellectual enterprise, it had drawn along other forms as well. In launching their expeditions, the adventurers needed first of all to command a knowledge of navigation and of mathematical geography. This knowledge, which we may call the tactics of enterprise, we have seen in process of organization. They needed, in the second place, what we may call the strategy of enterprise: that is to say, the knowledge of oversea geography and especially of economic geography that might locate the markets to be attacked and so direct the expedition to its several destinations. We may suppose that the Russia Company looked after the organizing of this knowledge. The reports of its agents were regular, as we find them printed later in Hakluyt's collections. They were probably digested by merchants or captains at home; but there is reason to think that the arrangement of the reports required a special kind of person, that it soon became necessary to call into being a new kind of geographical expert. That expert I shall presently picture in the person of the elder Hakluyt.

Adventurers needed, in the third place, some measure of public interest in their ventures. They had to secure what we now call publicity. I do not mean that the need for publicity was either consciously felt or consciously supplied. Probably it was not even thought about before the days of the younger Hakluyt, in the eighties. The fact remains that while there were practically no books of oversea interest before 1553, an important beginning was made in that important year.

The first book appeared shortly after the setting out of the Russian expedition which it was meant to commemorate. Its contents bore little relation to the northeastern plan; but the *Treatise of the New India* was an apt choice. No great research had been necessary to find the material. Sebastian Muenster's *Cosmography* had been a popular European work for a decade; and in selecting that last part of it which dealt with the early Spanish discoveries—of Columbus, Vespucci, and Magellan—the translator paid a serious compliment to the explorers who were now setting out for a new unknown.[6]

It was Richard Eden who thus broke the long English silence on the new worlds. Richard Eden of Cambridge was formerly a Treasury official, perhaps at this time private secretary to Cecil. Upon what encouragement he published the *New India* is not known. Another official had turned his hand to like translations. William Thomas, Clerk of the Council, had made one recently of John Holywood's medieval treatise *On the Sphere* and another of a late Italian voyage

[6] Eden's first two American works are reprinted in full by Arber, *op. cit.* Of his translation of Cortes only the dedication is reprinted, *ibid.* In Arber's introduction may also be found the letter to Cecil concerning the proposed Pliny. The facts of Eden's life, with documents, are given by Arber and in the *Dictionary of National Biography.*

to Persia, but he had not published them. Eden may have been subsidized, though one cannot be certain.

Eden's preface testified merely to "the good affection which I have ever borne to the science of cosmography . . and much more by the good will which of duty I bear to my country and countrymen, which have of late to their great praise . . . attempted with new voyages to search the seas and new found lands." When therefore "there chanced of late to come into my hands a sheet of printed paper . . . entitled of the new found lands," a pamphlet which Eden found unworthy, "I thought it worthy my travail . . . (as one not otherwise able to further their enterprise), to translate this book." The idea was apparently his own, but his later dealings with traders suggest that the first English book on the new worlds was favorably viewed.

For a second and much more elaborate book appeared from the same pen in 1555, the year of the formal incorporation of the Russia Company. It also was a translation. It began with the first Spanish history of the discoveries. Then the work grew under Eden's hands; he went on to much compiling from many and varied sources; and the book at length became a large and shapeless compendium of oversea knowledge.

It was called *The Decades of the New World,* which was the title of the collected news-letters sent from Seville by Peter Martyr to various princes of the church. Of these *Decades,* of which ten had been written by 1530 by the gossipy member of the Spanish Council of the Indies, Eden chose the first three, so carrying the story of the Spanish discoveries down to 1521. To them he added an account of Magellan's voyage round the world; the text of the Pope's Bull of 1493, which awarded the transatlantic world to Spain; an account from the Spanish of the subsequent disputes between Spain and Portugal; and further descriptions of the new world from the successive Spanish historians Oviedo and Gómara. These selections gave a rough summary of the western voyages. There was more to follow. For the English reader Eden added, from the Italian, an account of the Cabot voyages to Newfoundland; several descriptions of Russia; and, new and unpublished material, accounts of the two recent English voyages to Africa. For good measure Eden then threw in a treatise on metals, the Pyrotechnica, and some remarks by the Dutch geographer Gemma Frisius on the measuring of longitude.

My summary gives a coherent idea of Eden's table of contents, which followed no logical order of arrangement; and the book was as far from being complete as it was from being coherent. What it did accomplish was to present for the first time in English or in England a substantial body of information on the new age, and, in addition, to list for the first time the names of the major writers on it. The native reader was now referred to the Spanish historians Martyr, Oviedo, and Gómara; and he was referred above all to the great Italian collection of Ramusio which was now appearing, the first thoroughgoing assembly of the records of travel. With this book we may say that England woke to the new day. The fact that the world had materially changed was at length made plain.

With this substantial achievement we may sum up the embarking of England on oversea affairs and oversea knowledge. A strong company had been formed to develop the new trade, to exchange English woolen goods for Russian timber and for Oriental treasures bought in markets beyond Russia. In the company were represented not only the City but the court as well, and the sending of envoys between Moscow and London made the trade semiofficial. To guide the new venture the pilot major of Spain had been brought to England to add his wider experience to the more narrowly mercantile experience of the City; and after his death in 1557 he was replaced by men like the Boroughs, who, by their relations with the Admiralty, made the development of the art of navigation also semiofficial. To the organizers of trade and the organizers of knowledge we may now add the recorder, in the person of Eden, who, had he remained in England, might have held the post of historiographer, as Spaniards were holding that post in Spain.

The inference is plausible. For Eden, dedicating his *Decades* to Philip and Mary, was rewarded with a place in the royal treasury. He speedily lost the post on suspicion of heresy contained in the book itself; but he remained in touch with the Russia Company, for it was he who in 1561 translated the *Arte of Navigation* which Borough had suggested, and it is believed that he was made historian of the company. Nothing came of this appointment, unless it was Eden who organized the company archives in the form in which Hakluyt was later to publish them; and unless he intended his translation of Pliny, which he proposed to Cecil in 1562, to be a contribution to geography. Whatever his relations with the state and with trade, Eden suddenly shifted his allegiance. In 1562 he entered the Huguenot service; he was out of England for eleven years; and when he resumed his translations he was already near his end. His death in 1576 transferred to the younger Hakluyt the duties of historian; but to Eden remains the credit for breaking out a path from English insularity, for publishing the first important works on geography since Caxton.[7]

To fashion the experience of past ventures to practical ends—what I have called the strategy of enterprise—is still a third intellectual function, separate from the function of an Eden, on the one hand,

[7] Mention should also be made of these other less important works of the fifties: manuscript translation (about 1550) of Josafat Barbaro, *Travels to Tana* [Crimea] *and Persia* (1487), a modern geographical record; translation, *The Description . . . of Aphrique* (1554), from the French version of the next item; translation of Johannes Boemus [Beham], *Omnium gentium mores* (1520), as *The Fardle of Facions* (1555). See Appendix IV.

and from the tactical functions of a Cabot or a Borough on the other. Whether Eden was a strategist in this sense I do not know. He is believed to have seen to the collecting of the Russia Company trade reports, perhaps as a sort of librarian. It is not known that he went further, to organize for further commercial uses the information contained in the reports. Possibly he was beginning to do so, and when he left England in 1562 his place was more or less speedily taken by the elder Hakluyt. This is, however, mere conjecture, as is indeed much of the earlier history of the company, since Muscovy House vanished in the Great Fire.

The gap between Eden and the elder Hakluyt is at any rate not long, and I come at length to the career of the latter. It has not been traced before, nor has its importance been at all realized. I shall therefore give his story in some detail.

Of him rather less is known than of his more famous cousin. Indeed the two continue to be confused, whereas it will be seen that their spheres of action by no means coincided. The elder man probably did not, like the Cambridge group of whom I have spoken or like his Oxford cousin, approach geography through the university. On the contrary, he seems to have come to it in empirical rather than academic fashion, as a kind of agent of commerce. His empirical approach was not, on the other hand, that of a Borough or a Jenkinson, or even of a Gilbert preparing his own enterprises. It was not the approach of a man of action. Nor was he again, as were Eden and his cousin, anything of an editor or an historian. His rôle was singularly specialized and, it may be added, unobtrusive. He had not the pretension of the scientist. Indeed, we do not know that he had any interest in the mathematical side of geography. He did not display the authority of the man of action nor the ambition of the man of letters. His function was singularly a function *ad hoc*. He gathered other men's experience, especially in economic geography and, having gathered it, retailed it as a kind of consultant. How he came to play this rôle in the new drama of commerce and colonization it will take a new chapter to explain.

CHAPTER III

Richard Hakluyt of the Middle Temple

1535?–1591

In the fifteen-forties John Leland was touring England on his geographical mission. Armed with a royal license, he passed from town to manor, taking the voluminous notes which he arranged as his *Itinerary*. Arriving in Herefordshire on the Welsh border, he was entertained at Eaton Manor, near Leominster, by the head of the house of Hackluit, who gave him some information about the family. Mainly he learned that "the chief and ancientest of the Hackluits have been Gentlemen in times out of memory, and they took their names of the Forest of Cluid in Radnorshire, and they had a Castle and Habitation not far from Radnor."[1]

"Times out of memory" means in this case some three hundred years, as modern history finds the facts. When King Edward I completed the conquest of Wales, Sir Walter Hakelutel (or Hacklitel) was placed in authority in several of the Welsh counties, rising in 1303 to be Justice, or royal administrator, of West Wales. Since his time many of the name had been knighted for similar feudal services. They had been knit by marriage with the leading border families. Though the name had been spread through many counties, the seat of the family remained for three centuries near Leominster.[2]

The family may have been Welsh, but the name was not. As I explain more fully in Appendix I, Sir Walter was called anything from Hacklutel to Hakelute. This is Germanic and soldierly enough. The name became simplified to the informal Haclet, which shows the Tudor pronunciation; but I suspect that a late family tradition aimed to make the name Welsh, as Leland was told it was, perhaps because a Welsh king reigned. The family may even have tried to say Hak-e-lew-it, or Hakelwit; but ignorant bystanders called it Haklet, and so may we.

I note something of the family lineage in the Appendix, though it is not very clear. I shall therefore not set down the long list of knights and esquires and priests whose names are scattered through the state papers of four centuries. I remark only that the name was distin-

[1] John Leland, *Itinerary*, IV 178.

[2] The initial source of information on the Hakluyts of Hereford is the Herald's *Visitation of Hereford* (edited by F. W. Weaver, Exeter 1886). But the pedigree there set down does not go back beyond the end of the fourteenth century. I am not including here the plentiful Hakluyt references in the state papers, to which I refer in Appendix I. I note only, as an instance of their number, that there are eighteen references to the first Sir Walter (died 1315) alone, in the Patent Rolls, Close Rolls, Inquisitions Miscellaneous, Feudal Aids, and so forth, in the times of Edward I and Edward II.

guished, and I pass to the event which opens the history of Richard Hakluyt of Eyton, gentleman and geographer.[3]

The event is his admission to the Middle Temple. Born probably in the fifteen-thirties, he became a law student in 1555, the year of the incorporation of the Russia Company; and the Temple records describe him as the son and heir of Thomas Hackluyt, Esquire, of Eyton in Hereford. His family and his profession were both important to his career. One is sure that he was of the family since his father was Esquire. One is not sure of his exact place in the pedigree.

A reason is that there were too many younger sons in a prolific family. Another is that our lawyer was born a generation too soon. The Herald who visited Hereford in 1569 and established the Hakluyt family tree found a large number of Hakluyts. He ought to have noted Richard, an eldest son; but he did not. The Leominster church registers do not begin until after Richard came of age, and there is no help there. One turns to the Chancery inquisitions, where one finds all one needs to know about the main line of the family; but all they tell about Richard is that he was next of kin to the head of the house, Thomas, who was master of Eaton from 1538 to his death in 1586.

A number of Hakluyt wills are extant. Richard's own will identifies his father as the Thomas Hackluyt of Eyton who died in 1544. Other evidence, as I explain in Appendix I, identifies Thomas as the son of Edmond Haklett of Eyton, called Gentleman. Beyond Edmond I cannot go. He must have been a younger son of some head of the house in the fifteenth century and lived and owned land in Eyton, close by the original Hakluyt manor of Eaton on the outskirts of the market town of Leominster.

Whoever this Edmond Haklett was, he had three known sons. One was Thomas, father of the present Richard. Another was Walter, a priest. Walter held a Suffolk living from 1522; he took the degree of Bachelor of Canon Law at Oxford in 1530; he died in 1538. A third son, Richard, was apprenticed in 1510 to a member of the Skinners' Company of London, becoming later a member of the Company and a citizen; he died in 1557, leaving a family of young children, of whom one was to be the editor of the *English Voyages* and the principal character in this book.

Thomas Hackluyt, father of the law student, may be safely identified as a government official. The state papers of the reign of Henry VIII reveal his various posts. From 1526 until his death in 1544 he was clerk of the Council for Wales and the Marches. For at least part of that time he was also clerk of the Princess Mary's Council, and he seems to have been steward in Wales of the Countess of Salisbury. He may therefore have had some legal training, though there is no record of him in the Inns of Court. If he did follow the law, it is

[3] The facts of Hakluyt's life and family are vouched for in Appendix I.

natural that the eldest son of his large family should take up his profession.

The son Richard followed the law all his life. Except for a year's interim, he remained a Templar in good standing until his death in 1591. Aside from practicing his profession, he continued to be a country gentleman. An orphan after his father's death in 1544, he probably succeeded to a small property, becoming his own master at about the time he entered the Temple. He had numerous relatives. In his own family there were four sisters and, by his father's second marriage, four half-brothers and three half-sisters. His stepmother married again and had more children. There is no record of the lawyer's marriage; but the marriages of his brothers and sisters alone must have brought him into kinship with most of the neighboring families.

Richard had some standing in the community. In 1564 he was declared contingent heir of Eaton and in 1586 came down to conduct for the Crown the inquisition into the Eaton property required by the death of the head of the family. The deceased left a son, as it happened; and Richard did not inherit, keeping only his portion of Eyton. This property he seems mainly to have leased out, though in the eighties he took some interest in stock raising, which was a typical Hereford pursuit; and perhaps he retired then from London and the law to a gentlemanly rusticity.

The importance of this Hereford background to Hakluyt's career is undeniable. He belonged to the gentry, which was not a mere landowning class but an official class. For Hakluyts who had been knights and landowners since the thirteenth century, and had gone to the wars in Wales, in Ireland, and in France, enjoyed the favor of the King and the nobility. The King's esteem they had found profitable, and the King's enmity, when they sided against him as they did against Edward II, not too dangerous. They had held provinces and property for the Crown, they had received wardships and other kinds of fees. They had been rewarded by the nobility whom they served, or whose widows they married, with revenues and manors.

Furthermore, the Hakluyts had been long and regularly represented in official posts. Following the Hakluyts who were administrators in Wales there were Hakluyts who were administrators in Hereford and elsewhere. They had been King's yeomen, commissioners for troop and tax levies, justices of the peace. They had been sheriffs and knights of the shire in Parliament. It is true that not more than one or two in a century had really distinguished themselves. The memorable ones had been Sir Walter, Justice of West Wales under Edward I; Sir Edmund, soldier in Wales, Ireland, and France under Edward II; Sir Leonard, soldier, sheriff, and member of Parliament under Richard II; Ralph of Eyton, Esquire, sheriff, and member of Parliament under Henry VII. There were many of the house who did not distinguish themselves at all, even as wrongdoers; but they probably prided themselves on the three battle-axes of their arms and the hunting horn of their crest.

Richard Hakluyt's immediate family seems to have responded to the changing situation of Tudor times. One uncle was apparently, to judge by his degree in the Canon Law, a church official. His father worked into the new administrative machinery which replaced the older military system of government in Wales. The other uncle left Hereford and landowning to become a merchant in London.

It is altogether natural that the young lawyer whose ancestors had attached themselves to the feudal frame of society should attach himself in turn to the new economic structure. By inheritance and by family connection he was close to both the administration and Parliament, close to Westminster; and the new commerce was at least semi-official. By family connection he was close enough, if he cared to be, to the City. By profession he was placed midway between Westminster and London, in the Inns of Court; and there were plenty of lawyers, from Rastell to Chief Justice Popham, who were organizers of foreign projects.[4]

I suggest these contacts of Hakluyt because one finds among them his incentives to geography. What the incentives were exactly, I cannot say. His interest in trade and geography hardly appears before 1570. It may then have come from connections with Westminster. It may have come from legal connections with the City. What these connections were it now becomes necessary to explain.

2

And first his profession. Just what career his admission to the Middle Temple opened to him is not easily decided. It is difficult to trace the career of any lawyer in the century unless he happened to rise to the bench. For what we can find out about Hakluyt we must search in the records of the Temple.

First, and in the normal course of events, he was admitted. The admission was recorded, together with the names of the members who stood surety for his bills—room rent and "commons." Hakluyt was introduced by a Bencher, or governor, and sponsored by a member who was soon to become a Bencher. Normally a student came up from one of the preparatory Inns of Chancery; but Hakluyt is not recorded as doing so and may have come direct from school or university, though whence one cannot tell.[5]

Once admitted a fellow of the Society, the student was constrained

[4] For some of the relations between the Inns of Court and the expansion, see C. E. A. Bedwell, *Brief History of the Middle Temple* (London 1909): Chapter III, America and the Middle Temple.

[5] The most satisfactory account of the organization of the Middle Temple is given in Sir William Dugdale, *Origines juridiciales* (1666), particularly in his reprint of a manuscript of the time of Henry VIII. I have verified Dugdale by the Middle Temple Records.

to from four to seven years of lectures and moots, when he might be called by the Readers, or lecturers, to the "Utter Bar." Though now a barrister, he was still not permitted to plead. He must endure further training for two or more years before he was permitted by the Benchers to appear in court. No record was kept in Hakluyt's time of admissions to the bar. The call seems to have been the prerogative of the Readers alone; it was not until 1574 that the "Parliament" of the Temple began to ratify the action of the Readers. It is therefore not possible to say when Hakluyt qualified. The question might even be raised if he were called to the bar at all, since the occasional orders against idle members and the frequent fines assessed against absentees show the number of dilettantes among the Templars.

But no fines were levied against Hakluyt, or at least none is recorded. He seems to have kept his vacations, to have attended his lectures, and to have paid his bills. He seems likewise to have taken communion at the stated times in the Temple Church, and to have worn no extravagant hose, nor allowed his beard to grow for more than three weeks at a time, nor worn his gown outside the Temple nor his sword in Hall. He seems to have obeyed the laws of the Society.

What duly enrolled barristers did in their profession was a matter which did not further concern the record, unless a member was called to the bench and removed to Serjeants' Inn or was appointed Reader in his regular turn or otherwise called to the Temple bench. Whatever his prowess otherwise in the courts, no notice was taken of it. He might be awarded dignities in the Society as a result of his professional deeds; but the deeds were not recorded. The records kept were those which would be proper to a lawyers' club.

Of the ten entries in the record which relate to Hakluyt, the majority are of the usual perfunctory kind. He appears as surety for a new member. He changes his room or his roommate. He is ousted, in 1584, from his lodgings, which are "forfeited for discontinuance." This we should expect to be the last of him: he has probably returned to his lands and his cattle in Hereford. But he suddenly reappears in the striking entry of 1585:

"Thomas Morgan and Richard Hackluit shall henceforth be associate with this bench for their commons. None shall henceforth be so associate unless he give £ 10, or plate, or some provision for the table, unless he be a Reader."

And at the time of his death in 1591 he is again occupying his chamber with Delabere, his roommate since 1575.

The explanation of this entry is found in a resolution passed by the Society in 1568. It was "ordered that all who paid a fine for the omission of their readings, if hereafter they are promoted to the Bench on account of their age, skill in law, or dignity of their offices, shall be considered as Masters of the Bench . . . except that they shall have no voice, place, or seat in (the Society) Parliament." Those who had declined to take their turn as Reader, or lecturer, usually because of the expensive entertainment they were required to provide, and who accordingly dined at a table by themselves as Ancients, could be made associate Benchers, or governors of an honorary sort. Hakluyt's elevation may have been due to one of the three qualifications. Seniority was one and, now that he had been thirty years in the Temple, a plausible one. Skill in law or success in the profession was another. Public office, such as a law office under the Crown, was the third. The last is obviously not Hakluyt's case, unless public office be extended to mean political activities, since there is no clear record of his holding office.

The political activities remain to be considered, since it is impossible to trace Hakluyt's professional career. He may have been a successful barrister, if not so distinguished as to be called to the bench; but the facts are undiscoverable. Within the Temple, to sum up, he was probably called to the bar in due course. In due course he declined his turn as Reader and transferred, in the seventies, to the Ancients' table. Continuing in that presumable mediocrity, he was eventually called to be an associate Bencher. The crown of this respectable career was the emblazoning of his arms "in the first window of the south wall of the Hall." There Sir William Dugdale observed them a century later, and there the Herald copied down the "azure three battle-axes gules" which was the only memory left of their bearer.

3

If Hakluyt became a Bencher because he indulged a taste for political activities and honors, I cannot find that his indulgence was regular. He may have been, like his father, a permanent official; but, if he was, I find no record. Moreover, there are reasons for thinking that he was not an official. If he had been employed in the Customs, or in the Admiralty, or in any other of the government departments with which he had dealings, it is almost certain that his careful cousin would have given him the proper title in mentioning him in the *Voyages*. His cousin did not give him a title but referred to him regularly as of the Middle Temple or sometimes as of Eyton. Furthermore, the lawyer's dealings with the government themselves suggest an unofficial hand. They suggest, as an account of them will now make clear, that when he served the state he served it as a volunteer.

Hakluyt's dealings with the government are varied in nature. Both in Hereford and in the Temple he was associated with members of Parliament and officials. It is even possible that he sat in Parliament himself. A Richard Hakluyt, Esquire, sat for Leominster in the last Parliament of Queen Mary, in 1557; and though there may have been other Richard Hakluyts, he would be the likely one to represent the borough. Certainly his youth would be no barrier, as it was none to Philip Sidney. He was the head of his immediate family, the son of an official, the relative by marriage of most of the Parliamentary families of Hereford.

If the evidence is not conclusive, it is almost beyond doubt. But thereafter the lawyer is lost to sight politically for a dozen years. When he comes back into view, it is with the air of one outside the administration yet familiar enough with the administrators to address them personally. The familiarity does not appear to be that of a courtier, as one might expect. There is in fact no record of any relations with a patron, of any dealings at all with the nobility except as they were officials.

Hakluyt was known to Lord Burleigh, who was virtually Prime Minister, and addressed to him two letters in the course of the year 1571. The beginning of the first suggests his unofficial standing. "Right Honorable," it reads, "knowing that a letter might have more apt access unto your Lordship than I, and that less to your trouble, I thought good to send this inclosed note, beseeching your Honor to construe my meaning in the best part." To those who are familiar with the manners of the time, the words are ordinarily respectful, but no more or less. They suit a gentleman who, in modern terms, "takes the liberty" of submitting an idea to a high official of his acquaintance.

The letter itself, written on the last day of February 1570–1571, enclosed some military intelligence which Hakluyt had just had from Spain. "Before Christmas," he wrote, in the breathless style of the time, "there arrived from Grand Malaga a young man a kinsman of mine, by whom I understood that the bearer hereof he left in service in Spain with such a one as had great doings for the King there, and that he meant shortly after to be in England. And sir, conceiving thereof that it was possible that he should understand some secrets, I examined him after his arrival and gathered the effect of the enclosed note." [6]

The enclosed note was testimony to a Spanish mobilization order, obtained by "harkening and listening at a lock hole." It was quite exact, showing that Philip II had ordered the assembling of large forces—57,000 men, with ships and munitions—to be used against "the enemies of Christianity." Nor was this the only alarming news which the government was receiving. Ten days before Hakluyt sent his witness to Burleigh, an English soldier of fortune, stranded between Spain and France, dispatched an account of another danger. The danger came from Thomas Stukeley, swashbuckler in ordinary, who was living in Spain on a royal pension. He was raising a force of 10,000 men, it seemed, for a descent on Ireland; and, when the

[6] The justification of these statements is given in Appendix I, section 5.

stray Englishman refused to join his legion, Stukeley was so menacing that the soldier made a quick and secret escape to the frontier.

It was probably the news about Stukeley that most roused the English government. There was trouble enough with Spain already, trouble that was to end in war. England had intercepted the pay of the Spanish army in Flanders on the pretext of saving it from pirates on the Narrow Seas. The Spanish ambassador was stirring up trouble with Scotland. Moreover, Ireland was already in insurrection, fanned by a Breton noble who, it was alleged, was set on by Spain. If now Stukeley were to descend on Ireland and if the Spanish navy were being mobilized, though ostensibly against Turkey, then there was danger indeed. The government took immediate alarm. Ten days after the receipt of Hakluyt's letter, the Queen herself wrote to the ambassador in Paris that she was sending off an envoy to Spain to make inquiry and was also mustering troops in Ireland.

The alarm was needless, as it happened. As soon as the envoy reached the Spanish border, he began to hear news which minimized the Stukeley danger. When he presented himself at court, the King was able to laugh it away entirely. And the innocence of Spain was completely proved in the following autumn when Spain defeated Turkey in the great naval battle of Lepanto.

Hakluyt had by no means given a false alarm, none the less. One could not be certain that Spain was really mobilizing against Turkey. Even though Hakluyt's news dated back to the preceding summer, it was valuable; for it was certainly the Admiralty's business to know what the Spanish navy was doing. By acquiring and transmitting so exact a piece of intelligence Hakluyt was performing an essential service.

He was not unaware of the fact. There is in the letter a certain tremulous eagerness, which a less naïve period than the Elizabethan would find amusing. "Thus being bold to trouble your honor," he concluded, after insisting on the competence of his witness, "praying pardon for my boldness and the rather because I could not wait as duty requireth to utter the same by mouth, I rest, wishing unto your Honor health and that this commonwealth may long enjoy you."

Burleigh seems to have been gracious in acknowledging the service; for later in the same year we find the lawyer venturing again to trouble his Honor and "to crave pardon of this my rude boldness." This time he was excited by corruption in the Customs of the port of London; and, in order to cut a Gordian knot, he finally carried his protest direct to Burleigh.

He had been called in, probably as a lawyer, to advise a puzzled officeholder. An "honest and virtuous merchant," as Hakluyt called him, Oliver Dawbeny of London, had been made "surveyor of customs and duties on all beer exported, . . . with order to the officers of customs to deliver him copies of their entries and their licenses; with power to search for concealments and to report offences in the Exchequer."

The office has a suspicious flavor. Dawbeny may have intended a public service; but one infers that he was to be paid by results and hence to do himself a service as well. This was a main motive of Tudor officialdom; but it is not surprising that Dawbeny got no help from the Customs officers on whose booty he was to privateer. They were conspicuously slow in opening their books to the new surveyor until Hakluyt, though he called himself the "meanest" of the commissioners, or subordinates of Dawbeny, allowed his indignation to burst the dam and to intercede for his client. The Customs intrigue was quite complicated in the telling and is harder to follow now. In sum, Hakluyt was able to declare categorically, despite the bureaucratic evasions, that "the book yet not brought forth . . . discovered the deceit of £7000 in wines within the compass of a year, and that in so excellent a sort as could not but have pleased the Queen's Majesty's eye and yours."

One is ready to believe the worst, with Mr. Hubert Hall, of the golden age of great Elizabeth. It is quite likely that the new Customer, or collector of the port, although he remained unmoved in his office until his death, was "in league," as Hakluyt protested, with the spoilers. It may even be that he made there some of the fortune which he left his son, Sir Thomas Smith, who was to be the Cecil Rhodes of his time. What the sagacious Burleigh thought of the lawyer's indignation can only be imagined. The tone of most of the petitions he received was highly emotional, bitter or self-pitying or supremely self-confident. He could not have been the administrator he was if he had been moved by such overwrought feelings. So in reading Hakluyt's outburst he must have smiled to himself over the picture of honesty which had in vain tried to make head against corruption. He would have been quite right in noting that men's passions were stronger than their logic; for certainly, to our age of innuendo, the Elizabethan document appears heated and illogical, as it certainly is diffuse. Burleigh may have relished the style, at the same time that he discounted the value, of the lawyer's peroration, which was an appeal for help "against these mighty bulls of Bashan that, propped up with spoil and wealth and great friends, would seem to overlook all men and make the world believe that the moon is made of a green cheese, while all men note their abundant spoil, and sore lament that so noble a prince is so spoiled of such caitiffs."

Whatever Burleigh thought, he probably concluded that the lawyer was an honest man; for the letter, right or not, is unmistakably honest. So was Dawbeny for that matter, or at least unfortunate. For when his office expired, the bulls of Bashan had reduced him to clamoring for indemnity, and Burleigh was hardened to such outcries.

I do not know that Hakluyt was habitually honest. Nor do I know whether Burleigh used his honesty again. He makes but one more official appearance, this time, ten years later, in a less delicate matter. In June of 1581 the Privy Council appointed a committee to report on the condition of Dover harbor. Flemish engineers had been brought to England to inspect it, and the committee was to consult the engineers and lay their recommendations before the Council. The committee included the chief officials of the Admiralty—the Lord Admiral, the Treasurer, the Surveyor, the Controller, and the Clerk of the Navy; two private persons, Edward Dyer of the court and Thomas Digges, military engineer; and lastly, "Mr. Haclette."

Perhaps Hakluyt's private interest in maritime matters placed his name on the list; or he may habitually have served on similar committees, of which the records are lost. He was not appointed for his engineering knowledge, as was Digges; for when the committee reported a month later, the report was signed only by Digges the engineer and Borough the Clerk of the Navy, and it was Digges who directed the actual work on the harbor. In any case, there was honor for Hakluyt, and recognition of some sort of ability.

One more letter to Burleigh closes the official record. The affair was this time a private one. Some of Hakluyt's cattle had been taken up, in 1587 and 1588, for the royal household. Hakluyt refused to accept the value set by the purveyor, whom he charged with "overdriving and underfeeding and misdieting" the cattle on the road from Hereford to London, in order to force down the price; and he insinuated to Burleigh as Lord Treasurer that the purveyor's honesty was not what it should be. The somewhat hysterical appeal, as we should think it, was answered by the treasurer of the household. This paper is much more temperate, since the treasurer, having insufficient funds to pay his bills anyway, held the post of vantage; but he did not avoid insinuating in his turn. It seems clear now that Hakluyt was merely standing up for his rights. He wanted to charge the market rate in Hereford. The purveyor expected to pay the market rate in London, which was lower. Without troubling to look up the household accounts, I think we may conclude at once, knowing the government's reputation, that Hakluyt did not get his money.

How much it mattered whether he did, one cannot say. One does not conclude, on reading the survey of his property, which seems to give him some six hundred acres of arable and pasture, and on reading his will, that he was a wealthy man. His bequests sound indeed rather scanty, though much of the property may have been entailed; but even an entail would not be likely to cover an extensive estate, since it derived from a younger son. One could make a number of

FIG. 8—London Bridge and the Pool in the year of Hakluyt's death. From J. C. Visscher, *London*, 1616. By courtesy of the British Museum, Print Department.

guesses about Hakluyt and his success or failure; but all that is really justified can be said briefly. In his profession of the law he was not outstanding, since his highest known achievement was his rank as associate Bencher of the Middle Temple; but he may have practiced successfully and won a name. In his relations with the government he may have been a useful man for odd jobs. Beyond that we may suppose him honest and God-fearing.

4

I can advance no theory to account for Hakluyt's interest in geography, which makes up his only further claim to fame. Agricultural and inland Hereford is not the place to look for oversea ambitions; and so far there is little else in the lawyer's history which would lead him to the search and discovery of the world. There are hints, of course. Hakluyt's uncle Richard came up to London to deal in skins and furs; and the Russia Company imported those commodities. One could hardly arrive in London (Fig. 8), moreover, in 1555 without becoming aware of the new enterprises. Court and City must have talked of investments, of the heroic deeds of explorers in Arctic ice and storm, of the books of Eden, which were made more vivid by the installing of a Spanish King of England who was also ruler of the Indies.

The law student must have been aware of these events, but we do not know that they yet held meaning for him. At the end of his first decade in London they had come to absorb his interest. By some accident of his profession, or perhaps by mere curious inclination, he suddenly shows himself drawn to the new cause.

The scene of the revelation is dramatic, and it is described with dramatic skill by Hakluyt's cousin the editor. It takes place in the upper chamber on Inner Temple Lane; the year is probably 1568. I give the editor's sonorous prose, written at the beginning of the *English Voyages:*

"I do remember that being a youth, and one of Her Majesty's scholars at Westminster that fruitful nursery, it was my hap to visit the chamber of M. Richard Hakluyt my cousin, a gentleman of the Middle Temple, . . . at a time when I found lying open upon his board certain books of cosmography, with an universal map: he seeing me somewhat curious in the view thereof, began to instruct my ignorance, by showing me the division of the earth into three parts after the old account, and then according to the latter and better distribution, into more: he pointed with his wand to all the known seas, gulfs, bays, straits, capes, rivers, empires, kingdoms, dukedoms, and territories of each part, with declaration also of their special commodities, and particular wants, which by the benefit of traffic, and intercourse of merchants, are plentifully supplied. From the map he brought me to the Bible, and turning to the 107 Psalm, directed me to the 23 and 24 verses, where I read, that they which go down to the sea in ships, and occupy by the great waters, they see the works of the Lord, and his wonders in the deep. Which words of the prophet together with my cousin's discourse (things of high and rare delight to my young nature) took in me so deep an impression, that I constantly resolved, if ever I were preferred to the University, where better time, and more convenient place might be administered for these studies, I would by God's assistance prosecute that knowledge and kind of literature, the doors whereof (after a sort) were so happily opened before me."

The conversion of his ward and cousin to the enterprise of learning is the first sign of the lawyer's avocation. He is now well past his moots and his legal readings, has probably begun to plead. Something has turned him to the study of commerce—perhaps some client like the merchant whom he aided in the Customs inquiry, perhaps an interest in the law of admiralty. From the study of commerce he has been led on to the study of geography or cosmography. But he has been careful to remember in his study the special commodities and particular wants of the nations. He has learned the intercourse of merchants, as the next chapter will explain. He has come to deal with the strategy of trade.

How and why will not be apparent for another decade. One would like to know the meaning of the letter which it is said was written to him in 1567 "on the fur trade," if there was such a letter. One would like to know more of the honest merchant Dawbeny who was collecting the beer tax, for Dawbeny had been overseas in the Newfoundland voyage of 1536. One would like to know why the young kinsman had been in Grand Malaga, for he may have had something to do with English trade to Spain. All these persons point a way to the lawyer's later actions, perhaps even guide him to what will be his second career. Did they not so soon drop back into darkness, they might explain what the lawyer was doing besides buying books of cosmography and expounding them to wide-eyed schoolboys.

It is not until 1578 that we find Hakluyt actually giving advice on the strategy of trade. Before that time there was one further step in his process of learning. To show that the lawyer had gone beyond reading in books, had gone out to gather knowledge for himself, we need to bring in one incident more. The younger cousin was to print in the *Voyages* a letter from an English merchant written to the lawyer in 1572. Despite the Spanish law on aliens, Henry Hawks had lived five years in Mexico. Perhaps the young kinsman from Grand Malaga knew him. Perhaps the lawyer, excited by his piece of Spanish intelligence, had gone after more of the same kind. At any rate he ordered from the merchant an account of Mexico.

The description was partly geographical, concerning the travel routes in New Spain; and mainly commercial, dealing with Mexican products and the methods of Spanish trade. I doubt that the report was in itself significant. English merchants had occasionally made their way to the West Indies in the time of Philip and Mary, to leave their reports behind them in the younger Hakluyt's *Voyages*. English merchants in Spain could easily get information of the same sort for the use of their government or their business friends at home. And the slave-trading John Hawkins must have gathered at least as useful information on his recent voyages.

But it must be emphasized that the Tudor geographer's task was precisely the collection of all possible testimony on unknown lands, just as it was the task of the Admiralty to collect all possible testimony on the doings of foreign fleets. Whether Hawkins knew more or less of Mexico than Hawks, Hawks could not be overlooked. When knowledge of the country was scarce enough at best and was filtered through Spanish censorship to the rest of Europe, the geographer must be something of a reporter. The younger Hakluyt in particular was to develop a passion for interviewing; and this interviewing of Hawks is typical of both Hakluyts.

As a typical empirical process, the episode may further explain why John Dee, for all his acquaintance with the leading Continental geographers, took no larger part in the English expansion. On the Continent the geographer was very likely to be at once a map seller, an instrument maker, and an employment agent for land and sea pilots; and he therefore "employed at this task [of map making] the leisure of caravan leaders and sea captains: and the experience of these travelers brought the geographer an unceasing stream of information which thus went to enrich his collections."[7] Of such an industry there is as yet no sign in England; but merchant companies and the state kept the reports of oversea agents; and the two Hakluyts, though they did not become professional map makers, were to build up their knowledge from such reports. So far as we know, Dr. Dee did not gather reports, and his geography remained at best secondhand and academic.

Whether the report of Hawks was obtained for any other purpose than the geographer's private information does not appear. The paper does not seem to have found its way into the state archives, as did so many similar papers, and was therefore not sent in as Admiralty or Foreign Office intelligence. Nor does it seem to have been meant for any commercial venture of the time, unless perhaps for Drake's first warlike voyage—his raid on Panama of the same year. There is no evidence that it was meant for Drake, to whose purpose it is not notably germane; and indeed Drake had already been in Mexico himself with Hawkins. I conclude that the report was obtained in what was now the lawyer's ordinary routine of inquiry, and that, being treas-

[7] General Wauwerman's article on Mercator, in the *Biographie nationale de Belgique*, contains this information. I have looked through his diffuse work on *L'École cartographique belge et anversoise* (Brussels 1895) for his proofs, which are not very satisfying. See his Chapter XIV.

ured in his *dossier,* it at length came duly into print in the *Voyages* as a sign of English interest in America.

So far, then, there is little that is conclusive of Hakluyt's connection with trade. He has been shown established in the right place, midway between London and Westminster, and bound to both by numerous personal ties. He has learned something of the new geography, something sufficient to prove at least an amateur interest. He has collected information of the sort that would be useful to a consultant geographer. Whether he has yet been consulted, regularly or casually, the record does not say. Not until the year 1578, when his schoolboy cousin had become a Master of Arts and was already introducing the new geography at Oxford, do we find the lawyer suddenly launched upon the full tide of his activity.

CHAPTER IV

The Elder Hakluyt and Trade

1567–1585

With the year 1575 begins an important new turn of the wheel of English trade overseas. The Russia Company, after twenty years of activity in Russia and beyond, was finding its trade too expensive, and English merchants turned more and more directly toward the Orient. In 1575 an emissary was dispatched to Constantinople. In 1579 the Turkish trade was again opened to English merchants by the Sultan. In 1581 Russia Company merchants and others formed the Turkey Company. In 1583 the new company dispatched overland the first English traders to India. In this development the elder Hakluyt, and in its last particular the younger, had their share.[1]

At the same time the original plan of trying the sea routes to the East was resuscitated by the new generation. The northeast venture, on which the Russia Company had been built in 1553, was again attempted by an expedition of 1580. The northwest venture, which had been abandoned for nearly half a century, came to sudden life in Frobisher's three futile voyages which began in 1576, and again in Davis' voyages ten years later. A plan for southwestern discovery and settlement was submitted in 1573, and Drake made his successful voyage around the world from 1577 to 1580. Various plans followed his return, several expeditions got as far as America, and Cavendish repeated the Drake exploit.[2] In all except the southwestern ventures, the elder Hakluyt, and in one case the younger as well, had a hand.

Still another plan was revived. It was clear that the unknown continent across the Atlantic might be of use in this expansion toward the East. At the worst it might provide a stepping-stone between England and Cathay, especially in view of Verrazano's ancient map (Fig. 3), which made the present site of New York an isthmus beyond which lay the Pacific. At the best there was always the chance of discovering, in the unexplored region between Florida and Newfoundland, a second Mexico or Peru. America thus promised both trade route and treasure-trove; and it was Gilbert who proposed to

[1] Of the numerous works on the expansion, the most profitable for this chapter have been: W. R. Scott, *Joint-Stock Companies to 1720* (Cambridge Press, 1912, 3 vols.); A. J. Gerson, *The Organization and Early History of the Muscovy Company*—E. V. Vaughan, *English Trading Expeditions into Asia*—N. R. Deardorff, *English Trade in the Baltic*, constituting the University of Pennsylvania's publication *Studies in the History of English Commerce in the Tudor Period* (New York 1912); Albert L. Rowland, *England and Turkey*, in *Studies in English Commerce and Exploration in the Reign of Elizabeth* (University of Pennsylvania, Philadelphia 1924).

[2] Now discussed by J. A. Williamson in *Sir John Hawkins*, Book III, Chapter 4 (Oxford 1927).

establish an American colony for both purposes. With his projected colony of 1578 the elder Hakluyt was concerned; with his attempted colony of 1583, the younger Hakluyt; and both Hakluyts were concerned with the Raleigh colonies that followed.

How large a part in these new enterprises to East and West was played by the lawyer who had friends in Court and City can be judged only by those of his memoranda that were subsequently printed by his careful cousin. There are seven such documents; three deal with the Levant and Persia ventures, one with the northeast expedition, three with the westward voyages. I shall take them up in that order.

The first paper is a short note of instructions given in 1579 to a dyer, one Morgan Hubblethorne, on his mission to Persia to investigate methods of dyeing in that remote country. The second, of 1582, is a short note on the woolen trade, which was intended for "a friend that was sent into Turkey," presumably as a company factor. The third, also of 1582, is a similar though much longer note, written for "a principal English factor at Constantinople." [3]

The purpose of the three notes was identical. England, as Hakluyt wrote in the first, was acknowledged to produce "the best wool and cloth of the world"; but English dyeing he admitted to be inferior. "Therefore it is much to be wished," he pointed out, "that the dyeing of foreign countries were seen, to the end that the art of dyeing may be brought into the realm in greatest excellency . . . for which cause most principally you are sent over at the charge of the City; and therefore for the satisfying the lords [of the Council], and of the expectation of the merchants and of your company, it behooves you to have care to return home with more knowledge than you carried out."

The note written in this cavalier fashion touches a crucial question of the new trade, the question of competing successfully in the manufacture and sale of woolen goods. The world knows how the competition succeeded, and it is therefore less aware of the contempt in which English woolens were often held in the beginnings. England had of course learned from the Flemings; now it might learn from the rest of the world. Hence the investigation into Persian methods, which the Privy Council itself took a hand in imposing on City recalcitrants.[4] Hence the recommendation to the friend that was sent into Turkey, who was advised to collect samples of all the dyestuffs there in use, even to the herb sesame, which Hakluyt had learned was to be found in a certain town in Egypt. Hence the recommendation to the principal factor at Constantinople, for whom was laid down a complete program of inquiry. He was to investigate the woolen in-

[3] The three eastern notes of the elder Hakluyt are printed in the *Voyages*, III 249, V 229, V 231, respectively.

[4] The letter of the Privy Council to the Warden of the Dyers' Company is summarized in *Acts of the Privy Council 1578–1580*, p. 147, under date of May 31, 1579.

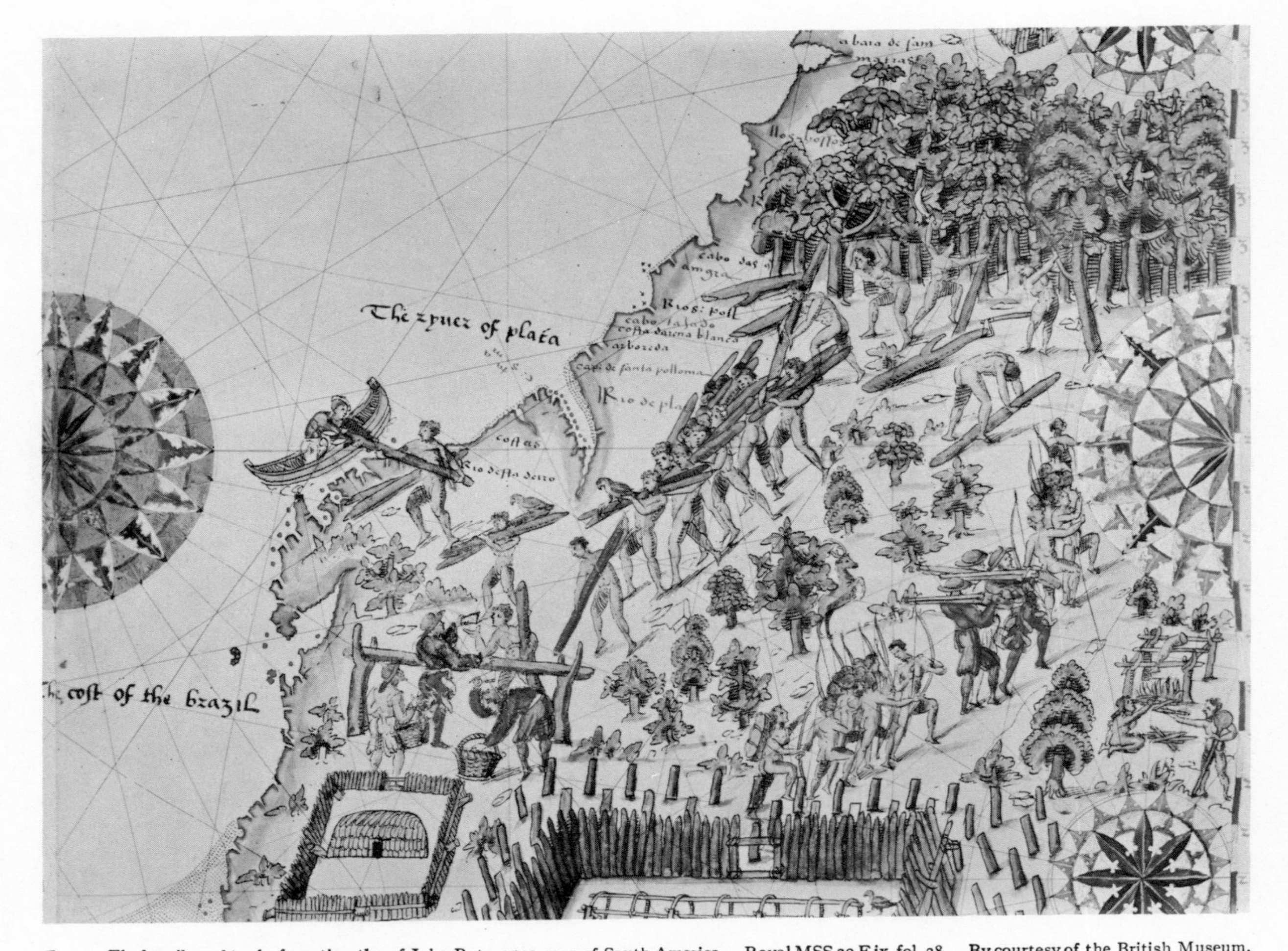

Fig. 9—The brazilwood trade, from the atlas of John Rotz, 1542, map of South America. Royal MSS 20 E ix, fol. 28. By courtesy of the British Museum.

dustry at home. Arrived in Turkey, he was to ship home sample dyestuffs; to kidnap, if he could, expert Turkish dyers; and especially to acquire samples of Turkish cloth, "to be brought to the Dyers' hall, there to be shown, partly to remove out of their heads the too too great opinion they had conceived of their own cunning."

The plan therefore called for an educational program. English conceit was evidently as great a handicap as English ignorance, and it is clear that there was much ill feeling aroused by Hakluyt and the progressive manufacturers, whoever they might be. To make his program complete and progressive Hakluyt had quite clearly informed himself on dyestuffs, as they affected both the merchant and the geographer. Evidence of his research is found in his special anxiety over blue. The current blue dye, woad, which was imported from Bordeaux and the Azores, was expensive. The substitute logwood (Fig. 9) was unsatisfactory; and the investigators in both Persia and Turkey were to find out about anile, or indigo, a promising alternative.

Hakluyt's notes might be those of an alert merchant. One infers from their tone of authority that they were written by the expert for the signature of the merchant or of the Dyers' Company or perhaps of the Privy Council itself. The fact that the notes were written by the expert, and not by the merchant himself, is highly important. The merchant was not yet differentiated from the banker, the shipowner, the manufacturer; he was not even differentiated from the salesman; yet he was already finding his commerce too complex for his own unaided control.

Two examples will enforce the point. Additionally to his concern for dyestuffs, Hakluyt laid down detailed directions on the marketing of woolen goods. The friend sent into Turkey was informed of the special weaves which might, on the one hand, be most profitably sold and, on the other, most probably fit the demand. This was practical, over-the-counter advice, and it was given not by the merchant but by the merchant's expert. Likewise with the inquiry into dyestuffs. Any traveler might have heard of the herb anile; any sailor might have picked up the information that saffron was grown in Syria; and any merchant or merchant's clerk might have collected and systematized these and other facts of economic geography. Yet it was in fact the lawyer who collected them for the merchant and who added to them such fruits of his reading as the note on the herb sesame, which he found in a Saracen geography. Already, in short, the expert was needed; and what is more important, already he was employed.

How Hakluyt acquired this authority can only be surmised. I can hardly suppose that at this late date he got up his facts from the beginning. He had been collecting from Hawks a few years earlier; so he might well have been collecting for merchants for some time. But even if he had not, even if he had been called in at the last moment, he was not compelled to do all the organizing of material. There were facts enough in company offices, as the following parallel cases will show.

When the Russia Company sent out in 1555 its first trading voyage, it was already alive to the duty of inquiry. Its factors were then instructed to "learn and observe all kind of wares, as well natural as foreign, that be beneficial for this realm, to be sold for the benefit of the company, and what kind of our commodities and other things of these west parts be most vendible in those Realms with profit, giving a perfect advice of all such things requisite." This note was general; more specific instructions followed. In 1557, probably on the basis of the first reports, the company set up in Russia a rope factory with English workmen for a core; it also dispatched two coopers, together with a man to direct the cutting of yew timber. Also it sent out a skinner, "to view and see such furs as you shall cheap or buy," and especially ten apprentices to learn office work and the routine of buying and selling.[5] With this force in training in the new market the company continued to enforce the duty of inquiry. An elaborate set of instructions to its far-flung agents were sent out by the reorganized company in 1567.[6]

"Write us your opinions," runs one of them, item 16 in the long list, ". . . for what quantity of wares may be uttered in the Emperor's dominions, where the places of traffic be, and what quantity of wares may be uttered in every place, the colors and sorts of cloth and what other wares be most in estimation, and this to be done from year to year." The concluding phrase is important. For if this record were in fact kept from year to year, collation, the function of a Hakluyt, would sooner or later be necessary.

"We be desirous," it is declared again, in item 58, "to have a sea card [chart] made of the voyage on the Caspian Sea." "Send us a just note and counterpoise of all the weights and just standard of all measures, we mean as well those of Russia as Persia and Media," declares item 15. "Whether there may be any good canvas made of that country flax or hemp," is asked in item 20; "and a perfect card to be made of the journey" from the White Sea to the Baltic, in item 47; and, in item 63, "whereas there be slaves to be bought at the Caspian which have been at Ormuz (the staple of spices), and speak the Portugal and Persia tongue, we think it good you gave order some of them be bought, by whom to the state of Ormuz trade might be opened. . . ."

The manner of these remarks is exactly the manner of Hakluyt. The document may even have been his, so similar is it to his undoubted

[5] The instructions to the first factors are in the *Voyages*, II 284; the 1557 instructions, *ibid.*, II 381.

[6] The instructions, dated 18 April 1567, are contained in MS Cott. Nero B. xi, fol. 321. They were printed in *Hakluyt Society Publications* 73, p. 206.

papers. Perhaps as early as 1567, when he was able to lecture his cousin on geography, he had become a company consultant.

If the answers to these queries were well kept, there is in any event no need to look farther for the sources of Hakluyt's information. The company records would be opened to him; and then, for the special function which distinguished him from a company scribe, he could draw upon his books of cosmography for supplement. Hence his knowledge of dyestuffs; and hence a growing body of special geographical knowledge.

2

That Hakluyt's familiarity with the woolen trade was a mere special phase of his knowledge is made clear in the second new enterprise of the expansion, the northeast expedition of 1580. For this venture of the Russia Company there was gathered the sum of English and foreign experience, now concentrated in mainly English hands. No longer was it necessary to call in a Sebastian Cabot to dictate ways and means. In nearly thirty years of voyages around the North Cape English mariners had gained their own first-hand experience. The first document to follow the company's instructions to the captains, as the younger Hakluyt later printed the record, was properly enough the sailing instructions given by the company's most distinguished navigator, William Borough. In third place came the advice of John Dee, who gave his idea of the Siberian coast. Fifth in order was a note from the venerable Mercator, still the leading geographer of Europe. And in fourth place stood the directions of the elder Hakluyt.[7]

His notes clearly mark the broader nature of his function, limited by the nautical experience of Borough on the one hand and the cartographical experience of Dee and Mercator on the other. A first section of his paper related to the surveying of unknown shores, with an eye to sites for a combined naval base, trading post, and colony. A second section provided for the inquiry to be made in the East into articles of supply and demand, such as "the ornaments of their houses within" and "all such things as are brought into the markets." In the major section of the memorandum were listed the articles that experience preferred for exotic trade and not only textiles and hardware but articles of advertising value as well, such as coins of the realm, dainties "for banketing on shipboard persons of credit," maps of England and London "of the biggest sort"; "and let the river be drawn full of ships of all sorts to make the more show of your great trade and traffic."

The notes were again clearly of the kind that could be gathered only by close acquaintance with the details of foreign trade. To matters of trade he confined himself. He was not concerned with navi-

[7] The various instructions to the northeast expedition are given in the *Voyages*, III 251 ff.

gation, with physiography, with discipline. These were taken care of by his collaborators; but, again like a merchant, he instructed his salesmen on what they should take to sell, how they should approach their clients, what they should look for as articles of barter, and how they should choose warehouse points. The barrier between the geographer and the trader has here again worn very thin and typically so; for in just such a dual capacity might have acted Anthony Jenkinson or any other intelligent trader, had he been called on to bequeath his experience to his successors.

As the Levantine notes have shown Hakluyt's knowledge of the woolen trade, so these northeastern notes show his acquaintance with trade in general. The list of exports made out by him for the last section would stock a peddler's pack; the organizers of the expedition needed only, in loading their cargo, to mark the quantities opposite his items. The program of inquiry, set down in the second section, was vague enough and necessarily so, since the far Northeast was a blank on the most ambitious maps; but as an outline it showed the expert had studied his records. The locating of strategic points for stations was clearly defined in the first section; and this advice could have come only from close study of the Russia Company's experience in establishing "factories." The divisions of the memorandum illuminate the empirical method, and the link between purely economic geography and the more general science is formed by such notes as this: "To note the Islands, whether they be high land or low land, mountain or flat, gravelly, clay, chalky, or of what soil, woody or not woody, with springs and rivers or not, and what wild beasts they have in the same. And whether there seem to be in the same apt matter to build withal, as stone free or rough, and stone to make lime withal, and wood or coal to burn the same withal. To note the goodness or the badness of the havens and harbors in the Islands." Or, more succinctly, this: "If you arrive at Cambalu or Quinsay, to bring thence the map of that country"; and this: "If you take Ortelius' book of maps with you to mark all those regions, it were not amiss." There is nothing haphazard about this plan for gathering knowledge.

These evidences of Hakluyt's study of foreign trade might well suggest that he held some sort of permanent post with a merchant or merchant company. The suggestion, logically though it might read today, still disregards the fluidity of function in Tudor times. It is quite possible, of course, that Hakluyt was, if not a regular employee, at least a promoter or a shareholder and additionally a consultant. I can find no evidence that he was so involved in trade, though the records of the various companies are hardly complete enough to enable me to be sure. In such records as we have, however, of the Russia Company, of Frobisher's Cathay Company, of Gilbert's colonies, of the Levant Company, and so on, his name does not appear; and there is no real reason why he should not have been merely the consultant.

That such a function was possible is amply testified by the career of the younger Hakluyt as well as of others. It will be seen, for example, that when the younger man was consulted by the East India Company he was addressed as a purely private person. He gave the desired information and was paid a substantial fee. The same process may account for the older man's relations to traders, the same intermittence of function justify his remaining unattached and yet being at times indispensable.

3

The section of the northeastern notes that relates to the locating of trade posts is the bridge between English commerce and English colonization. The founding of a Russia Company station at St. Nicholas on the White Sea is the exact precedent for the founding of a settlement on the American coast. In the view of the "adventurers," or investors, at any rate, the two enterprises were identical in character; and, in turning back from Hakluyt's notes on eastward expansion to his notes on westward expansion, we discover an identical approach. In the second case as in the first the program took up the site of the trading post or colony, an inquiry into the local products, and a statement of suitable English exports.

The Turkish instructions were written in 1579 and 1582; the northeastern in 1580; the American, to which we now come, in 1578 and 1585. In order of time the American interest thus had first expression. With the first Frobisher expeditions, in 1576 and 1577, which opened the American ventures, I find no record of Hakluyt's dealings: yet the papers of the Cathay Company, which backed the enterprise, have been preserved. As has been pointed out, the northwest idea was justified at length in Gilbert's *Discourse,* which proved, with a wealth of illustrations from ancient and modern geographers, that a Northwest Passage was as plausible as the English Channel. Though the book was not published until 1576, after the first enterprise had been launched, it had been in manuscript for ten years and had doubtless influenced the courtiers and merchants who pooled their subscriptions.[8]

The new northwest voyages focused many lines of experience, as the documents show. Court and City subscribed with alacrity, even if most of the subscriptions remained unpaid. The chief adventurer and sufferer, Michael Lock of the City, was the son of a merchant in the wool trade to Flanders and the brother of a prime mover in the African voyages of the fifties. He had himself spent fourteen years

[8] The records of the Cathay Company are printed in *Hakluyt Society Publications* 38 (1867), entitled *Three Voyages of Martin Frobisher.* A valuable discussion of the company is in Scott, vol. II, part I, Chapter 3.

as a factor in various markets of southern Europe, and he was an eager student of geography. The chief enterpriser, Frobisher, was already an experienced navigator; and it is recorded that high naval officials like William Borough and Sir William Winter and Russia Company agents like Jenkinson and Thomas Randolph supervised the equipment and personnel of the expedition.

With such mercantile and nautical experience may be aligned the aid lent by books to the voyagers. The ship's library was well supplied. It contained "a very great carte of navigation"; Mercator's "great map universal in print"; and three other small maps, printed. In nautical information it added a Spanish text on navigation, not that of Cortes but one by another India House pilot; the recent *Cosmography* of Thevet, French geographer royal, and his earlier *New World,* an account of the French colony in Brazil, neither book a very happy choice; "a cosmographical glass," doubtless Cunningham's work in mathematical geography and astronomy; the "castle of knowledge," an astronomy text of the same earlier period; and finally, bought very cheap, the still accredited travels of John Mandeville. It was not a very authoritative library and not nearly as informing on either East or West as was certain material about to be published.

This new material we may include with Gilbert's *Discourse* as part of the publicity brought forth by the northwestern ventures. Published in 1577, the *History of Travel in the East and West Indies* was in part a reprint of Eden's *Decades,* in larger part a work of northwestern publicity addressed to various noble ladies by Richard Willis, who was apparently a tutor in a noble house. As a reprint, the *History* was superior to the original in being arranged by countries; whereas, as has been said, the *Decades* were not arranged at all. As publicity, the *History* was especially pertinent in the item that immediately followed Peter Martyr's three Decades. This was a discussion by Willis of the Northwest Passage problem, written for and addressed to the Countess of Warwick, one of Frobisher's shareholders. Equally obvious in motive was much material on the East: an account of China, an account of Japan, a description of Persia, narratives of Jenkinson's voyages to Asia for the Russia Company. Inspired by the same motive as Eden's *Decades,* that of printing timely information, the *History* thus proved far more relevant and may therefore be thought valuable support for an expedition that hoped to reach the East. Purely as geographical information, on the other hand, the *History* furnished an important supplement to Eden, whose *Decades* had covered in the main the western lands. In the history of English records of discovery, therefore, the *History of Travel* may take its place as the second significant book.

The intellectual support of Frobisher already appears large. In the organization we have reckoned the City experience, particularly of Lock. In what I have called the tactics of enterprise we have recorded the presence of mariners and land captains, reinforced by certain academic authorities like Thevet and Mercator and Cunningham. In what I have called the stategy of enterprise we may infer the economic-geographical knowledge of Lock and others, again reinforced by academic authority. In the publicity we reckon, finally, the Gilbert and Willis productions, together with others not yet mentioned. To all these authorities we must now add two native consultants of a less obvious sort—Dr. Dee, whom we should expect to find drawn in the wake of court interest, and the elder Hakluyt, whom we should expect to be drawn in the wake of mercantile interest.

Dee became in the first place a shareholder in Lock's Cathay Company. His economic interest was in all likelihood a result and not a cause of his intellectual interest; he was probably adviser first and investor second; but the two interests combined to enthrone him in a veritable wisdom seat, whence issued a flood of advice to successive captains of enterprise.

Some of the advice was written. It was probably Dee who early drew up a statement, still kept in the archives, of what was known of the Northwest Passage. "A note of certain navigations," it was called, "heretofore attempted for the discovery of a passage through the straits out of the North Sea into the South Sea." [9] Thevet, Mercator, Cunningham, Dee: here was indeed reliance on academic authority.

Much of Dee's advice was oral. A picture of him *in cathedra* has been preserved in his Diary. We read that at the end of June, 1578, after the third and final Frobisher expedition had sailed, he "told Daniel Rogers, Mr. Hackluyt of the Middle Temple being by, that King Arthur and King Maty both of them did conquer Gelindia, lately called Friseland [Greenland or an imaginary land near it], which he so noted presently in his written copy of Monumetensis." [10]

The concourse at Dee's house is interesting, even if the occasion was not momentous. The elder Hakluyt had just been advising Frobisher, as will be told. The younger Hakluyt was perhaps present, for the note on Arthur's fantastic voyage duly found its way to the first page of his *Voyages*. Daniel Rogers of Oxford and of Walsingham's staff, the third person, was a relative by marriage of Ortelius, the Flemish geographer, who had recently been made geographer royal of Spain; and it happens that Ortelius had visited England and had

[9] The memorandum is catalogued under State Papers Domestic Elizabeth, 106, 77.

[10] Dee's Diary was printed as *Camden Society Publications* 19 (1842). The reprint is declared incomplete by Charlotte Fell-Smith in her *Life of Dr. John Dee* (London 1909), whence I have the reference to the visit of Ortelius and the later information. I am still following the authorities on Dee mentioned in the notes on Chapter II.

met Dee in the year preceding.[11] Now it was not the part of a Spanish official to encourage English expansion; yet Ortelius could hardly have helped yielding some advice to Dee at the time of his visit. At any rate, this brief bit of geographical gossip shows something of Dee's new importance, as it shows how much gathering and gossiping of geographers may have been taking place.

Dee was in fact to be much wrapped up in the northwest idea during these dozen years of experimenting, dealing with it both as a promoter and as an unofficial geographer royal. As a promoter, he had subscribed some sixty pounds to Frobisher and may even have paid them in. But even before that subscription he had appeared, in 1576, as an authority on navigation. Despite the nautical experience that Frobisher and others could command, Dee was called on to give lectures in the art to Frobisher's company. With his usual passion for the pen Dee did not stop there. He developed an extensive treatise, the *General and Rare Memorials pertaining to the Perfect Art of Navigation,* which spread with his passion to unprintable dimensions. Only the first section, the *Petty Navy Royal,* a plan for a mosquito fleet which had nothing much to do with the case, was published. The second section, the *Perfect Art of Navigation,* was too long and required too many figures to be rescued from manuscript, where it still lies. The third section Dee kept a mystery, perhaps because it may have dealt with matters of foreign and therefore anti-Spanish policy. The fourth section, on *Famous and Rich Discoveries,* apparent propaganda, likewise remained in manuscript. In intention Dee covered the whole field of tactics and much of publicity.

Most of this writing was probably done for royal perusal. At any rate, the Queen speedily called on Dee for his official advice. Late in 1577, when Frobisher was extending his plan to include a colony in the frozen Northwest, Dee was summoned to Windsor, where he "declared to the Queen her title to Greenland," and so on, that is to the Frobisher region. The colony was not, as it happened, established; but Dee, once installed in his semiofficial seat, was called into further inquiries when Frobisher's plan yielded to Gilbert's. Gilbert himself came to consult Dee in 1577, the year of his own patent. In 1578, probably to justify the grant, Dee drew up a paper on the Queen's title to North America. (It was probably of this paper that the note on Arthur's voyage was an echo.) The paper itself seems not to have been presented to the Queen until 1580, by which time Dee was thoroughly enmeshed in Gilbert's web. To accompany the paper, he drew up an American map, incidentally consulting one drawn by Gilbert's

[11] The life of Daniel Rogers is given in the *Dictionary of National Biography;* of Ortelius in *Biographie nationale de Belgique.* Letters to and from Ortelius were printed by J. H. Hessels, *Abrahami Ortelii epistolae* (Cambridge 1887). The younger Hakluyt's meeting with Ortelius is mentioned in the former's *Discourse on the Western Planting,* in 2 *Collections Maine Hist. Soc.* (Cambridge, Mass. 1877), II 102.

Portuguese pilot;[12] and in addition to the paper and the map ("for copy whereof," as he later wrote, "I have refused an hundred pounds in money offered by some subjects of this kingdom") his busy pen turned out tracts on the "hydrographic description of the Atlantis," or West Indies, and even on "spreading the gospel to the [American] heathen."

These are the consultations of which we have record; but a great deal more of riding out to Dee's house on the Thames is to be inferred. We know from the Diary that Gilbert was one visitor. Walsingham, Principal Secretary and a leader of the colonial party, was another. In 1582 one of Gilbert's chief backers, Sir George Peckham the Catholic leader, came to Dee to inquire for himself into the English title to America. And sea captains like the younger Hawkins came as well. The oracle's importance increased with his company. He took larger holdings in the ventures. By 1580 he had been granted by Gilbert the royalties on all lands north of 50 degrees in the abandoned Frobisher region. This grant became the entering wedge for the new Northwest patent. In forming the Northwest Passage Company, which received its patent in 1585, Dee was preëminently active. Repeated conferences with Gilbert's brother Adrian, with Walsingham the chief friend at court, with the merchants of the City and of the Russia Company in particular give hints of Dee's organizing activities. At length, in January of 1583, "I, Master Adrian Gilbert, and Jone Davis went by appointment to Master Secretary (Walsingham) to Master Beale his house, where only we four were secret, and we made Master Secretary privy of the Northwest Passage, and all charts and rutters (routiers) were agreed upon in general."

So Dee played his leading part: as adviser in navigation to the Frobisher sailors; as adviser to the Queen on questions of title and to Gilbert and his backers as well; as geographical adviser to the Russia Company in its Northeast Passage expedition of 1580; and finally as general adviser to and as a principal organizer of the company which sent John Davis to discover Davis Strait in 1585. Thus his importance grew from stage to stage. To the Frobisher voyages, as has been said, Dee subscribed sixty pounds. In the Gilbert colony he was granted royalties from all the lands between Labrador and the pole. In the Davis voyages he began, at least, with the share of a principal. And in connection with all three he earned the good will of the Crown, which was expressed long afterwards in a substantial benefice. Had he remained in England, he would doubtless have taken a conspicuous part in Virginia as well, the fourth American venture before the Armada. But in the critical year 1583 he left his secret meetings and agitations for the more alluring promises of Continental courts. When he returned six years later he was apparently out of

[12] Dee's consulting of the Fernandez map is explained in the *Narrative and Critical History of America*, IV 96. The map is in the British Museum.

touch, and his wisdom was replaced by the wisdom and perhaps the disdain of a younger generation. He had been an oracle once, but he had given up earthly wisdom for spiritual; and the authority on crystal gazing and spiritism ceased to be consulted on the terrestrial science.

4

Even in the heyday of his opportunity Dee had not been a sole authority. In general geography and in the history of exploration, on which depended the establishing of title, he was potent. In matters affecting navigation, the tactics of trade, he was also potent; as was witnessed by his sharing in the council which planned for the Davis voyages "all charts and rutters." There still remains the strategy of trade; and here the elder Hakluyt was again needed.

He was needed to summarize the experience of the Russia Company in organizing its posts in the frozen north of Russia, for the third Frobisher voyage of 1578 planned to leave a handful of men in possession of the frozen north of America. For their guidance the elder Hakluyt drew up a paper, which, when first published by his cousin in 1582, bore the mystifying title of instructions "heretofore to be given to one that prepared for a discovery but went not" and which, in a later printing, was less reticently headed "Notes framed by M. Richard Hakluyt of the Middle Temple Esquire, given to certain Gentlemen that went with M. Frobisher in his Northwest Discovery, for their directions."[13]

The paper furnished a thoroughly practical program for the colonizer. Assuming that he had settled the direction of the voyage; that he was an organizer of men, of commerce, and of the gold-mining industry which he hoped to carry on; and that he had arrived on the unknown shore: his instructions carried him on to a self-supporting colony.

First he must consider a site. Certain requirements must be met: a harbor protected against sea and enemy; a river affording access to the interior; an appropriate climate; proximity to water, food, fuel, and building material. Anyone may say now that such requirements were absurdly incongruous with what Frobisher already knew of the ice fields of the Northwest. Doubtless the voyagers hoped to reach something better than a frozen land, some miraculously open climate on the road to Cathay.

The site fixed and the settlement made, the second problem was the economic structure of the colony. Hakluyt had not, of course, grasped the first principle of colonization, which he might have learned from foreign experience outside the tropics, that colonies must first of all be able to feed themselves. But that principle could not to be learned from Russian experience, which relied on the natives,

[13] The elder Hakluyt's doings are accounted for in Appendix I, section 5.

and was in fact to be established only slowly and painfully by the lessons of starvation. He had at any rate realized that the colony could not be a mere trading post like the Russia Company stations. It must on the contrary develop production of its own that would not depend, like the Spanish colonies, on native industry. His second step therefore forecast such autonomy. Judged from all reports, the commodities that could be produced in America were, as he listed them, timber, hides, salt, grapes and olives, dyes; and the colonizer would prepare to investigate immediately. The most obvious was timber. Timber was a Russia Company staple; and the first act of the colonizer should therefore be the setting up of a sawmill.

This was the substance of the instructions, to which were added remarks on preserving peace with the natives. It is clear that in essence the instructions stressed the value of inquiry both before and after settling. Timber once provided for, the colonists would look about for other commodities. The instructions thus demonstrate the practicality of the advice. In particular it should be said that virtually no mention was made of treasure hunting, which effectually wrecked the first colonies. Treasure hunting had baited the hook of the Cathay Company. Michael Lock, the mainstay of the company, though a merchant of many years' standing, had profound confidence in Frobisher's ore. But it was not on the geographer's advice that gold was made an attraction. If there was anything visionary in his plans, it was not the *feu follet* of gold; it was rather his failure to realize the need of a transatlantic food supply. The lesson was not obvious, and Hakluyt must not be blamed for not having learned it. He must rather be esteemed for applying the experience of the Russia Company to the handling of New World products as he knew them and for producing a program at once clear and feasible.

It may be added that the programs of later experts were formed on essentially the same plan. The promoters of Gilbert's colony, Carleill and Peckham, adopted the idea of a staple product, timber or fish. The younger Hakluyt enlarged the program to include furs, the value of which he learned in France. In summing up English experience, the elder Hakluyt paved the way of his successors. Their recommendations led in turn to the local investigations which the Raleigh colony observer, and later the Virginia Company, were to make in the new country. And the result of these investigations was in turn to be recorded in the national experience.

5

Meanwhile there was first-hand knowledge of America in England, and in the year in which Hakluyt wrote the colonial program for Frobisher he set to work to gather it. Undoubtedly he aimed at guiding the Gilbert project, which replaced Frobisher's. Having launched, as it were, the Northwest Passage idea in his *Discourse,* Gilbert turned to the idea of a colony in temperate latitudes. In November of 1577 he had conference with Dee. In the following June he was granted a colonial patent. In November of 1578 he set forth an expedition, which however returned in the following February trying to hush up the news of its disastrous encounter with Spanish ships off the coast of Spain. Again attempting to sail in the spring of 1579, Gilbert was "stayed" by the government, which was not desirous of provoking Spain further. The enterprise, though it was supported by a large group of adventurers, thus failed to reach America at all; and though the evidence is curiously elusive, since it was hushed up, the profits of privateering seem to have proved more attractive, as in so many other instances, than the profits of settlement.[14]

In any case the expedition was well supplied with knowledge of its destination. Gilbert himself, as is proved by the *Discourse on the Passage,* was widely read in the Continental geographers. He had gone to Dee for advice. He had been provided with a Portuguese pilot, Simon Fernandez, who was to guide all the Gilbert and Raleigh colonies.[15] In addition to this experience at his command, he learned what the elder Hakluyt could find out for him.

This was perhaps the most useful knowledge of all, since it was first-hand. It is characteristic of Hakluyt's method that he should make straight for the direct evidence. Newfoundland, which was Gilbert's aim, had been visited by a London expedition in 1536 as well as by the numerous fishermen who spent the summer months in drying their catch on its shores.

Of the remote expedition Hakluyt was able to find a survivor. I take it at least that at this time he obtained the account of it printed in his cousin's *Voyages.* The survivor was the London merchant, Oliver Dawbeny, who may have given his information at the time of the customs scandal; but, since Hakluyt was gathering other Newfoundland information in 1578, he probably sought out Dawbeny then. The information happened to have no great value. Either the aged survivor had forgotten his distant experience, or, as is more likely, the experience was not extensive. Indeed, the only lesson the old venture might teach the new was that when supplies ran out the voyagers could eat one another or else that they could steal from fishermen. Gilbert was to make use of the latter lesson.

That ancient voyage of 1536 had apparently done little exploring for anything but food; and, as the younger Hakluyt was to write in this connection, "it is much to be marveled that by the negligence

[14] For Gilbert's ventures my main reliance has been W. G. Gosling, *The Life of Sir Humphrey Gilbert* (London 1911), which, though badly arranged, has certain documents additional to those given in *Prince Society Publications* 19 (Boston 1903).

[15] Fernandez has been discussed at length by B. F. De Costa in *Ancient Norombega* (Albany 1890), a reprint (revised) from the *New England Historical and Genealogical Register,* April, 1890.

of our men the country in all this time hath been no better searched." The lawyer was however able to find a Bristol gentleman, Anthony Parkhurst, who had sailed with Hawkins and for some reason had explored the island of Newfoundland; and Parkhurst gave him as specific a report as could be expected. The report showed the number of vessels in the various fishing fleets, the vegetable and animal products of the island, and the possible mineral products. It recommended the occupying of a base in the Gulf of St. Lawrence, if not farther south, and professed its author's willingness to explore the St. Lawrence River.

Parkhurst's report may not have been the first made by an Englishman on the geography of Newfoundland, but it is the first on record. It was written to the lawyer's order, as is stated in it; it was ordered for the guidance of some enterprise, which can only be Gilbert's; and it was ordered in such a way as to draw Parkhurst, with his experience, into the venture. For, he concluded, "if you and your friend shall think me a man sufficient and of credit to seek the isle of St. John or the river of Canada [the St. Lawrence], with any part of the firm land or Cape Briton, I shall give my diligence." The record does not show whether this offer was taken up; but, as some scouting was done before Gilbert took his colony over in 1583, the enterprising Parkhurst may have been mustered in as he suggested. In any case he subscribed to the 1583 colony; and to Hakluyt may go the credit not only of gathering Bristol experience for Gilbert's purpose but also of gaining Bristol support. The consultant thus easily merged with the promoter, as was also true of Dee and the younger Hakluyt; and the combining of functions serves to mark the lawyer as linking Bristol and, one supposes, its fishing industry, to oversea expansion, as he had previously linked the woolen industry.

Hakluyt was thus one of the engineers of English colonization in America. If we omit the plan of 1563 to preëmpt French Florida for English uses,[16] we may date the first project in 1578, when Frobisher planned a settlement in the frozen North. The details of this project were laid down by Hakluyt. The second project is of the same year, when Gilbert planned a settlement in Newfoundland. For this project Hakluyt obtained the available English information from a survivor of the 1536 voyage and from a Bristol gentleman who had been to the fishing banks. His information also served, as we may now add, for the second Gilbert attempt of 1583, though Gilbert was now considering a more southerly settlement, and the information needed supplementing from other sources. There is no evidence that the lawyer was involved in this extra harvest. His younger cousin, now Master of Arts and geographer on his own account, was very actively

[16] For the attempt to captur• Ribaut and French Florida see Woodbury Lowery, *The Spanish Settlements Within the Present Limits of the United States, Florida 1562–1574* (New York and London 1905).

involved in it; and, in so far as the older man inducted the younger into his career, the former's connection with colonizing may be considered still unbroken. Probably his *dossiers* were still in active use, his advice still painting a background of experience, for the colonizers; and in any case he was again brought forward in the cause of the fourth project in 1585.

6

His contribution was a pamphlet of the prospectus type, which was entitled by a later hand *Inducements to the liking of the Voyage intended towards Virginia.* The purpose of its writing does not appear in the printed version, which was not made until 1602; but the date 1585 is the date of Raleigh's first Roanoke colony, and the pamphlet must have been written in Raleigh's interest. The most striking pamphlet of the sort had been presented to the Queen in the previous summer by the younger Hakluyt, already a sort of official adviser for Virginia; but the younger man had thereupon returned to Paris, and I take it that in his absence the elder was summoned to prepare a paper as bait for investors.

The *Inducements* will be considered later, along with its companion work, the discourse to the Queen. For the moment it is enough to say that, as it was not apparently printed at the time, neither was it included in the younger Hakluyt's *Voyages* in 1589 or in 1600. When it did appear in 1602, it was a weapon in the revived campaign for colonies. To draw new subscriptions to new enterprises a brochure was put forth in that year which contained accounts of the latest westward voyages and which added, in a second edition, this early prospectus. The campaign was successfully carried on, in part by the younger Hakluyt, to the founding of Jamestown; and thus, long after his death, the geographer who had drawn up the first substantial project for an English colony had his part in the first success.

The contribution of Richard Hakluyt of the Middle Temple was thus notable. Whatever the occasion for his mingling in trade, this country gentleman and lawyer managed to have a finger in many of the significant ventures of his time. With the Raleigh experiment, however, he seems to have stepped out of his vocation, leaving his mantle to the more illustrious younger man whom he had trained. That, at any rate, is the conclusion suggested by our evidence. Yet it is clear that his activities were more extensive than we can now assert. One has had to infer that he burrowed extensively into the documents of traders; and his increasing knowledge may have led to an increasing demand upon it in ways which we cannot fathom. There are many memoranda, trade reports, trade projects, studies of trade policy in the state papers, on which he may have advised, which he may even have written. But no one can say now. One thing at least may be said.

I make no doubt that it was in no small part his labor which went into his cousin's *Voyages*. Without his accumulation of documents, or at least his organizing of documents, the Russian section of the *Voyages*, for example, could hardly have been as thorough as it was. Without his plowing, it is difficult to conceive of the *Voyages* being harvested.

The enigmatic geographer is revealed in one more geographic enterprise before his death in 1591. In an undated letter ascribed to the year 1590 he laid before the venerable Flemish cartographer, Ortelius, a plan for a world map. It was Ortelius who had published the first modern atlas, engraving not his own maps but the best he could find. To him, then, Hakluyt turned with another new idea on map making. In conjunction with John Ashley, merchant of London, the lawyer required a map that could be conveniently used by merchants and students whose houses were "not large enough nor light enough" to admit the usual bulky kind. He suggested the use of rollers. The specifications for the frame occupied a large part of the letter; but quite as much space went to justify a plainly marked Northwest Passage on the map itself. I do not know if the map was ever executed. But the final gesture of the geographer is significant of the acclimatization of the science that had taken place in his lifetime.[17]

[17] Hakluyt's letter to Ortelius is given in Hessels, pp. 415–418. That the elder and not the younger Hakluyt wrote it is proved by the writer's reference to himself as "incumbens legibus." The interest in the Northwest Passage may date the letter earlier than 1590.

CHAPTER V

An Apprentice to Geography

1552?–1582

For the purposes of his career the younger Richard Hakluyt was ushered upon the stage at exactly the right moment. Had he been born fifty years earlier, he would have lived in an insular England. Had his career begun instead in the seventeenth century, he would have been, like his successor Purchas, a mere worker in archives. As it happened, the span of his life, from 1552 to 1616, paralleled the rise of a larger England, an England stretching fingers of empire to East and West.

The beginning of the Russian trade in 1553 marked the first step of the eastward expansion. Before Hakluyt's death, the merchants trading to Moscow and Bokhara and Aleppo had planted the seed of the eastern dominion. Of the westward movement, the first stirring was recorded in 1555 by Eden, forerunner of Hakluyt. In the preface to his second English book on the new worlds, Eden then wrote:

> " beside the portion of land pertaining to the Spaniards, . . . there yet remaineth an other portion of that main land reaching toward the northeast, thought to be as large as the other, and not yet known but only by the sea coasts, neither inhabited by any Christian men."

It was still during Hakluyt's childhood that the first English plan for a colony in this region was hatched by the French experiment in Florida, though the plan reached no farther than to the bribing, in 1563, of the French captain Ribaut. And it was between 1576, the year of Frobisher's first voyage to the Northwest, and the year of Hakluyt's death in 1616, that the foundation was laid for an English North America. Of this important era Hakluyt was an eyewitness.

To the career of eyewitness he devoted himself from an early age. Indeed his self-dedication is the earliest known fact in his history. The story of his cousin's lecture over certain books of cosmography and of his immediate resolve to prosecute that knowledge and kind of literature is in fact the only record in his early history. The fact is characteristic. For as he looked back twenty years from the height of his great book, where he recorded the experience, it appeared then that his life, or the only part of it worth telling, began in his sixteenth year on the day when his cousin revealed to him the magic of seafaring and the mystery of maps. I have quoted his words in speaking of the elder Hakluyt. In speaking of the younger it is only fair to think that the incident may have been rose-colored by time. There

FIG. 10—A galleon, *circa* 1550. From British Museum, Cotton MSS Aug. I ii 46.

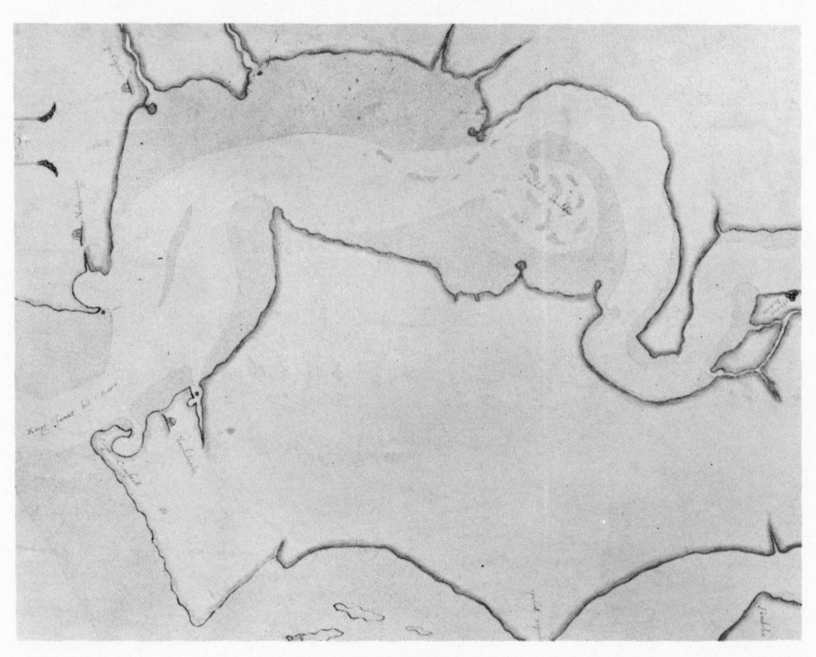

FIG. 11—The James River, 1608. From a map of Virginia by Robert Tindall, 1608. British Museum, Cotton MSS Aug. I ii 46.

may have been numerous visits to the room in the Middle Temple where maps were spread upon the board. It is very likely that the story was embroidered, when the man came to tell of it, by the clerical or the literary touch, which would lead the anecdote to end, in picturesque climax, with a reading from the Psalmist on those who go down to the sea in ships.

The central fact of the story which opens the *English Voyages* is yet unmistakable. It was the cousin who shaped the lad's career. Some such special influence is needed to explain the firmness with which the idea seized and held him. For Westminster School, and even more the University, was far from the echoes of oversea adventures. The Hawkins slave ships of the sixties may have caused some little stir at court. The pompous formalities of the "opening" of Russia, with its exchange of compliments and envoys, may have excited London. The yearly sailings for Africa or Russia may have caused a bustle along the river down below the bridge (Figs. 10, 11). But if the Westminster youths were stirred by foreign excitements, it is likely that they were stirred by the combats of the Narrow Seas, by the exploits of the Huguenots in France and of the Sea Beggars in Flanders rather than by the remote wealth of Persia or the French treasure seeking in Florida.

The mature Hakluyt was to kindle to these far ventures, which grew more exciting with Drake's exploits of the seventies, during his Oxford period; but the fire of epic interest was only smoldering while Hakluyt trained himself. In his own story, as he wrote, Westminster and Oxford were but interludes, mere intervals between the vision which his cousin had flashed before him and the fulfillment of it. Westminster and Oxford were good for him, he thought, only as they left him free to follow his bent. Otherwise, it was fate and the cousin who combined to equip him for his career; and the story of his career is the only story we really know in his long and active life.[1]

2

If I have correctly guessed the ancestry of the younger Richard Hakluyt, he was the grandson of Edmund Hakluyt, Esquire, of Eyton, and the son of Richard Hakluyt, merchant, of London. The record will show that he enjoyed the benefits of both connections. He could draw on the mercantile interest, which had already profited his cousin of the Middle Temple; he could command the dignity of the landholding family of Hereford, which enabled him to sign himself gentleman; and he could thank his fate for the cousin, who was probably his guardian after the early death of his parents and who combined in his own career the influence of the governing and the mercantile classes.

[1] The evidence for Hakluyt's life and actions is given chronologically in Appendix II.

As Thomas Hakluyt, the father of the lawyer, had become a salaried government official instead of a soldier administrator, so Thomas' brother Richard broke even more brusquely with all the traditions of his battle-axe ancestors and became a merchant. In 1510 he apprenticed himself to a member of the Skinners' Company in London, or, in modern terms, went into the leather business. We suppose him then in his teens; later he became free of the company and of the City. Late in life he married an unknown Margery, who bore him four sons and one or two daughters before he died in 1557 and she died soon after.

We suppose further that the Skinner was not unsuccessful. All four sons could afford a University education, and they owned some property in Hereford. Of property in London there is no sign. Richard the father gave over the title of Esquire which his father wore; his sons resurrected the family tradition, and at Oxford the youngest signed himself gentleman. From the University the sons went on to various gentlemanly careers. The eldest, Thomas, passed from Westminster School to Cambridge; thence he transferred to Oxford after taking his Master's degree, and died there soon after. The second, Richard, went to Oxford and became a clergyman and a geographer. The third, Oliver, studied medicine at Oxford and retired to Hereford to build a practice, a family, and something of an estate. The youngest, Edmond, went on from Oxford to an indeterminate career which would have set him down in the law if he had not died at Eyton in his early thirties.

The opportunities of the four sons of the Skinner are significant. Whatever the merchant's worldly state, it is unlikely that his sons would have opened the doors of education if their grandfather had not been Esquire. One of them might have joined her Majesty's forty scholars at the refounded Westminster School. One of them might have been elected to a studentship at either University, since the School held six appointments yearly.[2] But it is not likely that all four would have succeeded had there been no family prestige to whisper in the ear of authority. That prestige we suppose to have been personified in the lawyer cousin; and his guardianship, whether legal or only voluntary, we may now trace in his bringing up of his young namesake.

The first fact in the life of the youngest of the Richard Hakluyts, who was born in 1551 or 1552, is his presence at Westminster School, which we may place in the sixties. His elder, Thomas, was there until 1567, when he departed for Cambridge. The two youngest brothers entered before Richard left for Christchurch in 1570, and they had both followed him to Oxford by 1575. Richard's appointment as Student of Christchurch was the better one, the major election from

[2] See John Sargeaunt, *Annals of Westminster School* (London 1898), p. 57.

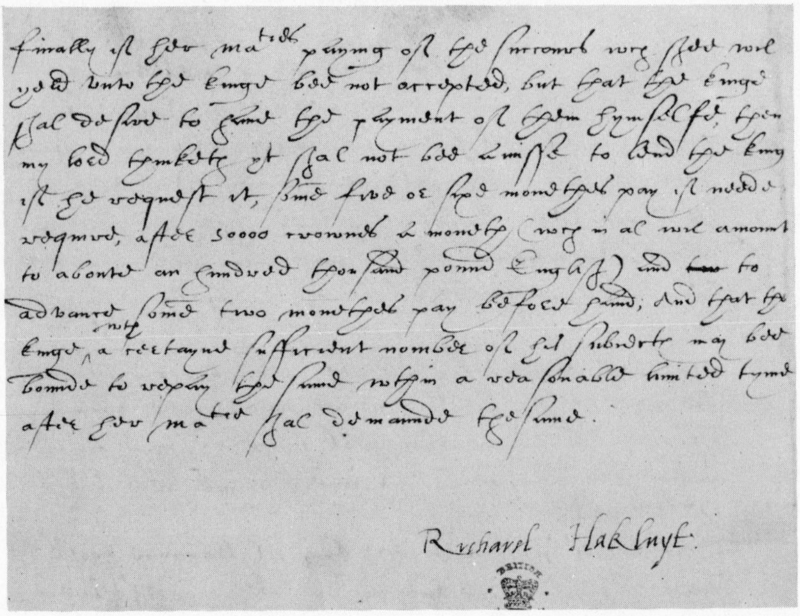

finally if her Matie paying of the crownes wch shee wil
yeeld unto the kinge bee not accepted, but that the kinge
shal desire to haue the payment of them hymselfe, then
my lord thinketh it shal not bee amisse to lend the king
if he request it, sume fewe or three monethes pay if neede
requyre, after 50000 crownes a monethe (wch in al wil amount
to aboute an hundred thousand pounde English) and ~~two~~ to
advance some two monethes pay before hand; And that the
kinge wth a certayne sufficient nomber of his subiects may bee
bounde to repay the same within a reasonable limited tyme
after her matie shal demaunde the same.

Richard Hakluyt.

FIG. 12—Holograph of Richard Hakluyt, lawyer. From his letter to Lord Burleigh, 28 February 1570–71. Public Record Office, London: State Papers Domestic Elizabeth 77,18.

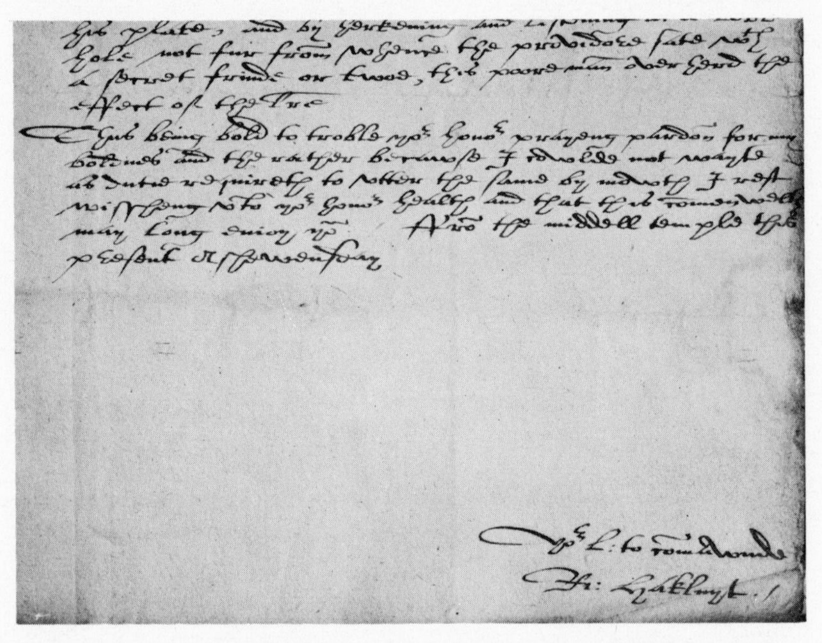

his estate, and by pertaining and [illegible]
hole not far from whence the providore hath not
a secret frinde or twoo, this poore man doeth heare the
effect of the Ltre
Thus being bold to trouble yor honor praying pardon for my
boldnes and the rather because I would not wayte
as duetie requireth to pester the same by mouth I rest
wisshing unto yor honors health and that this commonwelth
may long enioy the. From the middell temple this
present Wednesday

Yor L: to commaunde
Ri: Hakluyt.

FIG. 13—Holograph of Richard Hakluyt, preacher. From his report to Walsingham, July 1588. British Museum, Harleian MSS 288, fol. 213b.

Westminster. By its terms the incumbent was to be made comfortable at Oxford for as long as he remained unmarried. In Richard's case, the Studentship allowed him to take his degrees in due course, in 1574 and 1577; to take orders, at the hands of his Dean who was now advanced to be Bishop of Salisbury, at some time between 1577 and 1583; and to continue to write himself of Oxford until he had reached his middle thirties. His educational history is thus far simply told. Like his brothers, Richard was a Queen's Scholar at Westminster. Like one of his brothers, he passed directly from the royal school to a royal studentship in the late King's foundation at Oxford. His story is the story of a continuing subsidy paid to his family name.

The second fact in Hakluyt's life is his visit to the Middle Temple. Doubtless it was not the only fact in his early dealings with the lawyer. When we spoke above of the family prestige, we implied that the prestige was made deed by the Hakluyt who lived in the Middle Temple and was known to Lord Burleigh. Probably the lawyer cousin had taken up his charge long before the talk on geography. He was "overseer" of the will of the Skinner, "to be aiding, assisting, and comforting" the widow; and, when the widow died soon afterwards, it was probably part of the duty of an overseer to look after the orphans.

The bond was certainly close between the lawyer and his cousins. He left his property to them when he died; and the youngest of them, who himself died soon afterward, provided for a monument to his "dear cousin." The testimony is brief but sufficient. In Richard's case the bond is even closer (Figs. 12, 13); for, in addition to whatever duties of a guardian the lawyer may have assumed, there must be reckoned the decisive scene when the lawyer spoke things of high and rare delight to his young kinsman. From that conversion flowed a constant resolution, and the lawyer channeled and guided the resolution. Henceforth until the young kinsman came mentally of age the lawyer watched over the young mind.

We read further of the younger man's story, as he wrote it in the *Voyages:*

"At Christchurch in Oxford, my exercises of duty first performed, I fell to my intended course and by degrees read over whatsoever printed or written discoveries and voyages I found extant, either in the Greek, Latin, Italian, Spanish, Portugal, French, or English languages, and in my public lectures was the first that produced and showed both the old imperfectly composed, and the new lately reformed maps, globes, spheres, and other instruments of this Art for demonstration in the common schools, to the singular pleasure and general contentment of my auditory. In continuance of time, and by reason principally of my insight in this study, I grew familiarly acquainted with the chiefest Captains at sea, the greatest Merchants, and the best Mariners of our nation."

So the exercises of duty seemed to him, when he wrote of them some fifteen years later, to be a mere trial, a seven-year study of the humanities which was essential but only preliminary to his main progress. In those seven years he would be introduced to a certain body of knowledge. He would read the Latin and Greek classics which had been added to the Aristotle of an earlier time. He would learn some mathematics and some natural science, he would read philosophy. But he would be trained particularly in the arts of logic and rhetoric. Argument, disputation, debate would be the educational method; and it is possible that not a little knowledge filtered past the screen of dialectic.[3]

Although the candidate for the two degrees was obliged to "respond," to "determine," and to preside over disputations, it is not likely that Hakluyt used his chance to lecture on geography until after he had been licensed Master of Arts in 1577. In the two following years he was required to act as "regent master," or lecturer, in training for the teaching career which the degree permitted him; and I suppose that he then avoided the divinity schools and fell to his intended course in languages and science. He could then turn his lectures to cosmography. Perhaps by way of commentary upon Ptolemy he explained the new lately reformed maps, and thus, for the first time as he thought, he let in at Oxford the light of the new science.

The lectures, and the singular pleasure of his auditory, he may have thought, sanctioned his choice of a career. Certainly they marked a distinct stage in his apprenticeship, which in our view of his history runs throughout his later Oxford period down to 1582 or 1583. They may also have given him a sign not only of what he could but of what he might do, once the apprenticeship was over. For it may well have appeared to the young Oxford student that his passion for geography would lead him to the promised land. Naturally he would not see very far ahead, unless his cousin were a prophet. But one fact was patent, that there were no professional geographers in England. The Continental nations would indeed have laughed at the idea that England had need of geographers. "But the English of all others," as Hakluyt later heard in Paris, "for their sluggish security and continual neglect of the like attempts, especially in so long and happy a time of peace, (were) either ignominiously reported or exceedingly condemned." The "like attempts" were "notable enterprises by sea"; and in their absence there could have been no need of geographers.

We have seen that there were notable ventures and that there were geographers by avocation; for England was becoming an independent maritime nation. It was still dependent, to some extent, on foreign shipping. Aside from the vessels that carried wool to Flan-

[3] The clearest statement of the Oxford curriculum, though of a slightly later period (1590–1620), is in the introductions, by Andrew Clark, to the *Register of the University of Oxford*, Oxford Historical Society (1887), vol. II, part I.

ders or brought back wine from Bordeaux, England's dealings with the outer world were still carried on in large part by Dutch and German shipping; and Dutch and German sailors were themselves only middlemen, who transshipped the goods brought from the Levant and the Indies by the master mariners of Italy and Spain and Portugal. But Englishmen were pushing farther overseas in the seventies. In the Huguenot wars they met with sturdy Norman seamen, who ranked only after the Iberians in their knowledge of remote lands. As a result of the religious wars in the Low Countries, English ships were gradually taking over from the Dutch the distributing of oversea products from Spain and Portugal to northern Europe and thus widening their knowledge of ocean routes and foreign lands. The Venetian trade was drying up at the source. The German importers of the Steelyard were steadily losing their commercial privileges. English merchants who had sent ships into the White Sea were now sending them into the Baltic. English shipbuilding had been much improved. Finally, the expansion eastward of the search for markets began a new oversea expansion of English trade from about 1575, a contest with the Mediterranean nations for the trade and trade routes of the East. English commercial independence was being achieved in Hakluyt's early years.[4]

This fragment of history may explain why the younger Hakluyt could follow a new profession, why he could prepare for it in leisurely fashion at the university. So far as we may learn of his preparation we judge that he mastered the rudiments of his science. Certainly he was familiar with the works of the leading scientists, or at least he could prefix an imposing list of them to his first serious publication in 1582. How "sound" he was as a geographer it is more difficult to know, for he never expounded his geography in a public system, never gathered together a treatise, never drew a map himself. Other men, his contemporaries, show a more abstract interest. Wright explained and applied the so-called Mercator projection. Hues, like Dee, wrote treatises on the use of the globes. Hariot passed easily from geography, which brought him an early subsistence, to the mathematical studies which anticipated Descartes. But of Hakluyt all that we are told of his proficiency in the pure, as opposed to the applied, science is that he lectured at Oxford. It is easy to believe that his audience responded. We cannot know that there was a further demand for lectures of the sort; and it was not until the foundation of the Savile chair of astronomy in 1619 that lectures were regularly provided.

Hakluyt may have hoped for some such chair for himself. I doubt it, since in none of his urging of endowments for this and for that did he later appear to put himself forward as a candidate. It

[4] See again J. A. Williamson, *Maritime Enterprise;* and E. P. Cheyney, *History of England from the Defeat of the Armada to the Death of Elizabeth,* vol. I, Chapters 15–20 (New York 1913).

turned out that his career was not to be academic. Under his cousin's presumable guidance he was to follow his cousin's model by attending to applied geography. Applied geography, meaning mainly economic geography, was still to be studied empirically; and the most useful key to the study was linguistic. Hence Hakluyt learned, as his story naïvely recites, all the essential European tongues, for in the narratives and reports of explorers lay buried the facts he was to assemble. The library of travel was already large. It was growing by leaps as nation after nation was drawn into oversea enterprise. To acquire a knowledge of geography, to learn the languages, and to begin to assemble his materials might well take Hakluyt a full seven years.

The guiding hand of the cousin must be seen in the direction of this apprenticeship. Oxford could hardly direct it. It could give the student whatever we may agree to call mental training; but it is doubtful if Oxford was interested in the reform of Ptolemy, and here the cousin alone could step in. To the cousin Hakluyt owed the first inspiration. To him was doubtless due the plan of general study, which centered in geographies and grammars. To him was unmistakably due the specialization in applied geography that would bring clients, and due not least of all the introduction to clients who would need specialists. To him was perhaps due finally the qualifying for holy orders, which would free the geographer from the uncertainties of patronage. The plan was admirable. To judge by the results, it reduced to a minimum the false starts and waste motions that may hamper the beginning of a career.

3

The most fruitful period of the elder Hakluyt's expert career was that about 1580, which was a critical period in the expansion. So well was cast the horoscope of the younger Hakluyt that he was approaching professional maturity at exactly this time. There could hardly be too many hands at work on the harvesting of geographical information, and he was easily drawn into the field. He was still the apprentice, his knowledge still untested by action; he was now to be made acquainted with other sources of knowledge than books.

He must know his colleagues, so to call them. He probably met Dr. Dee, who was known to the lawyer. He met Ortelius, the Flemish geographer, who was in England in 1577. What passed at this meeting we do not know, or whether it was arranged by the lawyer or by one of the Fleming's relatives in England, whom the clergyman certainly knew later. The royal geographer of Spain may have talked graciously to the young man; a few years later Hakluyt wrote down something Ortelius had then said about Dutch colonial projects. He probably met the French geographer royal, if Thevet was really in

England in 1582; certainly he was to see much of the Frenchman in later years in France.

The most impressive event of all in Hakluyt's early career was his correspondence with Mercator in 1580. This grew out of the northeast expedition of that year, for which, as we have seen, the Russia Company sought many advices: from Borough the navigator, from Dee the academic geographer, from the elder Hakluyt the strategic geographer. In order to extend the net as wide as possible, the younger Hakluyt tried to add the experience of Mercator, the leading geographer of Europe.

It was very likely his own enthusiastic idea which led him to write to Mercator, posing certain questions on Siberian coasts and currents. It certainly was of no use to the expedition, as the watching cousin, with his tongue in his cheek, perhaps expected. For the letter reached Duisburg too late for an answer to arrive in time. At any rate, the old man, with nearly fifty years of research behind him, answered graciously and at length to his young and unknown correspondent. Hakluyt kept and printed the friendly letter and fittingly enough, for the mere writing of it was a kind of welcome into the profession. The transaction was the first professional employment of the student. No one but himself may have taken it seriously. But it was a sign that he had given advice to merchant adventurers. It might mean also that he had done other things for the expedition, that he had perhaps helped his cousin to write the latter's memorandum. The exchange of letters was not the end of Hakluyt's acquaintance with Mercator, which he apparently continued through the geographer's nephew and successor, who was then in London.

For a young man under thirty an acquaintance with geographies and geographers was still not enough. He must also collect and collate the reports of travelers, to which end he had learned his many languages. That he had been doing so is witnessed by the second step in his active career, which he took in the same year with the letter to Mercator which is the first step. He published at Oxford a small volume containing two narratives of American travel. The choice shows that Hakluyt was already drawn to the special American field which was to be his main concern.

The narratives reported the discovery of the St. Lawrence River in Canada in the years 1534 and 1535. Sufficient reason for their publishing may be found in the current English interest in that part of America. The northwest voyages of Frobisher had failed to find either gold or a passage to China; and, though they were shortly to be revived in the voyages of John Davis, the project of an American colony in their stead had been brought to the fore by Gilbert. Gilbert aimed vaguely at the country north of Florida; and aside from the information to be had in England, which we have seen the elder Hakluyt collecting, there were but two descriptions of the region. We must except the reports of Spanish explorers, which were sadly diluted by the official historians. For other North American information one could go only to the letter of Verrazano, who had explored most of the Atlantic coast, and to the reports of Cartier, who had sailed three times to the Gulf of St. Lawrence and had twice ascended the river to the height of Montreal. Verrazano's results had already been given in Eden's *Decades.* Cartier's reports, of which only the first two out of three had been printed in France, completed the story.[5]

The translating of Cartier was done by John Florio, from the great Italian collection of Ramusio. Because Hakluyt's name does not appear in the volume, his share in it has been generally overlooked. The work was none the less his own idea. In dedicating his next book in 1582 Hakluyt was to write that "the last year, at my charges and other of my friends, by my exhortation, I caused Jaques Cartier's two voyages . . . to be translated out of my volumes." So the undertaking was Hakluyt's own, and the method of it is easily seen. Florio, the son of an Italian Protestant refugee, was then an undergraduate at Oxford. Hakluyt may have been studying Italian with him or his father, and the choice was an obvious one for the task in hand. One does not need to suppose that Florio was interested in geography or in America. The chances are that he was not, since he never returned to it; and he seems to have been no more than an agent.

That he was only an agent is suggested by the subject, for the future translator of Montaigne was not likely to be interested in two bare narratives for their own sake. It is suggested also by Florio's preface, which addressed the book to "all Gentlemen, Merchants, and Pilots, . . . or whosoever desirous of new Discoveries." Moreover, the book was definitely aimed to arouse interest in the American projects under way. "For," as the preface further declared, "here is the description of a country no less fruitful and pleasant . . . than is England, France, or Germany, . . . which opportunities . . . might suffice to induce our Englishmen not only to fall to some traffic with the inhabitants, but also to plant a colony in some convenient place." The voice is the ventriloquist's.

The modest book so sponsored is not in itself of great importance. Books on the discoveries were becoming plentiful in English, as will soon be shown; and to the public view this could be only one more volume, though an appropriate one. In Hakluyt's history, however, the event has its meaning. The expert was stretching his limbs. After the consultant came the editor. The letter to Mercator marked the one function; the Cartier marked the other. Hakluyt's career was already double.

[5] The principal authority on the growth of European knowledge of North America is Justin Winsor, *Cartier to Frontenac* (Boston and New York 1894); and also the earlier volumes, II, III, and IV, of his *Narrative and Critical History of America* (Boston 1884–89).

4

Still a third strand was being woven into Hakluyt's training presumably by the providence of his cousin. He had become a student of geography and had lectured on it; he had studied his languages and collected something of a library, if the phrase "my volumes" was not too ambitious. Even more important was acquaintance with travelers. In a time when the earth had grown overnight to beanstalk proportions the geographer must be, as we have seen, something of a reporter. Perhaps as something of a reporter Hakluyt now, to use his own later magniloquence, "grew familiarly acquainted with the chiefest Captains at sea, the greatest Merchants, and the best Mariners of our nation."

Of this widened circle of acquaintance we have little evidence that goes back before 1582, the year when Hakluyt was definitely caught up into the colonial plans of Gilbert and Walsingham. The consulting of Mercator suggests that the cousin had already found a way for him into the merchant group that centered in the Russia Company; and it may be that he was already, for one purpose or another, going over the records of traders. That he was his father's son may have helped him to relations with the City. At least, the cousin could insure that the City should remember him.

The dedication of the *Divers Voyages,* which he was to issue in 1582, gives hints of such relations. Hakluyt had then made the acquaintance of "merchants of credit that have lived long in Spain"; some of them were perhaps the translators of whom a word will soon have to be said. He had talked with Stephen Borough, most distinguished of Russia Company captains, who perhaps was still cherishing his ambition to be pilot major of England. He had interviews with Sir Francis Drake himself, returned in 1580 from his journey round the world, interviews which concerned a school for pilots. He "had great conference in matters of cosmography" with the Portuguese ambassador. Such a conference would have yielded small information a year or two before, when Portugal swayed a vast empire and was jealous of rivals; but the ambassador was now a refugee from a country which had been swallowed by Spain, his sovereign Dom Antonio was counting on English naval aid, and he showed himself to Hakluyt "most privy to all the discoveries of his nation."

One acquaintance was more than casual. This was with Michael Lock, merchant and traveler and principal investor in the Frobisher voyages, which had virtually ruined him. In that venture he must at least have met the elder Hakluyt and hence the younger too. His relations with the young man, which must have been enlightening in many ways, are clearly shown only by his part in the *Divers Voyages,* for which he made the map. Lock had seen much of the world as an agent in foreign parts and had seen rather too much of the ways of speculative enterprise; and he was keenly interested in geography. The disillusioned merchant helped the young scientist with his book, and the friendship between them continued throughout a long lifetime.

It may be added that Lock was the stepfather of the man who later became Sir Julius Caesar and a law officer of the Crown, and also that Caesar was an Oxford contemporary of Hakluyt. These facts weave a final strand in Hakluyt's training, the necessary acquaintance with men of position and influence at court. His cousin was again able to put him in touch with the right people: with City merchants on the one hand, whose business affairs were then as always affairs of state; with Middle Templars of influence on the other, of whom more than one, like Sir John Popham, later Chief Justice and a leader in Virginia, were to count in colonial enterprise. But the younger man's expensive education could also be turned to profit. Among Oxford contemporaries there were few who might be immediately useful; but the few were important. Gilbert had of course gone down before Hakluyt's time. Raleigh had left Oriel for the Huguenot wars in the year before Hakluyt matriculated. But there was Caesar, who was just beginning practice in 1581; there was Edwin Sandys, later prominent in Virginia, although he was first to spend twenty years in orders; and of main importance at first there was Philip Sidney.

That generous youth was a member of Christchurch, where he lived during part of Hakluyt's time, from 1568 to 1572. The geographer was to dedicate to him the *Divers Voyages,* as to one "which hath been always so ready to pleasure me and all my name." To Sidney's father-in-law Walsingham, Her Majesty's Secretary, was to be due Hakluyt's official recognition, his entrée into colonial circles. Very little more can be learned. Hakluyt is mentioned only once in Sidney's letters and then favorably though not too familiarly. One gathers that Sidney did his duty by his fellow collegian and effectively, but no more.

One must speak at this point of another courtier, Edward Dyer, the winning friend of Sidney and a favorite of the court and the Queen. Dyer may have become known to the younger Hakluyt through the elder, since both were named on the Dover committee of 1581. He is the one man of whom the geographer ever wrote with more than formal enthusiasm. In the preface to the *English Voyages,* he singled out Dyer for a friendly rather than an official acknowledgment, writing in these terms: "In respect of a general encouragement in this laborious travail, it were gross ingratitude in me to forget, and willful maliciousness not to confess, that man whose only name doth carry with it sufficient estimation and love, and that is Master Edward Dyer. . . . Both myself and my intentions herein by his friendly means have been made known to those who in sundry particulars have much steaded me." Sidney was dead, of course, before the *Voyages* were well started; but, even so, he would probably have been mentioned in the preface if he had been as kind as Dyer. One regrets that no more is known of the dealings of Dyer and Hakluyt. Hakluyt did not lack friends; but they seem always to have been professional ones, and the gracious figure of the courtier brightens the picture for only a moment.

Last and most impressive on the list of the Oxford group may perhaps be placed the adventurous Earl of Cumberland. That picturesque sportsman and soldier took his degree at Cambridge, being there attracted to mathematics. Having received his M. A. in 1576, his daughter recorded, he went over to Oxford to study geography and especially to consult "ancient maps and divers papers" in one of the colleges. The remark is tantalizingly left unexplained. Why one should travel to Oxford for geography is unaccountable if it is remembered that it was Cambridge that had led the revival, in John Dee's time, of the science of Ptolemy.[6]

One is tempted, of course, to infer that word had come to Cambridge of Hakluyt's studies and perhaps of his public lectures. The conclusion is not so fanciful as it sounds. For Hakluyt's eldest brother Thomas was a contemporary of the Earl and a member of the same Cambridge college. Not only were they contemporaries: if the Earl journeyed to Oxford in 1576, he would have found there or perhaps even accompanied there the same Thomas Hakluyt, who was just transferring. An acquaintance of some sort is nearly certain. Even if the Earl had not known of Richard Hakluyt but had some irrelevant motive in visiting the other university, he could hardly have failed to discover Hakluyt on arriving. Indeed, the ancient maps and divers papers may very well have been Hakluyt's own.

If I relate this incident it is not to prove anything very serious. It is only to suggest the numberless ways in which the young geographer might establish his circle of influence. The Earl was to be a Queen's favorite. He was to send out or to command no less than twelve expeditions during the Spanish war. He qualified, at least in the eyes of an admiring daughter, as "the most knowing and eminent man (in knowledge of navigation), of a Lord, in his time." How much a Lord had to know to surpass his peers is dubious. If he knew any thing at all of seafaring, he could be useful to Hakluyt. Whether he was useful to Hakluyt, or Hakluyt to him or to his ventures, one cannot say.

[6] See G. C. Williamson, *George, Third Earl of Cumberland* (Cambridge 1920), pp. 10, 11.

5

These various strands of Hakluyt's training may now be seen gathered up in the event that marks the end of his apprenticeship: the publishing in 1582 of the *Divers Voyages touching the discovery of America.* At the age of thirty, Hakluyt now reached a position of independent professional importance. His maturity was now declared.

No more favorable moment could have been chosen for the book. The year 1582 was decisive for American enterprise. To the unprejudiced the decision should have seemed altogether adverse. The Northwest Passage, which made the first motive in the American complex, had not been found. Frobisher had tried it again for the Cathay Company in 1576 and the two succeeding years. Like the Cabots he had tried in vain; but the Passage remained on every map, and Adrian Gilbert and John Dee were putting their heads together and were soon to form a new company to send out new expeditions in search of it. Frobisher had also looked for gold in the frozen North; he had not found it, and the Cathay Company was bankrupt in consequence. But the tale of every traveler argued fabulous treasures in the unknown continent; and every tale was believed, if only because the conquerors of Mexico and Peru had had as much, or as little, to go on.

If these lessons of experience were not enough, the menace of Spain might seem to close the case against further enterprise. This was a positive lesson, which had already been rudely learned by the French. Except indeed for the exploits of Drake and others in the seventies, which were spectacular rather than conclusive, the only challenge to Spanish supremacy in the New World had so far been delivered by France. French pirates had roved the Atlantic for half a century before Drake, and the result had been the birth of a Spanish fleet in the Atlantic; French colonies had been settled in Florida in the early sixties, but their brutal extinction by Menéndez was a lesson to be seriously pondered by colonizers.

Such lessons are not, however, apt to be taken seriously by those whose interest it is to take them lightly; and English commerce was not ready to consider the case closed. Its appetite for profits was whetted but by no means satisfied. The Russian trade had brought in large returns. England was displacing Dutch and German ships in the carrying trade; but the English commercial position was still precarious. The large returns from Russia came from Oriental products; and, whether the products were procured through Russia or through Asia Minor, the obstacles of time and space and dangerous transit were many. The carrying trade between Lisbon or Cadiz and northern Europe depended upon Spanish good will, which was not large, and upon competition with Germany and Holland, which was not easy. It was not therefore difficult to defy the lessons of experience on eastern and American markets. It was on the other hand easy to allege many benefits to the nation, in wealth, in prestige, and in self-defence, to justify the ventures of those who would profit by a reopening of the American case.

The profits were proved by Drake's voyage round the world, which returned ten thousand per cent. This handsome figure interested the Queen, who made large investments in piracy, and encouraged the anti-Spanish party, which was naturally the colonial party. With the active aid of the government, expansionist plans were accordingly pushed after Drake's return. Dom Antonio was to sanction expeditions to his lost possessions of the Azores and in South America, Africa, and India. Fenton got to South America in 1582. William Hawkins reached Porto Rico. Drake planned the conquest of the Moluccas and instead descended on the West Indies in 1585. Cavendish finally sailed on the southwestern voyage in 1586.

In 1584 a new patent was granted for the northwest discovery as well, a patent under which John Davis was to lead three voyages in the following years. These expeditions were all meant to reach the East. A parallel series looked to America, no longer a mere station on the China route. Throughout the year 1582 the plans of the Gilbert colony went steadily forward. In the preparations there appeared as a leading actor Sir Francis Walsingham, Secretary of State and enemy of Spain. Principally he tried to gain Catholic support for a colony that might draw off Catholic disturbers of his peace. Incidentally he enlisted Hakluyt in the venture.

This official recognition may have been due as much to personal influence as to personal merit. Yet it is not to be doubted that the *Divers Voyages* counted. It is not clear where the idea of the book came from. Since it was opportune, we may fancy that either or both of the Hakluyts hit upon it and that the colonial party was not slow in supporting it. As American propaganda the book was excellently planned. Its author at once outdistanced by the plan alone his forerunners in publicity, Eden and Willis.

The modest title of *Divers Voyages touching the discovery of America* framed the plan of much of Hakluyt's later work. The filling in of the plan was rather haphazard, as if the writing had been hastened to meet the market; but there was good reason for including all the rather miscellaneous material and particularly the narratives which justified the title. But, as what Hakluyt did in the *Divers Voyages* must be judged by what there was to do, I must first carry on the story of oversea publicity from the point at which it was left by Eden.

The latter's two books on America had been coincident, as we have seen, with the beginning of the Russian trade. For twenty years thereafter there was little further publishing. Then, with the new cycle of commerce, began an outburst of books, which was later, under the younger Hakluyt's impulse, to grow into a steady stream.

The thin trickle after Eden was largely journalistic, as shown by the bibliography.[7] Two narratives of French Florida, hastily written and hastily translated; a belated account of the other French colony, which had been settled and wiped out in Brazil in 1555; a record of Hawkins' last disastrous voyage to Mexico in 1567—these slight works made up the additions to the literature of travel before Frobisher. In addition may be noted a continuing interest in navigation, which is marked by two original English treatises in 1573 and by the plan worked out by Sir Humphrey Gilbert by 1570 for the teaching of navigation and geography to the wards of the Crown. Finally there may be noted a faint flavor of the revival of learning in the publishing in 1565 of an abstract of Pliny from the French and in 1572 of the *Survey of the World* by Dionysius of Alexandria.

With the Frobisher voyages the floodgates opened. Gilbert's *Discourse on the Passage* was followed by a seemingly concerted attempt to bring England up to date on the record of the discoveries. Translators set to work with a will. There was none ambitious enough to attempt a complete record, which was to be Hakluyt's achievement. Yet nearly every substantial book on at least the Spanish discoveries, and some on the Portuguese, was tackled and, in whole or in part, made English.

First in order of translators comes Richard Willis. For a noble pupil this otherwise unknown translator put out a new *Decades* and, in what is the second important English book on the new worlds, considerably expanded and improved the first, which was Eden's. To the Spanish portions of Eden, as taken from the official histories of Peter Martyr, Oviedo, and Gómara, he indeed added little; but for the first time in English he published material on the East. Pereira's description of China, Maffei's description of Japan, Varthema's recent overland journey to India were taken from foreign sources, the last in Eden's own translation. From English sources he took the first printed record of the Persian journeys of Jenkinson and Willis' own summary discourses on Cathay and the Northwest Passage. In Willis' book Asia and the roads to Asia were for the first time made real to the English reader.

Willis' *History of Travail* was put out as publicity for the Frobisher voyages. So also, and with greater or less appropriateness, were the books that followed. An account from Gómara of the conquest of Mexico; the record of the conquest of Peru; a work on American drugs; a geographical survey of the West Indies—all conveyed much encouraging information on American wealth, while Las

[7]See Appendix IV.—The name Willis below should be Willes.

Casas' episcopal denunciation of red slavery called up a virtuous and patriotic hatred for Spain. To these records of the West were added substantial further accounts of the East: a chronicle of the Portuguese voyages, a much more ambitious history of the discovery and conquest of the Portuguese Indies, and Marco Polo himself passed through the Spanish into English.

All this publishing, to which must be added the accounts of Frobisher's voyages and numerous editions and reëditions and translations of works on navigation, testifies to a conscious propaganda or a sudden popular demand or both. That the bulk of the translating was done by English merchants who had lived long in Spain suggests a combination of these motives. Their employment argues that more than linguistic ability was required, that some expert sense of trade values and of geography dictated the choice of both the translators and the works translated.

At any rate, the output of volumes is remarkable, and it was upon this flood that Hakluyt's own publications were to be floated. He must, however, steer his own course; and his special training served him in laying it down. Accounts of the East or Spanish West might be all very well for general information or general interest; but with the shift from Frobisher to Gilbert, from a passage to China to a colony in North America a practical geographer must ask himself the practical question: What precisely is known of North America? Willis had asked himself, or been asked, a similar question about the East and the Passage and thereby shown himself a conscious propagandist. Hakluyt asked himself this new question and in the event became the second and greater propagandist. The answer was to be found piecemeal in the Spanish histories; but, as these were compilations and as the original narratives of the Spanish explorers were sequestered at Seville, the question must be carried back to other original narratives of other explorers. Those narratives it was important to explore and then to publish.

By some such reasoning the *Divers Voyages* must have been shaped. The elder Hakluyt had tried English sources. Gilbert and the active Walsingham were tapping original sources of their own by examining stray travelers and by sending ships to reconnoiter beyond Newfoundland. The younger Hakluyt recurred to the written record. He gathered from it first all that could be found of the Cabot discoveries, which established English title. Then the relation of the mythical fifteenth-century voyage to Greenland of the Zeno brothers, which, taken with the Frobisher narratives recently published elsewhere, summed up the knowledge of the frozen North. Then came Verrazano's account of the first exploration of the American coast, in 1524, which, with Hakluyt's recent Cartier, contained all the accessible information on temperate North America. For good measure, Hakluyt added the rare narrative of the beginning of Ribaut's colony of French Florida.

This was far from being a complete collection of American voyages (Fig. 14); but it seems to have been as complete as was permitted either by Hakluyt's knowledge—for there was much hidden away in manuscript—or by official censorship. The great gap was formed by the omission of all references to the main French colony in Florida. To account for that omission we may suppose that no one was anxious to emphasize such a signal failure. We may realize also that French Florida became Spanish territory and was legally closed to England. For other omissions, we may note the failure of Hakluyt to obtain for this volume, as he did for a later, the account of John Hawkins' second voyage, which had made a point of stopping at the French colony and had brought home encouraging news of the country. The same motives may have prevailed in this case also and likewise decided the omission of a confidential account of Florida written twenty years before and now kept in the archives.

At any rate, the collection contains all that Hakluyt seems to have been able or permitted to print. Its material was certainly picturesque if not, considering the limitations, of great use. It did at least answer the question on sources. With this material the geographer was not, however, content. Having first given chapter and verse for his researches in an impressive and pedantic list of the geographers and travelers on whom he drew, he composed a still more impressive list of American products. This list he probably intended to be the most tempting part of his prospectus; and he added a discussion of the Northwest Passage, which might furnish other bait to those who doubted the fabulous American treasure. The list and the discussion look pretty dubious now; but it must be asserted that they were fully justified by Hakluyt's authorities, which, if not unimpeachable, were yet unimpeached. In his assembling of the list of products and thus analyzing in print the reports of travelers we must again note, as of special meaning, the typical empirical method of the two Hakluyts. Even in the discussion of the Passage Hakluyt moved empirically. For instead of the authority of the ancients, which Gilbert's *Discourse* began with, he relied upon explorers and in second place upon the modern geographers.

This material, then, composed of original narratives and of facts assembled from them, forms the strictly informative and the major part of the prospectus. As such, it brings into print as much of the answer to Hakluyt's question as was printable and not yet printed in English. He was still not content. To strengthen the case he went farther, as is usual in a prospectus. It may not have been thought judicious, at a time of strained relations with Spain, to add a statement of colonial policy, as Hakluyt was free to do in later works;

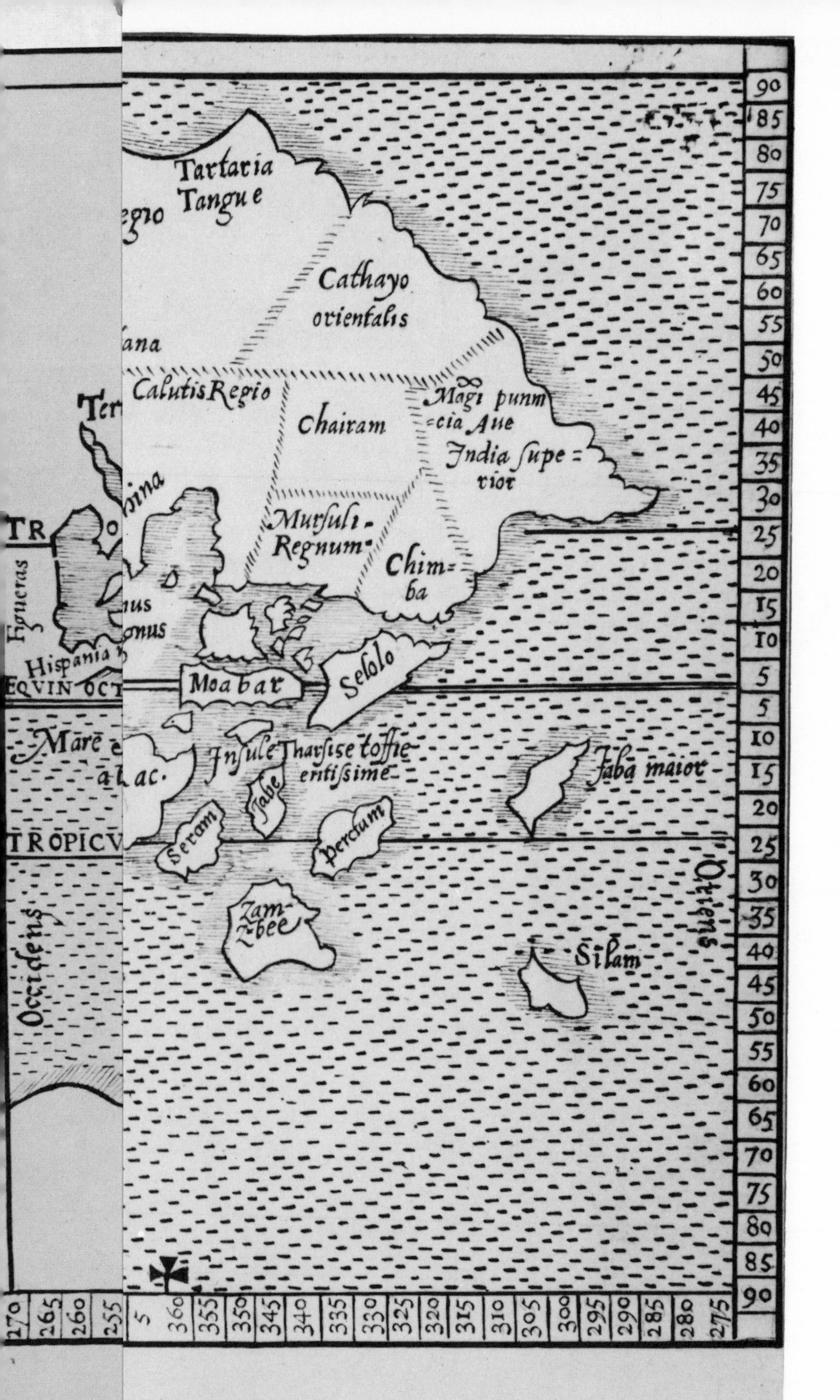

rom Siuill in Spayne by maister Robert Thorne
forking Henry the 8. to Charles the Emperour,
e may seeme rude, yet I haue set it out , be-
stood without the same. The imperfection of
me the knowledge of Cosmographie not then be-
antes, as nowe it is.

, Glasgow.

but there were other ways of appealing to the national pride. For this emotional turn, well known to students of publicity, Hakluyt counted, for one, upon the Cabot narratives and, for another, upon an earlier English work of propaganda which had not yet been printed.

This was the *Book of Robert Thorne* of Seville, of 1527, which has already been mentioned. There was little present value in the Thorne letters. The map of the world which Thorne had surreptitiously obtained was antiquated by fifty years of discovery. His plan of exploration over the pole had been several times tried and had so far failed. His plan of exploration to the Northwest was still being tried and was still failing. The matter of colonization, which was the matter in hand, he had not even mentioned. Yet his book could still be revived as the earliest statement of an oversea policy that had been written by an Englishman, and it contained the memorable words, which Hakluyt now put in circulation: "There is no sea innavigable, no land unhabitable." In the eyes of modern eulogists of the expansion Hakluyt has justified his calling by printing this one resounding sentence.

It was probably from his acquaintances among "the greatest Merchants" that Hakluyt obtained this discourse, which had been kept these many years in the family of Thorne's executor. It was from his guide and cousin that he obtained two other manuscripts, which expanded still further the plan of the collection. One manuscript was the guide to explorers which had been written by the older man for the late northeast expedition. The other was the guide to colonizers written by him for the last Frobisher voyage. With the list of American products the two papers combined to answer the second question of the colonizer, What is to be looked for? as the travel records answered the question, What is known? With this explanation I think the *Divers Voyages* loses what appears at first to be its miscellaneous character. It was guided by a plan; and the fact that it had a plan immediately takes Hakluyt out of the class of the rather aimless compilers who preceded him and places him at once in the company of the organizers of intelligence.

In summary, the *Divers Voyages* is seen to play a number of tunes, all of which will continue to sound in Hakluyt's story. The collector of voyages is represented in the narratives of Cabot, of Verrazano, of Ribaut, and of the Zeno brothers. The collector of voyages for a conscious purpose is revealed by the common subject of these narratives, the American scene. The geographer is represented by the note on the Northwest Passage. The consultant is apparent in the instructions for the northeast discovery, in the list of American commodities, and in the colonizing instructions. Finally, the nationalist and expansionist is observed in the *Book of Robert Thorne,* a statement of nationalist policy.

To this grouping of motives in this first essay in publicity will correspond the pattern of Hakluyt's future activities. He will appear most actively as the organizer of publicity, though an organizer on a much larger scale than would be imagined from this first volume. In a character of hardly less importance he will appear as an organizer of knowledge, a rôle he began to play when he wrote the letter to Mercator. In a part of lesser but still considerable importance he will appear as an organizer of enterprise, the agent and the spokesman of an expanding England. The age of thirty finds his energies definitely set upon these several courses.

CHAPTER VI

The Beginnings of Virginia

1583

Seven years make up the second period of Hakluyt's career, the years between the slim *Divers Voyages* of 1582 and the *English Voyages* of 1589. The first book closed his apprenticeship; the second established his fame. Between them were seven years of research, of which five were spent in France. From the research flowered five other books of increasing importance. Many labors also in the cause of the new commerce punctuated the period, making it active as well as fruitful.

The seven years are the best known, as it happens, of Hakluyt's life. He kept no diary as did John Dee, which might reveal the daily doings of a geographer. But by reason of his mission to France he wrote letters; and the letters reveal as fully as a diary the comings and goings of the scientist. It is from the diary of the one, indeed, and the letters of the other that we can add flesh and blood to the picture of the new kind of scientist, whom we can see otherwise only in skeleton in the records of Eden and of the gentleman of the Middle Temple.

Their earlier sketches dissolve at once into the portrait of the young clergyman; or, to change the figure, the younger expert speedily overtakes and all but eclipses his forerunners. Except for his pamphlet on Virginia, the lawyer is seen no more after 1582 in the records of trade. To judge by his suspension in 1584 from the Middle Temple, he was for a time absent from London, retired perhaps to look after his land and his oxen in Hereford. His connection with the Russia Company seems to cease before 1582; and that company needed rather the diplomat than the economist at the time when it was struggling for its foothold in the Russia of Boris Godunov. With the related Baltic trade of the new Eastland Company the elder Hakluyt seems to have had no connection, nor was the younger put to work for either of the eastern enterprises. With the new Levant trade the lawyer likewise ceases relations, unless perhaps he kept in touch with the factors for whom he had made memoranda and whose notes came into print in the cousin's *Voyages*. In the Davis voyages to the Northwest neither Hakluyt seems to have been employed either as promoter or consultant. But in the remaining enterprise, in the affair of the American colony, there was major service to be rendered. In that task the younger Hakluyt came at once to the fore.

The eastern, or Levantine, and the western interests thus engaged and long continued to engage the younger Hakluyt, stepping now into the shoes of the elder. The eastern, which was at first a minor motive, may be mentioned first and so for the time disposed of.

For thirty years the restless fingers of the merchant had been fumbling at the gates of the East. Three voyages, in 1553, in 1557, in 1580, had tried the Northeast Passage. Three Frobisher voyages had tried the Northwest, and three more were about to be launched. Drake had penetrated the Southwest, and after many trials Cavendish was on the point of following him. But as yet there was no opening the gates by sea. The merchants had also tried through Russia, aiming at Persia and Bokhara and reaching them; but the route was incredibly circuitous, and it was with the aim of trying again the Levantine route instead of the Russian that many of the Russia Company merchants turned to making up the Turkey Company of 1581.

Once settled in Constantinople and organized to trade with the Turkish dominions, the company proceeded immediately to its further aim. Early in 1583 a commercial mission was dispatched to Syria, thence to travel overland to India. Of this romantic journey to the East, from which only one man who went the whole way returned, little needs to be repeated here. The mission brought the first English buyers to the markets of India. It brought almost the first recorded Englishmen to the peninsula. It succeeded, in short, in its mission. I wish to note especially the knowledge and experience which such a mission needed to command for its setting out, leaving the results of the journey to a later chapter.[1]

As might be expected, that knowledge and experience was summed up mainly, if not entirely, in the personal history of one of the leaders of the party of five. John Newbery, merchant, "right beloved friend" of Hakluyt, had been in the Near East, where Englishmen had occasionally wandered. He had just returned from what looks like a preliminary reconnaissance as far as Ormuz on the Persian Gulf. He had pushed to within striking distance of India by the overland route and knew his farther way by sea.

He still needed to know, when he should have reached the peninsula, the markets and their commodities. Much of this information he must have learned from Italian and Portuguese records; notably, I suppose, from the two Portuguese histories which had recently been done into English and from the story of that earlier overland traveler, Varthema, which Eden had translated and Willis published. Much more of it he must have picked up on his caravan journey and

[1] The Newbery documents are contained in the *Voyages*, V 275 *ff.*, and amplified in *Purchas His Pilgrims*, IX 483 *ff.* and X 165 *ff.* The Stevens letter is printed in the *Voyages*, VI 377; an account of Stevens as missionary and poet is given in H. G. Rawlinson, *British Beginnings in Western India* (Oxford 1920). An account of the Newbery mission has been composed by J. H. Ryley in *Ralph Fitch* (London 1899)—Fitch being the only man to return. There is also a narrative in the *Dictionary of National Biography*, art. Fitch.

FIG. 15—View of Dartmouth Harbor, *circa* 1550. British Museum, Cotton MSS Aug. I ii 39.

FIG. 16—View of Exeter Harbor, *circa* 1550. British Museum, Cotton MSS Aug. I ii 39.

from the merchants in the Levantine markets. But his information could never be too exact or too complete.

I am inclined, therefore, to assign some importance to the advice given to the mission by the younger Hakluyt. Whether this was his first dealing with the Levant Company; whether he was acting for his cousin, who had just drawn up the notes for the new company agents; whether he was asked for information or gave it without asking—none of these questions can be answered. All that the record says, in a letter written back from Syria, is that Hakluyt asked the traveler to look for an Arab geography and that he gave the traveler two notes made by voyagers in the East.

One note was from the first Englishman to go out to the East. This was Thomas Stevens, a Jesuit sent to the Portuguese capital at Goa, which was Newbery's goal. Arriving in India in 1579, Stevens had written home to his father, a London merchant. This letter Hakluyt gave to Newbery. It could not have helped him very much, for Stevens' account was mainly of his voyage by sea and very little of India. If it did not give information the letter did, however, establish an acquaintance in Goa, an acquaintance which was to be of the utmost value to the pioneers in allowing them to perform their mission at all.

The other note I imagine to have been more informative, the note of "Francis Fernandes the Portugal." The fact that Hakluyt did not later publish it suggests that it had more than a little commercial importance. I take it, therefore, to have contained somewhat the same details of markets and prices as Hakluyt was afterwards to furnish to the East India Company. To be more explicit, it came, I suppose, from a Portuguese pilot who had been in the East; and it came to Hakluyt, I suppose further, in one of several ways. It might have been captured at sea, say by Drake, to whom Hakluyt was already known. It might have come to Bristol or London merchants who traded with the Azores and with Spain (Figs. 15, 16); and we have seen that the elder Hakluyt had acquaintance at Bristol. It might have been written to command by a mariner who, like the Simon Fernandez employed in the American voyages, had been brought into the English service. Or it might, finally and perhaps most plausibly, have been submitted by one of the Portuguese naval officers who were now flocking to England in the wake of their deposed king. In any event the note may have had some importance for the mission, and the consulting of Hakluyt was proof that he was at least in touch. It was also an earnest of further and more important consultations when the enterprise should come to be clothed, at the end of the century, in the majestic garments of the East India Company.

2

For the moment the eastern interest had to wait, though it was not to be lost sight of. For the moment the American interests held the field. It was now reaching its climax in the ambitious plans of Gilbert and Walsingham for an American colony. In these plans the young clergyman takes on an importance one would not expect in a man who was not a courtier or a court favorite like Dee, and who was not on the other hand a merchant. Again one supposes the guiding hand of the cousin, putting forward the younger man either to shield his own retirement or, if he himself played an unrecorded part of the project, to supplement his own labors.

I must not exaggerate the value of a man who could supply only a little information to a complex enterprise. The work of Gilbert and Walsingham fell to many subordinate hands. Some were busy with the teasing forth of reluctant subscriptions, others with the rounding up of soldiers, sailors, and colonists and with the allotting of places in the semimilitary system. To others again must have been assigned the providing of ships and supplies, the planning of the oversea organization, the arrangement of trading and industrial activities. To still others must have been allotted the less obvious tasks of pacifying hostile friends and deceiving suspicious enemies like the Spanish ambassador. In so wide-reaching a movement, involving City and court, we shall be fortunate if we find even a few traces of one who was an organizer merely of knowledge; we shall be impressed if we find any traces of him at all.

From the most likely place we find him strangely absent, and that is in the organizing of actual information for the voyage. Yet the organizing of that information was done thoroughly or at least was recorded thoroughly. The voyage of 1583 was not a first attempt. Gilbert's first expedition, of 1578, was already fairly well fitted out with information, as we have shown. In the interval there had been added the experience of an exploring voyage of 1579, which had been little more than a rapid round trip, and of a probable fishing voyage of 1580, which had gone down the coast of Maine. The two books of Hakluyt, the Cartier and the *Divers Voyages,* made a further contribution. Yet even this body of information was not left to casual sifting; for we find a suggestion in the late summer of 1582 of what looks like a full-dress session of a committee of inquiry.[2]

There is preserved in the state papers a document endorsed " Sun-

[2] The report of the committee is contained in State Papers Domestic Elizabeth 175, 95, and State Papers Colonial, America and West Indies, vol. 1, no. 2. Extracts are given in Gosling's *Life of Sir Humphrey Gilbert,* already mentioned. The full Ingram testimony was printed in the 1589 edition of the *Voyages* but omitted from the final edition because (Purchas, XVI 112) of "some incredibilities of his reports." The testimony has been reprinted, privately, from a British Museum MS by P. C. G. Weston (1856); from a Bodleian MS in *Magazine of American History,* IX 168 (1883). The other witnesses, Fernandez and Walker, are discussed by B. F. De Costa in *Ancient Norombega* (Albany 1890), reprinted (revised) from the *New England Historical and Genealogical Register,* April 1890.

dry reports of the country which Sir Humphrey Gilbert goes to discover." The paper shows that a last effort was being made to scoop up whatever knowledge of America still lay dormant in odd places. As we know from Hakluyt, the inquiry was thought important enough to attract the Queen's Secretary, Walsingham, to sit with Gilbert and the latter's chief supporter, Sir George Peckham. This record alone shows that the Elizabethans were not, and my entire book aims to show that they were not, by any means careless venturers into the unknown. The presence of the Secretary at the session called to examine travelers proves that they were not careless, as does the presence of the same Secretary at the meeting with John Dee over the northwestern plans. The very passion of the Elizabethans for documentation begins to become in itself adventurous. And this inquiry in the late summer of 1582 is especially impressive as the last intellectual adventure of the intellectually impassioned Gilbert.

The history of his adventure in search of knowledge of America proves him to have been no mere swashbuckling visionary. In the early days of his soldiering in Huguenot wars and Irish ambushes he had worked on the problem of expansion. At first it was the Northwest Passage. As early as 1566 he was one of the signers of a petition for a Passage venture, and probably at the same time he was working over the geographical classics to write his *Discourse* proving the reality of the Passage. So convinced was Gilbert of the value of his study that he recommended for a proposed Queen's Academy, for the instruction of wards of the Crown, a thorough course in geography and navigation.

All this labor marks him out before 1570 as the most persistent amateur in the new study. The record shows him to have been no less studious afterwards, when he had seen the Cathay Company launched, had dabbled in the plans for a Southwest Passage Company, and had gained his own American patent and led a first voyage in that direction. He had been seen at the house of Dr. Dee, been seen too consulting other experts. He had sent out Simon Fernandez in 1579 on that Portuguese pilot's first apparent voyage to the New World. Now in 1582, on the eve of his final and fatal voyage, he was still acquiring knowledge.

In this particular inquiry he and his associates sought the testimony of one David Ingram, seaman. Much was hoped from this man. For he said he had wandered overland from Mexico, in what casual or desperate fashion he could not tell, all the way to Cape Breton, in escaping from the Spaniards after Hawkins' broil at Vera Cruz in 1568. Such a man must be used; and as the questions put to him reveal the strictly empirical method of the inquiry, I quote from them as follows: "What he observed in his travels on the north side of the River of May (in Florida), where he remained three months or thereabouts. How long he traveled there. Whether that country be fruitful, and what kind of fruit there be. What kind of beasts and cattle he saw. What kind of people and how appareled. The buildings. Whether any quantity of gold, silver, pearl, or other jewels, and whether he saw a beast far exceeding an ox in bigness."

Ingram's manner must have satisfied the examiners, for they wrote down his testimony at length, and Hakluyt printed it seven years later as valuable. Only afterwards was it suspected that the seaman's remarkable story was fantastic if not fictitious. At least he furnished agreeable answers to the questions, answers that the examiners were delighted to hear. Yet, in saying so, I am far from belittling the method of the inquiry. Ingram said he had really seen turquoises and silver and buffaloes and other desirable things; and perhaps he had. The examiners were wrong only in thinking that the products all grew in more or less the same place. The idea was a cardinal mistake of the early colonizers. But it was not unreasonable. Ingram had walked across the continent, and no one could tell how far. If he had been more fortunate, he might have sailed across it, for it was still possible to believe that the Pacific stretched all the way across to what is now New York (Fig. 17). Most of all, Ingram's statements of what he had seen tallied with those of the Spanish explorers, as Ramusio's collection of travels would testify.

Ingram probably went back with honor to end his days in Barking, and Gilbert passed on to other informants. These were "certain that have traveled the aforesaid countries, with the note of such things as they have found there, over and above that which Ingram upon his examination did confess. Whose names are Vererzamis, Jaques Cartier, John Barros, Andrew Thevett, John Walker, of which number Sir Humphrey Gilbert did confer in person with the three last named." The first two of these will be recognized as the authors of narratives which Hakluyt had just published or was just about to publish, narratives which gave the first information about the northern coast and the River of Canada. John Barros should be some Portuguese pilot, whom I cannot locate. Thevet was the French geographer royal, who had had something to say in his *Cosmography* about the northern coasts; and it is possible that Gilbert had gone to Paris to see him. Walker had been to Maine in 1580, probably on a fishing voyage, and had seen silver there. In addition was cited before the examiners, or privately, "Mr. Secretary's man," otherwise Simon Fernandez, who had made the flying trip three years before.

I have dwelt on this episode because it proves how much of a geographical *dossier* had been built in England for at least fifteen years before 1582 for Gilbert's use and largely by his means. All the local sources of information had apparently been tapped. All the Continental authorities in so far as they were to be located in print had

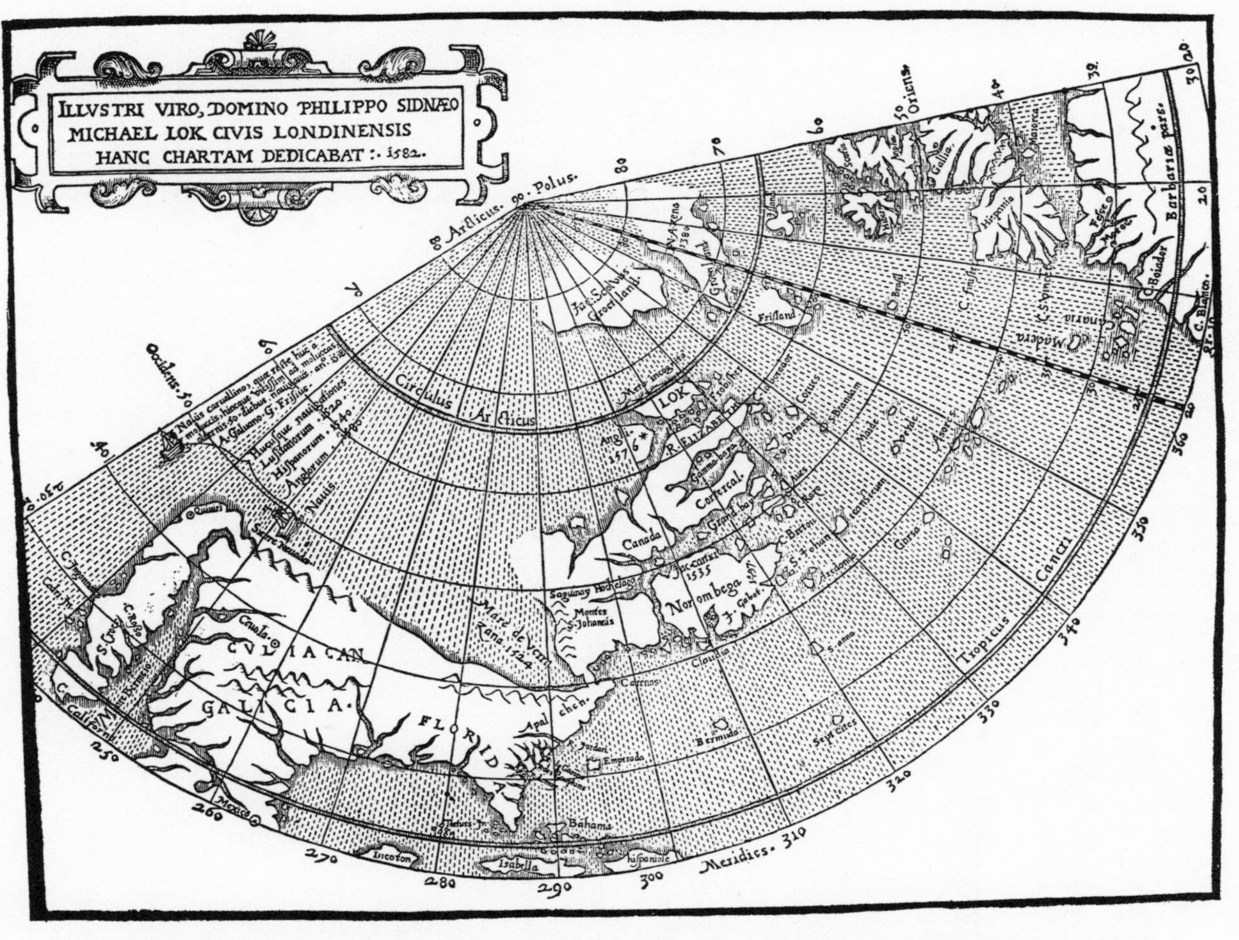

FIG. 17—Map of North America, by Michael Lok. From Hakluyt's *Divers voyages touching the discouerie of America*, London 1582.

likewise been gone over, if we may credit Dee and Gilbert and the Hakluyts with having thoroughly raked the ground among them. And not only was the ground gone over, but the gleanings were carefully hoarded in the younger Hakluyt's storehouse. His *Divers Voyages* gave the nation the key to the storehouse. His later works opened the door wide.

3

How he was aiding the Gilbert organizers—to return at length to that question—is still a matter of inference. He brought out in print at the time the Verrazano and Cartier narratives, together with other American material and especially the list of American commodities, which obviously drew from the list added to its record by the committee of inquiry. It is not likely that the material of the book was handed out to him with the request that he print it. He was probably active, not passive. At least he knew about the inquiry. Otherwise he would not have been able to say, when he later printed Ingram's testimony, that it had been delivered to "Sir Francis Walsingham, Knight, &c., and to Sir George Peckham, Knight, and diverse others of good judgment and credit." The words, if not those of an eyewitness, are those of a participant or at least of one who was close to a participant. Even if he were not himself one of the divers others, he or his cousin must have been able to supply the names and the date. Nor could he, again, have been out of touch with the colonizers when he printed, in the end of the *Divers Voyages,* the list of American products. It is quite possible that he compiled the list himself for the committee. Such was the sort of work that a studious man was qualified to do: it was the sort of work he was to do later. But the lack of direct evidence, and particularly the fact that the state paper is not in his handwriting, leaves the supposition merely pleasing.

The chances are that Hakluyt had his substantial part in these colonial preparations. At the very least he printed the *Divers Voyages,* which was no mean contribution and compared favorably with Eden's *Decades* and Willis' *History of Travail.* Of his following actions there can be no question at all. The use of Thevet as a witness is a key to the use of Hakluyt. The geographer royal of France was not particularly competent, since his knowledge of North America had been gained by a sojourn in Brazil. But consulting him supposes, on the part of the colonizers, a respect for the expert which could not fail to be extended to the young Oxford geographer. The net which Walsingham was swinging had a wide scope, and Hakluyt was easily slipped into it. Within the year after the *Divers Voyages* he was responsibly attached to the government service. Being recommended to Walsingham by two leaders of the enterprise, he brought into the venture a substantial subscription. He nominated the scientific observer who would go with the voyage, when Gilbert sailed in June of 1583, to gather first-hand knowledge of the new country; and his own sailing on a like mission was avoided only by a plan which sent him to another post.[3]

The first of these actions is related in three letters which were to be printed in the *Voyages*. It appears from them that Hakluyt had made a favorable impression upon Sir George Peckham, the Catholic leader, who was a figure of importance second only to Gilbert in the colonial plans. The impression may have been made by the *Divers Voyages* or by whatever part Hakluyt otherwise took in gathering information or by merely personal encounters. On the other side, he had made some sort of acquaintance with the corporation of Bristol, which was again, as always, at the center of American plans. In November of 1582 the mayor of Bristol wrote to Walsingham on business connected with the new colony. In the following March, the Secretary, finding the young man spoken of by Peckham as having "endeavored and given much light for the discovery of the western parts yet unknown," called him officially into the business in hand.

The letter of March 11, 1583, which marks Hakluyt's official recognition is indeed only a testimonial, enclosed in a letter which he was to carry from the Secretary to the mayor, and a perfunctory letter as well, since the Secretary ignored the book just published by Hakluyt. But the fact of the mission is clear. The bearer of an official proposal, Hakluyt proceeded to Bristol. Some two weeks later the mayor announced to the Secretary that "after some good light given by Master Hakluyt unto them that were ignorant of the country and enterprise and were desirous to be resolved," a fund of something like seven hundred pounds had been raised to fit out two ships.

This promoting episode, which was to be curiously repeated twenty years later, is striking enough. The mere academic expert had satisfied the citizens of the city which in England knew most about America. It is true that they had been used to supporting oversea ventures since at least the time of the Cabots and were probably quite free to be convinced. Hakluyt must still be credited with the stroke that fixed the subscription. As it happened, the subscription was not taken. It was not, the closing letter makes clear, destined to Gilbert's own voyage, as Walsingham had wished, but to the auxiliary voyage planned by Carleill, Walsingham's son-in-law. Carleill continued active in his own plans for at least another year. In September he was negotiating for Russia Company support in order to follow Gilbert. In the following spring, as appears from Hakluyt's second Paris letter, he was expected to lead his own voyage overseas. Meantime Gilbert's patent passed to Raleigh, and Carleill, diverted to the Spanish war, never carried out his plan. But such good will as was wit-

[3] The account of Hakluyt's doings 1582–1589 is verified in Appendix II, chronology.

nessed by the Bristol corporation would not be allowed to waste. Hakluyt's mission was turned to the profit of a later expedition.

It seems to have turned also to his own profit. When in the next year he was nominated to a church preferment, it was a place in the cathedral chapter of Bristol that was assigned him. He drew not only a thousand marks for America but an excellent post for himself.

To this doubly successful venture Hakluyt added another, which concerned Gilbert in general and Hakluyt's geographic interest in particular. For the advancement of learning it was desirable to have an educated observer sail with Gilbert. This observer was discovered by Hakluyt and introduced to the commander. A certain Hungarian, Stephen Parmenius by name, had somehow found his way to Oxford and to Hakluyt's intimacy. His qualifications as observer are not recorded; but his command of Latin verse, in which he published a eulogy of Gilbert and of the voyage, seems to have been thought enough for the purpose. He accordingly sailed with Gilbert in June.

Why Parmenius went instead of Hakluyt we are not told. Hakluyt intended going, for Parmenius spoke of his following in a later vessel, probably with Carleill. Hakluyt says nothing himself of his intention; but he ought to have been eager for a first-hand view of the country on which he was an authority. As it happened, he went to France instead of America. And fortunately enough, as it also happened, for he escaped the fate of Parmenius, who went down at sea with Gilbert's flagship.

Hakluyt's part in the Gilbert experiment was thus a minor one. By way of information he had probably said all he had to say in the *Divers Voyages*. Any Bristol fisherman who had sailed to Newfoundland might have said more. But he had at the least published the book, and Peckham thought that he had "endeavored and given much light" to the colonizers. As a promoter he had come late into a movement that had interested Gilbert for fifteen years; he was not a merchant or a soldier or an administrator; he had no standing at all as a man of action. Yet he had gone to Bristol and returned with a large investment, enough to equip another expedition the size of Gilbert's. He had arranged, finally, that a scholar should sail with the expedition to devote himself entirely to scientific observation. He had done more than any one would think possible.

As a result Hakluyt took on a certain importance in colonial circles. The fact is attested by the interests of the colonizers in him. Gilbert knew him at least well enough to accept an observer at his hands. Peckham was grateful to him. The merchants of Bristol listened to him obediently. Sidney, whom we suppose he knew at the university, was a titular subpatentee of Gilbert's colony and permitted the dedication of the *Divers Voyages*. And Hakluyt kept knocking at the door of Sidney's remembrance. A year later, Sidney wrote that "we are half persuaded to enter the journey of Sir Humfrey Gilbert very eagerly, whereunto your Mr. Hakluyt hath served for a very good trumpet."

So Hakluyt's radius widened. Sidney was more eager for military than for colonial adventure, as it happened, and tried to embark, with Carleill, in Drake's raid of 1585 on the West Indies before he went to his death in Flanders. Meantime Hakluyt crossed to other stepping-stones. He had made himself known to Drake, as will appear in another chapter. He had been found serviceable to Walsingham, under whose eye he was to mount steadily. He was to gather information, as he had gathered money, for Walsingham's other son-in-law, Carleill. He turned next to Raleigh, who succeeded to Gilbert's privileges and Carleill's opportunity. Before another year was out he became the spokesman for Raleigh in commanding the attention of the Queen herself.

4

As late as June of 1583, I repeat, Hakluyt was planning to sail for America. If the intention was serious, it was speedily abandoned. In the early autumn Hakluyt crossed instead to France in the suite of the new ambassador, Sir Edward Stafford. The change of plan involved in fact no change of aim. If he were not to go to America to observe directly, he could do as well for himself, if not better, by tapping the Continental experience. Hakluyt or another was needed to explore America. Hakluyt or another was also needed to audit the knowledge of America already achieved elsewhere. If Parmenius and after him Hariot took up the American mission, then Hakluyt was clearly indicated for the European mission. Stated thus after the fact, the case is doubtless too clean, the intentions of Hakluyt too much rationalized. The result is the same. From his new post of vantage Hakluyt could continue to focus for English use the oversea experience of France, Spain, and Portugal.

The account of the Paris mission will be given in a later chapter, leaving to this chapter the story of his further promoting. For the purpose of a summary, it may, however, be said now that he was to remain at the Paris embassy for five years, maintaining the while his close relations with the colonial party at home. Arriving first in France in October of 1583, he was to return to England in the following summer either for his private affairs or intentionally to knit relations with Raleigh. During this summer he wrote for Raleigh a brief for royal aid to the western planting. This discourse he presented in person to the Queen.

The *Discourse* summed up the investigations which Hakluyt had meantime been making in Paris and which he continued to make after he returned there in October of 1584. His English visits continued. He was at home in the spring of 1585, when Raleigh's colony sailed. He was there again early in 1586, and he seems to have stayed on until September, when Drake brought the discouraged colony back. He was again at home in the spring of 1587, when the second colony sailed. In the next year, the year of the Armada, he was twice in England on embassy business; and he returned to England definitively in the winter following the victory. In all he probably spent as much of these five years in England as in France and enjoyed full opportunity to carry on the work of colonizing.

The main object of this mission in France Hakluyt expressed as the "diligent inquiry of such things as may yield any light unto our western discovery." This was a varied task. As will be seen in the next chapter, it meant an interest in a complex of activities; navigation and maritime enterprise in general, as well as naval affairs; geography, particularly in its economic aspect; and oversea trade and its organization. These activities were all germane to his inquiry, and the geographer seems to have thrown himself whole-heartedly into his task.

The influence of a man who has made a vocation of his hobby is likely to be as wide as his personal circle; and we have already seen that Hakluyt's circle included men of influence. As the circle widens, the possibility of judging the effect of the influence diminishes. In Hakluyt's case one must suppose that his conversation reached many more men than can now be accounted for, as there is reason to believe that he talked colonies in and out of season. There was Walsingham for one, who was kept reminded by his agent of the colonial problem. There was Carleill, who seemed for a time to be the successor of Gilbert and to whom Hakluyt assiduously sent information. There was Sidney, whom Hakluyt "more than half persuaded."

There is record of another person upon whom Hakluyt more directly acted, whom indeed he brought to open his purse. This person, as Hakluyt wrote in his second Paris letter, was Horatio Pallavicini, the Genoese banker who was most useful to the English treasury. Pallavicini, who was later knighted for his support of the treasury during the war, was in France in 1584, attempting to collect debts for the Crown. On a favorable occasion Hakluyt buttonholed him. As a result of the chaplain's enthusiasm, he "replied very cheerfully that if he were moved thereto by the least word from your honor (Walsingham), he would put in his hundred pound adventure or more."

The stock which Hakluyt thus sold was apparently, like the Bristol subscription, destined to a Carleill colony. Possibly it was never paid in, once Carleill dropped the colonial project for soldiering. Possibly it was paid in to Raleigh, for there is no record of the financing of Virginia. In any case, the incident is important. If Pallavicini would listen to Hakluyt, so would others. What others can only be guessed, since Hakluyt was not usually at pains to record his conversations. There were others, the most conspicuous being the Queen herself. His argument before Her Majesty took shape in a lengthy discourse. But that royal interview we may leave to another chapter.

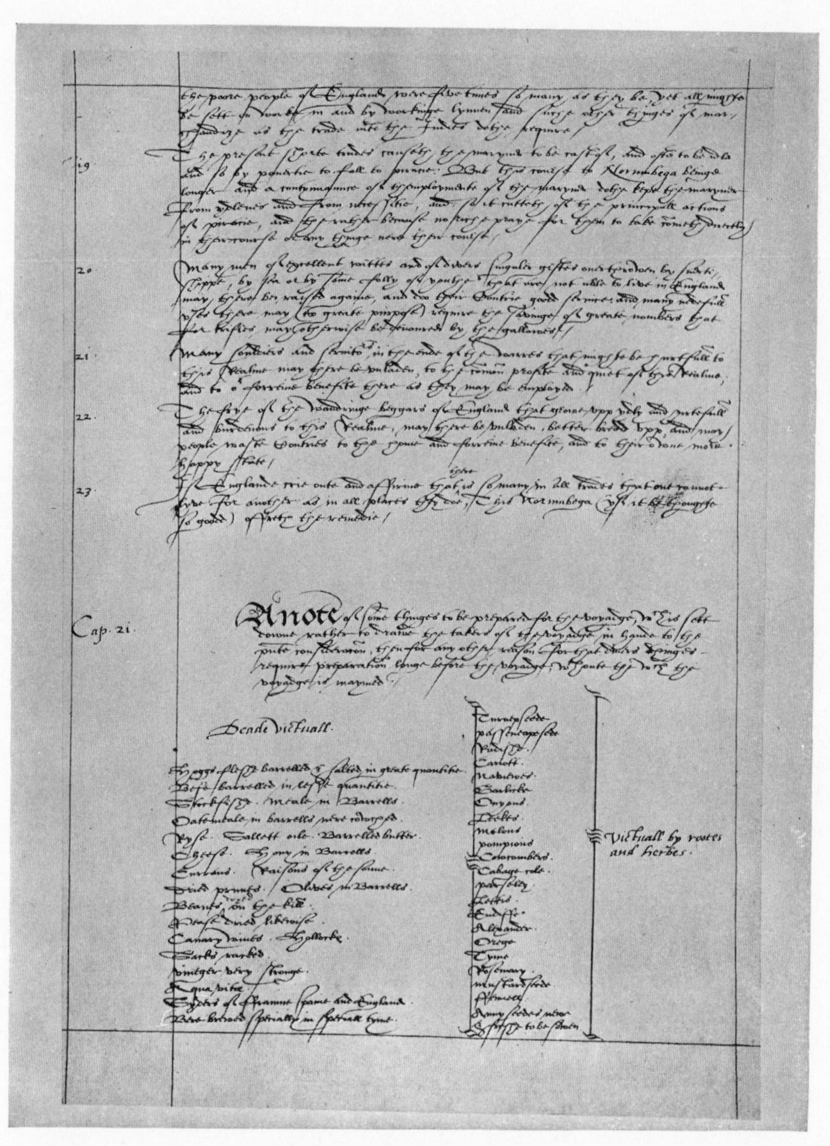

Cap. 21

A note of some thinges to be prepared for the voyadge

Deade victuall

Victuall by rootes and herbes

FIG. 18—A page from the *Discourse on the Western Planting*, 1584, Chapter XXI. By courtesy of the New York Public Library.

CHAPTER VII

The Discourse on the Western Planting

1584

Hakluyt's mission to France kept him as close to colonial enterprise as if he had gone to America instead. Though he arrived in Paris only in October of 1583, he was again in England in the following summer. Already the heritage of Gilbert, heroically drowned at sea, had passed to his half-brother Raleigh. On the New Year, March 25, 1584, the royal grant set up a new proprietor of the New World. In the next month a voyage of reconnaissance was dispatched to choose a southerly site for a colony. In September Hakluyt was given audience by the Queen, to whom he presented, in Raleigh's name, a *Particular Discourse on the Western Planting.*

If evidence were needed that the young geographer had attained his recognition, this fact would be evidence enough. When Raleigh, in gathering up the threads of enterprise, looked about for a spokesman, he inevitably found Hakluyt, whom he does not seem previously to have known. So the choice of Hakluyt for the writing of the *Discourse* stamps him as the acknowledged penman of the expansion.

The steps of his progress to a royal audience can be only conjectured. At some time during the summer the geographer must have been brought to Raleigh's attention and was speedily pressed into service for an appeal to the throne. The result was the *Discourse,* written, as the endorsement runs, "at the request and direction of the right worshipful Master Walter Raleigh, now Knight, before the coming home of his two barks," of the scouting vessels, that is, which returned in September.

To the audience and to the *Discourse* itself, which he never printed, Hakluyt makes but one reference. In a later letter to Walsingham from Paris, where he went back on October 15, he wrote: "two days before my dispatch, upon the sight of a couple of books of mine in writing [that is, in manuscript], one in Latin upon Aristotle's Politics, the other in English concerning Mr. Raleigh's voyage, the copy whereof I purpose to send your Honor immediately after Easter. . . ."

The commentary on Aristotle was an Oxford public lecture, attesting Hakluyt's political competence. The object of the *Discourse* (Fig. 18) is expressed in the last of the twenty sections, which is headed: "Certain reasons to induce Her Majesty and the state to take in hand the western voyage and the planting therein." It was an appeal for a royal investment in this as in other voyages of piracy and discovery like Drake's. The appeal was buttressed by the precedent set down in an earlier section: "God, which doth all things in his due time, . . . stir up the mind of Her Majesty at length to assist her most willing and forward subjects to the performance of this most godly and profitable action: which was begun at the charges of King Henry the Seventh, . . . followed by King Henry the Eighth, . . . and left, as it seemeth, to be accomplished by her."

On this theme Hakluyt built a complete and rounded argument for colonial expansion, in a document unique in its time, which spreads before the historian the full scope of the movement overseas. The now familiar case for expansion is here set forth in full outline, as if once and for all. The attractions of the purse are here, assembled from the shelves of experience which are heaped with profitable past adventures; a full statement of policy, to sound the national appeal; a glowing prospectus, to sound the private appeal. To these is added, in a subsequent copy which may have been the one promised to Walsingham after Easter, a plan of colonization, a complete program of settlement. Had the work not lain hidden for nearly three centuries, it would have proved a guidebook in colonial theory. It did remain unknown until the last century and so was robbed of its deserved influence. As it is, it affords an indispensable record of the motives and intentions of the first colonizers.[1]

2

The private character of the memorial, which was not to be seen by the general eye, permitted Hakluyt to state freely the case for a colonial policy. Such freedom was necessary if the *Discourse* were to discuss with any adequacy the great political obstacle to colonizing, the fear of Spain; and to the case against Spain a good half of the *Discourse* was dedicated. Hakluyt was apparently well fortified with argument by his naval friends, who seem to have belonged to the aggressive school of Drake. He devoted several sections of the twenty to the already familiar idea of a colony as a naval outpost. Given an American base, the argument ran, there was opened an easy channel to the West Indies, a channel for attack on the forts on land or for a swoop on the Plate Fleet carrying home American treasure. There was opened also a channel for a descent on the Spaniards who haunted the northern fishing banks and who supplied Spain with some of its food. With the resource of a colony England could strike at will at the root of Spanish power, which lay overseas.

[1] The bibliography of the *Discourse* is given in Appendix III. The "prospectus" portion of the paper is analyzed at length by George Louis Beer in his *The Origins of the British Colonial System 1578–1660* (New York 1908). But he does not, as it seems to me and as I have throughout tried to prove, give sufficient importance to the link between commerce and colonization. Beer admits the link (p. 64); but he makes the "sea dogs" rather more important than the merchants, while my thesis is that the merchants were all-important and that the "sea dogs" and colonizers alike were their agents.

Though bold, the argument was not of course new. The same plan had been proposed as early as 1577, probably by Gilbert, in two memoranda entitled, "How Her Majesty may annoy the King of Spain." [2] The argument was certainly doubtful in the abstract, doubtful at least until England should be able to rule the seas. It was certainly unsound historically. Hakluyt's royal reader had only to remember that Spain had once wiped out a similar French base in Florida. To strengthen his argument Hakluyt could have answered that with a little intelligence the French might have kept their foothold. But he preferred to overlook the whole French precedent, as he had in the *Divers Voyages*. He did consider, perhaps thinking it more to the point, the actual extent of the menace of Spain. Here he fancied he had important and gratifying information.

This information was presumably the fruit of his French mission, being a survey of the Spanish possessions as made by an "excellent French captain." Its tendency was to minimize the strength of the adversary; to support his proof by the analogy of the Portuguese possessions, which, Hakluyt had learned from a sure source, did not boast more than ten thousand men in the outposts of both hemispheres; and to call to mind the aid against Spain that could be expected from natives whom Spain had alienated. Nothing need be feared, he thought, from the nation that claimed monopoly of America, not even the claim itself, which two further sections discounted.

The rival monarchy was thus agreeably disposed of. It is to be said in Hakluyt's favor that he did not needlessly flourish the sword. Aggrandizement for its own sake was not the motive of this memorial. Aggrandizement was barely in question. Only the severely practical motives, or what Hakluyt considered the severely practical motives, were called into the argument. England had been headed for years towards war with Spain; a colony in America was a practical weapon against her. Even the religious motive, which Hakluyt of course placed first, became rather practical than sentimental. It was true, as Hakluyt admitted, that the Protestant nations suffered by comparison with the Catholic. It was sentimentally important that the leading Protestant country should bring up its missionary record to balance that of Catholic countries. That was obvious, if of minor importance. More to the point, in the pious first section, was the lesson of Catholic experience, which suggested that the settlement should precede the mission. The missionary, as Hakluyt read history, could not be effective unless he were protected by the plantation. The plantation was the thing.

[2] The supposed Gilbert documents on naval policy are State Papers Domestic Elizabeth, 118, 12. The *Calendar 1547–1580* and Gosling, in his *Life of Sir Humphrey Gilbert*, believe the erased signature to be Gilbert's.

3

If the trumpet of national prestige was thus barely audible, the theme of the national interest was loud enough. As a statement of policy the *Discourse* sketched a complete economic program, which would produce a self-sufficing England. The now familiar argument is as yet, in this first of English imperialists, ill-defined and implicit. Being no politician, Hakluyt struck out no conclusions on the might of nations. Being no maker of generalizations, he confined himself to the practical, to the lessons of experience which he had found in his texts. Taken piecemeal, his plan pointed to the shifting, one by one, of English markets from Europe to America. Taken altogether, had Hakluyt drawn out the consequences, the plan pointed to English economic independence of Europe.

Later publicists were to make of self-sufficiency an end in itself. For Hakluyt the end was hidden by the means, which made a sufficient problem. Knowing the inconveniences of England's foreign markets, he suggested their transfer to a new world. The Barbary trade was endangered alike by Moors and by Spaniards. The Levant trade and the Russia trade were expensively carried on. The Spanish markets, which accounted for half of English commerce, were precarious. Trade with the closer European neighbors suffered from various hindrances. If the same raw materials could more easily be got outside of Europe, if the same exports could more easily be sold outside of Europe, then England's foreign trade would run on a smoother track, England's growing industries would be unshaken by wars on the Continent. A steadier trade would insure, moreover, a steadier revenue; and economic health would insure to the realm political health.

So before the event Hakluyt wove a colonial policy out of economic needs, strengthened by the military and the religious inducements. Fourteen of the twenty sections of the *Discourse* are thus accounted for. A portion of the remainder must be used to prove that America was an economic reality. If the lanes of commerce were to be so radically changed, the markets must first be assured. So he must frame what we may call the prospectus portion of the paper. The point to urge in these three sections was that America produced every desirable commodity now drawn by England from Europe. Here Hakluyt was of course most in his element. From his bookshelves he could assemble an impressive list of authorities on American fruitfulness. Every commodity that England imported from Europe or through Europe from the East and West Indies could be equally well imported, he proved by his authorities, from an English North America and by an unhampered sea route. The export of English woolen goods could correspondingly flow into all the corners of the vast continent, to natives and to colonists. In the prospectus was the germ of the greater England, had Hakluyt released it.

Being no rhetorician, he did not release it. He was content instead with pouring out the flood of facts that proved what America was capable of. Drugs, spices, precious metals, furs, food, and all the resources of the animal and vegetable kingdoms had been marked down by observers in a country which answered in climate to the lands between Egypt and Archangel. Verrazano had observed a soil fit for wine, corn, and oil: agriculture promised. Coronado spoke of garnets and emeralds in the south, as Cartier spoke of silver, gold, and copper in the north: treasure invited. Furs and fish had already built up a French trade, tested by its profits. A wealth of forest offered fruits, naval stores, drugs. A wealth of animal life offered wool and skins as well as food. If these were not enough, there was still a Northwest Passage, beckoning with new and learned arguments to an East which supplemented a West.

The imposing list of products had grown since Hakluyt first printed it in the *Divers Voyages*. Fifty-four commodities, staple as well as rare, made an appetizing prospectus, which was as soundly documented as Hakluyt's researches could make it. Given the commodities, it was important that they could be had for little or nothing. Hakluyt furnished French experience to prove that point. His "friend Stephen Bellinger of Rouen" had sold in France for four hundred and forty crowns what he had bought in Maine for forty. Most of the products could be had indeed for the asking.

I do not know whether Hakluyt had full confidence in his rich list. At least it was as strictly tested, despite its fantastic ring, as experience would permit. A man who stayed at home must needs accept the word of the traveler, and, until the outlines of the world were sharpened by further travel, one miraculous discovery was as good as another. Paradoxically enough, experience was to prove, in the English experiment, a broken reed; and not to rely on experience was to be the only ultimate wisdom. Experience of America, which was largely Spanish, suggested mines and a large native population to work them. Both these possibilities still loomed large to the popular eye, as may be imagined. Both these possibilities, though he mentioned them, Hakluyt minimized. Instead he imagined the twenty-four occupations which would exploit the fifty-four commodities. He minutely divided the occupations among the extractive and agricultural industries, from mining to feather gathering. The elaborate division of labor would have seemed the height of irony to the settlers on a vacant coast. But a further irony of history has carried out the prophecy almost to the letter, as every commodity listed by Hakluyt has in its turn come to light in America.

The last section of the *Discourse* shows that in painting his vivid prospectus Hakluyt was boldly forecasting. For the immediate colonial needs he was careful to set down in supplement an immediate program. The colony deposited overseas must not be left free to hunt for gold mines. The planners of colonies, it should be emphasized, were not only treasure seekers. The adventurers who had scattered their money in Frobisher's gold mines demanded more plausible plans. These Hakluyt had ready.

French experience recorded an immediate profit from furs and skins; but if this trade failed, as there was no reason to think that it would fail, there was no deceit in the American forest. Furs, on which New France was to be founded, were not so much needed in England. Forest products were needed. The elder Hakluyt had pointed out this need in his colonial program, and timber was in fact to become the basis of some of the English colonies. With a saw-mill for timber, the *Discourse* then suggested, and with the proper workmen for extracting naval stores and "soap-ashes" or potash, England would take the first step to independence of the Baltic timber market.

For its success this program needed only the experience of the Russia and Eastland companies, on which it was based. To set a colony going was a less obvious task. Hakluyt was again ready. He had not so complete a set of instructions to present as his cousin had had in the earlier paper; but he added some details in an extra twenty-first chapter, which dealt with the actual supplying of the colony before it sailed, as the earlier instructions had dealt with the maintaining of the colony after it had landed. He made an especially careful list of needed food, food being, as it proved, the crucial question. On Hakluyt's plan the ideal colony would set forth like another ark. It would transport its familiar domestic animals and its staple grains and garden seeds. It would embark its hunters and fishers, its butchers and salters, its cooks and brewers. The bold requirements appear amateurish enough, ignoring the mere limitations of space. The plan cannot be compared with the finished statement of personnel which had been made up in France half a century before for a Cartier colony. But it was suggestive; and suggestiveness was a quality which might profit the military or naval leader of colonies, who would already know how to supply a body of men.

The striking merit which the modern historian may read into the *Discourse* is just this quality of suggestiveness, which is akin to the joy of making lists. For this quality was the albumen which might feed the colonial yolk. The yolk was the immediate program, the building of a colony on the resources of the American forest. As the colony grew, it would be able to feed on an ever-developing industry. To forestry would be added mining; to mining, fruit growing and cattle grazing; and so on, in even wider circles to the limit of exploitation. The possibilities were grandiose.

It is true that the plan was absurdly unfitted to the unit of one hundred men in the first colony. Their first care would be the raising of their own staple food and not much more. Yet the program was to work, if by slow degrees. Once established, Virginia was speedily to produce its own food and at the same time to develop a surplus staple, tobacco. Plymouth was to export timber immediately. And so with the other colonies.

4

The program was proved in the event to be practical; and the credit is to be given less to Hakluyt's imagination than to his good sense, which set him on the shoulders of his predecessors. For it must again be emphasized that if Raleigh's colony was a beginning it was also an ending. It was not a venture into the void. Its foundations had been laid by fishermen in the North Atlantic; by the discoverers of Russia; by wine traders to Bordeaux; by the merchant adventurers who had begun by sending wool to Flanders and were now buying silk in Persia and ivory in Guinea. If Hakluyt could suggest timber as an American staple, the reason was that the Russia Company had handled timber as a staple. The City and its emissaries had learned to set up trading posts in the inhospitable parts of Europe; they were prepared to set up plantations in inhospitable America as well.

Hakluyt did not build his program on air; he did not even build on his own foundations. There were programs ready to his hand, pamphlets which he later reprinted without, curiously enough, printing his own. In point of fact, almost any account of an oversea venture carried an air of propaganda. Eden's translations of the *Decades*, as far back as 1555, suggested in a preface that the wide stretch of the continent awaited the colonist; and Rastell's *Interlude of the Four Elements,* forty years before that, was intent on commerce if not on colonization. Best's account of the Frobisher voyages, and Hayes' story of Gilbert bore their implications. Gilbert's own *Discourse on the Northwest Passage* offered a foundation for one section of Hakluyt's *Discourse.* His plan of attack on Spanish America to "annoy the King of Spain" may have suggested other sections. But the most pertinent predecessors of Hakluyt were the two Gilbert enterprisers who had consulted him, Captain Carleill and Sir George Peckham. They had published their colonial programs in 1583, one before Gilbert's departure, the other after Gilbert's failure. Of these pamphlets which anticipated Hakluyt's, it is important to say a word.[3]

Carleill's discourse was a brief and businesslike address to the merchants of the Russia Company, designed "to satisfy merchant subscribers who are insistent about their interests." The argument

[3] The Carleill discourse was printed by Hakluyt, *Voyages,* VIII 134; the Peckham discourse *ibid.,* VIII 89. The elder Hakluyt's *Inducements* is accounted for in Appendix I. The full reprint of the Peckham paper, including the dedication and introductory verses, was made by the *Magazine of American History,* extra no. 68 (Tarrytown, N. Y., 1920).

was a pure appeal to the purse, and the corresponding part of Hakluyt's paper might have been taken bodily from it. Carleill argued the uncertainty of English foreign markets; Hakluyt argued the same uncertainties, though in different words and with more elaboration. Carleill sketched the American possibilities in a fashion which would most closely compare America with Russia. The argument of the easy and unhampered voyage was Hakluyt's argument as well. The commodities which Carleill promised from the North were the Russian commodities—fish, furs, hides, naval stores. The products which he promised, though with less certainty, from the South were the products imported from Russian and Mediterranean markets—wine, olives, wax, honey, and salt. The same exports sold in both markets, since all barbarians could use woolen goods if the climate were fit. The northern passage to Asia was as likely by the West as by the East. The possibilities of treasure were as unlikely. As for labor, it was reasonable to suppose that American natives were as employable as Russian.

The similarities of the two discourses are more apparent than the dissimilarities. If Hakluyt went into greater detail, suggested a wider scope, the reason is doubtless that he was not bound to the special audience of merchants and could therefore expand where Carleill minimized. The likeness of method, which is the essential likeness, cannot in fact be accidental. The one discourse borrowed from the other its structure and many of its arguments.

It is not necessary, though it is tempting, to believe that Hakluyt wrote both papers. If he framed a long discourse for Raleigh, whom he probably did not know very well, he could easily have framed a short discourse for Carleill, whom he did. The earlier discourse is not, however, in Hakluyt's style. It is marked by a conciseness which the scholar never attained elsewhere, by a directness which was not in his character as a writer. It is more likely that since the longer discourse was quite too obviously written in haste, its author drew freely upon the shorter one, that he virtually incorporated its methods in his own larger design. If the original design was his, the fact cannot be known.

The discourse written by Sir George Peckham, a principal landholder under the Gilbert patent, was of ampler scope and hence closer in aim to the later document of Hakluyt's. The worthy knight, ambling though his pace, yet struck perhaps more clearly to the point than either of his more ambitious colleagues. He was not concerned with changing the course of English commerce. He was concerned with a colony to which, with Walsingham's connivance, English Catholics could resort. As an American investor rather than as a trader he was stirred to read the lesson of Gilbert's failure and to align inducements for a sequel.

Peckham's plan was simplicity itself. Fish was his mainstay, as forests were the mainstay of the others. He would send settlers in the outgoing fishing fleet, stowing them apparently in the space reserved for cod on the return trip; and there would be no transportation charges. The settlers would catch plenty of food on their arrival at the Banks. They would need no means of defense in remote Newfoundland. They would gradually add to their fishing the other extractive industries. To merchant investors nothing could be less onerous nor, if Peckham's list of native products could be trusted, more remunerative. For to Carleill's cautious supply he added silks, dyes, palm wine, and precious stones, which "such persons as have discovered and traveled those parts do testify that they have found in those countries."

Peckham added some loosely gathered arguments to support an appeal to patriotism as well as an appeal to the purse. A reference to the persevering Columbus; a word on missions; a chapter on dealings with the natives; a statement of the English title overseas, based on Cabot and on the Welsh words left in American languages, it was thought, by the mythical Madoc of Wales; a statement of the profit to the English realm: the arguments could not but anticipate Hakluyt, since they were obvious enough. That Hakluyt stood at Peckham's elbow during their writing is yet plausible. The list of authorities might have been taken, with additions, from the *Divers Voyages,* if not from Hakluyt in person. A hint of a mysterious French trade, which was to recur in Carleill and be explained by Hakluyt, may very well have been contributed by the last. And Strongbow's plantation in Ireland was a colonial precedent to which Hakluyt was also to recur, in the preface to his *French Florida,* so suggesting that its use by Peckham was whispered by him.

A word may be added on a paper of the same kind, the *Inducements* which the elder Hakluyt wrote in 1585. The pamphlet struck a mean between the *Discourse* to the Queen and the paper of Carleill. The latter had been eminently conservative. Opening no glittering vistas whatever, it had confined itself to the authentic possibilities of American trade. A simple, cautious transfer of markets, with no dabbling in gold mines, was presented as a scheme which could certainly not fail.

The younger Hakluyt went to an opposite extreme. In his *Discourse* he poured his geographical knowledge, acquired from travel records and from travelers, and mixed with it the political arguments proper to an embassy official. For commercial enterprise, his *dossiers* told him, America was a promised land, to which might be diverted with ease all of England's foreign trade.

The elder Hakluyt knew too much about trade to be so easily dazzled by promises. At the same time, with the experience of the Russia Company at his command, he could advise the cautious and gradual exploitation of many more American resources than Carleill admitted. With Carleill he accepted only the products approved by English use, fish and timber. Unlike Carleill he could draw on his knowledge of current trade. He had not forgotten that England needed dyestuffs. Some of the valued vegetables might therefore be transplanted from Europe to the new soil. He presented likewise other products which the City found it difficult to grow. But as for flourishing his cousin's magic wand, he would have none of it. In his restrained fashion he allowed himself certain hopes which, if carefully nourished, might surprisingly flower. "And in time," he wrote, "such league and intercourse may arise between our stapling seats there and other posts of our northern America and of the islands of the same, that incredible things, and by few as yet dreamed of, may speedily follow, tending to the impeachment of our mighty enemies and to the common good of this noble government." "In time": so the lawyer qualified his only colonial enthusiasm on record. For his purposes and for the purposes of his merchant and courtier audience he was building on the instructions he had given to Frobisher seven years before, of which the emphasis rested on inquiry and careful experiment.

5

As an interpreter of experience the younger Hakluyt was dependent on other interpreters. Yet his work went far beyond theirs in scope and in documentation. His was a statement of a colonial policy; theirs were statements of a commercial policy. Their work was addressed to a class; his was addressed to a realm.

It did not, it must be said, go far enough beyond theirs. Though less diffuse than the amiable remarks of Peckham, the *Discourse* still remains confused in statement and incoherent in structure. Prospectus, program, and policy overlap and repeat; and the scale varies with Hakluyt's knowledge or interest. So disarranged is it that one suspects its author of never having brought it to the final stage, whether because of haste in the writing or simply because he could not bring himself to leave out the irrelevancies that fascinated him. The naïveté suggested by this conclusion is certainly not out of keeping with his character as elsewhere revealed.

It is especially to be noted that, despite Hakluyt's pains to put in every detail that might either impress or inform, he never got to the real purpose of the paper. If there were reasons why the colonial enterprise was dependent on state aid, Hakluyt left them to be assumed. The realm would profit by the enterprise, runs the sole discernible argument; therefore the government would be well advised to give aid. Had the Queen read Peckham's discourse, she could easily have replied that Peckham had made out a case against subsidy and that Hakluyt had not even gone to the pains of answering it. To point out this defect, however, may be to misinterpret Hakluyt's aim. His argument was aimed at the enhancement of the realm; but he and Raleigh may have been asking not a government subsidy but merely the Queen's private investment.

The royal aid was probably not forthcoming. Possibly the Queen might have come into a colonial scheme if the war had not intervened. Without waiting for an American naval base, Drake went off in the next year, 1585, on the great raid on the West Indies which effectively began the war with Spain. The colony had been started in the same year, and Drake stopped at Roanoke on his way home. If he expected to find a naval base, he was disappointed. The colony was discouraged, there were no supplies, and Drake brought all the colonists back to England with him. The second colony, of 1587, disappeared; and the fact that it could disappear showed that it was not needed as a base by the privateers who kept raiding the West Indies.

Whether Hakluyt had his colonial program accepted, we cannot very well say. We do not know whether the ships were supplied according to his plans. We doubt whether the Queen did more than encourage the noble enterprise now that she had a fleet on the Spanish Main, an army in Holland, and Mary Queen of Scots to execute at home. In general we suspect that Hakluyt's careful plan was neglected, partly because Raleigh was engaged in fighting as well as in colonizing, partly because of the difficulty of thorough planning on both sides of the water. The immediate utility of the *Discourse* cannot be tested; and, as we do not know who read it later, neither can its ultimate utility.

So the great statement of English imperialism seems to have failed of its immediate aim. The *Discourse* was consigned to the oblivion of the archives and, except as has been mentioned, was never again referred to either by Hakluyt or by his contemporaries. The fact that Hakluyt did not himself publish it is singular. The fact that his literary executor Purchas made no mention of it is baffling. Yet the writing of it was by no means a vain labor; although it did not come into print, we know that it was read by at least some of the expansionists—Raleigh, Walsingham, Leicester. Doubtless it was seen by the men of power in the later generation of the expansion, the men like Sir Thomas Smith who made Virginia a reality; and at the lowest estimate, its ideas were incarnated in the person of its author, who continued to preach from the same platform for the rest of his life until the word became deed.

However the *Discourse* aided the colonial cause, it at least aided its author. As a sign of royal appreciation the Queen presented Hakluyt, at the close of the audience, with the reversion of the next vacant prebend in Bristol Cathedral. We learn from a letter written by Hakluyt to Walsingham in the following spring that at Bristol there was some discontent with his claim; but the air was cleared, perhaps on the advice of the Secretary, by a personal visit which Hakluyt then made to Bristol, when he formally presented to the Chapter the mandate of the Crown. Fortune continued to favor him. Instead of the vain waiting for " these seven and seven years " which he had feared, he was gratified by a prompt death among the canons and, probably in 1586, was seated in the first stall of the Cathedral.[4] The sinecure was well deserved. With his increased resources he was able to press forward in his work of research and publication, to put forth into the main stream of his life's work.

[4] The details of Hakluyt's prebend are given in Appendix II, under the years 1584–85.

CHAPTER VIII

The French Mission: Investigation

1583–1588

Gilbert's hapless voyage of 1583 had been designed to explore the middle Atlantic coast, the land between Florida on the one hand and Norumbega and the St. Lawrence region on the other. The expedition reached no farther south than Sable Island, where the flagship was wrecked with all on board. So the ambitions that had been fed by great hope and care succeeded neither in settling nor in the further exploration that would make settling possible. The failure was completed when Gilbert went down in mid-Atlantic with the second of his three ships. When Raleigh took over the plan he was obliged to begin afresh by sending out another reconnoitering voyage.

There were undoubted limits to what such a voyage could discover. So Hakluyt went to France, to drain from that country the experience of the new world in which England was still so greatly lacking. He went to France to discover America. His mission was an exploring expedition.

The need of knowledge of America cannot be too strongly emphasized. Whatever was known of the Newfoundland region, the country south of it was virtually unknown in England. The turn south from that island made by Gilbert in the summer of 1583 was nearly as precarious as had been the turn east from the North Cape when it was made by the discoverers of Russia in 1553. Unless at Seville, there were no maps or routiers of the deceitful coast. Few Englishmen had been known to sail any distance from the fishing banks. Foreigners had been more active; but their records were not available in England. In making the turn south Gilbert had sailed into a void.

The explorers he had learned from reduced themselves in number to four; and three of them were inadequate. Verrazano's voyage of 1524, which had proved North America a continent by sailing from Carolina to Newfoundland, was a good beginning. The map built on it showed indeed the only substantial outline of the coast; but it was more valuable as a prospectus than as a chart. The southward voyage of Gomez in 1525 might have been more valuable; but its records, like those of other Spaniards who had sailed north from Florida, were kept secret in Seville. The narrative of Ingram was that of an eyewitness; but, if Ingram had crossed the continent from Mexico, his account was so bewildered that Hakluyt was later to omit it, for its incredibility, from his collections. There remained a third authority, the Portuguese pilot Fernandez. We are told that he had been to America; yet his only recorded voyage prior to 1583 had taken but six weeks, and he must have made no more than a quick trip to Newfoundland and back. Finally there could be mentioned John Walker, with whom the committee spoke by the mouth of Gilbert, and who had been to Norumbega, that is to Maine. His information may or may not have been important. He must have done some exploring, for he had seen a silver mine; but at the best he had been there only in summer. More information was distinctly needed.

If it be asked why Hakluyt went to France to discover America, it may be answered that he went there because he could not go to Spain. Spanish enterprise had explored the entire coast from Newfoundland to Mexico. Spanish expeditions had crossed most of the territory now included in the southern states; and in the very year in which Hakluyt went to Paris a Spanish explorer tried again the route from Mexico to New Mexico. On the coast, Spanish garrisons and missions had briefly settled, at various times, as far north as Jamestown; and nearly twenty years had passed since St. Augustine in Florida was made a permanent post. Moreover, Spanish America was organized with an elaboration, if not with an efficiency, that made it a reservoir of political experience, upon which Hakluyt later tried to draw.[1]

Spain, then, was the fountainhead of colonial experience, of experience in exploration, in geographical observation, in the settlement and organization of colonies. Had friendliness existed betwen the two nations, English enterprise might have laid out colonies on the Spanish pattern. As it was, the secrets stored in the India House at Seville continued to be closely guarded, even from the master in espionage named Walsingham. Sebastian Cabot had been lured from Spain, bringing his experience with him; but neither before nor since had any person of like standing been obtained. Foreigners were not welcomed in the Spanish Indies; and, though some had obtained passage, like the Henry Hawks whom the elder Hakluyt once examined, they were infrequent. After Cabot, the most important acquisitions were Portuguese, like the Simon Fernandez who has been mentioned. Indeed, it now appears that the flight to England, in 1581, of the Portuguese pretender Dom Antonio was of some importance to English expansion. With him came his naval officers, still the ablest seamen in Europe. Of their knowledge we may suppose Walsingham, or Hakluyt for him, to have made every possible use.

To judge, however, from the documents preserved, American intelligence was meager enough in Walsingham's reports, at least until Drake and other men of war, taking the seas from 1585 on, brought back a considerable material. Otherwise the Spanish censorship was

[1] The best account of Spanish North America is given in Woodbury Lowery, *The Spanish Settlements within the Present Limits of the United States 1513–1561* (New York 1901) and *The Spanish Settlements within the Present Limits of the United States, Florida 1562–1574* (New York 1905).

rigid. To evade it, England could not even depend on the diplomatic service; for no English envoy was at this time accredited to Spain, and when one was shortly afterwards sent he was to be *éconduit* without a hearing. The reports from Spain in the early eighties are therefore negligible in importance as in quantity. Save for an occasional timid letter from an English merchant in Seville, who used his space to complain of the danger of sending letters at all, Walsingham had no intelligence.[2]

There could therefore be no question of sending to Spain a young Protestant clergyman who had no special qualification as a spy, particularly if he could not be shielded by the diplomatic privilege. With Spain out of consideration, France was the excellent second best. It was nearer to Spain, and it was a focus of anti-Spanish intrigue by Dutch and Portuguese rebels. Stafford, the ambassador, we know to have pushed valiantly into the Parisian web-spinning. He bought his way into the Spanish ambassador's household on the one hand and took pay from him on the other. He kept in touch with Dom Antonio and with the plans of both England and France for attacking Spain with Portuguese help. How these plans availed Hakluyt will presently appear.

If France was thus nearer to Spain than England, it was also in a sense nearer to America. French experience of America was considerably wider than English. French experience of the Atlantic seaboard, which immediately interested England, was indeed almost as conclusive as Spanish. French fishermen had followed the Newfoundland route almost as long as the English, if not longer, and certainly in much greater numbers; and although fishermen have left curiously few records in the history of exploration, yet much might be learned at first hand from so continuous an experience as that, for example, of the Cartier family of St. Malo. French fishermen, moreover, were developing a considerable trade in furs, which took them down the New England coast and even, it is surmised, to the mouth of the Hudson River. It is not surprising that Mercator had drawn his authoritative map of northern North America from the " sea card " of a French mariner,[3] and it was wise for an investigating geographer like Hakluyt to seek the same sources. Furthermore, Cartier had not only made at least three voyages into the Gulf of St. Lawrence but had passed two inland winters in the country; and such experience was far more useful to a colonial expert than the report of a mere summer traveler. In sum, there were outside of France few guides to the country which was appropriately named New France.

On the southern half of the continent, which was called Florida, French experience was almost as serviceable as Spanish. A small

[2] See the Calendars of State Papers Foreign Elizabeth.
[3] Mercator's letter to Hakluyt, *Voyages*, III 275.

French post had in 1562 been set up by Ribaut in what is now South Carolina. In 1564 a substantial French settlement had been made farther south, on the St. Johns River in modern Florida. Their experience was especially valuable because of their failure; and there was always the chance of discovering survivors of those colonies who might have strayed into the country between Florida and New France, the country which was the English objective.

Not much information was likely to be gained, unless in Spain, of this intermediate region, which was not yet christened Virginia. What information there was was gained by the exploring vessels, the "two barks," of 1584, which decided on the Roanoke site. To this voyage, which, like the other Virginia voyages, was piloted by Simon Fernandez the Portuguese, Hakluyt does not seem to have contributed; but he must have hoped to discover in France various sources of information, in written records as well as in interviews. Verrazano might have left behind other documents than the map which Hakluyt had seen in England and the single letter which Hakluyt had published in the *Divers Voyages,* though Hakluyt was not to find them.[4] The last voyage of Cartier, in 1541, was still unaccounted for, as was also the Canadian colony connected with it. The full story of French Florida was yet unpublished. As late as Hakluyt's own time there were further French attempts at settlement, of which news might be forthcoming.

In these various ways France might yield much profit to a geographer and a propagandist and particularly to an intelligence agent. Much of the profit cannot be measured at this distance, since the sojourn abroad must have broadened Hakluyt's outlook as well as enlarged his information. How the change of environment affected his career as a scholar will be explained in the next chapter. The present chapter will sketch his activities in acquiring information for the colonial cause.

2

The evidence for the account of Hakluyt's five years in France is preserved in half a dozen of his letters, in the *Discourse on the Western Planting,* in an occasional mention of him in the foreign dispatches, and in casual remarks which he let fall in prefaces. Incomplete as it is, this evidence gives an ample picture of his actions during his first year and his last, from which may be inferred a panorama. The picture does not, as it happens, clearly define his function. He was later referred to by Purchas, his literary heir, as the embassy chaplain, or more correctly, in the fashion of the time, as the ambassador's chaplain. At times he acted as a secretary and he frequently carried dispatches back and forth.

[4] A new Verrazano letter was published by Alessandro Bacchiani in the *Bolletino della Società Geographica,* November 1909.

His embassy duties cannot be inferred from either his own or the ambassador's earlier letters. His own were mainly about colonizing. His utility would not, of course, appear in official letters, since he would report to the ambassador rather than to the Secretary at home. But he tried to make himself useful. "What I can learn among them of the religion (the Protestants)," he wrote to Walsingham, "I always bring unto my lord, which can judge of reports and advertise you of the truth." What he learned was probably not of great importance. Otherwise Hakluyt would have been more emphatic, since in this letter he was putting his best foot forward in frank Elizabethan fashion. His long absences on leave join with his failure to stress his importance in suggesting that he was, at first at any rate, foot-loose; and the gossip with which he filled up his few letters home to Walsingham was certainly not valuable.

Towards the end of his stay he seems to have shouldered more responsibility. By 1587 he had become useful as a courier. "I know the bearer is faithful," wrote Stafford to Burleigh in a letter he did not wish Walsingham to see, "and will deliver this into your own hands." [5] Such praise of common honesty was not, in the sixteenth century, unnecessary. Early in 1588 Hakluyt carried another personal message to Burleigh, this time from the Earl of Westmoreland, the senior Catholic exile, who was seeking repatriation. On his return to Paris he had a secret midnight interview with the Earl and wrote a further message to the Lord Treasurer. Almost immediately thereafter Stafford took up the matter himself and closed it, the baffled exile returning to the Spanish service.[6]

This is the only record of Hakluyt's acting on his own initiative in diplomatic affairs. Only once again does he appear in an important rôle. In May of 1588 he was trusted with an oral message hedged about with these precautions: "If lack of experience maketh that he cannot deliver so well matter of so great weight," the ambassador wrote, "necessity hath no law. I have taken his oath upon a book for secrecy; for his honesty I will answer." The matter was indeed highly confidential. It was nothing less than a virtual request by the King of France for Elizabeth's direct support against the League; but Hakluyt's task was again that of a courier, not of an agent. To judge by his writing out of the message when he got to England, he acquitted himself with credit. If his honesty was above reproach, so was his intelligence.[7]

These instances, which are perhaps only samples, of the chaplain's activities prove merely that an ambassador's servant would come to

[5] Stafford to Burleigh, 8 January 1586–7 (*Calendar*, p. 486).

[6] Hakluyt to Burleigh, in State Papers Domestic Addenda 1580–1625, 30, 96. And see the chronology, Appendix II.

[7] The message Hakluyt carried he wrote down in what is now Harleian MSS 288, f. 212 (see the chronology). I have not printed the document, since Hakluyt was only repeating a message.

handle some of his master's work—going about among the Protestants, carrying messages to and from home, convoying the ambassador's wife or son across the Channel, and even rising to the exercise of his own discretion. He may have had a further function, which was more closely related to his colonial researches while it was more normally diplomatic.

A man interested in voyages of commerce and discovery would naturally come into contact not only with merchants and their mariners but also, in an age when the same ships and crews were used turn and turn about for war and for trade, with naval officers. Now there was in Paris, during Hakluyt's sojourn there, a body of naval officers to whom he had access—the suite, namely, of the Portuguese pretender. Dom Antonio, driven out of his kingdom by Philip of Spain, was pathetically peddling at the neighboring courts his schemes for repatriation and revenge. He had been in England in 1581 to plan an allied naval descent upon the Azores. He was now in France, engaged in later hopeless enterprises; and Stafford was instructed to yield him soothing, if sterile, encouragement.

Now I have no idea that Hakluyt was specially commissioned to deal with Dom Antonio. Stafford himself frequently visited the forlorn refugee court at St. Germain. But Hakluyt did keep in touch with the pretender and his suite. "I have talked twice with Dom Antonio of Portugal," he reported within three months of his arrival in Paris, "and with five or six of his best captains and pilots. . . . The number of Portugals which hang upon the poor king are about an hundred or sixscore; divers of them are lately come out of the East India, overland. . . ." What he talked about was the Northwest Passage and other maritime matters; but a man disguised as a harmless scientist had plenty of pretexts for sly questioning on naval as well as marine business. I do not go so far as to say that the chaplain acted as a sort of naval attaché. But he might very well have done so, collecting not only the information which he picked up in Paris, from Portuguese and French alike, but that which came in to the embassy from the English agents at the ports.

At least, Hakluyt did collect a body of naval intelligence. Two important pieces of information are given in the evidence. In his first year he obtained from his "excellent French captain" the survey of the West Indies that has been mentioned. It was a survey of no great detail, but it might have some value, at least until Drake had obtained first-hand information in his raid. In the same year he seems also to have gained, from Dom Antonio's secretary and from Portuguese sailors returned from the East, an idea of the organization of the Portuguese colonies.[8] In 1587 he confirmed the information by "a secret

[8] Mentioned in the *Discourse*.

extract of the particular estate" of Portugal and "of every government and office subject to the same."[9]

Both these surveys Hakluyt thought valuable; and unless this was merely the impression of the novice, excited by all the web-spinning and inclined to value his own discoveries, the Admiralty could not afford to overlook them. The information on the Portuguese establishments in the East might not be of immediate importance; but it would be stored up against the day of use. The Spanish information, which Hakluyt thought important enough to include in the *Discourse*, may have been more immediately useful. In 1585 Drake was to launch his momentous raid on the West Indies. Thirteen years had passed since his last voyage to the Spanish Main. It is true that other Englishmen had been there since, and the Admiralty probably had plenty of information; but any such document as Hakluyt's needed to be respectfully considered by the naval commanders. When it is added that Carleill commanded the soldiery in that voyage and that Philip Sidney expected until the last moment to share Drake's command, it will be clear that Hakluyt and his information need not have waited in vain in the antechambers of power.

When Drake returned in 1586 after overthrowing most of the Spanish strongholds, Hakluyt was at hand to examine two of the prisoners captured in Florida.[10] Their depositions he was later to publish, together with the accounts of most of the naval enterprises of the time. Whether the examination was in any sense official is again an open question. Whether his copying or translating reports and captured documents for his own use was not also turned to public use is also an open question. A man who had the run of the Admiralty clearly had many occasions for usefulness. It is well known that journalists are often set to work nowadays on the levers of the state machine. So Hakluyt, who was a kind of journalist when he interviewed prisoners and made copies of documents, may well have been used and even officially directed by the authorities.

3

The presumption is strong, therefore, though it remains presumption, that as Hakluyt had something to do with domestic and foreign politics in and about the embassy so he had a good deal to do with naval intelligence, which makes use of many agents. These interests seem none the less incidental. While his long visits to England may have turned to Her Majesty's service, they may more likely mean that he was encouraged to go about his own business of colonial affairs. That is certainly the inference to be drawn from one of his first actions abroad. When he wrote to Walsingham in January of 1584, he

[9] Mentioned in the dedication of the *French Florida*, English version.
[10] September 1586 (see the chronology).

wrote to suggest his own going to America as an observer, supposing that "for obtaining leave of my Lord Ambassador here to depart, I doubt not but to find means of myself, seeing he may have enough to supply my room." At that time he thought his colonial activities most important.

This was his second attempt to acquire a first-hand knowledge of America; and, if he had sailed with Amadas and Barlow on the reconnoitering voyage of 1584, his knowledge might have obviated many of the subsequent mistakes of the Roanoke colonies. Not that Hakluyt was necessarily a trained observer, or that his knowledge was not in many respects ludicrously at fault. But at the worst he was still the best-informed man in England, except his cousin, if only from books and generally at second hand; and his intentions at least were scientific. "I know," he wrote to the Secretary, "that this present enterprise is like soon to wax cold and fall to the ground, unless in this second voyage all diligence in searching every hope of gain be used." His purpose, as he repeatedly declared, was the assembling of useful knowledge.

Apparently no one cared to pay Hakluyt's way in 1584; and when Raleigh's first colony sailed in the next year it was an Oxford contemporary, Thomas Hariot, who sailed as observer. Thus Hakluyt was recommitted to a career of research. His authority was in no wise lessened for that. Despite the increasing number of Englishmen who were gaining first-hand knowledge of the distant quarters of the world, the value of the man of research was still admitted. So in 1597 the Secretary was to require advice on Guiana from Hakluyt, who had not been there, in corroboration of Raleigh, who had. So again in 1600 the new East India Company was to consult him on their commerce, in corroboration of some of their own members who had explored and done business in the new territory.

These facts may prove that Hakluyt could make a reputation by staying at home. His method was simple; he consulted the right people. During his Paris period the right people were Newfoundland fishermen of the Norman and Breton ports and the merchants who distributed their fish and furs. They were French and Portuguese sailors, whose voyages covered among them most of the known globe, as those of no Englishman but Drake had yet done.

The importance of the Portuguese cannot be estimated, since Hakluyt left little record of their information. We have observed, however, that he had seen something of the Portuguese pilots, "one of whom was born in East India." In one of the interviews with Dom Antonio he was lectured on the Northwest Passage, a Portuguese chart serving as key. In 1586 he was employing a Portuguese map maker, whom he described in a letter to Raleigh as "the prince of Cosmographers of this age." He studied the Portuguese colonial administration, as has been mentioned. It was probably from the pilots that he began collecting the notes on eastern markets which he was later to turn over to the East India Company. So Hakluyt stored a knowledge of the East, from which no Englishman but Drake had yet returned. So from the premier globe-trotters of the time he gained his facts on world geography. So from the first navigators of Europe he learned, as he could have done from few Englishmen, the problems of the oceans. Hakluyt stayed at home to become the best-traveled man in England. If he used his opportunities as we suppose, the Portuguese association was enough in itself to justify his going to Paris instead of to Seville.

4

So much for the Portuguese. For the French, we have seen that Hakluyt obtained a French survey of the West Indies, which probably gave him little that was new in the way of commercial and geographical knowledge but which may have corrected some of his impressions. The French captain from whom he had the survey remains unidentified; but most of Hakluyt's American news came to him from the northern ports. These we know were watched by English agents, whose reports are preserved. For immediately on his arrival in France Stafford wrote home that "besides some friends on the Normandy coast I mean to send thither again, and have taken such order for Brittany, Rochelle, and Brouage that I hope nothing will be enterprised there without my hearing of it." From one of these watchers, who wrote to Stafford at the end of October of 1583, Hakluyt might have heard of a ship preparing at Honfleur for a voyage to "Peru." From the same report he might also have noted the size of the Honfleur fishing fleet, which sent twenty ships a year to Newfoundland.

This was the type of information most germane to his purpose; for English experience had not yet discovered the way to make American enterprise profitable. So Hakluyt tried to find out how American enterprise profited France. The extent of the fishing was easy enough to estimate from the agents' reports. Hakluyt took pains to record the fact that Frenchmen made as many as two trips a year to the Banks. But the fishing was only incidental in his inquiry; more important was the amount of trade with which the fisher supplemented his catch, and with this information Hakluyt speedily supplied himself. By the time of his first letter to Walsingham, in January of 1584, he had already visited the "French king's skinners" and obtained the facts on American furs. By the following summer he had seen his "friend Stephen Bellinger of Rouen," whose knowledge warranted a place in the *Discourse*. Bellinger had gone trading down the Maine coast in 1583, where he had bargained with forty crowns' worth of merchandise for furs and skins worth eleven times as much.

By such beginnings the outline of New France was already being sketched. By such beginnings the frame of New Netherlands would later be drawn. England was, however, to play a different game; and Hakluyt's mission was designed to turn up new cards. The fur trade was not to figure importantly in English America until the Hudson's Bay Company was founded nearly a century later. Meantime the search for more profitable products was in hand, as Hakluyt reported in the *Discourse*. He picked up a rumor that some Basque fishermen had found cochineal. Bellinger had brought back skins dyed in various colors; and in addition to his hopes for native dyes he was speculating on the value of castoreum, which came from the beaver. Moreover, Bellinger thought he had seen signs of silver ore, thus confirming the report of John Walker to Gilbert and strengthening the suspicion that the ore which the latter had collected and lost at sea was really silver.

Hard upon this last report from Bellinger came the news of a Spanish discovery of silver in New Mexico, news contained in a book published in Madrid in 1586 and hurried over to Raleigh by Hakluyt. The connection is not apparent to us, who know the distance from Maine to New Mexico. Hakluyt had no such knowledge. Indeed, he had good reason for believing the distance negligible. Ingram said he had walked it; and the story of de Soto's wanderings westward from Florida was not clear enough, in the account given by Oviedo, to prove that any great distance separated the coast from Mexico. Even if it did, a further hope remained. No one in England and probably few men elsewhere believed that much of the distance was overland. Hakluyt's French captain had reported an inland waterway from Florida to Mexico, a waterway built by the Spaniards to bring their treasure safely out into the Atlantic. Hakluyt was reassured of the existence of such a waterway in 1586 by Drake's prisoners from St. Augustine; and he was the more ready to believe it because he believed also in an inland sea covering most of the continent. He had the authority of Ortelius himself, as well as the map of Verrazano (Fig. 19) which he had imitated in the *Divers Voyages;* and he obtained an explorer's report at first hand. This came from a Breton whom he named in the *Discourse* and who told him that the inland sea had been seen from Montreal. Jacques Cartier's nephew was critical when he wrote to Hakluyt about it in 1587; but one could still believe what one wanted to believe. So Hakluyt summed up, when he wrote in 1587 the dedication of his *Florida,* by saying that "as the late experience of that skillful pilot and captain M. John Davis to the Northwest . . . hath showed a great part to be main sea where before was thought to be main land, so for my part I am fully persuaded by Ortelius' late reformation of Culvacan and the gulf of

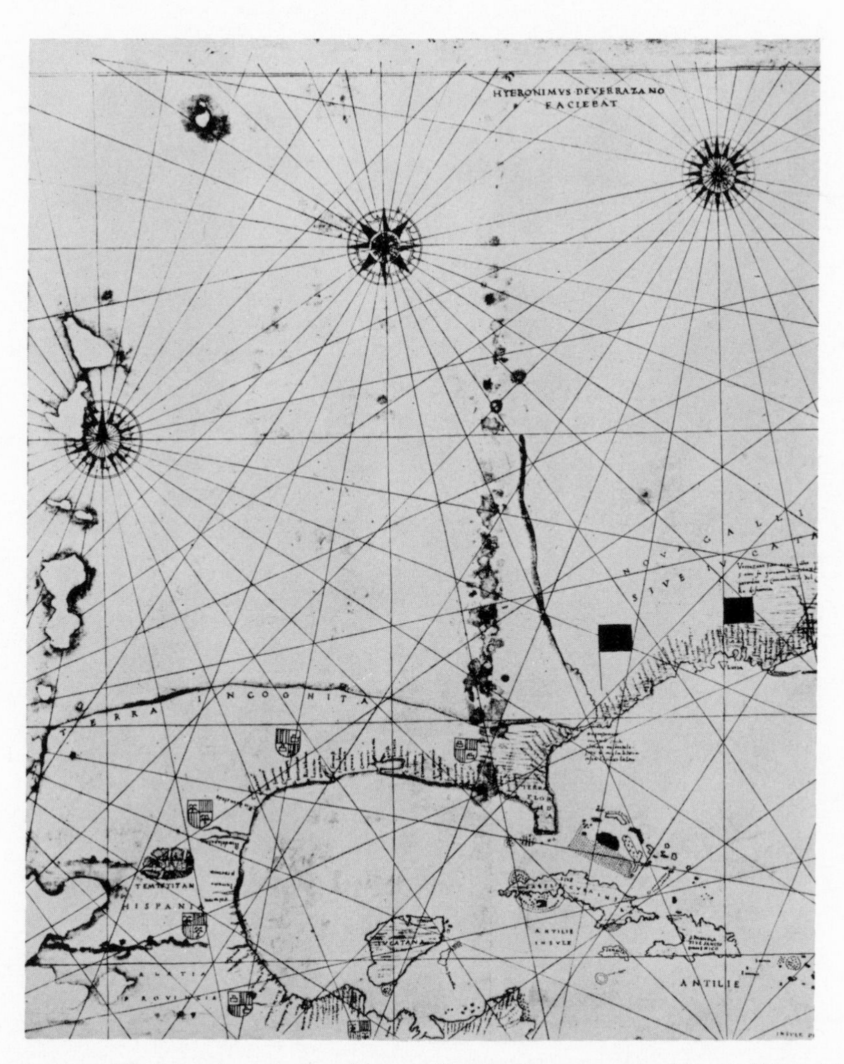

FIG. 19—A portion of North America, from the world map of Hieronimo Verrazano, 1529. From the Vatican Library.

California, that the land on the back part of Virginia extendeth nothing so far westward as is put down in the Maps of those parts."

We have passed over, as Hakluyt did, from the study of commodities to the study of trade routes, both of them carried on in the same scientific fashion. To the facts and the surmises of geography and trade Hakluyt was also able to add some information on foreign colonies and colonizing. We have spoken of his surveys of both the East and the West Indies. We may add that he acquired in Paris an important document on Mexico. This was nothing less than an illustrated native history of that country, translated from the native language and intercepted on the way to Spain by a French corsair.[11] An even more important discovery was one which could have been made anywhere, though more easily in Paris than in London. It was the book which he conveyed to Raleigh for its mention of New Mexican silver, the book of Espejo's journey into New Mexico in 1583. The information on this new exploration was rather belated. It was rather public than private and seems to have given Hakluyt no inkling that the journey was a prelude to an important extension of Spanish rule. The book was in any event a signal addition to the record.

With French colonial enterprise the case was different. Being on the ground and being in the confidence, it would seem, of Thevet, a fellow geographer, Hakluyt kept well informed. Of contemporary plans there was little to learn, for it was not until the end of the century that New France became possible. There were plans, however, and Hakluyt seems to have learned of them as much as is known to modern research. The Marquis de la Roche, who was a French Raleigh, had been watched by the English for some years. In 1584 there were rumors, which Hakluyt duly reported, that that nobleman was launching a new colony. He reported also the rumored colonial plans of the Basques of St. Jean de Luz. And of the court supporters of both these enterprises he heard from Thevet and so told Walsingham.

So he learned what there was to be learned of the current stirring toward America and added a great deal of information on the past. French colonial activity in America had been marked, through the century, by Roberval's Canada in 1541, by Villegagnon's Brazil in 1555, and by Ribaut's and Laudonnière's Florida in 1564. The Brazil experiment had been made known in English by translation from Thevet, but there was much to say of the others. Of Canada Hakluyt acquired the fragments of a report, which he presently published. There was little enlightenment in it, unless the routier of its pilot might be useful to Englishmen who thought of competing for New France. The discovery of the account of French Florida was, however, a distinguished achievement. The manuscript which Hakluyt found and published was nothing less than the full official report of the

[11] Published by Purchas, XV 414–568, in the English version made by Michael Lok.

governor of the colony and had the signal merit of revealing to the colonial expert all the lessons of experience the English might need to learn. The country was of the same sort as Virginia, and the natives shared the same plane of civilization as the natives of the new English territory. These facts marked off the experiment from that made by the Spaniards in the islands and in the southerly mainland. Of equal if not of greater importance was the lesson of French administration. Unwise relations with the Indians, the frittering away of energy in treasure hunts, the neglect of agriculture, and the consequent dependence on home supply—these were mistakes of moment, to be pondered by future colonizers; and the final disaster brought about by Spain, coupled with the discontent of the colonial personnel, was a serious warning to the provident. No similar lesson of experience was more applicable to English affairs, as Hakluyt specially insisted. If experience ever played a vital part in history, this experience summoned reflection.

5

A more complete *dossier* of colonial information could hardly have been gathered save at Seville alone. It is difficult to suppose that the task could have been better done. That the service of a *dossier,* like that of a dictionary, may be tested only in the long run detracts in no way from its value. What heed the venturers paid to this one we can hardly know. The bits of intelligence which Hakluyt writes of transmitting to Carleill in the winter of 1583–1584 may have served Raleigh when Carleill yielded place to him. Walsingham may have treasured his agent's statistics. Raleigh certainly acted on the suggestion, whether Hakluyt's alone or another's, that his second colony should be dropped on the Chesapeake instead of at Roanoke as Hakluyt advised in a letter of 1586. Raleigh gave the instructions, though the colony failed to regard them. The *Discourse* to the Queen, stuffed as it was with late information, may have earned re-readings by the lords of the council before it was shelved in the archives. The information was at least gathered and in quantity. Whether it was considered and acted on, it is not possible to say.

It is in its way startling that Hakluyt should ever have embarked on the mission, should ever have broached the idea of making a colonial *dossier*. The initiative I think we may assign to Hakluyt himself. He probably went to France because he wished to, not because he was sent. For it is doubtful that Walsingham, engrossed in anti-Spanish and anti-Catholic endeavors, should have taken so long a view in the subsidiary matter of colonies. Hakluyt knew what he wanted. I am inclined to think that Walsingham did no more than sanction the proposal, perhaps with some satisfaction that the able young university man would make one more in his corps of agents.

This view of the Secretary as being merely passive is borne out by the fact that he gave Hakluyt no instructions. Indeed, as is shown by Hakluyt's first letter to him from abroad, it was not until he was reminded that the geographer was under way that he showed his pleasure.

We have then but stray indications of the use and value of the colonial *dossier* which Hakluyt laid before his government. We cannot begin to estimate its value; and we can certainly not go very far in the estimate until we have reviewed Hakluyt's publications during this period, which make up the first consistent body of colonial literature in English. At the same time, we may say that the very fact of Hakluyt's diligence is startling enough. The first step in the English rise to maritime power we have correlated with the importing of foreign knowledge and foreign methods. The second step we have correlated with the growth of a native body of knowledge, gathered from native experience. This, the third step, is the sending abroad of a native expert, who should graft upon the maturing English stock whatever he might find abroad that was vital. His assembling of knowledge was as significant as the assembling of experience which had been made by men like the elder Hakluyt. From the younger geographer's labors and those of his generation was to follow the fourth step, the teaching of other nations by a mature England. In knowledge of the world and of the roads about it England was becoming adult.

Hakluyt's own profits from the French mission may not be so readily seen. The quantitative increase of information, important though it was, was not so important as the qualitative. The passage from England to France was, for a neophyte, the passage from a country which was beginning its seafaring to a country which had long been familiar with the ends of the earth. A Norman sailor had long since made the voyage to Sumatra. Norman corsairs had ranged the Atlantic since the time of Columbus and earlier and had even imperiled that sailor on one of his voyages. Normans and Bretons had placed colonies in North and South America and perhaps in Africa. If this were not enough for an avid inquirer he could add the master navigators of the world, the Portuguese whom he luckily found assembling in Paris about their exiled king. The young islander must have been vastly enlightened. From the voyages of books he rose to meet the men who had made the voyages. From the still rare English voyagers he expanded to intercourse with the many lords of the oceans. As education, the step was from the library to the laboratory. The effect must have been the effect of expansion, expansion to a wider view of the earth as seen by its masters. The result was saturation, which may be thought the final educative process.

CHAPTER IX

The French Mission: Publicity

1585–1588

Hakluyt had twice seized the idea of going to America as an observer. He had thought to go with Carleill when Carleill should follow Gilbert, and he hoped to go with Amadas and Barlow when they went exploring for Raleigh. Other occasions may have offered. But the fact remains that Parmenius and Hariot went instead. It is striking that the man who organized a school of oversea publicity never went overseas himself. For that very reason he obtained the more time for his other work; the first period of his productivity was the period of Raleigh's settlements in Virginia.

In obvious ways publicity was indicated as Hakluyt's work. There were already in America men who were investigating for themselves —not as carefully as Hakluyt would have liked, as he presently declared, but at any rate investigating. Raleigh saw to the sending over of the proper persons, taking a leaf perhaps from the French example or perhaps taking advice from Hakluyt. For the first, we know from Hakluyt that Raleigh was in these years maintaining in London the official artist of the French Florida colony of twenty years before.[1] For the second, we recall that Hakluyt had already urged an observer upon Gilbert. Raleigh's observers were two. Thomas Hariot was one, an Oxford contemporary of Hakluyt's and a sort of private scientist of Raleigh's for many years to come. Hariot was especially skilled in mathematics and perhaps reached geography through that study. He was to write and publish the first book on Virginia, the first descriptive treatise in England on the economic geography of the new worlds.[2] John White was the other observer, a man of talent with the brush as well as governor of the second Roanoke colony. With their observation in America a geographer in Paris could not hope to compete, though he was to do much towards preserving their records.

Hakluyt was in no danger from their competition. He was a professional geographer, trained as such from childhood. White was not a geographer at all. Hariot was a geographer for the occasion and, for all his life service in Raleigh's pay, remained the mathematician. Moreover, Hakluyt had his own mission to carry out. His task was to assure the permanence of the record by publishing it and by publishing systematically, not in the casual fashion of the translators of

[1] Mentioned in the dedication of *French Florida*, English version.

[2] Hariot's life has been written by Henry Stevens of Vermont (London 1900).

the seventies. With Eden's first book and Willis' second, with the whole flow of translations in the seventies, the record had been largely lined out. It remained for Hakluyt to complete it, to mark out a comprehensive course of publishing.

Such was the result of his work, though I have no idea that Hakluyt was yet thoroughly aware of it. His *Divers Voyages* had already concentrated the American record, the North American record that is. But that record was by no means all set down, and certain discoveries of his Paris period materially enlarged it.

Hakluyt's research and his publishing were two aspects of the same activity. A first example will illustrate. In 1586, the year of its publication in Madrid, there came into Hakluyt's hands an account of the Spanish journey into New Mexico made by Antonio de Espejo in 1583. The account added, as we have seen, to his information on Virginia and most especially because it recorded the discovery of silver in "the latitude of 37½ degrees." He was quick to act. "For the zeal he beareth to his country and countrymen," wrote a later English translator, Hakluyt "brought the same first into this court." The person to whom he brought it was doubtless Raleigh; and presently we find Hakluyt engaging for Raleigh a Portuguese draftsman to make a map showing the new discovery. So much for his investigating. Meanwhile the narrative was going through the press. "Within few months afterward," Hakluyt wrote later, it was "reprinted by me in Paris" in French. Early in the next year an English version was brought out, probably with Hakluyt's supervision.

This process was typical. Did a significant new work appear abroad, he had it. He brought it to the attention of those whom it might concern, like Raleigh, and translated it or had it translated with a view to final printing. Occasionally the translation, or notes from it, went from the recipient to the archives, where it stayed. Usually it was published, sometimes separately, sometimes with the other documents which Hakluyt was soon to collect for printing in the *Voyages*. In such fashion Hakluyt made himself a mouthpiece of knowledge, to be held first to the official then to the public, ear.[3]

Hakluyt did not work only from printed sources. The feat of his Paris years was his uncovering of the manuscripts that related the entire story of French colonizing in America. Searching, he found documents accounting for the first French colony, that which Cartier and Roberval had led to Canada in 1541. These were incomplete and remain so.[4] There was a portion only of Cartier's narrative, obtained from the Breton's descendant; a portion of a *routier* of the St. Lawrence, written by Cartier's pilot, who was a famous mariner in his time; a portion of Roberval's own report. These documents, which

[3] The bibliography of Hakluyt's work is given in Appendix III.

[4] See H. P. Biggar, edit., *The Voyages of Jacques Cartier*, in 11 *Publications of the Public Archives of Canada* (Ottawa 1924).

were too fragmentary to be published by themselves, Hakluyt later gathered into the *Voyages,* where they completed the story of French Canada to date. With the information from the French fishermen which he had set down in the *Discourse,* they finished a chapter.

The chapter of French Florida was more significant than the chapter of French Canada, since it more directly paralleled the Virginia enterprise. Ribaut's reconnaissance of 1562, similar in aim to the Amadas and Barlow voyage of 1584, had left a single record in England, whither Ribaut had escaped, a record which Hakluyt had reprinted in the *Divers Voyages.* Laudonnière's colony of 1564, which had been so dramatically stamped out by the Spanish heel, had so far found its only record in the narrative of a surviving carpenter, also printed in England; but the full report of the leaders existed only in manuscript. This report alone might have sent Hakluyt to France, since it filled the largest gap in his record of North America. Where he found the manuscript he nowhere says; but the credit may almost certainly be given to Thevet, geographer royal, whom he knew. For Thevet had himself been overseas in the French colony in Brazil whose record he had written. He must have known officially of the Floridian history; and he had lately supplied details from the history to an Italian compiler.

So the colorful story of massacre and revenge was rescued, as its French editor observed, "as from the tomb" and published at Hakluyt's expense in French and, in his own translation, in English. The volume seems to have had some success in France, as Hakluyt reported in his preface; indeed, the French edition is today the rarest of books. The success was in part due to the book's timely anti-Spanish and anti-Catholic theme. "By the malice," Hakluyt wrote in a preface, "of some too much affectioned in the Spanish faction (in France, it) had been above twenty years suppressed"; and there was a certain boldness in the revival. The boldness brought forth praise. "Monsieur Harlac, the lord chief justice of France," wrote Hakluyt further, "and certain other of the wisest judges, in great choler . . . asked who had done such intolerable wrong to their whole kingdom as to have concealed that worthy work so long."

Not only in France was the book a success; we shall see that the fame of the *Florida* was to spread to other countries and to start a travel collection rivaling Hakluyt's own. As a tale of combined Spanish and Catholic malignity, the book has made its permanent place in the American legend. It has been stamped with full dramatic values by the power of Parkman's retelling, and only within recent years have its barbaric colors been somewhat softened. In publishing it at the climax of the Raleigh enterprise and just before the Armada, Hakluyt fully proved his skill in publicity.

Yet it is noteworthy that Hakluyt left to others the sounding of the emotional trumpet. His preface to the English version is cool and edifying. "No history hitherto set forth," he wrote, addressing Raleigh, "hath more affinity, resemblance, or conformity with yours of Virginia than this of Florida." This was the declared ground of publication, an object lesson to the colonists, "whom, by the reading of this my translation, you will have forewarned and admonished as well to beware of the gross negligence in providing of sufficiency of victuals, the security, disorders, and mutinies that fell out among the French."

Not a word struck the spark of fortuitous emotion. If any feeling was designed, it was that aroused by the prospectus, which Hakluyt never forgot. He breathed hints, as Carleill and Peckham had done in their discourses, of "certain secret commodities," of which one was probably the sassafras bark, long supposed medicinal. He mentioned the hope of royal subsidy. He estimated ten thousand men as a sufficient military force to occupy the colony. One hundred were sent.

In short, every appearance of Hakluyt in print was tuned in the same key, the pressing forward of enterprise. Fully as important was the pressing forward of investigation. The colonists, he thought, "also might be put in mind, by the reading of the manifold commodities and great fertility of the places herein at large described and so near neighbors unto our Colonies, that they might generally be awaked and stirred up unto the diligent observation of every thing that might turn to the advancement of the action." This was scientific enthusiasm, which curiously outweighed the dramatic interest of the story. We need not think that Hakluyt was insensible to the excitement of history, since he himself so ably expressed it in his style. His task was of greater or at least equal magnitude, to interpret the lessons of history against the needs of the morrow.

So Hakluyt closed the historical chapter that dealt with North America in so far as it concerned the French. He had translated Verrazano and Cartier; he had completed the Canada record to date; he had printed the full story of French Florida. There was nothing left to record except the routine voyages of fishermen, nothing until Champlain should set out at the beginning of the new century.

3

The French record completed, Hakluyt passed to the Spanish. This is the obvious explanation of his reëditing, in 1587, the complete *Decades* of Peter Martyr. Although he was the first historian of the first discoveries of Spain, that worthy prelate had hitherto been published complete in only one edition, that of 1530. He appeared in English only in part. Three out of the eight books were translated by Eden in 1555, an abstract of the remaining books was added by Willis in 1577. The later historians, Oviedo and Gómara, had been substantially translated in the Frobisher period. The rest of the *Decades* had then to be issued if the Spanish story were to be as complete as possible.[5]

I repeat that this is the obvious explanation, that Hakluyt desired to complete the record of America, as he had completed the French portion of it and was to pass on to the English. Such a motive is to be found only by reading between the lines of his dedication to Raleigh and by viewing in perspective his list of publications. But motives may be mingled; and, to show that they were in this case, I need only say that the *Decades* were published in Latin, not in English, though Hakluyt was planning an English version; that they were published in Paris, not in London; and that the editor was after all more than a publicity agent, as he was more than the mere antiquarian which some of his commentators have thought him.

Most of all, I gather from his dedication as well as from his career, Hakluyt prided himself now on publishing a great work of geography as well as of history. He lauded Peter Martyr for his history, for "launching the history (of America) from its cradle, diligently observing the sequence of time and the exact description of place." He pronounced it significant that Martyr "depicts the whole body of that great America." "If we consider those things born in the earth," he explains, "the potency of plants, the fruits of trees, the strength of spices, the products of the fields, the splendor of metals, the breeding of quadrupeds, the birth of fowls, the nature of fishes, the birth, growth, maturity, life, and qualities of almost all living creatures: then not Aristotle, not Theophrastus, not Columella, not Pliny himself ever set down anything more learned or exact than did this our Martyr."

This praise of Peter Martyr as a new Pliny shows Hakluyt as primarily the scholar editing a scientific document; but, as I have said, motives are likely to be mixed, especially when one writes dedications to the great. Which was the dominant motive I cannot say, but I can mention the others. There was the patriotic motive, which flared out when Peter Martyr recorded the single English enterprise of the Cabots; and the combined patriotic and emulatory motive—"that other maritime nations, and first of all our English islanders, observing the beginning and the progress of Spain, may be incited to a like show of courage." The last motive rises to a climax in the eulogy of Raleigh, to whom the work was inscribed and to whom Hakluyt wrote, "this one thing I know, that you are embarking on the same plan which first the Portuguese, then the Spaniards at length brought to fruition by the devotion of their hearts."

[5] I have found useful, as an account of the growing Spanish history of America, the bibliographical chapters in the *Narrative and Critical History of America.*

Propaganda or not, the editing of Peter Martyr, the Pliny of the new world, was and is a solid achievement. The lively letters which the prelate poured forth over a period of years, detailing to the heads of the church the course of Spanish discovery, form a geographical classic. Now it had probably become a rare work in its complete form; and a competent edition, with notes and an index, was and always is a desideratum. By publishing it in the universal Latin, moreover, Hakluyt was increasing his momentum. The geographers of the Continent could now look upon and criticize his work. Ortelius wondered why he did it, which was not very critical of him. Hakluyt was clearly going back to the beginning, taking up the Spanish record as he had taken up the French and English. He was building a library of the new geography.

He did not, as it happened, go systematically forward with the history of Spanish America. The reason is doubtless the secretiveness of Spain. The Spanish voyages were accessible in the main only to the official historians, whose practice it was to digest, not to edit, the narratives. Some of the original records, like the recent Espejo and the much later found de Soto, Hakluyt was to obtain and publish, doing what he could. With the new histories, of Acosta and Herrera, he was to keep up as they came out; and large portions of them passed through his hands into the collection of Purchas, his successor. So he did his scholarly duty by the Spaniards; but he was at the same time the apostle of English expansion, and he was already turning to a larger and more apostolic task, the compiling of the oversea records of his countrymen. That task was to result in the *English Voyages,* his greatest work. Its story will be told in the next chapter.

4

All this publishing could not be done without collaborators. Of the *Decades,* for an example, Hakluyt wrote to Raleigh that it "will cost me forty French crowns and five months travail." If there were these difficulties with a mere reprint, what greater labors must have gone into the transcribing of manuscripts and even more into working over a readable translation such as Hakluyt's always was?

There must have been collaborators on the seven volumes which Hakluyt published by 1588. The first of these we have seen was John Florio, who did the early Cartier volume. In the *Divers Voyages* one finds no evidence that any other than their editor had done the translating, copying, and compiling, although it is clear that the elder Hakluyt and others had at least furnished much of the material. The English edition of Laudonnière's *Florida* was of Hakluyt's own translating and editing; while for the Peter Martyr, which was going forward at the same time, no collaborator is mentioned. Yet so much clerical work must have required help, at least for the *Decades,* which ran to more than one hundred thousand words.

Of the three remaining books a definite word can be said. The English Espejo carries in it no sign of Hakluyt's hand, nor do the French Espejo and Laudonnière, nor for that matter Florio's Cartier. It is possible that the English translator of Espejo, one A. F., had nothing to do with Hakluyt. Indeed, when Hakluyt came to reprint Espejo in the *Voyages,* he used a better translation, which he probably made himself. One is at a loss to know in that case what happened. Hakluyt has left no word of his part in the book; but it is hardly doubtful that the man who sent the book to Raleigh in the original, who had a map made for it, and who had it translated and published in French, would have seen to the translation into English. He may have been forestalled; but the probability is that the English Espejo was just as much his as the French, and that A. F. was a collaborator.

The collaborator on the French books was Hakluyt's "learned friend Martin Basanier," who called himself "gentilhomme" and mathematician. His Espejo, in 1586, says nothing of Hakluyt. It was dedicated to the Admiral of France. It acknowledged the help of an otherwise unknown Frenchman who "had experience of foreign sailors." But Hakluyt later declared that he paid for the book, apparently for the enlightenment of the French nation.

Basanier acknowledged Hakluyt's hand in the Laudonnière. Hakluyt rescued the manuscript, he said, as from the tomb; Hakluyt had Basanier edit it and dedicate it to Raleigh; Hakluyt paid for it. Basanier took most of the credit to himself, as was perhaps the way of the times. In fact, it was Hakluyt who saved Basanier's name to posterity. Otherwise the "gentilhomme" and mathematician would be known only for a mathematical work. Now he can be reckoned a man highly serviceable, if somewhat ungrateful, to the geographical cause.

Behind Basanier probably stands the French geographer royal, whom Hakluyt spoke of in his letters home. Thevet discussed matters geographical with Hakluyt; he gave news of French colonies past and present; he probably knew about the Florida manuscript, as I have suggested. He may have helped in getting hold of the Cartier manuscript and its fellows; and he supplied Hakluyt with at least one striking work in geography, the native history of Mexico which had come into French hands. He was not a collaborator, but he was a useful professional friend.

Editors and learned friends were not alone necessary. For completeness Hakluyt needed maps; and he himself, I repeat, did not make them. The Cartier had no map. The *Divers Voyages* had been furnished with two; one was the very sketchy and antiquated map

NOVVS
ORBIS

with which Robert Thorne illustrated his *Book*. The other was drawn by Michael Lok, merchant adventurer, as has been said; and I add in parenthesis that it was Lok who was to translate both the *Decades* and the Mexican history. No map went with the Laudonnière; but, though none was published, Hakluyt had a special map drawn to illustrate the Espejo discovery. To draw this map, as Hakluyt wrote Raleigh, he called in one Andrew Home, or Homem, the Portuguese, "prince of Cosmographers of this age", who must therefore be added to the editor's circle.

The map that accompanied the *Decades* (Fig. 20) was signed F. G., which is taken to mean Francisco Gualle, Spanish navigator. The map is considered a fine piece of engraving and in accuracy of detail ranks with the best American maps of its time. Indeed, the combined authorship should have been irresistible, the product superior to that of the best of living authorities. Thevet is now recognized as of inferior ability. Ortelius in Belgium was primarily an engraver, who took his maps where he could find them. Mercator in Germany was a really scientific cartographer; but even his resources might be taxed to compete with those of a specialist in discovery and a Spanish pilot on the Pacific Ocean. The success of the map shows the possibilities that were opened to Hakluyt had he cared to compete in cartography with the leaders of his day.

A still wider radius than that which includes the translators and draftsmen whom he employed takes in the men whom he encouraged to publish for themselves. How substantial was the aid he thus gave cannot always be measured. We have seen that in the case of Florio's Cartier Hakluyt claimed credit for the plan as well as for the expense of publishing; yet neither his initiative nor even his name was mentioned by Florio. If this nonchalance and that of Basanier be typical, the number of books that Hakluyt steered to publication cannot be fairly estimated. Indeed, considering the breadth of his interests and his acquaintance, one is tempted to think it larger than we know, to suspect that there are more volumes which need to be added to an already long list.

I have discovered a number, enough to show that Hakluyt was a veritable organizer of geographical publishing. His part in the Cartier has only recently been pointed out, and his share in the Espejo not at all. Similarly unnoticed have been several further works of this earlier period which were published under other names. One is an account of a voyage overland from Vienna to Constantinople by the same route as that followed by the first commercial mission to Turkey and therefore relevant to the Levant trade. The voyage was made in 1567 by an Italian, one Marc-Antonio Pigafetta. He would have destroyed his manuscript, or at least never thought of publishing it, had it not been that he "was exhorted principally by Mr. Richard Hakluyt, a young man endowed with a kind and noble mind, and not only learned in the knowledge of his calling, but also both learned in and devoted to matters of geography." The *Itinerario,* in Italian, was therefore brought to press in London in 1585.

Pigafetta was perhaps of the family of the Italian who sailed with Magellan and who wrote the only account of the first voyage around the world. One does not know why he was in London. One does not know how Hakluyt became acquainted with him, though the geographer may have sought him out to ask what he knew of the great voyage. In any case, the acquaintance continued. When Hakluyt came to publish his great collection of voyages, Pigafetta wrote for it an Italian sonnet in praise of the young man of kind and noble mind.

More remote, though still not irrelevant to Hakluyt's purposes, was a volume of *Certain brief and special Instructions for Gentlemen, Merchants, etc., employed in services abroad.* This was a traveler's handbook to neighboring countries and remains an interesting comment on land travel in the sixteenth century. Hakluyt would of course be interested in such a book; he would be specially interested because it had been taken up by a friend who was a traveler himself. The original had been done by a Dane, Latinizing his name as Meierus. The translating was done by the Reverend Philip Jones of Cirencester, who had gone to the Levant in a company ship and written an account of the voyage for Hakluyt. I imagine that Hakluyt suggested the translating, urging the man who had traveled to cast about for a book useful to travelers. I cannot prove that he did. All that is certain is that he advised his friend the translator in the choice of a patron. Hakluyt suggested Drake, or, as the preface delicately put it, Jones was "motioned to remember yourself (Drake) in the impression of this Index by my very good and learned friend Mr. Richard Hackluyt." But as patrons were fairly unreliable and especially likely to be so in the year after the Armada, it is possible that Hakluyt helped to pay for the book.[6]

5

With these widening activities Hakluyt's Paris years, which seemed at the first devoted to the massing of information, turned increasingly towards publishing; and by the time he returned definitely to England in the winter of 1588–1589 he had built a goodly edifice. It was to serve, however, only as the vestibule of the building he had planned, the *English Voyages.* The work was onerous both in time and in money. Besides accumulating the material he was to use in the *Voyages,* Hakluyt had translated the Laudonnière; he had edited the

[6] See the chronology, Appendix II, and the bibliography, Appendix III.

Decades; and he had set others to work, not without trouble to himself, under his remote or immediate direction.

He must therefore have gone to large expense. To meet it the Bristol prebend was opportunely conferred, especially as the appointment was followed at once by the outburst of books. The edition of the *Decades,* Hakluyt figured, cost him forty crowns, say ten pounds, perhaps half a year's income from his prebend. As much again may be taken as the cost of the other works together, not including the pay of assistants. The total makes an important figure.

Hakluyt seems to have borne the brunt of this expense himself. The French Laudonnière, he said in a later preface, was published at his charges; so was the French Espejo. So, one infers, were the other books, the *Decades* and the English Laudonnière at least and perhaps still others. There was nothing else for it but that he should foot the bill; for, he said later, there was no relying on patrons, meaning that in this period there was no help in Raleigh.

Many successive patrons were on Hakluyt's list. To Sidney was dedicated the *Divers Voyages.* After his death, Raleigh was the patron of the books of the Paris period, except the French Espejo, which Basanier dedicated to the Admiral of France, and the English Espejo of A. F. The first edition of the *Voyages* was to be dedicated to Walsingham. To Lord Charles Howard, Lord High Admiral of England, was appropriately to be addressed the first volume of the final *Voyages* at the end of the century. After him came Sir Robert Cecil, Secretary of State. To him Hakluyt complained, in dedicating the *Annals* in 1601, of his "being never therein entertained to any purpose until I had recourse unto yourself, by whose special favor and bountiful patronage I have been often much encouraged and as it were revived."

The implication is clear but unjust. No doubt Hakluyt looked back from prosperity to painful strivings to raise money for his books; no doubt he recalled only nominal gifts from the patrons to whom he addressed them. But it seems clear that he managed to forget the marks of favor shown him. These were ample enough. He probably did not inherit wealth. Otherwise he would not have asked Walsingham, in 1584, to pay his expenses to America. But he was subsidized to meet his successive needs. To his scholarship and studentship at school and university was added the chaplaincy which maintained him in France. Royal favor made him canon of Bristol; and we shall see that most of his important books were to bring him a corresponding mark of favor and reward.

Among Elizabethan men of letters Hakluyt was, indeed, especially favored by fortune. He had not to do precarious hack work for a publisher or a theater manager. He was never in want. He had not to trust, like John Dee, to the royal whim for his next meal, nor had he to live like Spenser in exile. His complaint may have meant that his reward always came late, that it ought to have been granted in advance as an incentive and a means. The fact remains that he regularly won the reward; and, if he was perhaps obliged to make sacrifices to get his work done, he was able to recoup his expenses, and eventually to live and die in comfort.

CHAPTER X

The English Voyages

1589

During his Paris years the plan of Hakluyt's life work gradually took new and larger shape. The seed sown by his cousin had grown into the study of the earth and its pathways. By the cousin's hand it was then trained to the study of the little-known pathways of the seas. Opportunity and occasion bent the young interest toward the western discoveries in particular, and the first fruits were the volumes that reported those discoveries.

If the principal theme had thus far been American, there were other themes and another focus. Hakluyt's first recorded action, the letter to Mercator, spoke for an interest in the Northeast Passage. A later action concerned the Newbery mission to the East. An interest in navigation and particularly in English navigation dated from the earliest book.

The scope widened still more, toward the end of the Paris period, to include the entire record of the English overseas, from the time of Arthur to the time of the Armada. Such was the grandiose interest of the book we may best call *The English Voyages.* Some of the incentives we have seen in the making. The patriotic motive had been expressed in the *Divers Voyages,* in the *Book of Robert Thorne.* Later we have seen Hakluyt mingling with "the chiefest Captains at sea" and with "the greatest Merchants" and learning from them and from the *dossiers* of his consultant cousin of the great swing of Elizabethan trade. We have seen him pass to France, there to meet with foreign enterprisers. There also in the years preceding the Armada he met with foreign disparagement.

The disparagement had its effect on the young man who had listened to the "chiefest Captains," and roused him to his great work. His sonorous prose is my authority. In France, he wrote in the dedication of the *Voyages,* "I both heard in speech, and read in books, other nations miraculously extolled for their discoveries and notable enterprises by sea, but the English of all others for their sluggish security, and continual neglect of the like attempts, especially in so long and happy a time of peace, either ignominiously reported or exceedingly condemned: which singular opportunity, if some other people our neighbors had been blessed with, their protestations are often and vehement, they would far otherwise have used."

He then quoted the slighting words of a French historian, who in effect called the English lazy despite their superior shipbuilding and discipline, and went on to point the moral of the disparagement. "Thus both hearing and reading the obloquy of our nation," Hakluyt wrote, ". . and further not seeing any man to have care to recommend to the world the illustrious labors and painful travails of our countrymen: myself being the last winter returned from France . . . determined notwithstanding all difficulties to undertake the burden of that work."

So the foreign travel turned the voyager back to his own country, and the man who had begun by compiling the record of the new worlds passed to compiling the record of England. The plan must have been shaped at an early date in his Paris years, if the great labor involved allows the inference. Its earliest mention occurs in 1587, when Hakluyt wrote in dedicating the *Decades:* "we shall attempt, in the light of your favor, to publish the maritime records of our own men, which are hitherto scattered and buried in dust."

With the sounding of the new motive, Hakluyt's work in France was done. Indeed it is likely, in view of the amount of compiling to be done in England, that the work in France was already becoming incidental. The long absences in England we can now interpret as being none too long for the consulting and copying of manuscripts; and the final return to England, in the winter of 1588–1589, was none too soon for the completing of the work in the course of the ensuing year.

2

The stout quarto volume which thus signalized the rise of England to maritime power was nobly entitled *The Principal Navigations, Voyages, and Discoveries of the English nation, made by Sea or over Land to the most remote and farthest distant Quarters of the earth at any time within the compass of these 1500 years.* The title was ambitious. Of the voyages of medieval Englishmen Hakluyt had as yet gathered only a handful. Only one-tenth of the volume's bulk was devoted to pre-Columbian travels, and the larger part of that tenth was taken up by Mandeville's ingenious compilations.

The fact that a volume of some seven hundred thousand words could be made principally of English enterprise in the sixteenth century is significant and is answer enough to the disparagement of foreigners. The very narrowness of the time limit suggests the speed with which the earth's surface had been explored. It suggests as well the tremendously increased difficulties of the chronicler. Hakluyt's predecessor and model, Ramusio, whose collection of travels had been first published in the fifteen-fifties, still clung to the plan of including the travelers of all nations.[1] There is some sign that Hakluyt had him-

[1] See the *Encyclopaedia Britannica* for Ramusio. The table of contents of his *Voyages* is given by Joseph Sabin in his *Dictionary of Books Relating to America* (New York 1868–92).

self once thought of continuing Ramusio's work. Florio's preface to the Cartier voyages had suggested the translating of the Italian book, since it was, he said, the main reliance of "the best Cosmographers of this age." The suggestion was doubtless Hakluyt's own. Had he been subsidized, as that preface hinted to potential patrons, he might have left the American field altogether and become one of the many translators of the period. But no subsidy appeared. Ramusio was not translated, nor did Hakluyt carry out Ramusio's full plan. It was not until he had reaped his own harvest that his disciple Purchas engaged in the larger enterprise of following the Italian.

The plan of the *Voyages* was still Ramusio's with modifications. That standard synthesis of the age of discovery had formed three sections of voyages: those to the East, those to the East and Northeast, those to the West. Hakluyt retained this grouping in the first edition of the *Voyages,* and it was not until the final edition that he altered it for patriotic reasons.

The framework was filled in, as in Ramusio's work, by a series of original narratives given in chronological sequence. Even more than Ramusio, who was less the scientist and more the official with scientific interests, Hakluyt emphasized the value of original sources. "I am not ignorant," he wrote in the preface, "of Ptolemy's assertion that peregrinationis historia, and not those weary volumes bearing the titles of universal cosmography which some men that I could name have published as their own, being indeed most untruly and unprofitably ramassed and hurled together, is that which must bring us to the certain and full discovery of the world." For Hakluyt the stage had been reached at which mere compilation ceased to suffice. The value of summaries and abstracts depended, as it always depends, upon the expertness of the summarizer, and the patience of Hakluyt the consultant had doubtless been badly frayed by the inefficiency of "those weary volumes." The historian's task did not yet call so much for interpretation as it called for mere recording. The historian must be preceded by the archivist.

An example may explain. Some of the Spanish explorers had given full accounts of their voyages, and these accounts were essential to the man who wanted to know just what they had discovered and where. But early in the history of the India House at Seville the task of making public the Spanish discoveries had been entrusted to official historians. For popular purposes the histories of Oviedo and Gómara were quite sufficient; but to the scientist they gave very little information of any kind. The voyage of Gomez from Newfoundland to Florida, a highly important voyage in the history of North America, was dismissed with a few lines in the histories. No critical reader of the account of it could discover more than a few generalities about the American coast; and generalities were the last thing Hakluyt wanted for the certain and full discovery of the world. What he did want was the full report of Gomez, accompanied if possible by a map and the ship's log. Only then could the Gomez voyage be of any use to him as a scientist and a historian.

It was archives that he wanted for himself. It was as an archivist that he conceived the plan of the *Voyages*. As archivist, Hakluyt's standards were more critical than Ramusio's, as was to be expected. The Venetian was not a consultant geographer. He had allowed accounts at second hand, had permitted the insertion of summaries and compilations. The Englishman allowed virtually no summaries or compilations in his collection. Except for the accounts of medieval travelers, which were necessarily derived from the chroniclers, the narratives which Hakluyt printed were the narratives of the eyewitness. The most striking example of his concern for the quality of the evidence was his journey of two hundred miles in search of the sole survivor of the early voyage made to Newfoundland in 1536.[2] Items in a foreign language he gave first in the original, following with a translation. Frequently he printed more than one account of the same voyage. The appropriate date headed every page, and an index was provided. The editing was in sum rigid and substantial.

As archives, the *Voyages* of Hakluyt went another step beyond the *Voyages* of Ramusio, a step which Hakluyt marked in the table of contents. Separately listed from the narratives proper, he included various illustrative documents, which surpassed in number if not in bulk the major items of the collection. He printed extracts from the state archives, in the form of patents, commissions to ambassadors, Admiralty instructions. He pillaged the records of private adventurers, such as the Russia Company, which gave him not only the narrative reports of their agents but also their commercial *dossiers,* itineraries, descriptions geographical and political of the countries to which English trade was carried. He added numerous private letters, such as those which told the story of his own and his cousin's activities. He reprinted various tracts which bore on enterprise, such as Gilbert's *Discourse on the Northwest Passage;* and, for further "stopping the mouths of the reproachers," he occasionally deviated to cite the tributes of foreign geographers to English enterprise. The result of such a plan was almost encyclopedic.

To illustrate the travels of medieval times, Hakluyt had so far gathered but few examples in comparison with the number that were to go into a later edition. Indeed, we may suppose the pressure of haste responsible for the fact that in the earlier period he did no more than scratch the surface, possibly with the aid of his friend Camden the historian. The section of southern and southeastern voyages, with which the volume opened, did no more than quote from the chron-

[2] *Voyages*, VIII 3.

FIG. 21—Plan of Hull, with fortifications, sixteenth century. British Museum, Cotton MSS Aug. I i 86.

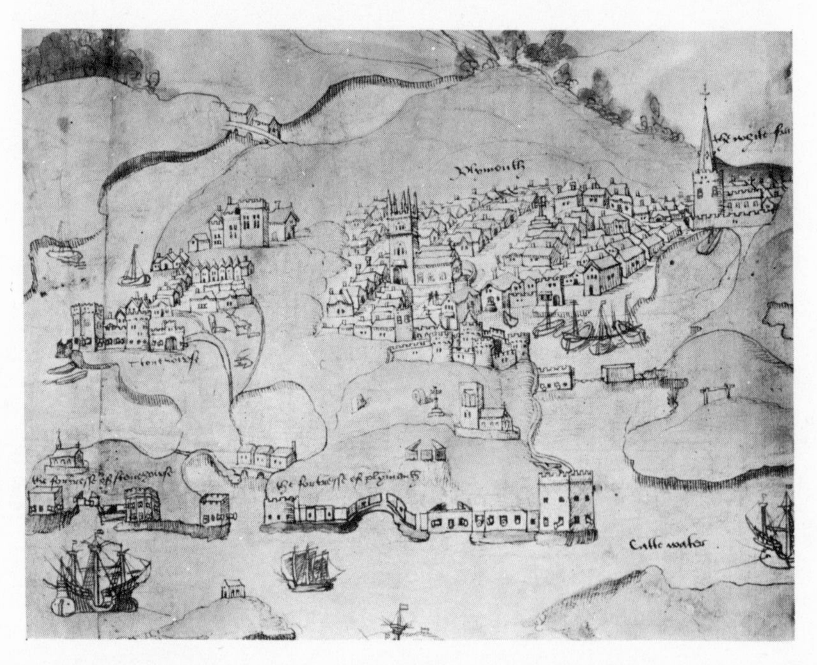

FIG. 22—View of Plymouth, *circa* 1550. British Museum, Cotton MSS Aug. I ii 38.

icles the brief records of early travelers to the Levant, of whom the Empress Helena was the first and the crusaders the largest in number. Mandeville was reprinted complete in Latin, though he was not to appear in the final edition.

The story thus brought perfunctorily down to Hakluyt's time could now proceed in earnest. Of the annual voyages to Barbary or Guinea which were inaugurated in the fifteen-fifties Hakluyt was able to obtain reports, in part from his predecessor Eden, in part from his own Bristol or London connections (Figs. 21, 22). The narratives were in many cases the official reports of the expeditions, made to the merchant adventurers or even to the Privy Council by the leader of the voyage. In some cases the report was noted as written to Hakluyt's order. In other cases the report was written down by Hakluyt from dictation. The majority of the narratives, however, give no sign of his part in their making. Generally, we may assume, he found the manuscripts ready to his hand. Otherwise he would have had to shoulder the burden not only of collecting but of ordering; and the number of narratives is too great, and the difficulty of obtaining them to order too evident, to have permitted him otherwise to bring the volume to press in any reasonable time.

That the collector was allowed access to the merchants' records is convincingly shown by the narratives of another section of the south-eastern voyages, the narratives of the Levant. Hakluyt had not yet worked up the stray records of the first half of the century; but from the beginning of the English negotiations with the Sultan in 1579 he was able to trace the documentary progress of the Turkey Company. The correspondence of the Sultan and the Queen; the patents issued by both sovereigns; the account of the first voyage for the new company; the commission of the first ambassador; trade notes on the markets of Algiers and Alexandria; a statement of the Sultan's civil list—documents such as these could hardly be obtained elsewhere than in the state or company record offices. Similarly Hakluyt obtained such reports as were at hand of the still unfinished Newbery mission, which he had seen off to the East and whose history he now detailed in official reports and private letters.

The Levant records, it should however be remarked, were not so complete and were not made so complete in the final edition either as were the records of other countries which we may next consider. One reason may have been that a certain censorship hedged about the new trade, which had to consider the strong and jealous foreign competition. Such a reason may have dictated the omission of the elder Hakluyt's trade notes on Turkey, which waited until the final edition. Another reason may have been that the Turkish trade was a settled one, having been in the hands of the Italians since the Crusades and recently of the French, and therefore needed small illumination. Hakluyt may therefore have felt justified in making no note of the annual voyages except for noteworthy reasons, such as the interception of a Levant convoy by Moors or Spaniards or the deviation from Turkey proper to Jerusalem or Cairo.

Political reasons also may account for the omission of many African narratives. Mr. Williamson's study of Hawkins has brought to light several voyages of the sixties and eighties which Hakluyt left out, perhaps because he wished to avoid disturbing the new entente with Portugal and Dom Antonio. It may not have been politic to remind Englishmen of the inhospitality of the Portuguese in Africa. Hence, it may be, the omissions; hence the condensing of the John Hawkins narratives which Hakluyt did print; hence also the failure to record any of the Portuguese missions which came to England to complain of the English in Guinea.

Though the southerly records were slight, the records of the voyages to the North and Northeast were ample. Following the *Book of Robert Thorne,* the documents presented a continuous and complete story of the annual voyages to Russia since its "discovery" in 1553. There is no question that Hakluyt was allowed to ransack at will the records of the Russia Company, and not only of the company but of the company's major agents whom Hakluyt mentioned, such as William Borough, later of the Admiralty, and Anthony Jenkinson, who had extended the Russia trade to Asia.

The documents thus collected were encyclopedic in variety. The series began with the code of sea discipline drawn up by Sebastian Cabot in imitation of the Spanish code which he had spent most of his life in administering. Of the perilous first expedition for which the code was drawn Hakluyt printed the reports of the leaders; and of the results of the voyage he collected documents so varied as to include the letters interchanged between the sovereigns, the instructions to factors, the Russian patent and the English patent, the instructions to pursers, and even notes on Russian money from an obscure German source.

Then followed the narratives of the successive Russian voyages, often duplicated and often supplemented by instructions and trade reports. The arrival of the first Russian ambassador in London in 1556 was duly recorded as "registered in *procès-verbal* by John Incent, notary." The trading license given by "the Hircanian king" on the way to Persia was followed by a list of Persian prices. Letters from factors gave sprightly news of foreign oddities, particularly the letter in fluent verse which was written by Turberville from Moscow in 1568. The instructions given by the elder Hakluyt were supplemented by answers to technical inquiries, as on the equipment needed for whaling, given by navigators like Borough.

In sum, Hakluyt could have added little else that was relevant to his scheme. Had he been able to include the home records of the Russia Company, he would have furnished a complete chapter of economic history. But such was not his purpose, which was oversea history, and was probably not within his power, since the Russia Company was not revealing its internal history. As a view of English enterprise in Russia itself, his story was nearly final.[3]

A like finality was achieved by the western section, which was somewhat larger than either of the others. Beginning with the mythical voyage of Madoc and the parleys of Columbus with Henry VII, he amplified the Cabot records, which were and remained secondhand, in order to buttress English claims to America. He noted the Newfoundland voyage of 1536, which he had been at such pains to discover. He obtained the reports of the Hawkins voyages which marked the first shock with Spain, as well as the reports of the escape from captivity of some of Hawkins' men. Having thus brought his story down, in a strict chronological fashion which he was to discard in the final edition, to the proper beginnings of English colonization, he reprinted Gilbert's *Discourse on the Northwest Passage;* detailed the voyages of Frobisher from the printed accounts; published in reprint most of the documents on the Gilbert colony, including the prospectuses of Carleill and Peckham; gave the connected narratives of the Raleigh colonies, adding the first book on Virginia, which Hariot had just published; and accounted for the three recent explorations of John Davis to the Northwest and for the circumnavigations of Drake and Cavendish.

A mosaic of this sort it would be tedious to discuss adequately. To do so would mean to consider each item in the long list, would mean to edit the entire collection. Such editing is still necessary. Hakluyt himself presented the documents without comment, except for an occasional marginal note. Many of the documents have been exhaustively edited in modern times, especially by the devoted labors of the Hakluyt Society. But the complete task is well-nigh prohibitive, as the Society must have found when it reprinted the complete work and took eleven volumes to the mere reprint.

What I have tried to do in this rough summary is to trace in the mosaic some sort of pattern. The pattern shows the aims of the designer. These were to examine the commercial expansion of England to distant lands that had been going forward in Hakluyt's own lifetime and to make collection of the documents, maritime and commercial, that would record the expansion. For the historian these documents would illuminate, and still do illuminate, a significant turning in the history of England. For the geographer they would record the new English experience of the world. For the casual citizen, unin-

[3] Compare the Hakluyt Society edition of *Voyages to Russia and Persia, Publications* 72–73 (1886) and the University of Pennsylvania Studies mentioned in the notes on Chapter IV above.

terested in Russian trade routes and the export of woolen goods, they would form a pleasing record of adventure and adventurers. For all three, the *Voyages* would be a monument to the national glory.

3

Such a monument could have been built only by one who had been trained to the task in the fashion I have described. From childhood Hakluyt had, as he grotesquely phrased it, "waded in the sweet study of the history of Cosmography." By developing his study into a vocation, by becoming a professional swimmer, he had obtained a grasp of his art that set him off from the mere dilettante. By his professional and social connections he had gained the coöperation of the experts in his study, without which his work would probably have been incomplete and certainly perfunctory. For the southeastern section of the *Voyages* he had thus had the help of Richard Staper, a main promoter of the Levant Company. For the northeastern he had called on William Borough and Anthony Jenkinson, captains of land and sea enterprise. For the American division his "chiefest light hath been received from Sir John Hawkins, Sir Walter Raleigh, and my kinsman." And it was Sir Francis Walsingham, Secretary of State, who delivered to the Stationers' Company the official license to print.

Such a monument could have been built only by a man of immense industry. The mere physical labor of preparing seven hundred thousand words for the printer was enough to make us hope that Hakluyt was not often obliged to ride two hundred miles for a single document. The printing of Peter Martyr was to cost seven months' work; but the *Decades* contained only about 130,000 words, and Hakluyt's edition of it was only a reprint. The *Voyages* contained 200,000 words of reprint alone, not from one book but from a score; and of that number one-tenth was translated from a foreign original. The remaining half-million words of the volume were printed from manuscripts. Of these words 17,000 had again been translated, making a total of some 40,000 words of translation alone, in itself enough for a small volume. Of the manuscripts in English, it is not possible to say whether Hakluyt had to have them all copied for the printer; but at the best, supposing him able to send the originals to the compositor, the labor of supervision bulked enormous.

If then we may take as a measure the time required to prepare and print the *Decades,* which was seven months, we may suppose that the *Voyages,* which was five times as long, required for the printing alone at least a year. It is now clear that Hakluyt must have resigned his diplomatic post and returned to England in order to give to the printing his undivided time. The greater part of the preparation of the copy must correspondingly be placed farther back, at least as far back as the mention of the project in the *Decades* in 1587. The accumulating of the material had doubtless been carried on, in more or less methodical fashion, for several years before that. Probably it could not have been accumulated at all, had it not been for the serried ranks of the Russia Company records, which Eden had perhaps helped to organize, or for the systematic researches of the elder Hakluyt.

Hakluyt spoke in the dedication of the huge toil and the small profit to ensue. I may add a note of the probable expense. If we may make rough comparison with the cost of the *Decades,* we must put the cost of the *Voyages* at not less than forty or fifty pounds, or some two to three hundred pounds in modern equivalence. What the arrangement was with the publisher, we cannot say, or what the hopes of the patron, Walsingham. It has already been suggested that Hakluyt himself bore the expense, which was not light. We have seen that he was to speak bitterly of his poor and inadequate reward. He was none the less rewarded.

He had recently given up the studentship at Christchurch, perhaps in order to be free to marry; and, when he gave up his Paris chaplaincy as well, he was left with only the prebend at Bristol, which could not have been worth more than fifteen or twenty pounds a year. He was given one additional preferment on the publishing of the book. In April of 1590 he was made rector of Wetheringsett in Suffolk, being presented to the living by the ambassador's lady. This benefice, together with the prebend, was to constitute his main support for the next decade. Hakluyt probably felt that a man approaching the age of forty was entitled to a more substantial reward for the great work than a mere benefice, worth probably not more than ten pounds a year. Walsingham was dead, Raleigh was unsatisfactory, and it was not until a dozen years later that Hakluyt was taken up and amply endowed by Sir Robert Cecil. Certainly there was for the moment small profit to ensue for his huge toil.[4]

Whatever the reward, any man might be proud of the achievement, the merely literary achievement, of the *Voyages.* Of their larger values it may be well to postpone discussion until the final edition is considered. It may be enough now to speak of the timeliness of the work. The choice of the year following the Armada is significant. For the story of England's rise to maritime power, which was Hakluyt's theme, is the swelling prologue to the conflict with Spain. The later edition was to detail the story of that conflict as well. But in its first form the *Voyages* was well calculated to strike the note of national pride. This note Hakluyt sounded in the passage which has been quoted and which was echoed by Spenser. To the larger view the *Voyages* was a noble addition to the company of books illustrating the national glory that were so notably produced in the last years of the century. With the chronicles of Holinshed and Stow, with Cam-

[4] For the living, see the chronology, 1590, in Appendix II.

den's *Britannia,* with the historical plays of the new theater, and with Spenser's *Faërie Queene* the *Voyages* takes its acknowledged high place.

As the note of national pride resounds through these works, so does it more than occasionally pierce the monotone of Hakluyt's wilfully matter-of-fact narratives. The death of a Willoughby in Arctic ice or of a Gilbert in an Atlantic storm has worked no less powerfully on the national imagination than the last combat of the Revenge, which his later volumes were to record. These were the dramatic moments of the prose Odyssey. No less impressive were the exploits of scores of heroes bound on missions of trade and exploration, which were no less arduous for being successfully and even profitably survived.

CHAPTER XI

A Consultant Geographer

1589–1597

Hakluyt has been declared in modern times to be "the man who more than any other took upon himself the toil, and earned the credit, of establishing England's first colony." To this topic, to his part in Virginia and other imperial undertakings, we may at length turn.

The story of his concern with oversea enterprise has been, as we have brought it down to 1589 in these pages, the story of one man among many who worked for English expansion. How he worked for it has been shown. As a classifying intelligence he ranged the experience of the past and supplied it to the men of action. His studies at home and in France served to the further assembling of experience. The *Divers Voyages* and the *Discourse* and the books of the Paris period were the chief public contributions to the plans then under way. They constituted his raw materials, and it was as important that they should be made public as it was that his conclusions should be made known.

Thus far Hakluyt was the consultant, the adviser; but it is seldom a simple task to dissociate the consultant, the man of learning, from the man of action. As in the individual organism so in the social organism action leads to knowledge, and knowledge spurs to action. Hakluyt's functions have thus been shown blended. His constant concern with the problems of enterprise could hardly have failed to arouse in others the interest that feeds action. Such an interest he stirred in Sidney. Such an interest he thought he generated in the mind of the Queen's banker Pallavicini.

In some cases Hakluyt became the full-fledged man of action. For the Gilbert colony he obtained the investment of Bristol. For the Raleigh enterprise he wrote the *Discourse,* which may be reckoned not only a summary of experience but a bid for royal subsidy and therefore a piece of promoting.

These we concede to be only specimen cases, which may or may not span Hakluyt's reach. Were his personality more fully illumined, it might be more possible to judge the radius of his influence, which would vary with his enthusiasm. He was not certainly the silent listener pictured by Professor Raleigh. He was not, at the other extreme, a leader and organizer of men, like the soldiers Gilbert and Raleigh, like the merchants who fortified their cause with ships and money and men. Something between the two he must have been: a dealer in facts, for one thing, who may well have been employed to mold his facts into plans; a dealer in projects, for another, who may have had a larger success in bringing his projects to market than we can now begin to reckon.

At the least, he took upon himself the toil; but the credit which he earned must depend upon our view of his versatility. It does not at all follow that the man who devotes himself to an idea is responsible for its success. It does not follow even if he is publicly associated with the success. He may in such a case have really worked behind the scenes or he may simply have been found useful as a figurehead. In the later history of the Virginia experiment Hakluyt does appear as an associate of its success. Whether or not he was a figurehead the story will attempt to decide.

The formal change from personal to group control of the American project was made in the last years of Raleigh's interest in it. The step was taken in 1589, somewhat less than halfway between the Gilbert patent of 1578 and the Virginia Company patent of 1606. Under Gilbert's title and Raleigh's it was the individual who controlled the enterprise, into which he called the aid of investors in court and City. Gilbert's funds had been built up by nobles like Burleigh, Leicester, and the Sidneys; by the Catholic subscription of Sir George Peckham; by contingents of Southampton and London and Bristol merchants. In like fashion Raleigh probably enlisted his supporters, though we do not know them; and, had his colony succeeded, as later proprietary colonies like Maryland and Pennsylvania succeeded, there would have been no need to change the plan.

The colony did not succeed. The first settlement, of 1585, whose morale failed with the failure of supplies, was brought home by Drake in the following year. The second, of 1587, was cut off by the Spanish war; and, whatever might be its future, it had certainly yielded no returns within two years after its settling.

The presumption is that by that time Raleigh was discouraged. If it be true that he had poured into Virginia the immense sum of forty thousand pounds, he had reason. Whatever profits had been made had come from the incidental privateering; and to a man of many enterprises the colonial project, however honorable, may have seemed the least desirable. At any rate, he proceeded, in the spring of 1589, to throw it over.

Raleigh had already begun to delegate his powers. In 1587 he had assigned the control of affairs in the colony itself to the governor and twelve assistants, chosen on the traditional guild model. Now he assigned all his further interest in the colony to a company of nineteen, whom he described as "merchants of London" and to whom he paid, as if for a ransom, the sum of one hundred pounds. He was still the titular patentee, reserving for himself the traditional fifth part of all treasure that might be turned up by the new directors; but in this reservation he was merely securing the rights of the Crown. He became therefore the merely nominal link between the Crown and the colony.[1]

Hakluyt was one of the nineteen directors, but it is difficult to say what his place was in so mixed a company. The mainstay of the board was undoubtedly the two merchant princes. One was William Sanderson, patron of Davis' voyages to the Northwest. The other was Thomas Smith, soon to become the director of most of the oversea companies. Others on the list bore familiar City names and were also to be members of the Virginia Company. These adventurers were men of financial standing; and, had Hakluyt been joined with them alone, his importance in the plan would be assured.[2]

The group was not, however, homogeneous. Indeed, its personnel suggests either that the modern device of the "dummy" director is not very modern or else that the board was filled in with technical experts and employees. The inference is already confirmed by the inclusion in the contract of the governor and assistants, the employees overseas. It may be the reason as well for the inclusion of Thomas Hood, mathematician and protégé of Smith; of Richard Wright, the later paid secretary of the East India Company; and of Hakluyt.

How Hakluyt came into this group we do not know, as nothing more explanatory than the contract itself has been saved. It seems dubious that he was named by Raleigh; for such a place it would have been more natural for Raleigh to name his own private expert, Thomas Hariot, who had himself sailed with the first colony and who had just published his book on Virginia. As a technical expert, Hariot should thus have outranked Hakluyt in Raleigh's choice. The *Discourse* may have turned the scale in Hakluyt's favor, together with his Paris publications, which were dedicated to Raleigh; with his scholarly reputation, earned by the edition of Peter Martyr; and, probably not least, with the fact that he was a gentleman and canon of Bristol.

Hakluyt had come formally into the circle of enterprise. From a casual consultant he became a director of Virginia. The year that established his literary position was also the year that established his active importance.

What he did with the new opportunity is again lost to the record. Seventeen years later a new company grasped the Virginia nettle, and in that new company Hakluyt was again placed among the leaders. The connection was thus kept unbroken, but only an occasional spot

[1] Raleigh's assignment was printed in the 1589 edition of the *Voyages* and reprinted in Ebenezer Hazard, *Historical Collections*, I (Philadelphia 1792). For the history of the Virginia colony I rely on the narratives in Hakluyt.

[2] The biographical dictionary appended to Alexander Brown, *The Genesis of the United States*, II (Boston 1890) is always useful for the lives of the colonizers. I have had sometimes to supplement it from company lists, mainly in William R. Scott, *The Constitution and Finance of English, Scottish, and Irish Joint Stock Companies to 1720* (Cambridge 1910–12).

of light flecks the long obscurity. All that one can be sure of is that Hakluyt must have been active, if not directly in colony planning at least indirectly in keeping himself remembered by the planners. Only inference of this sort can span the gap between the Raleigh assignment and the company charter.

There was need enough for activity on the part of the adventurers who relieved Raleigh. The new heirs to a third of America must have thought themselves mere receivers in bankruptcy. The assets were dubious; the liabilities were a colony of one hundred men, women, and children who must be rescued from the dangers of Indian, Spaniard, starvation, and disease. For I doubt not that the sentiment had already crystallized that was to be expressed by Bacon: "It is the sinfullest thing in the world to forsake or destitute a plantation once in forwardness." [3]

Governor White had already tried in 1588 to relieve his colony and his family, but the expedition had not reached Virginia. Later attempts were stopped by the war; and it was not until 1591 that it was possible, by Raleigh's influence, to divert a privateer from the West Indies to an incidental call on the Virginia coast. The search for the colonists was halfhearted. The omens were doubtful enough when the cabins of Roanoke were found abandoned. Indeed, the diversion probably cut down the profits of privateering, which were only one hundred per cent.[4]

This expedition was the most the colonizers achieved by way of looking after their colony, if indeed such credit as there is should not be given to Governor White alone. So far as the evidence goes, the project was hatched exclusively between White and Raleigh. Finding that certain ships were prevented by naval orders from a privateering cruise, White "acquainted Sir Walter Raleigh therewith, desiring him that as I had sundry times before been chargeable and troublesome unto him for the supplies and reliefs of the planters in Virginia: so likewise that by his endeavor it would please him at that instant to procure license for those three ships to proceed." [5]

Such was the account which White wrote to Hakluyt to explain the voyage; and it appears important not only that Hakluyt, a director, needed the explanation but that neither he nor any others of Raleigh's assignees seem to have been concerned or consulted. The assignees do not even appear to have raised funds for the undertaking. The privateering venture was already made up; the funds had been put in, perhaps by some of the assignees, perhaps by Raleigh himself, but for an entirely different purpose from colonial relief. When Raleigh reported to Burleigh on the profits of the expedition, in a letter

[3] Bacon's Essay *Of Plantations* (1625).

[4] Raleigh to Burleigh, 16 October 1591: printed in Edward Edwards, *Life of Sir Walter Raleigh* (London 1868), II 43.

[5] *Voyages*, VIII 404–406.

which has been saved, he reported on a matter of pure privateering. There is no reason, then, to believe that the assignees had any connection with this single attempt to discharge their receivership.

For this sinfullest negligence the Spanish war has been given as an excuse, but it is an excuse that will not bear the light. The fifteen-nineties were a period of considerable enterprise, which was not privateering alone. Fishermen were still going west, as Hakluyt recorded in his later *Voyages;* expeditions were being sent out to the East Indies; Raleigh himself was turning his versatile attention to Guiana. If the Virginia group is to be absolved, it cannot be absolved by the plea of a war emergency.

The colonizers were doubtless learning the lesson that, in Bacon's later words, "the principal thing that hath been the destruction of most plantations hath been the base and hasty drawing of profit in the first years." Since there was no base and hasty profit, since there was in fact no profit at all, the Virginia directors seem to have forgotten the plantations. They may have attempted relief; but Hakluyt recorded nothing of their attempts. They may have evolved elaborate plans to further the settlement; but no plans are known. The colonists remained forsaken, and to this day their fate is unknown.

What the directors may at best have done, since they did nothing here, was to keep American interest alive until the Virginia Company was launched; but of this possibility nothing again is known. The same must be said of Hakluyt's personal actions. Except for obtaining from Governor White the record of the last desperate voyage of relief, he is not seen to move again in Virginia affairs until thirteen years after his nomination to the directorship. That period is mere darkness.

2

I have said that the end of the century was a time of fast developing enterprise. The most spectacular was again the enterprise of the spectacular Raleigh, who sought to recoup his Virginia losses in a South American El Dorado. With these voyages, which began in 1594, Hakluyt seems to have had small connection aside, of course, from his constant concern with gathering records for publication. Indeed, there is some reason to think that he now stood outside Raleigh's circle.

The reason is that Raleigh continued to employ Thomas Hariot in the business of Guiana, as previously in the business of Virginia. As evidence there remains a letter which Hariot wrote to Sir Robert Cecil, now Secretary of State, after Raleigh's failures. In the letter, written in July of 1596, occur these sentences: "Concerning the Eldorado which hath been showed your Honor out of the Spanish book of Acosta, which you had from Wright, . . . I shall show you that it is not ours—that we mean—there being three. Neither doth he say, or mean, the Amazons river and Orinoco is all one—as some, I fear, do aver to your Honor." [6]

Here is question of the doubt raised by Raleigh's failure in the mind of Cecil, who was privately as well as officially interested. What is significant is that Hariot was here speaking for Raleigh and speaking against some one of Cecil's advisers who had small faith in Raleigh's plan. That someone I take to be Hakluyt.

The case is not proved, but it is probable. On a geographical matter of this sort, involving the study of the Spanish travel record, Cecil must needs have consulted a competent geographer. Now we know that he did in fact consult Hakluyt. In the state papers is preserved the relevant document, a paper labeled: " Notes concerning Sir Walter Raleigh's discovery of Dorado, translated from Acosta, Seville 1590, by Richard Hakluyt." [7]

The paper is given a tentative date of 1590, presumably because of the date of Acosta's book. This date can hardly apply, since Raleigh seems not to have considered Guiana before 1593. The document would therefore not be earlier than 1593 or 1594, when Raleigh sent an exploring voyage to Guiana. It was probably made for Cecil, since the letter of Hariot mentions Acosta as the source of Cecil's information. What happened was probably this. The Acosta book, the *Natural and Moral History of the Indies,* was submitted to Cecil by Wright, the letter explains, Wright being the navigator. It was then turned over to Hakluyt for an abstract, though it is likely that he had had the book himself as soon as it came out. The abstract submitted, it opened the controversy over the site of El Dorado which called for Hariot's protest.

If the sequence be fanciful, at least Hakluyt did make the abstract of Acosta, and he was at the time or later consulted by Cecil. In writing the dedication of the second volume of the *Voyages,* in October of 1599, he mentioned to Cecil that " it pleased your Honor in summer was two years to have some conference with me and to demand mine opinion touching the state of the country of Guiana." The date pointed to, 1597, is a year out of the way of Hariot's letter, which was 1596; and the advice of Hakluyt may in fact have been given later, in 1597 or 1598, when Cecil made difficulties over Raleigh's proposed new voyage. It is not, however, essential to link the state paper with any conference between Hakluyt and Cecil. It is certain that Hakluyt did advise the government of Acosta's information, which was the most up-to-date, and that he was once consulted by Cecil.

This is the sum total of what is known of Hakluyt's concern with Guiana, amounting to no more than submitting an opinion, as a

[6] Hariot to Cecil (Cecil Papers): printed by Edwards, II 420.

[7] State Papers Domestic Elizabeth, 235, 43. The notes were printed in the *Voyages,* XI 16–19.

friendly or a neutral or perhaps a hostile expert, on the soundness of Raleigh's knowledge. He may have been hostile not merely as an adherent of Cecil, who became his patron, but as one in the counsels of Sir Thomas Smith, director of most of the expansionist enterprises, who yet remained aloof from Guiana. To both Cecil and Smith, Raleigh may have seemed a mere adventurer; but this is conjecture. It need not be assumed that Hakluyt was acting in an unfriendly way to Raleigh, even if Raleigh did suspect Cecil's good faith. He will presently be shown negotiating with Raleigh on North American affairs in what seems like unimpaired friendliness. That he was not, as Hariot was, the confidant of Raleigh in the Orinoco voyages is the most that can be said.

Hakluyt was not, we infer, needed as an adviser of Raleigh or anyone else. For Guiana was not a new country nor was it unknown to English voyagers. Southampton and Plymouth merchants had been to Brazil in the fifteen-thirties and knew the way. In the sixties John Hawkins had marketed his slaves along the Spanish Main, guided by Spaniards or by Englishmen from the Canaries. Much more intimate knowledge of the Caribbean coast had been gained recently by Drake's raid of 1585. That expedition had halted for some weeks in Cartagena, the Spanish capital of New Granada to the west of Guiana, and even talked of retaining the conquered city.[8]

The raid was the first of a series of naval voyages, in any of which information may have been gathered of the empty coast between the Orinoco and the Amazon and of the inland El Dorado. As Hakluyt collected the reports of these voyages, he must have taken the necessary notes on their information and been able to supply them on demand. He had done so, we suspected, for the use of the Drake raid, in presenting his French captain's survey. He was to print an especially elaborate routier of the West Indies and also a long list of Spanish documents captured by the futile Virginia relief expedition. When, then, Raleigh sent out his preliminary Guiana voyage in 1594, went himself in 1595, and sent Lawrence Keymis in 1596 and Leonard Berry in 1597, he may have been drawing on Hakluyt's knowledge as well as on the first-hand experience of his mariners.

The chances are that he did not. "Many years since," Raleigh wrote in dedicating his *Discovery of Guiana* in 1596, "I had knowledge by relation of that mighty, rich, and beautiful Empire of Guiana, and of that great and golden city which the Spaniards call El Dorado . . . conquered, reëdified and enlarged by a younger son of Guainacapa Emperor of Peru, at such time as Francisco Pizarro and others conquered the said Empire."[9] He had read the Spanish histories, particularly of the conquest of Peru, either in the original or in the

[8] Sir Julian Corbett, *Drake and the Tudor Navy* (London 1899 edit.), II 50.
[9] *Voyages*, X 340.

recent English translations. He may have been specially stirred by the new Acosta, shown him perhaps by Hakluyt, as he had previously been shown Espejo's *New Mexico* when that book was fresh from Spain; and he may have been moved also by the new *Elegias* of Juan de Castellanos, a Spanish priest in Venezuela, which was to be republished in part in Hakluyt's Guiana narratives.

He had further sources. "I sent my servant Jacob Whiddon the year before," Raleigh wrote further in the same place, "to get knowledge of the passages, and I had some light from Captain Parker, sometime my servant." Spanish and English knowledge were thus at Raleigh's hand. Some perhaps came from Hakluyt, more perhaps from Hariot or Wright. Still more came, it is likely, from his own study, which was essential to one who was to lead in exploring the Orinoco. Most important of all in determining the course of the exploration should naturally be counted Raleigh's own encounters, once he had arrived on the spot, with Spaniards and natives in the new land itself.

What balances Hakluyt's side of the account is the fact that he was professionally a collector and could be relied on as such. He could still have been relied on without any acknowledgment by Raleigh; but the most that can be said is that he was competent to advise.

With Guiana publicity Hakluyt seems to have had no special concern. Raleigh was quite capable of writing and publishing his lengthy *Discovery of Guiana*. So was Keymis, his lieutenant, of writing the account of the second voyage, since his Latin verses to the *amantissimus* Hariot prove him a scholar. These pamphlets of record and of propaganda owed to Hakluyt, it is likely, only their reprinting in the *Voyages*. There too was first published the account of the third voyage, left in manuscript by the waning of Raleigh's interest.

We have little record of Hakluyt's concern with the later Guiana enterprises, trade and colonizing, except for his printing of the narratives.[10] He printed the account of the rather aimless voyage, in 1595, of Robert Dudley, son of the late Earl of Leicester, who yielded to Hakluyt's urging and wrote down what he himself thought "not worth the registering." One is immediately tempted to suppose that Hakluyt advised the youth on this his trial voyage. The youth himself was the son of that Countess of Sheffield who was mistress of the Paris embassy when Hakluyt was chaplain. He was but newly down from Hakluyt's own college in Oxford, which he had entered, it is true, after Hakluyt resigned his studentship. He was brother-in-law of Cavendish, the circumnavigator, who was a cousin of Hakluyt by marriage; and he thought of himself as carrying on Cavendish's labors.

One would like to suppose an influence, to fancy the picturesque lad shaped by Hakluyt's knowledge, especially when we find that Dudley said of himself, "having ever since I could conceive of any-

[10] On the Guiana voyages see J. A. Williamson, *English Colonies in Guiana* (Oxford 1923).

thing been delighted with the discoveries of navigation, I fostered in myself that disposition." But Dudley left no acknowledgments to Hakluyt. Of his first voyage he wrote, "I called to me the advice of sufficient seamen"; and he may have used a chart of the West Indies which was made for him by Thomas Hood, not by Hakluyt.[11]

Little is left then but the fact of Hakluyt's importuning Dudley for his narrative; the likelihood that the youth had at Oxford devoured the first *Voyages;* and the relationship by marriage. The gaps in the evidence are tantalizing. For Dudley was no mean figure in enterprise. It was he who was to send out the second trading voyage to India; later, in his long Italian exile, he was to become a geographer of importance.

The case lights up the difficulty of divining Hakluyt's personal relations, which must have been significant. Known though he was to all the men of importance in the state and in oversea affairs and useful though we have shown him to have been to them, our lack of written records prevents our writing his full history. Beyond the evidence we cannot, of course, go, to magnify his importance; but we can insist that what we here prove of his part in the expansion is at best a bare minimum. His real achievement is only too easily conjectured.

When we turn to the later Guiana voyages, we drop into an even less tolerable darkness. After Raleigh gave up Guiana there were frequent trading voyages to the coast; but there is not even a record of them in such of Hakluyt's papers as Purchas saw fit to publish. Hakluyt at least collected the relations; but it is hardly likely, as Englishmen took more and more often the short voyage to the Spanish Main, elaborately described in Keymis' description, that Hakluyt would need to be consulted. He may have been useful to the Leigh brothers, who went trading and colonizing from 1602 to 1606. He was known to them, for he had a note from Charles Leigh of an earlier voyage to Newfoundland, and he was to obtain their Guiana records when they had finished; but the shears of Purchas have clipped whatever the records contained of personal dealings. Of the Harcourt colony of 1609 to 1613 and of the Sir Thomas Roe exploration of 1610 Purchas has kept no relation at all; and Harcourt's own *Relation* shows no dealing with Hakluyt. Guiana passes out of his record in 1607, the last date of his collecting accounts of it; and his whole connection with the equatorial kingdom, from Raleigh's beginnings on, remains subordinate and incidental.

3

Hakluyt's energy had not yet aided in establishing either a North American or a South American colony; and it was not until the new

[11] A. H. Markham, in Appendix A of *Hakluyt Society Publications* 59 (1880), under the year 1592.

century came in that the foundations of the British Empire were to be firmly laid. The story of East India and of Hakluyt's part in it will be begun in the next chapter. The story of an achieved Virginia and of Hakluyt's part in it will be told in due course thereafter. Meantime another story remains to be related, which will surprisingly illuminate Hakluyt's profession.

The story relates nothing less than an international consultation. Its partial record is preserved in Dutch documents. Holland was already, in the midst of its war of independence, overtaking England on the road to empire. The Dutch pioneer in India, Linschoten, who had rescued the English pioneers at Goa, returned to Holland in 1593 to steer the new mercantile nation overseas. In 1595 a Dutch fleet sailed for India, the forerunner of the elaborate voyages that were immediately to make Holland the strongest European nation in the East. In the previous year a vigorous effort was made to turn the Dutch trade with Russia, which had followed at some distance the English discovery of that country, into a new search for the Northeast Passage. None of the voyagers succeeded in passing Novaya Zemlya; but the Dutch acquaintance with the northern seas endured.

It was after the first voyage that a difference in Dutch opinion called Hakluyt into distant consultation. The merchants of Amsterdam proposed sailing north around the obstacle of Novaya Zemlya. The merchants of Zeeland insisted that the voyage should pass the straits between the island and the Russian mainland. The former plan was supported by Plancius, a preacher geographer like Hakluyt. The latter plan sought the support of the Englishman.

How or why is not clear, since some of the correspondence has perished. At any rate, a refugee in London sought Hakluyt out and laid before him the need of the Zeelanders. What happened then is told in the letters from the intermediary to the Treasurer of Zeeland, which give the fullest picture we have of Hakluyt at work.[12]

The intermediary was Emanuel van Meteren, dean of the refugee colony in London although he was naturalized an Englishman. As a brother-in-law of Ortelius, the Antwerp geographer, he was easily known to Hakluyt, who had had some dealings with their nephew Ortelianus, another refugee. And as the author of a history of the Low Countries, from which Hakluyt was to reprint his account of the Armada, he was probably linked in the circle of antiquaries and chroniclers whom we project into Elizabethan London. He had also religious and business ties, not only in secret with Antwerp but more openly, or at least under cover of the military alliance, with his compatriots in Holland.

The Treasurer of Zeeland knew him; and, on his request, van

[12] The letters of van Meteren are printed in *Linschoten-Vereeniging Werken* XV, vol. 2 (The Hague 1917), pp. 201–210. See Appendix II below for the chronological details.

Meteren wrote to Hakluyt, who answered as follows. I translate the letter back from the Dutch version in which it has been saved.

Written at Wetheringsett near Ipswich,
6 December 1594

"Good Master Emanuel, to answer to the principal matter of your friendly letter of the 27 November touching an extract from such authors or from the opinions of persons of experience who have written or recorded anything on the Northeast Passage, you must know that to make such a sum or extract as it should be made is a matter which needs good observation and judgment, much reading, much speech, and many conferences with persons who have sailed thither; by means of which I find and can show by good proofs that your cousin Ortelius and other cosmographers have greatly erred in their descriptions, as well of the northeast as of the northwest parts of the world. As concerns others who have presumed to make maps, they are indeed but muddlers, and such as but counterfeit or copy the works of others, and not good geographers.

"You know both the great and the long travail which I have taken or used in these studies and how I have spared neither cost nor toil for a space of twenty-six years at the least,[13] to inform myself of these secrets. All the fruits of this my labor I am ready to declare in writing to you, if they wish me to do so, at the first opportunity, with notes and the quotations from the passages in my authors in the margin, and also will I help them to buy such books as are to be found printed of that matter, and as for that which is not yet printed I shall send them in brief compass the substance thereof in writing. But all this cannot be done without suitable time, and I must needs therefore come to you in London and there remain three or four weeks at the least, which you know will cost. Therefore touching the reward of my labor, I believe I shall well deserve twenty pounds sterling. But it may so happen that my advices will give your friends such light and courage that it shall profit them many thousand pounds. And to speak briefly and freely to you, I will not communicate all my secrets in that matter of so great import under the sum of twenty marks at the least. And let me first, I pray you, have in all haste a final answer from your friends to fully resolve me what my modest reward shall be, for else I should be loth to spend my time and mind therein. If that my labor may be rewarded as I truly think to deserve, I shall at once come to London upon the assurance of your next letter, and bring with me all my principal notes, and shall not return again before I shall in all dispatch and diligence have satisfied your friends' demands, and I shall conceal nothing that shall serve to further such a very Christian, profitable, and glorious enterprise. But herein

[13] This statement would give 1568 as the date of Hakluyt's beginning to study geography.

I pray you to be secret, for it imports much to me, and as the Italian hath it, Il savio e secreto.

"You would do well to inform your good friend in my name that he has wandered far in many places from the course of John de Plano Carpini, because (unless his copy differ greatly from mine, which is printed in Italian), he will find that he did not journey by the Mediterranean Sea, but by the north side of the Euxine, and across the River Volga not at Astracan but farther to the northward, and did not reach Bokhara but journeyed many days having the northern Ocean on his left hand, going eastward,[14] and he made many times mention of the Scythian or northern Ocean. But of this matter I can hereafter write you better and more particularly, [when I] can refer to the author's own words. I would know in what tongue they have the . . . of Plano Carpini, whether in Latin as I have seen it, and if it be printed, where, when, and by whom printed.

"Concerning Abilfeda Ismael, if it is not to be had from the Heidelberg Library of my friend Master Paul Melissus, then I can direct him again to one of my friends in Venice who hath copied it in the Latin.

"Herewith expecting your full and speedy answer, I commend you to God's grace."[15]

I have tried to recapture Hakluyt's words from their strange disguise. In so far as I can trust their present faces, they carry an air of anxiety. The geographer is anxious to be consulted, as I think there can be no doubt, and reasonably enough. He is anxious also about his pay, and even more reasonably, as will appear.

The anxiety spreads to van Meteren. "Your Excellency will be pleased to command what I shall reply to him," he wrote back to the Treasurer, "and the sooner the better. He asks at least twenty marks. . . . I believe that no living man is more zealous in learning of voyages, or, for a learned man, more able to speak thereof. He is the most skillful inquirer that I ever knew, and I have known him full twenty years."

It was not until the sixth of January that the Treasurer wrote to authorize Hakluyt to proceed. Meantime the geographer's anxiety drove him up to London. "My letter," wrote van Meteren on the 18th, "met him on the road, and he came to me. He has his notes and books here and thinks to have them ready, according to his promise, within eight or ten days, and immediately wanted to be paid before he leaves. I have promised him, and shall draw on your Excellency or on the adventurers."

Hakluyt's interview with van Meteren follows. "I have been this whole day with him," continued the latter, "and he has shown me

[14] A now obvious misreading of the route of Carpini, which led to the capital of Mongolia.
[15] My thanks are due to Professor A. J. Barnouw for correcting my translation.

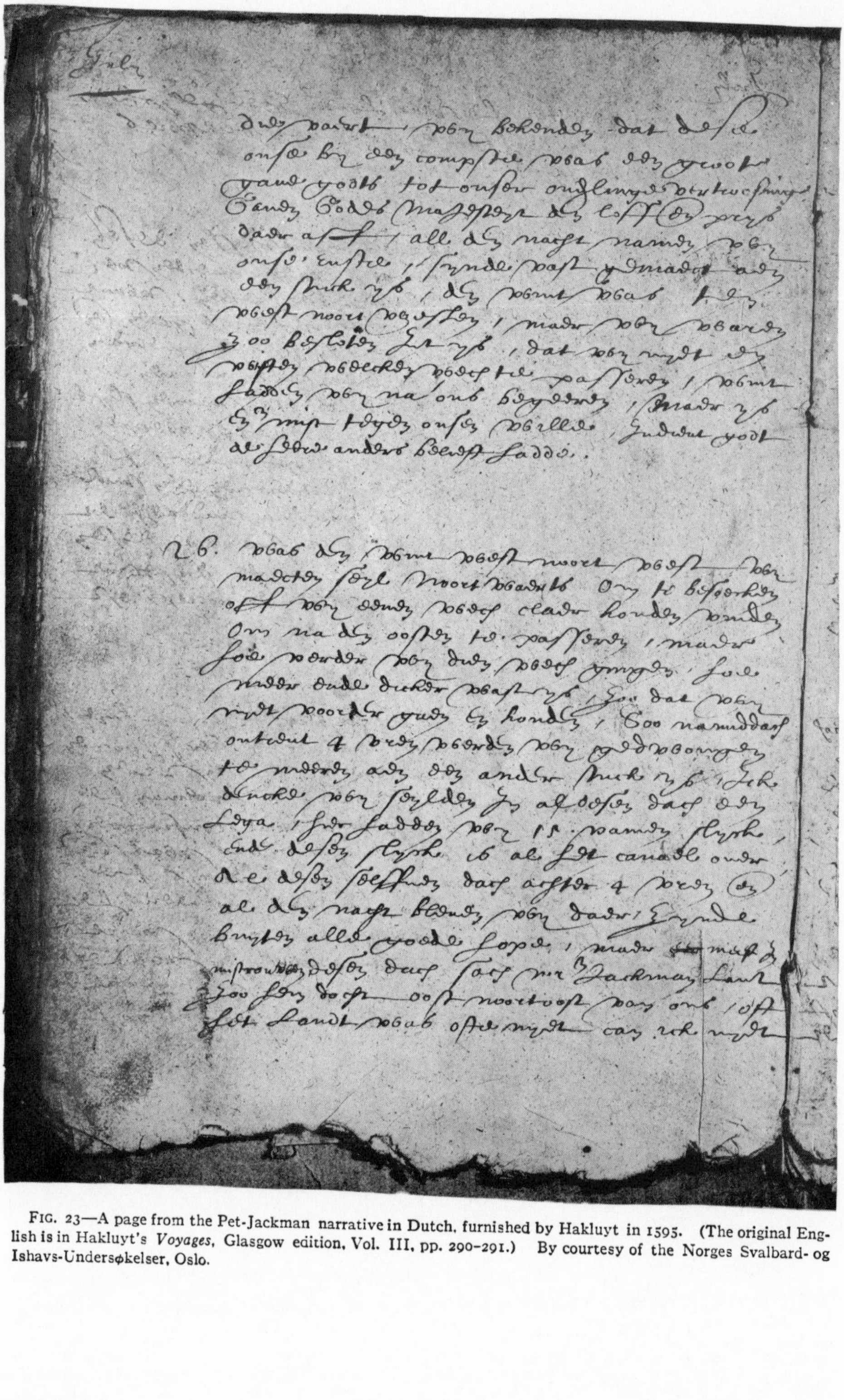

FIG. 23—A page from the Pet-Jackman narrative in Dutch, furnished by Hakluyt in 1595. (The original English is in Hakluyt's *Voyages*, Glasgow edition, Vol. III, pp. 290–291.) By courtesy of the Norges Svalbard- og Ishavs-Undersøkelser, Oslo.

what his notes will be. First he cites all the opinions on the North-east Passage that are in the old Greek and Latin authors, with notes of the places, and so following up to our own time. Nearly all who have written thereof have the same opinion, that there is a passage, and he did not doubt it, and said that once our people have reached the straits, they must immediately fall into the South Sea. . . . It is his opinion that one must sail farther and search out and so attain Cathay. He does not believe that there is any passage farther north."

Then come the modern authorities: an English factor who had followed the coast, the medieval monk whom Hakluyt's letter mentioned, and the Saracen geographer. "These notes," he went on, "will be from all those who have written of these routes, taken here and there. Hakluyt had often read these over, and has been the instructor of all these English voyages of discovery, but now they are all out to get a scanty profit from war, which grieves him."

Hakluyt was anxious and eager to pour out his information before his brother scholar, and not only on this but on other projects. "He has also," van Meteren echoes his enthusiasm, "the whole voyage round the world of Cavendish, very detailed and in short space giving account of all the harbors, islands, soundings, heights, and latitudes of the places where Cavendish was. He has also a map of China, made in that land on paper made of bark, that may be copied and that should well serve those who are sailing thither by the Cape of Good Hope. If your Excellency or your friends there wish to go to the expense (of copies), please let me know at once, before he leaves here. He is prepared to make his book of voyages more than half as large again. As it is in places very detailed, it would be useful to the voyages."

No word came back from the Treasurer. Three weeks later, on the 8th of February, van Meteren wrote again. The work was done (Fig. 23), being "nine or ten sheets long in all," and Hakluyt had gone back home to Wetheringsett. The Cavendish journal, which was of course irrelevant, Hakluyt had pressed on the historian too; and he recommended the buying of certain books, Ramusio's voyages, Giles Fletcher's suppressed book on Russia, and others. The notes were to be sent over with the first convoy.

The work done and presumably sent off, the question of pay continued to be an anxious one. "I have thought good," wrote van Meteren in the same letter, "not to give him that money until I was certain." And a week later he wrote again. "The man requires twenty marks for his toil. It seems to me well worth it, since he has paid out ten pounds sterling, besides what more he has promised to pay if it be your Excellency's intention to pay him in full. . . . In payment for this expense I have drawn for fourteen pounds sterling upon (?)egnier van Coolgie, wherefor I have sealed him a bond." And there the letters end.

The consultant energy of Hakluyt is nowhere better seen than in this urgent task. On the 27th of November van Meteren broached the plan. It was not until the middle of January that he was engaged, although he had probably been working at home on the material. Coming up then to London, he spent three weeks, instead of the ten days he had expected, in gathering his notes and having them turned into Dutch or perhaps Latin. To pay him, van Meteren bound himself in a respectable sum of money, mostly for expenses. The chances are strong that he was never repaid.

To do his work well Hakluyt not only drew upon everything in print and manuscript within his reach but also suggested books and promised a map of China. He went further and urged upon the Dutch, whose first voyage to India was going forward, the record of Cavendish in the East. Probably he would have been eager to draw up advices for that voyage, too, as he was to do for the English East India Company; and it is possible that he did.

As we reconstruct the contents of the notes on the Northeast Passage, we imagine the nine or ten sheets as beginning with citations from Ptolemy and other classical geographers and from modern scientists like Mercator. Undoubtedly the letter which Mercator once wrote to him was set down in full. Then from the Russia Company records in his book he probably copied long selections, giving in full the journals of 1556 and 1580, when the Passage was attempted, and the notes of instruction. How he got these done into Dutch is not told; but, since van Meteren complained that some of the notes were in English, I judge that the Englishman took it as part of his task to translate the body of them. That task would account for much of the rather large expense of ten pounds.

In some such way Hakluyt drew up his twenty marks' worth of advice. What use was made of it cannot be so easily conjectured. Probably it proved the case for the Zeelanders, since Hakluyt approved their plan to van Meteren. The ships which sailed in July did try the straits which would bring them into the South Sea, instead of going round Novaya Zemlya. But this year the ice was heavy, and the ships did not get through. In the following voyage in 1596 Hakluyt's plan was abandoned, and the voyage aimed to outflank Novaya Zemlya by the north. Barents and his crew were forced to spend an arduous winter in the ice, and there was no more searching for the passage in Hakluyt's time.

So both plans had failed, and none was to succeed until the days of steam. In those later days Hakluyt's share in the Dutch enterprise was finally confirmed. In 1871 a Norse explorer discovered in Novaya Zemlya the winter quarters of the Dutch pioneers. In the hut were many properties abandoned by Barents nearly three centuries before. Two maps, which Hakluyt may have supplied, were later found here, and a manuscript version in Dutch of the account of the English voyage of 1580. This I take to be the most useful of the notes which Hakluyt hurried up to London to make; and it was thought useful enough to accompany the third voyage, which had discarded Hakluyt's plan but retained his knowledge.[16]

That the plan did not work is not to be charged against him. He had gathered the experience of Europe and was to continue to gather it by adding the special experience of the voyages he had advised. The record of the three Dutch voyages was speedily published. As speedily, Hakluyt prepared for its translation into English, as will be seen. Unresting were his labors for empire and for learning.

[16] The narratives of the Barents voyages, together with the story of the discovery of the winte quarters, are given in *Hakluyt Society Publications* 54 (1876), and with more material in the Linschoten Vereeniging volumes.

CHAPTER XII

The Eastern Empire

1583–1614

As America was one constant focus of Hakluyt's interest, so the road to India was the other. His apprentice years were illumined by the Frobisher search for the Northwest Passage, and late in life he was to take part in the new enterprises in that direction. His earliest consultation had involved the renewed English attempt on the Northeast Passage, and he has just been shown enlightening the Dutch on the same problem. The overland route to the East had also gained his early notice; and now with the fifteen-nineties, the English were finally coming to the southeast voyage around Africa.

On this project the oversea energies of the City would soon need to be concentrated. The older trades were falling into unprofitableness. The Russia Company was passing through lean years of struggle and competition, from which it was not to emerge until it went in for whaling in the next reign. The Levant Company ships were running with difficulty the gauntlet of Gibraltar. Enemies and competitors spurred to new initiative.

Privateering was one such remedy. As long as the war with Spain lasted and the privateers succeeded, it was cheaper to spoil the Spaniards of the riches of West and East than it was to collect the riches at the source. But the war would not last. It would not always be profitable; and a steadier market must be found than the Azores, whence one could hope to swoop on the Plate Fleet from the West, though the English privateers never did; or where Indiamen could be, and three times were, intercepted.

New markets were vain to seek in the West. In North America there was no market of consequence. Frobisher's Meta Incognita had failed to yield treasure. Gilbert's Newfoundland yielded only fish. Raleigh's Virginia yielded nothing at all. Farther south there had been some idea of holding the Spanish Main, which was not feasible. Raleigh was to try Guiana but never to find the great and golden city. There remained the East.

England had already reached out to India in the northwest projects which began with John Cabot and in the northeast projects which began with Sebastian Cabot. These plans added northern America and Russia to the English sphere, but they did not reach India (Fig. 24). English contact with the East properly began with the simultaneous voyages of a pirate and a priest. In 1579 Drake crossed the

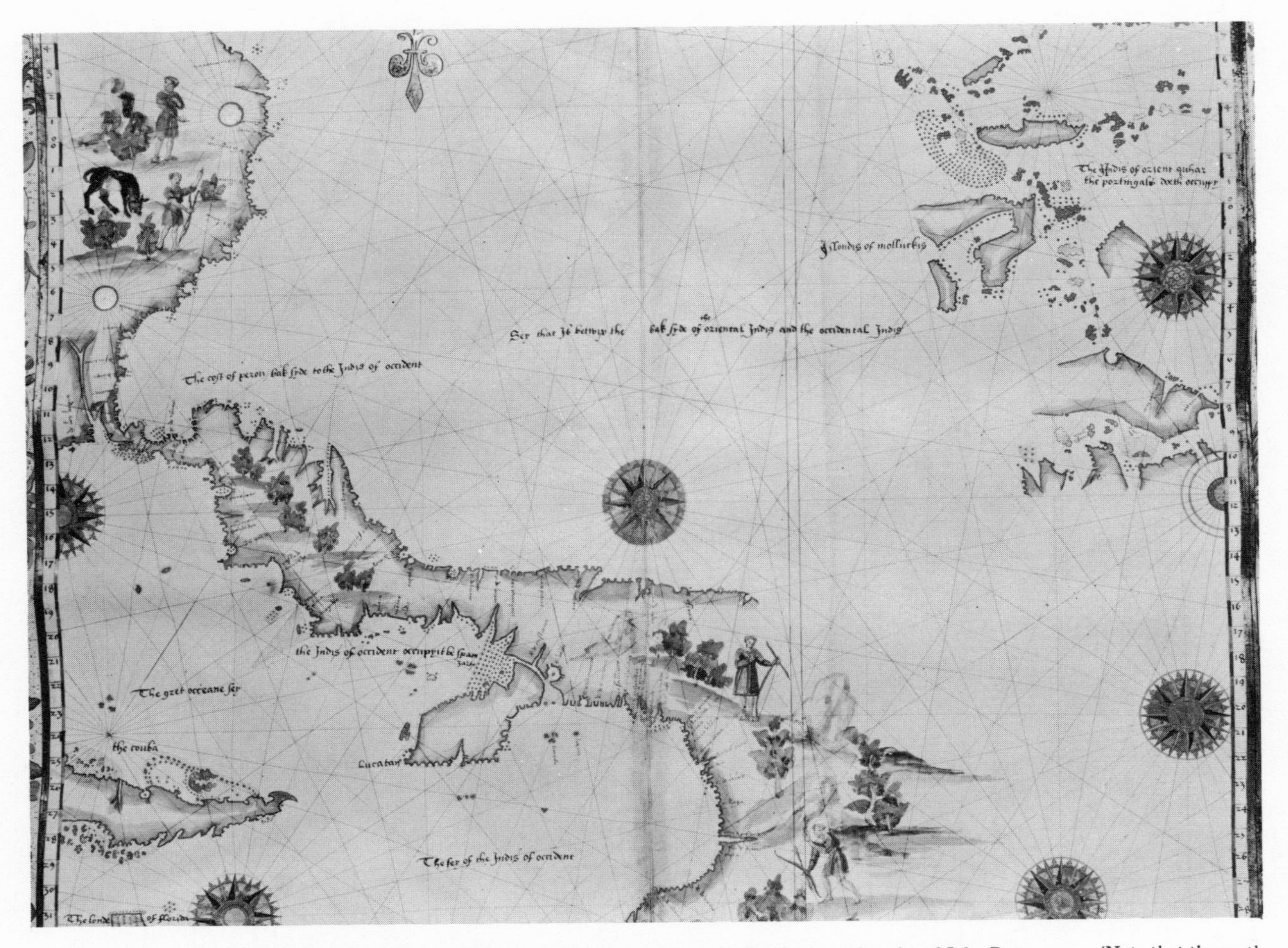

FIG. 24—Central America and the Moluccas, showing underestimate of the width of the Pacific, from the atlas of John Rotz, 1542. (Note that the south is at the top.) Royal MSS 20 E ix, ff. 7b–8. By courtesy of the British Museum.

Pacific to the Spice Islands, to lay a basis for future trade.[1] In the same year Thomas Stevens, S.J., arrived at Portuguese Goa to begin a long and illustrious career. Drake's profitable voyage was followed by the expedition of 1582, which started for the Southeast, made for the Southwest, and spent itself in dissensions before it reached the Straits; by William Hawkins in 1582–1583, who likewise failed to pass beyond the Atlantic; by an expedition planned for the Moluccas in 1584 and converted into Drake's West Indian raid of the following year; and by Thomas Cavendish, who in 1586 set out in turn to a successful circumnavigation.[2]

Father Stevens' first letter home from Goa was given by Hakluyt to the Newbery mission of 1583, which was to reach India overland for the Turkey Company. The first survivor of that mission, who had gone only part of the way, returned in 1589 and had his story printed in the *Voyages*. The second, who had traveled over most of the mainland of India and into Burma, returned in 1591. Meantime Drake's capture in 1587 of the East Indiaman San Felipe brought in a prize of one hundred thousand pounds. The Pacific piracy of Cavendish was found profitable on his return in 1588. The book of Caesar Frederick, the Venetian trader to India, was translated in the same year; and the organizing of a direct trade with the East was definitely begun in October of 1589.

The beginning is a memorial addressed to the Privy Council by "divers merchants." It is a dull document, intended to prove at painful length "no voyage into those parts to be doubtful, being orderly attempted"; to set down the places which the "Portingals" did and did not command; and to request a license for three ships. There followed ten years of experiment, of battering incredibly small ships around Africa. Not until 1591 did the three ships sail, under Sir James Lancaster, a seaman with a mysterious Portuguese past. Despite storm and scurvy one ship returned in 1594 to prove by the profits from its pepper the truth of the divers merchants' petition. Meantime the veteran John Davis was sent out in 1590 by west-countrymen, but his single ship was turned back by storms at the Canaries. Cavendish and Davis started in 1591 for the Southwest Passage; but the expedition returned baffled by the storms of the Straits, leaving Cavendish's body in southern seas. To point the opposite moral, Sir John Borough captured in 1592 a fabulously rich Portuguese carrack, the Madre de Dios, with a booty of one hundred and fifty thousand pounds. Ralph Fitch returned at last from the Newbery mission to India, and the Levant Company which sent him had its charter extended to take in the eastern lands.[3]

[1] See H. R. Wagner, *Sir Francis Drake's Voyage around the World* (San Francisco 1926).

[2] J. A. Williamson, *Sir John Hawkins* (1927), is the authority on these newly discovered plans and voyages.

[3] The record of most of these expeditions is made up from Hakluyt and from the able summary in

So these gropings towards the East seemed to show more profits than losses, provided only that the attempts were "orderly." While Raleigh hunted for El Dorado, the eastern expeditions continued. In 1593 a Hawkins of the third generation, Captain Richard, went forth to survey the Spice Islands but was captured off Peru. In 1594 Lancaster was sent to rifle the returning Portuguese off Brazil. In the same year, Robert Dudley started for the Straits in succession to his brother-in-law Cavendish; but the Queen's command limited him to the Spanish Main. In 1596 he then equipped three further ships; but they tragically disappeared after pillaging the Portuguese in the China Sea. In 1597 a great store of spices was captured in the naval raid on the Azores.

Most stirring incentive of all, the Hollanders were vigorously combining to build an independent Malaysian trade. In 1595 four ships sailed; in 1598, twenty-two ships in five squadrons, one of which followed Drake and Cavendish round the world; by 1601, sixty-five ships in fifteen squadrons. This disquieting example and the annoying rumor that the Hollanders were even buying ships in London for their new project set in motion the final elaborate plans that led in 1600 to the firm foundation of the English East India Company.

2

So far in this painful period I can find small trace of Hakluyt. At least he gathered information, and he may have dispensed it. He had copies of Father Stevens' first letter home from India. He had letters from the Newbery mission as well as the full reports. He talked with the Portuguese pilots returning from the East to Paris. He was on hand to collect information from naval raiders, especially from the captors of the East Indiamen. He took down or copied the reports of Cavendish, Lancaster, Davis.

What he did with the information is, before 1589, less clear. Certainly he gave advice to Newbery. Whether he furnished it to Cavendish and the others is unknown. What printed information he had he published. In the 1589 *Voyages* only the few Newbery letters and the report of Cavendish were included. With the most substantial book of the eighties that concerned India, the English version of Caesar Frederick, he had no evident concern. But he did see to the publishing of Mendoza's *China,* which supplemented Frederick's *India:* especially, wrote the translator, "for the illuminating of the minds of those that are to take the voyage next in hand to Japan, China, and the Philippines," that is the voyage intended by the petition of 1589. This was the latest information, the translator "passing over Paulus

Sir W. W. Hunter, *A History of British India,* I (London 1899). Also valuable is H. G. Rawlinson, *British Beginnings in Western India* (Oxford 1920), as is M. Epstein, *The Early History of the Levant Company* (London 1908). I add the 1590 voyage of John Davis from the *Geographical Journal,* II 146–149 (1893).

Venetus [Marco Polo] and Sir John Mandeville because they wrote long ago of those regions." But Mandeville went into the *Voyages,* and Marco Polo had been recently done in English. So it was with the history of the Portuguese discoveries. The gaps were filled in, and the record of the East was reasonably complete.

Hakluyt's hand would be especially visible, if at all, in the petition of 1589. He would certainly have been the one to know where the Portugals had their stations and where they traded under protest. For we remember that in 1587, when he was dedicating his translated *Florida,* he had a full report of the Portuguese colonial stations. Moreover, he had talked in Paris with the Portuguese mariners; and the petition mentions a queen of Sumatra "who was living about six years past," that is at the time when the Portuguese started home.

Hakluyt could have been consulted in the drawing up of the document; but it must be conceded that there were many other Englishmen who might also have been well informed. None of them would have known as much. Even Cavendish, who had just returned in 1588 from his circumnavigation, had not touched India proper, though he might have picked up a complete enough account of the Portuguese trade. In any case, whoever furnished the information, it was certainly not Hakluyt who wrote it down. The paper is not in his hand nor is it in his style. The writing is dull and formal, while Hakluyt usually managed an enlivening phrase. Again, there are no authorities cited, and Hakluyt lived for authorities.[4]

In the voyages that followed the petition I can still find no account of Hakluyt before the actual organizing of the company. The single ship of 1590 was sailed by John Davis, who probably hoped to capture Portuguese guides on the way; and it was sent out by John Sanderson, merchant, who had lived three years in the Levant and may have had many tricks in his own sleeve. The successful trial voyage of Lancaster must certainly have called for much information in the form of academic notes or direct knowledge from the previous voyage of Cavendish by the Straits or the contributing presence of Englishmen or Portuguese who had sailed the way before. The evidence is lacking; but Hakluyt could not have been far in the background, especially with his Mendoza and his Mandeville.

For it must be repeated that he was known, directly or through his cousin or another, to most of the adventurers and enterprisers in this direction as in others. He had special acquaintance with the Levant traders, in whose books he had rummaged for travel records. Cavendish was related to him by marriage, and he knew the Davis and Cavendish and Lancaster personnel well enough to get from them reports of their voyages. At court he was equally well known. Though Wal-

[4] The petition of 1589 is in *Calendar State Papers Colonial East Indies 1513–1616*, par. 239. It is now catalogued as C. O. 77, vol. I, no. 8.

singham and Sidney and Leicester were dead by 1590, he was known to Burleigh and was presently to be advising Burleigh's son Robert Cecil, Secretary of State and his most fruitful patron.

It is more than likely that Hakluyt, having returned to England at the beginning of 1589, was consulted on these initial expeditions. He certainly gathered knowledge that would serve. He reaped an especial harvest from the captured carrack of 1592. One gets the impression that, while the sailors looted the pearls and spices of that prodigious prize and while Robert Cecil sped posthaste to Plymouth to set a guard, Hakluyt was picking up the documents and maps on board. At least he used them with effect later, probably through the kindness of the Admiralty. If he gave the knowledge he thus acquired to the new company in 1600, it is likely that he had given it earlier to the 1596 expedition.

But these are all conjectures. What we know as certain of the first ten years of the groping towards India is simply that Hakluyt saw to the putting down of the records. He got official reports of the several voyages; he gathered regional information from voyagers and from foreign books as they came to his hand. By 1598 the record has cleared. The facts of the geographer's mission become indisputable. Whatever a closet expert could contribute to the elaborate new organization of the East India Company, that did Hakluyt fully contribute. In this one case we have a full-sized example, perhaps exceptional, perhaps typical, of the scope of his activities.

3

In August of 1597 an English agent in Amsterdam reported the return of the first Dutch voyage to the Spice Islands (Fig. 25). The English voyage of 1596 was still to be heard from; but the news from Holland seems to have stirred London. By November the printed report of the Dutch voyage was being translated into English, and it appeared in the following year. In February of 1598 the great new work on the East, Linschoten's *Itinerary,* was being translated in its turn, to appear in the same year. In 1598 also John Davis enlisted as chief pilot in one of the new Dutch expeditions, to gather the experience which he was to use in the first English fleet sent out by the new company.

How soon the merchants responded to these reports is not recorded. Certainly there was much activity and a considerable amount of organizing in 1598 and 1599. In September of the latter year, the movement came to a head. It was then reported to a gathering of merchants that thirty thousand pounds had been subscribed, an immense capital which had been surpassed only in the Spice Islands plan of Drake in 1584. Committees were appointed, and a record book was

1926, pp. 424–426.

begun. Internal organization being thus achieved, a petition for a patent was drafted and presented to the Privy Council.

On this promising action then descended a year's delay. The long naval war with Spain had reached the stage of negotiation, and Spain's right to trade dominion in the East demanded respect during the peace discussions. Peace was not actually signed until 1604 and then without settling the rights of foreigners to trade in the new worlds preempted by Spain. Meantime the English merchants tried to have the question settled. Early in 1600, being held up by the negotiations, they wrote a memorial to request that England obtain in the peace terms the right to trade in the Archipelago, which was not effectively controlled by Spain.

Here Hakluyt seems to make an effective reappearance. He it was who had helped to spread the news of Holland's new success. There is nothing to show that he had taken the report of the first Dutch voyage to the translator; but he did take the book of Linschoten, as will be shown in a later chapter; and both books were published by the same printer. The account of the second Dutch voyage, that of van Neck, was translated by his persuasion. But this publicity was only the beginning of his work for the new eastern enterprise.[5]

The records of the company are preserved, and they show that Hakluyt was continuously employed in the organizing period. He was present at the last of the four meetings in the autumn of 1599, when the final terms of the patent were to be arranged with the Privy Council. Though it is not clear what he was there for, since he was not formally a "committee," probably his geographical knowledge was being used. He may have helped in drawing up the petition for the patent, and he may have attended the conference of the merchants with the government over the petition. At the least, he was definitely in the company councils.[6]

After the meeting of October 16, 1599, the entries in the minute book cease for a year, the year of imposed delay; but Hakluyt was not to be idle. Such is my inference; for I have every reason to believe that the memorial which was then presented to the Privy Council, on the claims to be presented to the peace commissioners, was Hakluyt's own composition.

For this statement there is no direct evidence, and it has not previously been made. The case seems to me sufficient. The paper, written early in 1600, is entitled "Certain Reasons why the English Merchants may trade into the East Indies, especially to such rich kingdoms and dominions as are not subject to the King of Spain and Portugal; together with the true limits of the Portugal's conquest and jurisdic-

[5] For the publications see the next chapter.

[6] The early history of the company is given in Hunter. John Bruce, *Annals of the East India Company* (London 1810), prints many documents, including the memorial of 1600 (p. 115) and the answer. The minutes, 1599–1603, are printed in Henry Stevens, *The Dawn of British Trade to the East Indies* (London 1886).

tion in those oriental parts." With these reasons it was hoped, rather naïvely, that diplomacy would persuade Spain to give up the monopoly of the East, supported though it was by the Church and by a century of possessions, and so enable English merchants to make their handsome profits in peace and legality.

The style of the paper in its very title seems to point to Hakluyt, and, as one reads on, the likeness is confirmed. Certainly the style is not of the legal variety; nor is it that of the sprawling merchant hand. It bears all the marks of the educated and professional writer.

Moreover, the opinions of the paper are fully buttressed by a list of authorities, as in Hakluyt's *Divers Voyages* and his various notes of advice. The printed authorities, Portuguese, Spanish, Italian, Dutch, are separately listed. The voyages of the English and Dutch are elaborately mentioned—Drake, Cavendish, Fitch, Lancaster, the first two Dutch voyages "in print," an English witness from one of them, the reports of the third Dutch voyage just returned. The Hakluyt manner is unmistakable.

Finally, the petition is written in a hand which is almost certainly his. I do not press the point and would not without the aid of a professional paleographer; but to press it is hardly necessary, for the qualities of style and the method of presentation are striking evidence of Hakluyt's authorship. Again the conclusion opens the door wide to conjecture. If this long unsuspected document be really Hakluyt's, how many others of the same kind did he actuallly compose? How many may he have written of which no record now remains? How many notes of advice may he have dictated to how many adventurers and enterprisers and even officials in the period when he lurked at the heart of the expansion movement?

The fact that the memorial was referred for reply to Sir Fulke Greville is further significant. The friend of Sidney was an able official. He was something of a scholar as well as a man of action and had lately taken Hawkins' place as Treasurer of the Navy. But he could have been no more than an amateur in geography; and, when he made his hasty reply, on March 10, 1600, he was able to draw the facts for his corroborative survey of the Spanish-Portuguese empire only from three of the many authorities cited by the memorialist.

The reference to Greville seems in itself to show that Hakluyt wrote the memorial. If he had not been the author, he would almost certainly have been chosen to write the answer. He was just publishing his final *Voyages*. He was known, of course, to many of the Privy Councillors, including the Lord Admiral, and to the Secretary Cecil; and in May of that same year he was to be specially noticed by the Council as a deserving subject. Only in case he was already spokesman for the company would he be overlooked by the Council when an expert was needed. In any event the Greville answer could find no fault with the facts of the memorial, and Hakluyt remains the reliable authority.

The memorial, of course, accomplished nothing. The peace conference had no issue, and there was no hope anyway of Spain's blessing the English trade to the East. In the autumn of 1600 the plans began to revolve again, and the patent was finally delivered on the last day of December.

In the meantime there was much consulting. On October 2, 1600, the two survivors of the Newbery mission were cited before the committees to "confer of the merchandise fit to be provided for the voyage." In addition Hakluyt was called in, if indeed he had not been in almost continuous consultation. In the minutes of January 29, 1601, we read: "Mr. Hacklett, the historiographer of the voyages of the East Indies, being here before the Committees and having read unto them out of his notes and books divers instructions for provisions of Jewels, was required to set down in writing a note of the principal places in the East Indies where Trade is to be had, to the end the same may be used for the better instruction of our factors in the said voyage."

The note covers a multitude of advices. For a little later, after the first expedition had been sent off, we read again, under date of February 16: "There is given to Mr. Hackett by the assent of this assembly for his travails taken in instructions and advices touching the preparing of the voyage and for his former advices in setting the voyage in hand the last year the sum of ten pounds, and thirty shillings for three maps by him provided and debited to the company."

These entries illuminate more clearly than any other evidence the part for which Hakluyt had cast himself. The organizers of the new trade, having collected the evidence of merchants and travelers, summoned also the knowledge of the closet expert. At an early meeting of the directors he was present and probably prepared to testify. He perhaps drafted the memorial which declared the possible range of the enterprise, which opened up the whole extent of the eastern markets. A fortnight before the departure of the expedition, he made a public report to guide the leaders of this latest and largest of oversea enterprises.

Upon the presentation of the public report Hakluyt was commissioned to submit it in writing. His final memoranda included three maps, which we suppose were destined to supply each of the three ships. The ten pounds which he received as fee, though the figure is smaller than the one he quoted to the Dutch venturers, we can now measure by comparison as a handsome one. Not only was it large in itself, as representing a modern equivalent of sixty to eighty pounds, but it was much beyond the reach of other professional men. The lawyer who drew the patent received only four pounds. Some years later, the navigation expert of the company was assigned a salary of only fifty pounds a year, "to examine their journals and mariners and perfect their plots [charts]."

The accident which has preserved this unique record of a geographer's relations with his client has also preserved the geographer's notes, thus rounding off the episode. The Hakluyt manuscripts which passed from Selden's library to the Bodleian are without doubt the original memoranda for the East India Company.[7] The earlier entry in the minutes speaks of "provisions of jewels"; and one section of the Bodleian papers contains a list of Oriental precious stones, with the prices marked in Portuguese currency. The entry also requires a "note of the principal places in the East Indies where Trade is to be had"; and a further section of the Bodleian papers is entitled "the chief places where sundry sort of spices do grow." Moreover, the margin of the manuscript is marked: "This note was made in February 1600," that is 1600–1; and reference is made in it to "the great Italian map, taken in the Madre de Dios, which I have translated and caused to be drawn for the company."

As these two sections of the report deal with imports, a third section discusses "commodities of good request in the East." For the facts in these notes Hakluyt gives, as always painstakingly, chapter and verse. His earliest authority on the East is Oviedo's Spanish history of the Indies, published some fifty years before. Then follows Ramusio's *Voyages;* and, after a reference to Drake's voyage, the rest of the evidence is made up from the period of Hakluyt's own maturity. The trial voyage of Lancaster; the Dutch experience, particularly as it was contained in the new standard work of Linschoten; Mendoza's *China;* the Venetian experience of Caesar Frederick—these sources, all of which Hakluyt had published in English, explain the expert's international reach, explain the fashion in which the national geographer assembled for English use the experience of all maritime Europe.

To the printed sources of information he added, from the insatiable stores of the archivist, two manuscript documents of foreigners, captured doubtless at sea. Signed by "Nicolas Sobras," one was entitled "A Remembrance of what is good to bring from the Indyas into Spain." The other carried a like title. Both listed the prices of precious stones and were therefore sources for Hakluyt's own summary of the jewel markets. So, with the help of his privateering countrymen, the Englishman profited by enemy researches.

Still a fourth miscellaneous section of the report is headed "Certain notes gathered of such as have had much familiarity with the Portugals that trade in the East Indies" and contains a further list of exports, additional to those noted down from books. Doubtless it was made up from Hakluyt's own inquiries of travelers, English and other,

[7] They are Bodleian MS Arch. Selden B. 8. They were printed in *Hakluyt Society Publications* 7 (1850).

dating possibly back to his conferences in Paris with the exiled pilots of Portugal.

The interpolation of these personal testimonies, however valuable they may be as archives, is yet a characteristic weakness of Hakluyt's. He had gathered all the details that could be gathered in Europe of European trade with the East; but he had by no means clarified his knowledge so that it could be readily used by traders. I have said in discussing the *Western Planting* that Hakluyt never quite got his facts into focus. In any one case his faulty arrangement might be laid to haste; but the excuse certainly cannot cover a multitude of cases nor can it apply to such notes as these made for the East India Company.

Not only is the plan broken up by the two insertions of Spanish trade notes, which, like eccentric circles, do not fit into Hakluyt's own scheme—they might be justified by the geographer's passion for archives or more likely by his sense of the conviction carried by authentic foreign evidence—but the expert's own compilations are singularly illogical in their plan. Just as the added chapter of the *Western Planting* is little more than a series of haphazard jottings, so the eastern notes, though reasonably divided as spice imports, jewel imports, exports, are generally unusable. The list of jewels is, it is true, clearly arranged, though twice repeated in the Spanish inserts; but the "places where sundry sort of spices do grow" are given not geographically but by commodities—pepper, cinnamon, cloves, and so on. The list of exports is arranged by authors and therefore repeats itself; while Hakluyt's own list of exports, the notes of such as have had familiarity with the Portugals, yields no visible arrangement at all. The traders who were to use the lists must have had to spend much time in rearranging. They must note in a new list or on the map the commodities which any given place might either buy or yield. They must bring into some kind of purchasable order the cloths, saffron, ivory, copper, lead, wine, olive oil, coin, mirrors, glass, emeralds, helmets, stockings, sweets, playing cards, paper, iron, beads, tinware, linen, pins, cheap jewelry, ironware, armor, wax, pewter, bells which the ships would stock before sailing.

Hakluyt was not yet skillful enough to digest his material. A further mental process remained for the purchasing agent or supercargo before whom the memoranda were laid. A further sorting was required before the appropriate pockets were filled. I suppose that the inductive process had not yet been thoroughly mastered; that it was not yet thought needful to take down the scaffolding and sweep up the chips. I do not know whether the same criticism may be made of all the other experts, of one kind or another, of the time. Possibly one must ascribe to the inductive scientist a mental adolescence corresponding to the adolescence of his art. The merchants, in their invoices and bills of lading, often followed a like haphazard plan. The criticism holds for Hakluyt's cousin also, whose memoranda were ill-arranged and undigested.

The criticism, whether it prove to be typical or merely personal, may seem of minor importance, as compared with the much greater importance of the soundness of Hakluyt's judgment. The arrangement of evidence is not difficult to learn. The testing of evidence, for admission or exclusion, is an obviously much harder task, and it may at once be said that Hakluyt's evidence was strongly supported. There is a vast difference between the *Discourse on the Western Planting,* written about an unfrequented country, and the East India notes, compiled from the experience of a century. If the Portuguese, who had been in the East for that length of time, contributed the smaller part of Hakluyt's evidence, they at least contributed bona fide market information on the buying of precious stones. Such information may not have been needed, since the Newbery expedition had gone out to buy jewels; but at least it was confirmatory and certainly complete. As to spices to be imported, there were not only the cargoes of the captured Indiamen to be relied on but also the notes of a Venetian who had traded in the East in the sixties and seventies, of a Dutchman who had lived at the Portuguese capital in India in the eighties, of the Dutch who were already deriving wholesale profits from the Spice Islands. It was not hearsay that Hakluyt submitted to the merchants who were investing thirty thousand pounds in India: it was the experience of a secular commerce.

Nothing more could be demanded; but whether the company thought its large fee well spent we are unable to say. The first voyage was thoroughly profitable, and one may suppose that Hakluyt's facts counted for something in its profits. Many of his facts may have ceased, with the fluctuating of markets, to be valid; but they were a sufficient springboard.

4

When the English themselves had scraped acquaintance with the islands and the islanders, there was little more for the home expert to do than to keep on compiling the reports. He did so, and he was further consulted on occasion. It remains to speak of several further incidents of the relation between the company and its historiographer, incidents that are curiously casual and yet speak of a perhaps deeply rooted connection.

The most important item concerns the third voyage, sent out after the three-year interval required by each voyage, in 1607. As the story was later printed by Purchas from Hakluyt's manuscript report of the voyage, the expedition was delayed below the equator by "gusts, calms, rains, sickness, and other marine inconveniences." The vessels were off Sierra Leone; and the master, "having formerly read well of the place, sent for the Book"—that is, said Purchas, the *English Voyages*. By using information in it, it was possible for the master to bring the ships to safe harbor, to refit, and to take in fresh supplies before setting forth again. "This saved the company, as Sir Thomas Smith affirmed to me," Purchas wrote on the margin, "£20,000, which they had been endamaged if they had returned home, which necessity had constrained if that Book had not given light."[8]

The event is striking: the *Voyages* had become the Book. It was carried on board the India fleet as a matter of course; it was a very present help in time of trouble. How many like uses it was put to one cannot imagine. At the least, it had become indispensable in a ship's library and in this one case increased the profits of the voyage from 195 per cent to the 234 per cent which has been estimated.[9]

One other casual note enforces the moral. To the first station in India proper, at Surat on the west coast, the company sent out in 1611 a consignment of literature. This included the tracts of Mr. William Perkins, "together with Foxe's Book of Martyrs, also Mr. Hakluyt's Voyages, to recreate their spirits with variety of history." Pleasure was to be permitted with instruction under the strict and pious discipline of the company; but it is not recorded whether the Book added again to the profits of the station. At any rate, the Book had followed its heroes to the ends of the earth.[10]

Their careers Hakluyt continued to follow from his cloisters in Westminster. To him came all the records of the succeeding voyages, to be consigned to future publication by Purchas. Further services he may have done to the company, like or unlike those recorded; but only one more record is known. On January 22, 1614, it was ordered that a book of exercises in "the Malacca tongue," "supposed very fit for the factors to learn," be printed. The exercises had been set out by Hollanders in parallel columns of Latin and Malay. The Latin had been made English by a company factor, and the translation, getting somehow to Hakluyt, was shown by him to Governor Sir Thomas Smith. Now the exercises were to find their way, in the edition printed for the company in 1614, to the eastern isles from which the English were soon to be swept away by the Dutch. For their use the company minutes give the credit to Hakluyt.[11]

With this extremely casual yet significant event I have completed the story of Hakluyt's known relations with the East India Company. His place in this episode of the expansion is clear enough to typify his career as consultant. He was not a leader or even a partner in

[8] *Purchas His Pilgrims*, II 502.
[9] Hunter, *History of British India*, I 291.
[10] *First Letter Book of the East India Company*, 419: quoted by Hunter, I 274.
[11] *Calendar State Papers Colonial East Indies 1513–1616*, par. 682.

trade. He was not an investor, though his knowledge may have been as useful in stimulating investment as any commercial motive. His rôle in the record is narrow but within its limits is without question effective. When I suggest that he was at the elbow of Sir Thomas Smith, a Jacobean Cecil Rhodes, I suggest the much greater reach which one may assign to his enthusiasm.

CHAPTER XIII

The Advancement of Learning

1589–1600

The story of Hakluyt's labors in the cause of empire runs side by side with the story of his labors in the cause of learning. The closing years of the century lead him to the pinnacle of both labors. He is a director of Virginia and adviser of the East India Company. As a scientist, he rises in the fifteen-nineties to the climax of the complete *English Voyages*. This book is the full fruition of his earlier work; but, as he brings his toil to its climax, he also widens his scope and his aim. Not one man but many must serve the advancement of learning. Increasingly Hakluyt urges others to labor in the cause. He becomes a director of research.

One notes first the expanding of his circle of influence from national to international. He is now one of the leading historical geographers of the century of discovery. There are three of special eminence, three contributors of moment to the scientific record. The great collections of travel narratives are those of Ramusio, Hakluyt, and de Bry. Something has been said of Hakluyt's debt to Ramusio. The Italian's work supplied an early feeding ground for the geographical student at Oxford. It supplied a number of documents for Hakluyt's own work, beginning with Florio's Cartier. Principally it supplied the model and the inspiration for Hakluyt's own *Voyages*.

As Ramusio inspired Hakluyt, so Hakluyt was now to inspire de Bry. Theodore de Bry was a citizen of Liége and had established himself as an engraver at Frankfort. His art expanded readily to a wide intellectual range. Ortelius, for an earlier example, had stepped from engraving to cartography and numismatics. De Bry had become interested in discovery, which he approached rather for its pictorial value than, like Ortelius, for its map-making opportunities. In the later fifteen-eighties he was evolving his plan for a new travel collection in four languages, which was to be distinguished by the engravings. In pursuance of the plan he came in 1587 to London and necessarily to Hakluyt.[1]

De Bry's first volume was planned to take up French Florida, undoubtedly because of the stir just made by Hakluyt's Laudonnière. How he learned of the pictorial opportunities of that story is not known. At any rate, it was in London that he found, perhaps after

[1] See the chronology, Appendix II. De Bry's English *Virginia* was reprinted in facsimile (New York 1871, and other editions). White's illustrations, now in the Grenville collection, were reproduced in the *Century Magazine* (November 1882, May 1883.)

a hunt for him in Paris, the official artist of the French colony of twenty years before. Jacques Le Moyne de Morgues had laid his drawings before the King of France and had been urged to publish them; but he had been unable or unwilling to find a publisher. Coming to London, probably as a religious refugee, he had been taken up by Raleigh, at whose "no small charges," as Hakluyt wrote in his English *Florida,* de Morgues' pictures were "lively drawn in colors." Still de Morgues seems to have lacked a publisher despite the subsidy from Raleigh; and it seems to have been Hakluyt who found de Bry for him.

At any rate, de Bry went to London and made an arrangement with de Morgues. Before the plan could proceed de Morgues died, and de Bry came back to London to procure the drawings from his widow. This time, if not earlier, de Bry certainly met Hakluyt. The year was 1589. Hakluyt had just been made a partner in Virginia; Hariot's description of Virginia was just published; putting Virginia foremost, Hakluyt delivered de Bry to Governor White, the official artist of Virginia.

The result of this mediation was a change of plan. De Bry had the Florida drawings and was to have Hakluyt's help in issuing them. He also had the Virginia drawings and put them out first. In 1590 he published in the four languages, Latin, German, English, French, Hariot's description of Virginia, together with White's drawings, mainly of the natives of the place. This first volume of the *Peregrinations* was followed in the next year by the second, de Morgues' drawings of Florida.

We suppose Hakluyt responsible for this plan, having interested de Bry in Florida by his book on the French colony. He was certainly responsible for the first volume and for procuring the illustrations for it. He collaborated on the English version, for which he translated from White's original Latin the legends of the pictures. He had an unknown part in the French version, being described in it as "the cause of the advancement of the present Treatise." He may further, it is thought, have modified White's map of Virginia and generally lent a critical eye to the editing; and he arranged that the work in its four versions should be dedicated to Raleigh.

To Hakluyt's example, as well as to his initiative and collaboration, were due then not only the first issues of the *Peregrinations* but perhaps the whole idea of the series as well. As publicity the achievement was striking. The first illustrated book on the new world was a book on Virginia. The publication in four languages, as one of a distinguished series, notified the European world of the beginnings of a new England overseas. And notice was not merely given of a political event. To the modern view it is also evident that England was discovering a science as well as an art, was preparing itself, by the new interest in geography typified by Hariot's book and White's studies, to take its intellectual as well as its political place among the western nations. A later Englishman was to lament that Hakluyt's own collections were written in the vernacular rather than in the universal Latin tongue.[2] In maneuvering Hariot's and White's Virginia into first place in the new polyglot series Hakluyt was fully answering that charge.

I cannot find that he had an obvious hand in any of the later *Peregrinations.*[3] Yet one can imagine the effect on the newcomer in Hakluyt's field of the Englishman's enthusiasms and his continuing labors. His example, at the least, can be observed in the later volumes of the de Bry series, which run a close parallel to Hakluyt's own volumes. After the Virginia and Florida issues, de Bry passed to the travelers of other nations, mainly the Protestant ones; but he returned in his eighth volume to English exploits. Drake and Cavendish were represented by narratives which appeared also in Hakluyt, though some of them were also printed separately. Raleigh's *Guiana,* which Hakluyt was to reprint, found place there also. The series of eastern voyages, which the sons of de Bry initiated in 1598, also paralleled Hakluyt. In the year following the appearance of Pigafetta's *Congo* in English, for which Hakluyt was responsible, the de Brys reissued it. Likewise with Linschoten's *Indies;* and, though in both cases the de Brys followed another than the English version and though there is no proof of influence, it is more than possible that the parallel was intended. As an editor of works of travel, Hakluyt had learned his business. The de Brys were learning theirs. Just as he presided at the birth of the series, so it is possible that he gave advice on its upbringing. At the least he set an example.

2

So the bond was knit between the geographer and the engraver, between the plain *English Voyages* and the stately illustrated folios of the *Peregrinations.* That the foreign example influenced Hakluyt's further plans does not appear. If it did, if Hakluyt tried, for example, to publish his illustrated native history of Mexico, he was unsuccessful. A map was the most he could provide by way of illustration, and a sensible index the most emphatic sign of his individual aim. If he was enlarging the plan of his work he was enlarging it in another way, by widening the scope of his material.

The plan of American publicity had in the *Voyages* been expanded to cover generally the record of the English overseas. But, as English enterprise threatened to spread to all four quarters of the world, to

[2] George Hakewill, *An Apology . . . of the Power and Providence of God* (Oxford, 3d edit., 1635), p. 311.

[3] The arrangement of the de Bry volumes is explained in the catalogue of the John Carter Brown Library.

follow Drake and Cavendish to the East as well as to the two Americas, a skilled publicity might well extend its plan to include information, whether English or not, about the whole unknown world. Historical geography might take the same course, since it was less directly interested in guiding enterprise and more directly interested in the geographical record for its own sake.

With the year 1589 may be marked the firm beginning of the new motive, already sounding in the *Voyages*. Restricted though the narratives in that volume were to the foreign fields known to the English, they covered a wide area of the globe. What we may call the universal motive now comes gradually to take equal place, in Hakluyt's publishing, with the other motives. The American subject, though still of importance, is accompanied by the world-wide subject. The English discoveries are supplemented by the European.

The new motive appears with the issue in 1589 of Mendoza's *China,* for which Hakluyt arranged. The Spanish monk Gonzalez de Mendoza, who had published in 1585 a work on that "mighty kingdom," owed to Hakluyt a speedy introduction to England. At the latter's "earnest request and encouragement" the book was translated by Robert Parke and published at the end of 1588 or beginning of 1589. The encouragement seems to have had, I may say incidentally, a curious limitation. Included in the Mendoza was Espejo's *New Mexico;* but, instead of using the published version of that journey or Hakluyt's own and better translation which was to appear in the final *Voyages,* Parke retranslated it from a French intermediary, while he translated the *China* from the Spanish. The procedure was curious enough and resulted, as it happened, in a distinctly inferior translation.

With the Mendoza, Hakluyt was revealing the East to England. It is true that a good portion of the work dealt with Spanish America —not merely the Espejo, which was irrelevant, but the *Itinerary of the New World,* an account of the journey by the Spanish West to the Far East. It was this account which Ortelius said was the best description he had seen of Spain's possessions. These two journeys, however, were but a small part of the book. The major part related the travels in China of the first organized body of missionaries sent to that country from Spain; and the information obtained by the careful Augustinian friars made up the most substantial news of China since Marco Polo. Aside from Polo and from Mandeville there had been available in English only the account of a Portuguese traveler of the early part of the century, published by Willis. In publishing Mendoza, Hakluyt was further carrying on the Eastern publicity movement of the seventies and carrying it on by means of the most informing book of his time.[4]

The book was followed by others which also illuminated the newly

[4] See the Hakluyt Society edition, *Publications* 14–15 (1853–54).

interesting regions of the world. Despite the war with Spain English trade was feeling its way to the East. How English ships gradually paced off the sea lanes to India has been shown in the last chapter, and it has been noted also that Hakluyt was adding their records to his archives. But England was not the only country to follow the Portuguese carracks. The pioneer Hollander in India, Linschoten, had reached Goa in the eighties in a Portuguese ship. Hakluyt brought his *Itinerary,* of 1595, to an enterprising printer, "which he wished might be translated into our language, because he thought it would be not only delightful but also very commodious for our English Nation." So the book was turned over to a translator and appeared in 1598, as did also, probably by the same process, the accounts of the first and second Dutch voyages to India.

Together with these Dutch works must be listed the book of the Venetian Caesar Frederick (as he was anglicized), published in 1588 to give an account of his overland journey to the East. The book was immediately done into English, though I cannot find that Hakluyt moved the translation. The chances are that he did; but at least he reprinted the book in the final *Voyages.* The importance of the Linschoten and the Frederick is shown by Hakluyt's use of them as the main sources of his notes for the East India Company. For the English inquirer as well as for the scholar they became immediately standard.

India and China were thus added to Hakluyt's growing series. To map out the globe he still needed Africa. He accordingly began the record of this continent with Pigafetta's *Report of the Kingdom of Congo* of 1591, an account of a recent Portuguese journey into the interior of the continent, which has become a classic. This explorer Hakluyt escorted to Abraham Hartwell, a clergyman and translator of some achievement, "intreating very earnestly that I would take him with me and make him English"; and the book was published in 1597.[5]

The Pigafetta was followed by another and much more elaborate work. About the year 1597, Hakluyt relates in a preface, he took into his service a young Cambridge man, probably the son of a prebendary of Westminster in Hakluyt's school days. John Pory was to be a later leader in Virginia; but Hakluyt apparently hoped to turn him into a geographer by a species of apprenticeship. What Pory did for Hakluyt is not clear. He may have assisted in compiling or translating; but the chances are that he was commissioned to prepare a work of his own on Africa, a sufficient task to fill in the entire three years during which we are told he was associated with Hakluyt.

In fact, Pory translated the classic work on Africa, a work com-

[5] The Pigafetta volume has been retranslated by Margerete Hutchinson (London 1881). See Appendix III.

posed early in the century by a "Moor" known as Leo Africanus. The plan developed under Pory's hands; and, when the volume came to print in 1600, it contained not only Leo's book but a large body of supplementary information on Africa which had been gathered by Pory. Hakluyt wrote a testimonial for the book by way of a foreword and obtained for it the patronage of Sir Robert Cecil, now his staunch supporter.[6]

The method of this volume suggests that Hakluyt was working towards a higher stage of scientific presentation. He had hitherto carefully restricted himself in his own books to the *peregrinationis historia,* the archive method, eschewing those weary volumes of the compiler. But in this volume inspired by him the disciple went beyond the archives to a partial digest of the record. Leo's narrative was only a starting point, from which Pory passed to a virtual treatise in descriptive geography. Why Hakluyt never did this himself is an unsolved question. As the most competent geographer in England, he was the man indicated to write an English geography of the world. He had the material. He produced it for the occasion. But he never set down for others the broad geographical summaries he must have made for himself. The work of Pory may be taken as a sign of what Hakluyt might have done had he been so inclined.

At least he was active enough as a director of publicity. Leo's *Africa* had long awaited introduction to England; Pigafetta's was a new and important work. Mendoza's *China* and Frederick's and Linschoten's *India* were the most important new works on the East. There was one other new work which Hakluyt should have added, Acosta's *West Indies* of 1590. Hakluyt had the book, since he made notes from it for the government. But if he intended to have it published, as I do not doubt, he did not succeed very well. It was not until 1604 that the translation appeared and then without assigning any credit to Hakluyt. I can hardly suppose that Hakluyt had nothing to do with it. It is hardly plausible that he should have let the book go, publishing only his notes on Guiana which he had taken from it. But there is no clear connection between him and Grimstone the translator.

With such possible exceptions, Hakluyt was comprehensive in his publishing. He saw to it that the records of travel were made complete, filling in the gaps, keeping up to the moment the English geographical library. He justified in ample measure the epithet I assign to him, that of director of geographical publicity, of director of the advancement of learning.

[6] See the Hakluyt Society edition, *Publications* 92–94 (1896).

3

The intellectual size of a scientist is measured not alone by his height, his contribution to knowledge; it is also measured by his breadth, his wider interests and enthusiasms which join him with others in the common intellectual cause. He has not only to survey the highway and to build it; he has also to cajole others into frequenting it.

The rôle of popularizer we have assigned to Hakluyt as his especial task. The term director of publicity implies as much; and, whatever his value as a collector of knowledge, it is clear that he made no new synthesis, no original interpretation, of his changing science. Still it must be clear that he was no mere amateur, recording without understanding the knowledge he popularized. His long consultant record would acquit him of any such charge.

His popularizing was then the special function of one who was also a trained scientist, much like Huxley's popularizing. In both cases the scientist was equipped with a superior literary power. Of such men especially does one expect a breadth of intellectual interests; and Hakluyt's science of cosmography was broad enough to cover a cluster of sciences. On descriptive and economic geography he published none of his own observations; but he was regularly required to make them, and his editing of the treatises of others required a special competence. The history of cosmography, the "sweet" study which he called his major interest, was another distinct enthusiasm. The mathematical side of his science he seems to have paid least attention to, but he did attend to it; and his enthusiasm overflowed the frontiers of his science.

How far it reached one cannot say, for there are only glimpses. Hakluyt was probably not a Bacon, universal in interest; but he was fitted for a seat in Solomon's House in the New Atlantis, not only because of his industry but because of his enthusiasm, which, though Bacon said nothing of it, would be quite as important there. As witness to his enthusiasm for learning I quote this passage from the preface of the first edition of the *English Voyages.* "And whereas," ran the expression of an almost naïve delight, "in the course of this history often mention is made of many beasts, birds, fishes, serpents, plants, fruits, herbs, roots, apparel, armor, boats, and such other rare and strange curiosities, which wise men take great pleasure to read of, but much more content to see: herein I myself to my singular delight have been as it were ravished in beholding all the premises gathered together with no small cost, and preserved with no little diligence, in the excellent cabinets of . . . M. Richard Garth, one of the Clerks of the petty Bags, and M. William Cope, Gentleman Usher to . . . the Lord Burleigh."

The same great pleasure in biology and anthropology has been seen before when Hakluyt was praising Peter Martyr, a second Pliny, for his wealth of observation. The same interest shines through a casual view of him engaged in a discussion of fossils with the nephew of the Flemish geographer Ortelius.[7] In making up the final *Voyages,* again, he is found discussing a treatise on tropical medicine and apparently urging the physician to whom he referred it, and who did not think much of it, to prepare a better one. A member of Solomon's House could have shown no more interest.

How wide his net was thus spread over cognate sciences it is difficult to say, for these hints of his enthusiasms are casual, and it is not clear that they bore fruit. Such is not the case, however, with the mathematical branch of his science. How much mathematics he knew and how well he could apply it to his study, we cannot say. There are many documents in his *Voyages* which would serve a mathematical geographer—tables of distances, for example, and observations of latitude. Probably they did serve him in his compiling of advices. With the more complicated uses of mathematics there is no record of his concern. There is only the supposition that, when the Mercator projection was being worked on by Wright, it was Hakluyt who aided in that design, though probably only in the details of the drawing and not in the projection (Fig. 26). Hakluyt might have used his mathematics had he wished; but he put by at least one opportunity.

At the outset of his career we find the geographer concerned for the art of navigation, or more precisely for the dissemination of the art. His concern endured for at least two decades, and the effort he expended is enough to rank the art as one of his major interests.

His plan carried on Borough's earlier idea of a state school for navigators. An earlier chapter has explained that idea and its failure and has suggested that private initiative meanwhile did what it could. The conscious expression of the need for the art was found in the textbooks. Bourne's and Blundeville's books on navigation were almost as popular as the Spanish texts, and by the nineties John Davis was making original contributions to the art. With him, it may be said, English nautical knowledge had become in less than half a century very nearly self-sufficing.[8]

Yet it is clear to Hakluyt that a rising maritime nation demanded more than casual instruction, and the demand became with him a lifelong preoccupation. The first sign appears in the *Divers Voyages.* Hakluyt had already talked with Stephen Borough and had got hold of the Spanish treatises on navigation. Thus primed to speak by the enthusiasm of youth and the experience of Borough, Hakluyt went to

[7] See the chronology, 1589, in Appendix II.

[8] The best discussion of the development of nautical science is probably in the *Encyclopaedia Britannica,* art. Navigation; and for the medieval and renaissance periods, the introduction by A. H. Markham to *Hakluyt Society Publications* 59 (1880), with complete bibliography.

FIG. 26—The Molineux globe, 1592. By courtesy of the Honourable Society of the Middle Temple.

Drake himself in 1581 or 1582. The hero fell in with the scheme for a state school "in the most bountiful manner at the very first," promised an endowment of twenty pounds a year, and asked Hakluyt to find him a lecturer. Hakluyt "brought him one," though he does not say whether it was Hood or Hariot or even Dr. Dee. Whoever he was, he found the sum only half large enough, probably because of the expenses of lecturing. Upon his demand for more, "the matter ceased for that time."

This attempt seems to have come the nearest to success of all of Hakluyt's known plans of the sort. He continued his efforts. Drake remained favorably disposed. As Hakluyt wrote, "the worthy and good knight remaineth still constant, and will be, as he told me very lately, as good as his word." Having gathered thus much help, the young man tried to influence Walsingham; then he "had some speech with Alderman Barne and other"; and, going to Paris, he discovered there a substantial precedent, which continued his urging upon the government "again and again . . . the erection of that lecture of the art of navigation."

The urging is contained in his second extant letter to Walsingham, which is the next piece of evidence. The French precedent was not a direct example, as it happened, since it concerned mathematics rather than navigation; and, though pilots at Le Havre were just being required to take out a license, it was not until the next century that instruction was provided for them.[9] But Hakluyt learned in Paris how much better these things are ordered in France. He was impressed by the public competition for the chair founded by the will of the late philosopher Ramus. He noted that this chair was additional to the royal lectureship at the Collège de France. And he thereupon expanded his scheme to include a royal lecture in mathematics at Oxford and a royal lecture in navigation at London.

The new plan required one hundred pounds annually and was not very likely to succeed in a country where twenty pounds was all Hakluyt could get. Yet he continued his pleading. In the discourse to the Queen he managed to slip in a word, which he strengthened by referring to the Gilbert expedition, deprived of its flagship by unskillful piloting. No success followed this appeal. Hakluyt continued to keep abreast of the subject. He continued to learn the details of the Spanish system, questioning one of Drake's prisoners. He gathered log books and *routiers* from English and foreign captains and printed them. And he continued to plead in vain.

"When I call to mind," he wrote at length in 1598, in the dedication of the final *Voyages*, "how many noble ships have been lost, how many worthy persons have been drenched in the sea, and how greatly

[9] See "L'Enseignement de la Science Nautique au Havre-de-Grâce" in *Bulletin de géographie historique* (1910), p. 92.

this Realm hath been impoverished by loss of great ordnance and other rich commodities through the ignorance of our Seamen, I have greatly wished there were a Lecture of Navigation read in this City, for the banishing of our former gross ignorance in Marine causes, and for the increase and general multiplying of the sea-knowledge in this age." This argument, which he addressed to the Lord Admiral, has lost in vigor and has become almost plaintive; but it has gained in dignity.

One infers that Hakluyt had learned the lesson of official obduracy, which refused to be melted by mere warmth. The changed tone reveals a changed argument. No longer does Hakluyt deal in the phrases of his letter to Walsingham, which pompously ran: "In my simple judgment it would be the best hundred pounds bestowed these five hundred years in England." Now he reduces the argument to the plain lesson of experience. He states to the Admiral the precedents, Spanish and English, for state control of mariners. To Cecil, in the dedication of the last volume, he pointed out the value of the Spanish regulations which appeared in it, in terms which one almost suspects of irony: "And for an appendix unto the end of my work I have thought it not impertinent to exhibit to the grave and discreet judgments of those which have the chief places in the Admiralty and marine causes of England (the Spanish orders). . . . Which, if they find good and beneficial for our seamen, I hope they will gladly embrace and imitate, or finding out some fitter course of their own, will seek to bring such as are of that calling unto better government and more perfection."

The hope was vain; but, as a matter of fact, affairs had much improved in Hakluyt's time, according as English pilots replaced foreign pilots in English ships of long voyage. Doubtless the "means of breeding up of skilful Seamen and Mariners in this Realm" continued to be largely haphazard; but signs may be read of more conscious education, for which Hakluyt's urging may have counted.

In 1584, we learn from Stow, there was begun "a mathematical lecture, to be read in a fair old Chapel builded by Simon Eyre within the Leadenhall, whereof a learned Citizen [of London] born, named Thomas Hood, was the first Reader. But this Chapel, and other part of that hall, being employed for stowage of goods taken [1587] out of a great Spanish carrack, the said lecture ceased any more to be read, and was then in the year 1588 read in the house of Master Thomas Smith in Grasse-Street."[10] Elsewhere we learn that the lecture included "the chief mathematical sciences, viz., geometry, astronomy, geography, hydrography, and the art of navigation."[11]

In the same year in which Hakluyt was setting forth the French precedent citizens of London were following it. When the navy later

[10] John Stow, *A Survey of London* (1633 edit.), p. 65. The lecture was published in 1588 or 1589.

[11] Sir George Buck, "The Third University of England," appended to the Stow-Howes *Chronicle of England* (1615), cap. 31.

preferred storage space to education it was a merchant prince who, as he had probably endowed the lecture in the first place, removed the classroom to his own house. There is no way of knowing what Hakluyt had to do with the enterprise; but it is hardly open to question that he had managed to add to Drake's twenty pounds a like sum or so from Thomas Smith, his later associate in Virginia.

If so, then Hakluyt had succeeded. He had not achieved state instruction; but he had seen set up a lecture of the sort he wanted, read by a lecturer who was certainly qualified and who may have been the one he presented to Drake. He got what he wanted; but perhaps the navigators did not go to hear Dr. Hood.

How long the latter continued to hold forth in Grasse-Street or elsewhere is not known. He published a number of books on the art, including the first lecture read at Smith's house. Perhaps he gave up when Sir Thomas Gresham's college was at length opened in London at the end of the century, with its lectureships in mathematics and astronomy. The latter could not have satisfied Hakluyt, or he would not still have been urging in 1598 and 1600 a state endowment. At any rate, navigation was being taught. In 1616 the East India Company appointed its own pedagogue, the expert Edward Wright.[12] With the establishment in 1619 of a chair of astronomy at Oxford the theory at least of navigation was finally sanctioned as a part of the higher education. Hakluyt's purposes had so far triumphed.

The study of the art was not left merely academic. Doubtless the rank and file of seamen continued to depend on the rule of thumb; but some exceptions allow us to suppose an increasing theoretical study of the art by its practitioners. Thomas Hood was perhaps not a navigator; but he had sailed round the world with Drake before he started to lecture at Leadenhall, and his thorough reëditing in the nineties of the first English text on navigation is a sign of the expanding English knowledge. Edward Wright was a professional navigator, though a sailor who was called Edward Careless may not have been a very good one. He was a man of considerable talent and knowledge of theory, at any rate, for it was he who worked out and explained for the first time the theory of the map projection invented by Mercator but never elucidated by him. John Davis, of the Northwest Passage and all the seven seas, is perhaps the most brilliant example of the new age; for, although he was a sailor and an explorer all his life and died in service, he found time to contribute his own independent treatises to the nautical art and to perfect its instruments of observation. In knowledge as well as in action, men like these were making England a seafaring nation.[13]

Hakluyt was of their company. He printed Davis' log books and

[12] East India Company court minutes, in *Calendar State Papers Colonial East Indies 1513–1616*, p. 284.

[13] See note 8 above.

treatises. He is thought to have aided Wright on the projection. He was joined with Hood, at first perhaps as instigator of Hood's lectureship, later as a fellow director of Virginia. He was joined, moreover, with their wealthy supporters. William Sanderson, merchant prince, was a patron of Davis' voyages to the Passage and likewise of Molineux' first English globe. Sir Thomas Smith, leader of the Virginia and the India and many other companies, was the patron of Hood and Wright. Both Sanderson and Smith were partners with Hakluyt in the first Virginia directorate. A Hakluyt devoted to his calling and influential with his friends could not but have helped this flowering of English knowledge from the bud of action.

CHAPTER XIV

THE FINAL *VOYAGES*

1598–1600

The diversified decade after 1589 begins now to seem the most important period of Hakluyt's career, the period of fruition. We have already assigned him activities enough to occupy him, as a partner in enterprise and as a prime mover in the advancement of learning. But over and above these concerns, the decade was full enough of the labors of the archivist. The amplifying of the *Voyages* was to be his great and in a sense his final task.

Meantime there were personal cares to be allowed for, as he himself gave them: "my profession of divinity, the care of my family, and other occasions [which] might call and divert me from these kinds of endeavors."[1] We cannot estimate how burdensome these cares were. He was probably taking his profession seriously. The first two years of his tenure of the stall in Bristol Cathedral he had spent in France; but perhaps he was obliged later to certain duties. He had probably retired to his Suffolk living about as soon as it was given to him; at least, he was living in Wetheringsett by 1594. Once there, of course, he would take up his duties as a country parson. He had no curate in 1603; it is reasonable to suppose that he had none before that time and that he looked after his two hundred communicants and their families with some earnestness.[2]

The family cares do not seem overwhelming. His cousin Richard the lawyer died in 1591, bequeathing his property to Hakluyt's brothers Edmond and Oliver. Hakluyt himself, as eldest surviving son of the Skinner, was presumably taken care of already. Edmond in turn died in 1593, leaving his property and its administration to Richard. These were cares of a sort.[3]

The clergyman was, moreover, married and a father. There is no record of his first marriage. It may have happened as early as 1588, when he resigned his Oxford studentship, which required celibacy. It may have been as late as 1594, in time for the birth of his only known child about 1595. There is no certain record of his wife's identity. A plausible tradition has it that she was Douglas Cavendish, a member of the Suffolk family and cousin of Thomas Cavendish the circumnavigator. Hakluyt's living was in Suffolk, and his uncle Walter had

[1] Dedication of the final *Voyages*, vol. I.

[2] Archbishop's Return, 1603, in Harleian MSS 595 ii fol. 168: printed in *Proceedings Suffolk Institute of Archaeology and Natural History*, XI 26 (1901–03).

[3] See the chronology, 1591–97, in Appendix II.

held the living of Shotley in that county, close to Trimley St. Martin, the seat of the Cavendishes. Douglas' father Richard, lawyer and author, had however moved from Suffolk to Hornsey, near London. One may take one's choice as to the story of their meeting, of the betrothal and the marriage, and of the family behavior.

At any rate, the clergyman married the daughter of a gentle house, if the tradition be correct, and a house of some personal distinction. Douglas Hakluyt bore him at least the one son Edmund and died in 1597. Her death may easily have been the climax of a series of domestic difficulties, if "the care of my family" was not a mere phrase. At all events, the clergyman lived during the decade at his country parish; performed his duties as pastor, brother, and husband; and made his excursions, when need was, to London, Bristol, and Hereford.

The "other occasions" remain unexplained. Hakluyt's relations with the state and with trade appear to have shrunk after Walsingham's death and Raleigh's abandonment of Virginia. But he may have done some special service to the state or to a private individual like the new Secretary, Cecil, his future patron. He may have had business over Virginia, which, though futile, may have taken time. And, in urging others to research and publishing, he may well have spent much labor in the cheerful unremunerative task of advising and revising. One is tempted to dismiss these burdens as magnified, especially since they are mentioned as a kind of apology for the delay in completing the final *Voyages*.

A careful consideration of the labor of these years does not, however, prove Hakluyt any less active than he had been in the vigorous eighties. In mere quantity the additions to the *Voyages* were no slight task. And there was not merely quantity. The first edition advanced no claim to completeness. For the second and final edition it was essential that its editor should give utmost care to making his greatest work as comprehensive and therefore as fully matured in both plan and product as was possible.

So the three final volumes were not to begin to appear until 1598, to represent Hakluyt's most important, as well as his last important, publication. They were entitled now *The Principal Navigations, Voyages, Traffics, and Discoveries*—the *Traffics* added—*of the English Nation* (Fig. 27), and the compass was now expanded to 1600 years. Between the first edition and the second stretched a decade; but the product of the decade summed up the careful accretions of a lifetime. All that Hakluyt had so far published was included. What is more important, all that he had learned as student of geography, as consultant geographer, as editor—all his experience went into the enlarging of the plans and the filling in of the material of his main achievement.

Arthur Gorges.

THIRD AND LAST VOLVME OF THE VOY-AGES, NAVIGATIONS, TRAF-fiques, and Discoueries of the *English Nation*, and in some few places, where they haue not been, of strangers, performed within and before the time of these hundred yeeres, to all parts of the *Newfound* world of *America*, or the *West Indies*, from 73. degrees of Northerly to 57 of Southerly latitude:

As namely to *Engronland*, *Meta Incognita*, *Estotiland*, *Tierra de Labrador*, *Newfoundland*, vp *The grand bay*, the gulfe of *S. Laurence*, and the Riuer of *Canada* to *Hochelaga* and *Saguenay*, along the coast of *Arambec*, to the shores and maines of *Virginia* and *Florida*, and on the West or backside of them both, to the rich and pleasant countries of *Nueua Biscaya*, *Cibola*, *Tiguex*, *Cicuic*, *Quiuira*, to the 15. prouinces of the kingdome of *New Mexico*, to the bottome of the gulfe of *California*, and vp the Riuer of *Buena Guia*:

And likewise to all the yles both small and great lying before the cape of *Florida*, *The bay* of *Mexico*, and *Tierra firma*, to the coasts and Inlands of *Newe Spaine*, *Tierra firma*, and *Guiana*, vp the mighty Riuers of *Orenoque*, *Dessekebe*, and *Maramnon*, to euery part of the coast of *Brasil*, to the Riuer of *Plate*, through the Streights of *Magellan* forward and backward, and to the South of the said Streights as farre as 57. degrees:

And from thence on the backside of *America*, along the coastes, harbours, and capes of *Chili*, *Peru*, *Nicaragua*, *Nueua Espanna*, *Nueua Galicia*, *Culiacan*, *California*, *Noua Albion*, and more Northerly as farre as 43. degrees:

Together with the two renowmed, and prosperous voyages of Sir *Francis Drake* and M. *Thomas Candish* round about the circumference of the whole earth, and diuers other voyages intended and set forth for that course.

Collected by RICHARD HAKLVYT *Preacher, and sometimes* student of Christ-Church in Oxford.

1617

Imprinted at London by *George Bishop*, *Ralfe Newberie*, and ROBERT BARKER.

ANNO DOM. 1600.

FIG. 27—Title page of the *Third and Last Volume of the Voyages*, 1600.

2

The final *Voyages* was to be, in the first place, complete. Rough measurement reveals that the new edition contained more than twice as much material as the earlier one.[4] For one method of expansion, Hakluyt stretched back into history. In part with the aid of his friend Camden, the historian, he added a quantity of medieval records to the hastily gathered and sketchy notes of 1589. For the north and northeast section, which he now placed first as signalizing the uniquely English achievement, he cited numerous voyages of the time of the early kings; added many documents of the later middle ages which concerned English trade with Germany and the Eastland; and discovered additionally two lengthy medieval narratives of journeys to the Tatar East, the first important narratives of the sort, though not of Englishmen, between Roman times and the time of Marco Polo. The new material effectively doubled the size of the medieval section.[5]

The medieval section of the southern and southeastern voyages was similarly replenished. Sir John Mandeville disappeared without apology; and, to fill his room, Hakluyt included numerous new items of medieval pilgrims and crusaders and added the narrative of a follower of Marco Polo to the East. Polo himself, being easily accessible in a recent English edition, was not included, though Hakluyt had made, or was to make, a new translation. Indeed, the inclusion of any foreigner was a step away from the original plan, a step taken for reasons which will be shown. Finally, in the scanty medieval section of the western voyages there was added the early Greenland venture of the Zeno brothers, taken from the *Divers Voyages* and for the same reasons.

The new matter increased the medieval portions of the work from some 75,000 to some 250,000 words. This addition, which was large enough in itself to make a good-sized work, is yet slight in comparison with the gigantic size to which the *Voyages* had now grown. The original three-quarters of a million words were now more than doubled; and in the process the additional modern voyages, those of the six-

[4] I give a table showing approximately the number of words in the various sections of the two editions.

	Medieval		Modern		Total	
	1589	1598	1589	1598	1589	1598
North and N.E.	4,250	175,000	210,000	315,000	214,250	490,000
South and S.E.	65,000	65,500	140,000	325,000	205,000	390,500
West and S.W.	1,000	7,350	279,000	812,000	280,000	819,350
All sections	70,250	247,850	629,000	1,452,000	699,250	1,699,850

I have not deducted for the duplication involved in printing translations along with the original. Such allowance would reduce the final total to about 1,500,000 words.

I note in addition that some 170,000 words, or about one-tenth of the final bulk, illustrate naval and military achievements; 425,000 words, or one-fourth, include the travels of foreigners; 350,000 words, or one-fifth, are translation, of which 250,000 are by Hakluyt himself.

[5] C. R. Beazley, *The Dawn of Modern Geography* (London 1897–1906, 3 vols.), is the indispensable authority on the course of medieval geography. I follow his estimates of the value of individual works printed by Hakluyt from the medieval period.

teenth century, are found to fill more space than the whole of the original book. Of these additions perhaps a third was designed to bring the records up to date. More light was thrown on the Russia Company under the recent difficulties made by Boris Godunov. A fuller view was given of the Levant trade, now reaching into the third decade of the company. Above all, an elaborate account was given of the new achievements on the Spanish Main, particularly of Raleigh's tropical adventures.

But additions of this sort cannot yet account for the vast expansion of bulk. To account for that expansion a new purpose must be invoked, or rather several new purposes which are implicit in the original plan. When the first edition was being compiled, England was aware of having become a maritime power, and the purpose of the compiler had been to "publish the maritime records of our own men." When ten years later the second edition was being put together, England was beginning to be entitled to call itself not merely a maritime power but a naval power contesting equal rank with Spain; and not merely a naval power, but a power groping farther and farther into the distant quarters of the earth for trade and colonies, reaching to Guiana in the Spanish dominion, reaching openly to East India by way of the Cape and thus to the Spanish dominion again. England was becoming an imperial power.

A feeling of the new national importance may then be taken as one cause of Hakluyt's expanding the scope of his volumes. To illustrate the naval power of England by recording its naval history was to add another element to the plan of the *Voyages,* limited hitherto to trade and discovery. In the medieval sections it was possible to include accounts of the conquests of Arthur by sea, of the capture of the Isle of Man, of the size of the fleet under various kings, of the military and naval expeditions of crusaders and later adventurers to the Southeast. It was possible to include enough, in short, to give a full account of Englishmen going to wars beyond the Narrow Seas. In the sixteenth century the records were of course more ample: of Englishmen fighting in defense of Rhodes against the Turk; of Englishmen fighting for the Spaniard in Africa; of Englishmen privateering against Spain; of English fleets descending with Drake on the West Indies, with Drake and with Essex on Cadiz; and finally of English fleets defending the Narrow Seas against the great Armada itself.

The illustration of English imperial power is less obviously explained than that of its naval power; but I think the motive can be recognized as the third element in the plan. "Albeit my work," wrote Hakluyt in dedicating the last volume, "do carry the title of The English Voyages, as well in regard that the greatest part are theirs, and that my travail was chiefly undertaken for preservation of their memorable actions, yet where our own men's experience is defective, there I have been careful to supply the same with the best and chiefest relations of strangers." The direct reference in this passage is to the American record. For example, "there is no chief river, no port, no town, no city, no province of any reckoning in the West Indies, that hath not here some good description thereof"; and so on over the entire American hemisphere, wherever the Verrazanos and Espejos and men like them had been.

As far as the American voyages are concerned, the foreigners were then included when they described countries that were already beckoning to the English imperial imagination. "No sea innavigable, no land unhabitable" had been the motto of the *Book of Robert Thorne* of Seville. "No country beyond the reach of the English flag" might well be the motive of Hakluyt in relating the voyages of strangers. For a glance at the first volumes discovers extensive narratives of foreign voyages to the East, together with descriptions penned by missionaries and traders in the eastern countries which, like the western continent, were on the point of opening their markets to the English. Altogether, the reports of strangers fill not less than one-fourth of the total bulk of the book. The final reason for them is that the book was in fact, from sheer empirical necessity, not merely a history of travel and a history of commerce and a history of naval warfare overseas; it was also, in intention at least, a geographical description of the new worlds as now fully opened to the English.

That it was not completely so may at once be stated. The compiler's main concern was with the English voyages. They were to be given complete. Whatever he added to them, by way of information useful to future English voyagers, was added arbitrarily. One may mention particularly the Danish description of Iceland which went into the first volume. The subject was hardly relevant, though hardly on the other hand irrelevant, to the main purpose. Iceland was important to the fisheries, and the fishing fleets were important to the navy; but Iceland was not of particular concern to the expansion and was not a new discovery. But the description of Iceland was newly published, and Hakluyt was nothing if not contemporary. Moreover, in its pages "a great number of none of the meanest Historiographers and Cosmographers of later times . . . are by evident arguments convinced of manifold errors." If "*peregrinationis historia* . . . is that which must bring us to the certain and full discovery of the world," then Hakluyt was advancing to that discovery as far as his limitations of subject could permit. Throughout his volumes his ultimate homage was paid not merely to the national need and the national renown but fundamentally to the advancement of learning.

3

When a century later John Locke or another writing more or less in his disguise summarized the literature of travel, he passed this judgment upon Hakluyt. " The collection is scarce," was the best he could say for the *Voyages,* " and valuable for the good there is to be picked out; but it might be wished the author had been less voluminous, delivering what was really authentic and useful, and not stuffing his work with so many stories taken on trust, so many trading voyages that have nothing new in them, so many warlike exploits not at all pertinent to his undertaking, and such a multitude of articles, charters, privileges, letters, relations, and other things little to the purpose of travels and discoveries." [6]

What the eighteenth-century critic said with his eighteenth-century liking for neatness is doubtless still said. It may well be taken as a starting point for whatever needs to be said here by way of evaluation of the *Voyages.* The discussion in an earlier chapter of Hakluyt's method should make it clear now that the eighteenth-century critic was peevishly ignorant of the art of history. Even " the so many stories taken on trust," which is the most damaging remark in the list, is hardly warranted. In an age of miracles no story was impossible, no story could be rejected as impossible, until it could be checked by further evidence. An editor was obliged to print whatever came in that was told at first hand. In some cases no more evidence might be available. In the American section of the first edition, for example, there was included the story of the escape of David Ingram overland from Mexico to Cape Breton. This seemed an authentic record, since Ingram had actually been left in Mexico by Hawkins, had been brought home to Europe by a French fisherman, and had been examined on his journey by Gilbert and others. How he made the journey and what he observed on the way were matters that could hardly be verified at the time. Only later accounts of the continent—Spanish explorations from the south, French and English from the east—could begin to give a basis of corroboration. How Hakluyt did test the narrative of Ingram we do not know. He omitted it from the second edition because of certain " incredibilities " discovered in it.

Even so, it is doubtful if he was really right in suppressing it. His task as archivist was to present the evidence. If his witness had really made the journey, as he falsely professed, then some of his evidence would be sound, and whatever was sound was needed to add to the existing store of knowledge. The same argument answers the critic's contempt for " so many trading voyages that have nothing new in them." Taking them as geography Hakluyt could not be sure that there was nothing new in them. Taking them as history he had the

[6] The essay, doubtfully attributed to John Locke and reprinted in his *Works,* was prefixed to Churchill's *Collections* (1704).

duty of recording them. As an inductive scientist he could really omit nothing.

The neat critic failed, in sum, to realize that Hakluyt was a historian of wide scope. He was a historian of travel, to be sure, with a prime interest in the knowledge of geography which is the fruit of travel; but he was a historian of much more than travel. The "warlike exploits" were essentially "pertinent to his undertaking," since he had become a naval historian and since a good deal of the most informing of Elizabethan travel was warlike. The "trading voyages that have nothing new in them" were equally pertinent, since he was a commercial historian and since most English travel that was not warlike was commercial. And "the multitude" of documents which were "little to the purpose of travels and discoveries" were very much to the purpose of the historian of trade.

Our critic might have urged, or perhaps did imply, that with such a manifold purpose Hakluyt fell between two stools. The answer is simply that he did nothing of the sort. He made a complete collection of English oversea voyages. Most of them concerned, and necessarily concerned, English commerce; and Hakluyt added all that he thought was relevant to the history of English commerce. Many of those voyages contributed as well to the history of geography, to the certain and full discovery of the world; but the discovery was not the achievement of Englishmen alone, and Hakluyt's contributions to it must be partial. Even so, they were extensive. The voyages of strangers were often gratuitous; and, when account is taken of the numerous new and newly discovered works of strangers which he printed in the *Voyages* or caused to be printed separately by others, one is justified in saying that he carried out the secondary motive, that of the geographer, as well. For, whereas the Englishman of 1575 had at his disposal but a scattered group of books of travel in English, the Englishman of 1600 had a complete library.

In reckoning Hakluyt's achievement, one may not then use the eighteenth-century measuring rod. One may not judge the *English Voyages* as a history of travel, for that it was not and was not meant to be, but as a history of English travel. It became in consequence largely a history of English trade or rather of that chapter of English trade that recorded the dealings of Englishmen in remote markets overseas. As such it has his limitations. The records of organization at home Hakluyt did not publish, except for such official papers as patents and privileges. The reason probably is that he was not permitted to publish any others, as he would not be permitted today. The reason may also be that he was not a modern economic historian and did not conceive of the importance of company ledgers and minute books. Many government documents he also omitted, such as his own *Discourse on the Western Planting;* but it will usually be found that these documents were confidential, just as the omitted company records were confidential.

Given these limitations, one is still impressed by the indispensability of his collections. The latest histories of Elizabethan commerce rely almost entirely upon Hakluyt on the one hand and upon certain state papers, which were not revealed until the nineteenth century, upon the other. And if it be objected that there are no other sources extant by which to judge Hakluyt's completeness, it may be answered first that his history remains adequate; and second, that the same conclusions may be reached in many cases. Raleigh's Virginia is recorded in the *Voyages*. The Russia Company history is recorded in the *Voyages* and in seemingly confidential state papers. The Frobisher enterprises are recorded in the *Voyages,* in state papers, and in company records which, now that they have been published by the Hakluyt Society, are seen to be clearly confidential; and so on for other enterprises.

How much farther, as a historian, Hakluyt might have gone we can not judge satisfactorily. The possibility still remains that among the documents to which he had access, which he did not print and which have been lost, were documents of importance. We know that he did make extensive searches. His Russia Company papers are exceptionally comprehensive. His American documents are rather less comprehensive; that is to say, one can imagine numerous reports which he might have had access to, but one can always imagine a censorship to hold them back. The records of the Levant and African trades are perhaps the scantiest, especially in the early years of the Tudor century; but we have Hakluyt's statement that he delved into the merchants' records, had the run of their offices, and was therefore unable to find any more documents bearing upon what was, until late in the century, an unorganized and casual commerce.

It is desirable at this point to consider another view of Hakluyt's labors, especially of their method. The picture which has been sympathetically drawn by Professor Sir Walter Raleigh[7] is a picture of a man eagerly interested in the accounts of travelers but interested only to listen and to note and, departing, to record. The picture is virtually of the silent man listening in a corner.

There is a certain symbolic truth in this delineation. Hakluyt was only incidentally a man of action, he was essentially the bystander who recorded. But the whole tenor of this book has shown that he was by no means a passive listener. The material he recorded did not come to him from mere acquaintance with the chiefest captains at sea. On the contrary, the whole record shows that Hakluyt went out and found his information. What he did in Paris may make one example, an

[7] Sir Walter Raleigh, essay introductory to the Hakluyt Society reprint of the *English Voyages* (1903–1905), vol. XII. The essay, entitled *The English Voyages of the Sixteenth Century*, was also published separately (Glasgow 1906).

example of diligently frequenting captains and spies and Rouen fishermen and king's skinners. The large number of documents captured at sea and therefore the property of the Admiralty or of private war makers, he must have bestirred himself to acquire. "Certain ancient Ligier books" of various London merchants in the Levant trade he had "diligently perused and copied out."

His materials did not come to him of their own accord. In fact, he was so much aware of his laboriousness that he wrote in the dedication to the first edition of the *Voyages:* "I now wonder at myself, to see how I was able to endure the delays, curiosity, and backwardness of many from whom I was to receive my originals." And again in the preface to the final edition: "What restless nights, what painful days, what heat, what cold I have endured; how many long and chargeable journeys I have traveled; . . . what variety of ancient and modern writers I have perused; what a number of old records, patents, privileges, letters, etc., I have redeemed from obscurity and perishing; . . . what expenses I have not spared; and yet what fair opportunities of private gain, preferment, and ease I have neglected: albeit thyself canst hardly imagine, yet I by daily experience do find and feel, and some of my entire friends can sufficiently testify." The entire friends have failed to do so. The complaint of hardships is certainly naïve in a work which is itself the record of physical toil and danger. But the evidence is unmistakable: Hakluyt was no silent listener.

To say that he was on the contrary an active and perhaps indefatigable collector is not, of course, to say that he was a successful one. It is clear that he was painstaking and within his limits competent. A final judgment on this score is not possible. It is easier to consider his conscientiousness. Many of his records have been reprinted from the original manuscripts or books, and some complaints have been made. In reprinting books or pamphlets, Hakluyt was accustomed to lop off prefaces and tedious introductions, the lack of which in his work frequently sends the modern investigator to the original. The editor's powers are, however, in this respect, discretionary. To a collector whose aim was essentially to print the records of Englishmen and others overseas, it was painful to present such rambling preliminaries as Sir George Peckham indulged in before getting down to his discourse on colonizing. Neither his reflections nor the panegyric verses were to Hakluyt's purpose.

For the modern scholar these irrelevancies may have ceased to be irrelevant. They may illuminate the motives and personality of the adventurers, they may even add precious and unsuspected information on the personnel of the ventures. But such information, concerning the home organization and not the oversea business itself, was not in Hakluyt's scope.

What Hakluyt did not do was to cut down the narrative itself.

Purchas, his successor, did and was praised for it by our eighteenth-century critic. The difference between the two men and their methods is here radical. Purchas, using in large part Hakluyt's own collections, was to write a history of travel and so to satisfy the amateur reader like our critic. Wherever possible he used the work of others, weaving it into his own frame. But Hakluyt was not writing a history. He was compiling archives of history and was obliged to print his documents complete. The conclusion is rather obvious, but for all that it should be expressed.

Some fault may be found with Hakluyt's accuracy as an editor, which is apart from his conscientiousness. He has been taken to task for altering the record of the first Cabot expedition to Newfoundland.[8] He has been accused by Professor Beazley, in our own time, of a general disrespects for his texts.[9] Professor Beazley reëdited many of them himself and should know. The Hakluyt Society editors of many more of Hakluyt's narratives have not been so critical; and, without going into more detail, one may admit that Hakluyt was uneven in his editing. If he was, it is safe to add merely that he was not better than his time.

At all events, the *Voyages* would still deserve the praise due an ample historical plan. The Tudor century was as much an age in which history was written as an age in which history was made. I am not thinking merely of the chronicles, though chronicle making expanded in the century to the elaborate proportions of a Stow or a Holinshed or a Camden. With the last, indeed, chronicling passes over into more than story and anecdote and becomes a political record. When I speak of the writing of history, I am thinking rather of the planned and organized record of which Polidore Virgil was the early spokesman and in the spirit of which were written such books as More's history of Richard III and Bacon's Henry VII.[10]

By comparison with these, perhaps, Hakluyt is not a historian in the full sense of the word, since he did not compact his materials into solid narrative. Yet his archivist method was even more valuable. He was not merely recording a different kind of history from that laid down by his contemporaries, avoiding the political and dynastic to focus on the commercial and the naval and the imperial; he was also preserving the fundamental sources of history, the original records. In the process he was rendering his work indispensable, as the work of few of his contemporaries is indispensable. Camden's *Annals* or Stow's *Chronicle* may be useful when they are not merely compilations at second or third hand; but the *Voyages* can only grow in importance and value as the importance and value of other historians diminishes

[8] Richard Biddle, *A Memoir of Sebastian Cabot*, Chapter 1 (Philadelphia 1831), answered by Charles Deane in 1 *Proceedings Massachusetts Historical Society*, XII 441 (1873).

[9] Introduction to *Voyages and Travels* (*An English Garner*) (1903).

[10] See the *Cambridge History of English Literature*, vol. III, Chapter 15: "Chroniclers and Antiquaries."

with every new discovery of Tudor documents and with every new rewriting of the Tudor record. It is hardly too much to say that Hakluyt's is the most important historical work of the century.

4

It is not so easy to estimate Hakluyt's value as a geographer. He was never to draw his observations together into a complete and systematic treatise, as did Pory, though he was often called on for the sum of his knowledge of a given region. His two outstanding papers of the sort are rather disappointing. The *Discourse on the Western Planting,* which tried to systematize the attractions of the new world of Virginia, is certainly not an example of either cautious inference or careful systematizing. The memoranda for the East India Company, which were likewise limited in geographical scope, were much more cautious but were hardly a satisfying piece of induction, as has been shown. As a man who laid down conclusions, who correlated his facts, he cannot be judged by any formal product to have been a successful scientist.

This statement made, one is free to admit the value of his collections as source material. "This proficience in navigation and discoveries," Bacon wrote in the *Advancement of Learning,* "may plant also an expectation of the further proficience and augmentation of all sciences."[11] The augmentation could come only after the piling up of innumerable facts; and Hakluyt certainly piled up the facts. Why he did not go on to organize them we are given no idea. In common with his time he perhaps thought geography merely an applied science and geographers merely engravers on the one hand or consultants on the other. Or it may be that he expected Pory to continue his work. At any rate, here was the heap of facts, and here was the empirical method used in assembling them.

In estimating the value of the *Voyages* as geography as I have already appraised them as history, I must consider mainly the method. Hakluyt's process was not in fact confined to merely printing accounts of voyages and then letting the accounts present their own unharvested information on geography. As he put in letters of instruction, patents, and other documents bearing on trade history, so he also put in documents bearing on geography, both descriptive and mathematical. One may mention various "tables of distances" which he found drawn up in the records: Russo-Persian distances, for example, supplemented by a list of "positions" of various towns on the itinerary; Brazilian distances; the *routier* of Cartier's pilot to Canada; and of course the extensive surveys of the West Indies. In economic geography one may cite the various trade memoranda of the elder Hakluyt as well as the numerous reports on foreign markets contained in the letters from

[11] *The Advancement of Learning,* Book II, A, II 14.

oversea agents. By way of complete treatises, moreover, while Hakluyt made none of his own, he was able to print many works of compilation: among them being treatises on Russia, on Asiatic Russia, on Iceland; on China, Japan, Corea, Pegu or Burma; on Newfoundland, Virginia, Brazil; besides much incidental information. Such treatises covered no small part of the earth's surface. Viewed as a whole, they could have enlightened any Englishman on almost any country where Englishmen or other western Europeans had yet been.

This statement means that, if we can hardly measure Hakluyt's merit as a geographer, we can at least praise him as an editor. The work he did was immense. In his own books and in the books which he brought to print in English he was editing a great geographical library. It was he who took hold of the casual and undirected labors of the translators and made himself responsible for a purposeful and directed plan of publishing. He brought chaos into order. He was a geographical society in his own person.

He did not look only to the recorded word; he looked for maps too and printed in his books the work of the first English cartographers. Again in this branch of the science he was not himself a creator; he was still the editor. If he drew no maps himself, he saw to it that the maps he used were the best.

English maps before his time had certainly not been good. The first since Columbus, that of Robert Thorne of Seville, was a mere sketch; but, as it was the first one, Hakluyt first published it in the *Divers Voyages*. There were early maps of foreigners that were good original works though left unpublished—those of Verrazano, of Jean Roze, of Sebastian Cabot, which reached England. In the Elizabethan period the maps now beginning to be drawn by Englishmen became again sketches—the one that accompanied Gilbert's *Discourse on the Passage,* the two that went into the book of Frobisher's voyages, and the navigator's maps that Borough made for Frobisher and Simon Fernandez made for Gilbert.[12]

Serious English cartography begins with the map of America drawn by Dr. Dee for the Queen in 1580. There was really no need for it, since the great atlas which Ortelius had just made up from the best maps attainable set a standard that a merely incidental geographer could hardly reach. At any rate, Dee's was the first respectable English map, and Hakluyt would have done better to print it in the *Divers Voyages*. Instead, and in order to present a particular theory about America and the inland sea, he trusted to the merchant Lok. His map, if not quite the wretched thing which Harrisse has called it, was taken from Verrazano's map of half a century before and was correspondingly antiquated.

[12] See J. G. Kohl, *Maps of America mentioned in Hakluyt* (Washington 1857); Justin Winsor, *The Kohl Collection of Maps Relating to America* (Washington 1904); and Henry Harrisse, *Découverte . . . de Terre-Neuve* (London and Paris 1900).

The Lok map was a mistake that Hakluyt never repeated. At all events the *Divers Voyages* is important cartographically. It printed the first modern English map of the world and was ambitious enough to print something like a respectable map of America, the first yet published in England. The Peter Martyr, which was the next book to have a map, went much farther though not to the glory of England. Hakluyt called upon a Spanish navigator for it, and the product compared favorably with the world map which he took from Ortelius for the first edition of the *Voyages*.

Hakluyt still had to rely on the maps of "strangers." Cartography was longer in getting a foothold in England than any other branch of the complex science of cosmography. I am aware, of course, that good maps were beginning to be made, if only of local interest. The attention to English history which had released a flood of chronicle writing had also released a respectable stream of writing on English geography: the *Itinerary* of Leland, Camden's *Britannia,* Stow's *Survey of London.* Together with the treatises went maps.

The first printed map of England was drawn by George Lilly, the schoolmaster's son, and published in Rome in 1546. A map of Britain by the Welsh antiquary Llwyd was included in Ortelius' atlas in 1573. The death in 1573 of Reyner Wolfe, which balked that enterprising printer's plan of a universal geography, at least brought to a head a briefer enterprise. A British cartographical survey was launched under court patronage; and from 1574 to 1579 the first of the professional English map makers, Saxton, drew and issued in an atlas a series of maps of the British Isles. In 1593 John Norden began a new series of county maps. In 1611 John Speed capped the climax of both enterprises with his *Theater of the Empire of Great Britain.*[13]

I cannot find that Hakluyt had any concern with these and other single works of chorography or local geography. I cite them merely to show that in England, as on the Continent, chorography was being taken up to parallel the growth of the larger division of the map-making art. Englishmen were learning to draw maps, as they were also slowly learning the art of engraving from imported Continental masters. And Hakluyt might have called on English cartographers, men with both knowledge and skill, to supply the maps for his earlier works.

I imagine that he would have done so, had he not been in France while he was planning and maturing them. Had he been in England, he might have taken a cartographer in hand and trained him. One was already in training during Hakluyt's Paris years, but he was not ready in time for the first *Voyages,* as Hakluyt declared in the preface. So

[13] See the anonymous article, *Elizabethan Cartographers,* in *The Antiquary,* VIII 213–215 (1883); Edward Heawood, *Some Early County Maps,* in *Geographical Journal,* 68, 325–337 (1926); A. W. Pollard, *The Unity of John Norden,* in 4 *Library,* VII 233–252 (1926); and Sidney Colvin, *Early Engraving and Engravers in England* (1906).

the Ortelius world map replaced there the expected new English one. It was of course the best map obtainable, if not up to date in detail.

The new English map was ready for the final *Voyages,* where it stood for as distinct an English achievement as the first English book on the new world or the first English lecture on the new geography. It was taken from a terrestrial globe of 1592, which is a sign of English independence in cartography. The globe, three years too late for the first *Voyages,* was made by Emeric Molineux of Lambeth, perhaps a man of Hakluyt's choosing, and at the expense of the merchant prince Sanderson, principal patron of the Davis northwest voyages and a director of Virginia with Hakluyt. It was Davis who gained the patronage of Sanderson for the globe project; and it is quite likely that Davis and Hakluyt collaborated with the cartographer.

The globe made, and engraved by Hondius the accomplished Dutch engraver and later the successor of Mercator in the supplying of maps, its reduction to a plane surface was a further task. Edward Wright, navigator and mathematician, seems to have had a hand in the reduction, since he was now reviving and explaining for the first time the projection invented by Mercator. Though it is not certain who actually drew the map that resulted, it is clear that it was the result of Molineux' globe, of Wright's projection, and of the possible advice in detail of Davis and Hakluyt.[14]

At any rate, it was Hakluyt who published in the *Voyages* the first large achievement in English map making, as it was Shakespeare who appropriately noted it, in *Twelfth Night,* as "the new map . . . of the Indies." Hallam has called it the best map of the sixteenth century; and, though his historian's statement has been seriously challenged, the map may pass for excellent. Excellence was to be expected from the collaborators; and Hakluyt's publication of their work is still another sign of his importance in organizing for English use the new English knowledge. He is again the excellent editor. Had he not published the map, it is doubtful if it would have been published at all. As it was, the map was stolen and published, though on another projection, by Hondius; and in its improved form it would probably not have appeared had there been no *Voyages* for it to accompany.

Again the *Voyages* stands out as the great English work of science of the Tudor century. It is a great work of history. It is the great source book of geography; and it includes the evidence of the ultimate English mastery of the science, which was due to Hakluyt more than to any other man.

[14]See the note by C. H. Coote, "The New Map of the Indies," in *Hakluyt Society Publications* 59 (1880). The challenge was made by the late Dr. Henry R. Wagner, who thought the map "by no means the best map of the sixteenth century and in fact [it] is not nearly as good as the globe" (private letter, 3 August 1936).

CHAPTER XV

The English Epic

It is at length time to speak of the *Voyages* as a work of literary distinction. So taken, the book may well seem at first recalcitrant to praise. Being a work of information, it starts with a manifest initial handicap. For, though it is true that a work of information may be melted and molded into form by a cunning mind, Hakluyt's work is not so molded. On the contrary, the very design asserts the handicap. The collection of more than one hundred long narratives is composed by nearly as many hands. Some of these hands were of exceeding skill, like Raleigh's and like Hakluyt's own in his translations. Some were crude and unfinished, like those of many of the sailors who copied their log books. The most were merely mediocre. Between the narratives are strewn multitudinous documents, some stately, some insipid. The whole is unrelated and unharmonized.

Such is the first appraisal. Of the individual parts of the immense series, more than one commentator has remarked the tediousness. More than one has equally observed the chaotic nature of the plan, a mere assembling of narratives in the order of time and of place, clearly devoid as a whole of the beginning, middle, and end which good narrative must possess.

The indictment is severe. To oppose it there stands out the simple phrase of Froude, who called the *Voyages* the prose epic of the modern English nation.[1] The phrase has been generally accepted as fitting the undenied impressiveness of the work. In what, it must then be asked, does the epic quality consist?

Broadly viewed, an epic must embody a theme of some consequence; it must fill its frame with events of moment; it must possess dignity. To the first of these tests *The Principal Navigations of the English Nation* answers by its title. Unmistakably there is a theme of consequence, a theme epic in scope could it be defined. The worthy Fuller aimed at a definition in a noble figure. "He set forth," wrote the biographer, "a large collection of the English sea voyages"; and "in a word many of such useful tracts of sea adventures, which were before scattered as several ships, Master Hackluit hath embodied into a Fleet, divided into three Squadrons, so many several volumes." [2]

The magnificent image strikes closer to the mark than many of the later commentators. Froude, for example, followed up his laudatory phrase by an account merely of the naval heroes. Of the comments

[1] J. A. Froude, "England's Forgotten Worthies," in *Westminster Review* (July 1852): reprinted in *Short Studies on Great Subjects*, I (London 1867).
[2] Thomas Fuller's *Worthies of England* (London 1662), under Hereford.

the least perfunctory is that of the Sir Walter Raleigh of our own day.[3] The theme of "the diffused and exciting tale," he decided, was the search for Cathay: its strands the search for gold, the missionary impulse, the scientific passion. There is much wisdom in this statement. To the adventurous splendor of the search for Cathay was paid the energetic devotion of Tudor merchants, mariners, and captains. The Russian and Persian enterprisers and the Levantine, the American explorers, traders, and even colonizers aimed in the first place at Cathay. Hakluyt himself made the study of Cathay and the way thither one guiding motive of his career. In so far as Tudor England looked forward, it looked forward mainly to Cathay.

But the theme is much foreshortened in this perspective, adroit though it is. Medieval England—and it has been seen that a tenth of the first *Voyages,* a sixth of the final *Voyages,* was medieval in subject—did not look to Cathay at all. The African voyagers of the sixteenth century certainly did not look beyond Barbary or Senegal even to the Cape, nor did they as a matter of fact lead on to the India voyages, which were prepared for rather by Levantine traders and by privateers like Drake and Cavendish. The American colonizers thought too much of Cathay for their own good, it is true; but they thought as much of America for its own sake. The naval adventurers thought little indeed of Cathay, preferring to pick up the Cathayan treasure by the process of piracy in the Atlantic rather than by long and costly voyages to Cathay itself.

The search for Cathay is hardly, inclusive though it is, inclusive enough. The motives given are still less adequate. The search for gold is not the same as the search for the many more treasures—the silks, the spices, the precious stones—that drove Englishmen overseas. The missionary motive was conspicuously absent from the recorded thoughts of most voyagers, as it was from their actions. The scientific passion was distinctly not an impelling motive to others than a few unusual seamen like the Boroughs, the Hawkinses, and John Davis. The canvas is still too large to be shrunk within this frame.

Our account of the *Voyages* will support such a conclusion without more insistence. The three Squadrons, it may be imagined, carried other orders than the command to Cathay. Rather they carried the sealed orders of fate, ignoring their destinations. Landing here, there, and everywhere over the remote globe, they found themselves anchoring in unexpected ports. The Cabots sailed for the East and found the West. Chancellor sailed for the East and found Russia. Frobisher and Davis sailed for the East by the Northwest and came thwarted home again. Alfred's missionary to the shrine of St. Thomas of India was followed seven centuries later by an English Jesuit and an English merchant; and only the last of the three returned. The story is singu-

[3] In *The English Voyages of the Sixteenth Century,* vol. 12 of the Hakluyt Society reprint of the *Voyages* (1905); also separately (Glasgow 1906).

larly complex in its conflict between intentions and achievements; but, failing or succeeding, the English voyager was its hero, and the English "search and discovery of the most unknown quarters of the world" was its theme.

The English nation embarking for the unknown, in fine, and it must be added in order to forbid the impression that the voyagers sought a will-o'-the-wisp as did the knights who sought the Grail, finding the unknown and making use of it. Chancellor did not stop on the unknown shore of Archangel but penetrated to Moscow for a license to trade, for a substantial gain; and Jenkinson pushed on to Bokhara for a like purpose. Exploration for a vain Northwest Passage discovered fishing grounds and laid a claim to a future New England. Slave trading in the West Indies paved the way of the privateer, whose hand, laid upon stolen but none the less tangible wealth, stretched to farther and farther distances. The search and discovery meant the dotting of the globe with the flag of the red cross of Saint George.

Thus seen, the epic story separates into the three stages already outlined. In the first stage England becomes a maritime power. Saxon and Norman travelers make their unexpected way to Madeira and Jerusalem, and even try for India. But they make no stay, establish no maritime habits, until the Bristol fishers dry their annual catch in Newfoundland and the Russia Company sets up its stations overseas. In the second stage England becomes a naval power. English sailors join battle in Atlantic and Mediterranean and Caribbean and even in Pacific to defend their explorers' rights. In the third and final stage England becomes a colonial power. The unknown East and West become known; England sets up its flag over its own stations and provinces in America and in India and becomes an empire.

This then is the epic theme, the search and discovery of the world leading to the radiation of English enterprise overseas. It is clear that, like the Iliad, the English epic is an unfinished story. The first *Voyages* substantially spanned the first stage of the theme, with some hints of the second in its account of the beginnings of the war with Spain and of the third in its record of Raleigh's Virginia. The final edition brought down the tale to the end of the second stage, the end of the naval war; but the third achievement was, like the capture of Troy in Homer's story, yet to be narrated. England was not yet established overseas, though Virginia had been attempted and the route of the Indiamen was planned. The story was still one of preparation to meet the unknown. It was to end when the unknown had become known; when England, knowing now its destination, had been prepared by the long course of experiment to reach it. Or perhaps it was not to end at all. Perhaps even the names of Franklin and Shackleton, of Livingstone and Bruce would not end the roll of the heroes of its story.

2

An epic tells a noble story of heroic characters (Fig. 28). If the story of the *Voyages* is England's quest of empire in the unknown, it follows that the heroes are legion. Explorer, captain, trader, settler —none stands on an eminence: for all meet the same enemies, which are the perils of nature and of the unknown. Enough praise has been given the fighting sea dogs—the heroes of the Armada and the heroes who singed the Spanish beard. They have their sufficient place, a Hawkins at bay at Vera Cruz, a Drake and an Oxenham swashbuckling in the Pacific, a Frobisher and a Grenville, as well as a Drake and a Hawkins, meeting valiantly a valiant end. But fully as important as these in the story are the explorers: Cabot and Chancellor, Jenkinson and Newbery, Frobisher, Davis, Cavendish, and many more, adventurers into the darkness. The traders and the settlers are heroes as well, dropped into the empty spaces of the globe to face, in nonchalance or despair or riotous merriment, the unknown dangers of fever and frost and privation and the incomprehensible alien.

Outstanding is the figure of Anthony Jenkinson, if only because, in the most coherent story of the collection, the story of the Russia Company, he appears as a permanent figure. He was more than a trader and peddler. He was more than an explorer who sought the way to Persia and Bokhara among unknown and dangerous tribes. He was more than a negotiator of treaties with the Czar and the "Sophy" of Persia and with numerous little princes along his route. As his own account shows, he was a symbol of the new England reaching overseas.

After his early voyages throughout the length and breadth of the Mediterranean, Jenkinson wrote, in his retirement: "I have sailed far Northward within the Mare glaciale, where we have had continual day and sight of the Sun ten weeks together, and that navigation was in Norway, Lapland, Samogitia, and other very strange places.

"I have traveled through all the ample dominions of the Emperor of Russia and Muscovia, which extend from the North Sea and the confines of Norway and Lapland even to the Mare Caspium.

"I have been in divers countries near about the Caspian Sea, Gentiles and Mahometans, as Cazan, Cremia, Rezan, Cheremisi, Mordoviti, Vachin, Nagaia, with divers others of strange customs and religions.

"I have sailed over the Caspian Sea, and discovered all the regions thereabout adjacent, as Chircassi, Comul, Shascal, Shirvan, with many others.

"I have traveled 40 days journey beyond the said sea, towards the Oriental India and Cathaia, through divers deserts and wildernesses, and passed through five kingdoms of the Tartars, and all the land of

FIG. 28—Sir Hugh Willoughby. The portrait at Wollaton Hall, from the plate in Richard Hakluyt's *Voyages*, Glasgow edition, vol. II, frontispiece. By courtesy of Lord Middleton.

Turkeman and Zagatay, and so to the great city of Boghar in Bactria, not without great perils and dangers sundry times.

"After all this, in An. 1562, I passed again over the Caspian Sea another way and landed in Armenia, at a city called Derbent, built by Alexander the Great, and from thence traveled through Media, Parthia, Hircania, into Persia to the court of the great Sophie called Shaw Tomasso, unto whom I delivered letters from the Queen's majesty, and remained in his court eight months, and returning homeward passed through divers other countries. Finally I made two voyages more after that out of England into Russia, the one in the year 1566 and the other in the year 1571. And thus being weary and growing old, I am content to take my rest in mine own house, chiefly comforting myself in that my service hath been honorably accepted and rewarded of her Majesty and the rest by whom I have been employed." [4]

Jenkinson left an honorable name, it was reported, in far countries, and either he had good fortune in his enterprises or he was nobly reticent about his hardships. Other men who followed him were not so reticent or so fortunate. "I have sown the seed," wrote one disgruntled factor from Persia, "and other men have gathered the harvest: I have travailed both by land and water many a time with a sorrowful heart, as well for the safeguard of their goods as yours, how to frame all things to the best, and they have reaped the fruits of my travail. But ever my prayer was to God, to deliver me out of those miseries which I suffered for your service among the heathen people."

And among compatriots as well: for "your worships must send such men as are no riotous livers nor drunkards. For if such men go, it will be to your dishonor and great hindrance, as appeared by experience the year 1565 when as Richard Johnson went to Persia, whose journey had been better stayed than set forward. For whereas before we had the name among those heathen people to be such merchants as they thought none like in all respects, his vicious living there hath made us to be counted worse than the Russians.

"Again, if such men travail in your affairs in such a voyage, you shall never know what gain is to be gotten. For how can such men employ themselves to seek the trade, that are inclined to such vices? or how can God prosper them in your affairs? But when a trade is established by wise and discreet men, then will it be for your worships to traffic there, and not before: for a voyage or market made evil at the first is the occasion that your worships shall never understand what gain is to be gotten thereby hereafter." [5]

Even the lesser deeds of lesser men are thus momentous. Again I pass over the major heroes—Frobisher and Davis, Willoughby and Pet, battling through ice to the Passages; Drake and Cavendish buffeted

[4] *Voyages*, III 196.
[5] III 43.

through Magellan's Straits. "Winds we have at will," ran the restrained account of Pet's voyage to the northeast in 1580, "but ice and fog too much against our wills, if it had pleased the Lord God otherwise." Bravery in the face of the elements needs no further insisting.

Or again I take Caesar Frederick of Venice, whose matter-of-factness is as English, in his exploring of India, as the manner of any Englishman in the collection. He is in the East Indies when he records that "we departed from thence with intention to go to an island to take in water, but the winds were so contrary that they would not suffer us to fetch it, so that by this means we were two and forty days in the sea as it were lost, and we were driven to and fro, so that the first land that we discovered was beyond Saint Tome, more than five hundred miles, which were the mountains of Zerzerline, near unto the kingdom of Orisa. And so we came to Orisa with many sick and more that were dead for want of water: and they that were sick in four days died; and I for the space of a year after had my throat so sore and hoarse that I could never satisfy my thirst in drinking of water: I judge the reason of my hoarseness to be with sops that I wet in vinegar and oil, wherewith I sustained myself many days. There was not any want of bread nor of wine; but the wines of the country are so hot that being drunk without water they will kill a man: neither are they able to drink them: when we began to want water, I saw certain Moors that were officers in the ship, that sold a small dish full for a ducat, after this I saw one that would have given a bar of pepper, which is two quintals and a half, for a little measure of water, and he could not have it. Truly I believe that I had died with my slave, whom then I had to serve me, which cost me very dear: but to provide for the danger at hand, I sold my slave for half that he was worth, because that I would save his drink that he drunk to serve my own purpose, and to save my life." [6]

There were dangers enough in settled countries. The fifth "voyage" to Persia was particularly beset. As the fifteen Englishmen sailed down the Volga in the summer of 1568, "it fell out in the way, before they came to Astracan by forty miles, that the Nagaian Tartars, being a kind of thievish and cruel people, made an assault upon them with 18 boats of theirs, each of them being armed, some with swords, some with spears, and some others with bows and arrows, and the whole number of them they discovered to be about 300 men. They for their parts, although they could have wished a quiet voyage and journey without blows and violence, yet not willing to be spoiled with such Barbarians as they were, began to defend themselves against their assault, by means whereof a very terrible and fierce fight followed and continued hot and sharp for two hours, wherein our men so well

[6] V 408–409.

played their parts with the calivers that they forced the Tartars to flee with the loss of 120 of them, as they were afterwards informed by a Russe prisoner, which escaped from the Nagaians, and came to them to Astracan, at which town they arrived the 20 of August.

"In this town of Astracan they were somewhat hindered of their journey" by nothing less than a six weeks' siege of the town by 70,000 Turks. The siege being raised, the Englishmen went on farther in their ill-starred journey: when, at Shavaran "(as they lodged in their tents) they were greatly molested with strange troops of sholcaves or foxes, which were so busy with them that they took their meat and victuals out of their lodgings, and devoured to the bare bones in one night a mighty wild Boar that was sent unto them for a present from the governor of the country. . . ."

At the holy town of Ardouil, where they arrived after wintering by the way, "they sojourned the space of 5 or 6 months, finding some traffic and sales, but to no purpose, the town being more inhabited and frequented with gentlemen and noblemen than merchants.

"The difference of religion bred great broils in this town whiles they remained there: for the brother sought the destruction of the brother, and the nearest kinsmen rose up one against another, insomuch that one of their company Lionel Plumtree hath seen in one day sometimes 14 slain in a garboil. And he being further desirous to see their manner of fight, or rather somewhat more curious to behold than mistrustful of their blows, was like to have borne a share in their bloody tragedy, being twice wounded with their shot and arrows, although not to the death."

After several years of marketing in various Persian towns, with attendant official difficulties, illnesses, and also profits, the English convoy had still to return across the Caspian Sea and up the Volga. "By reason of the variety of the winds and dangerous flats of the Caspian Sea, they beat it up and down some 20 days. And the 28 day riding at anchor upon the flats, certain Russe Cossacks, which are outlaws or banished men, having intelligence of their being there, and of the great wealth that they had with them, came to them with divers boats under the color of friendship and entered their ship, but immediately they took their hatchets and slew divers of the Russes that were of the ship upon the hatches: whereupon master Ducket, Lionel Plumtree, William Smith the master, a man of singular valor, and Amos Riall, being under the Spar-deck, did so well behave themselves that they scoured the hatches and slew 14 of the Cossack gunners and hurt and wounded about 30 more, being of them all in number 150 at the least, armed with calivers and other weapons fit for so villainous a purpose.

"M. Ducket notwithstanding and the rest aforesaid received divers wounds from the enemy, and were so hurt, and withal so oppressed with the multitude and force of them, that they were at last constrained to make an agreement with the Cossacks by rendering the ship into their hands, having received first their oaths sworn by their crucifixes not to do any further harm to their persons.

"Thus the ship being taken, and all the English grievously hurt, the Cossacks immediately discharged the ship of them, putting them all into the ship boat with two or three Persian targets full of horse flesh and swines flesh, without further victuals or relief: they being in that case, made the best haste they could to get to Astracan: and being come to the town, master Ducket made great suit to the captain to have men and boats set out for the rescuing and recovering of the ship if it were possible: who immediately sent out his son with forty boats and five hundred men to pursue the Pirates, and by good hap came to the place where they rid at anchor with the ship, but by reason of their foolishness in striking up the drums before they were come near them, the Cossacks discovering the boats cut their cables and put out to sea, whereupon the boats not being able to follow them returned again to Astracan. After which 60 boats more were sent out to pursue them again the second time: and that second army came to a place where they found many of those Cossacks and slew them, and found out the places where they had hid certain parcels of their goods in the earth in the chests of the ship: all which they recovered again for the English merchants, to the value of £5000 of 30 or 40 thousand pounds, but all the rest the Cossacks in the ship had carried away. . . .

"But our men being thus spoiled of their goods and wounded in their bodies, remained about two months at Astracan for their better recovery: and having gotten some reasonable strength, they then provided boats and went up the river of Volga to Cazan with such goods as they had recovered from the Cossacks. From Cazan they went towards Yeraslave, but in the way the ice intercepted them about the beginning of October, where suddenly in the night they were taken with a cruel and vehement frost, and therewithal the waters so congealed that their boats were crushed and cut in sunder with the ice, whereby they sustained both a further danger of life and loss of goods: but as much as they could preserve with much ado they conveyed over land in sleds to Vologda, and from thence sent much of it to Saint Nicholas to be laden in the ships for England.

"But Master Ducket, Lionel Plumtree and Amos Riall went with some parcels to Moscow, and there sold certain quantities of it to the Emperor, who pitying the mighty loss that they had sustained by his own rebellious people and subjects, bought himself as much as he liked and paid present money for the same. So that winter being spent out in Moscow, and such wares provided by them as served for England, they departed to Saint Nicholas, and there embarked in the month of August: and having endured a very terrible passage in nine weeks and three days [around the North Cape], with some hardness of victuals, contrary and furious winds, and other sea accidents, they arrived at London in the month of October, 1574, and so made an end of an unfortunate voyage: which if it had pleased God to prosper, that all things had come home as safely as they were carefully provided and painfully labored for, it had proved the richest voyage and most profitable return of commodity that had ever been undertaken by English merchants, who, notwithstanding all misfortunes, lost nothing of their principal adventure, but only the interest and gain that might have risen by the use of their stock in the mean time." [7]

From these Odyssean and not too unprofitable adventures one may turn to the tragic story unrolled before Cavendish at the Strait of Magellan and related with the unbelievable matter-of-factness that makes the dignity of the collection.

"The ninth day we departed from Penguin Island and ran south-southwest to King Philip's city which the Spaniards had built. . . . These Spaniards which were there were only come to fortify the Straits, to the end that no other nation should have passage through into the South Sea saving only their own: but, as it appeared, it was not God's will so to have it. For during the time that they were there, which was two years at the least, they could never have anything to grow or in any wise prosper. And on the other side the Indians oftentimes preyed upon them, until their victuals grew so short (their store being spent which they had brought with them out of Spain, and having no means to renew the same) that they died like dogs in their houses and in their clothes, wherein we found them still at our coming, until that in the end the town being wonderfully tainted with the smell and the savor of the dead people, the rest which remained were driven to bury such things as they had there in their town either for provision or for furniture, and so to forsake the town and to go along the seaside and seek their victuals to preserve them from starving, taking nothing with them but every man his arquebus and his furniture that was able to carry it (for some were not able to carry them for weakness) and so lived for the space of a year and more with roots, leaves, and sometimes a fowl which they might kill with their piece. To conclude, they were determined to have traveled towards the river of Plate, only being left alive 23 persons, whereof two were women, which were the remainder of four hundred.

"In this place we watered and wooded well and quietly. Our General named this town Port Famine; it standeth in 53 degrees by observation to the southward." [8]

Rarely, it may be said further, does a narrative, however plainly told, fall into the danger of the plainly told, the danger of dullness. It begins abruptly, as a rule, and without flourish. "The 14 of November 1582 we departed from Blackwall bound for the City of Con-

[7] III 150 ff.
[8] XI 298–299.

stantinople in the tall Ship called the Susan of London: the Master whereof was Richard Parsons, a very excellent and skillful man in his faculty. But by occasion of contrary weather we spent two months before we could recover the Cowes in the Isle of Wight. Where the 14 of January following we took in the worshipful Master William Harborne, her Majesty's Ambassador to the Turk, and his company, and sailed thence to Yarmouth in the foresaid Isle of Wight. The 19 we put from Wight. The 26 we did see Cavo de San Vicente. The same day we were thwart of Cavo Santa Maria. The 27 we passed by Tariffa and Gibraltar."

And so on in orderly log fashion and with just the flavor of names and dates exhaled by a log. Abruptly something more serious happened. "The first of February we put into a port in Mallorca called Porto de Sant Pedro: where they would have evil entreated us for coming into the Harbor: we thought we might have been as bold there as in other places of Christendom, but it proved far otherwise." Thence with resolute naïveté is told the suspicious maneuvering of the Majorcans. A portion of the crew was seized when they went ashore, there was much official protesting, and finally it was discovered at dawn that guns had been set to block the exit from the harbor.

"Now I think the harbor not to be above the eighth part of a mile over. Thus perceiving their meaning which was most plain: we agreed to take up our anchor and go out, and leave our men there, having none other way to take. . . . Then we weighed our anchors: but having little wind we towed the ship forward with the boat. The Viceroy himself was at the water side with more than five hundred men on both sides of the harbor as we thought. And when we came out with our ship as far as their ordnance, our Ambassador and the Captain being in their armor, the Master commanding of the company and trimming of the sails, the Pilot standing on the poop attending to his charge, with other very well furnished, and every man in order about their business very ready, they on land on the contrary part having a very fair piece mounted on the North side openly in all our sights, as the ship passed by, they traversed that piece right with the mainmast or after quarter of the ship, and a gunner standing by with a lintstock in his hand, about fourteen or fifteen foot long, being (as we thought) ready to give fire. Our whole noise of trumpets were sounding on the poop with drum and flute, and a Minion of brass on the summer deck with two or three other pieces, always by our gunners traversed mouth to mouth with theirs on land, still looking when they on land should shoot, for to answer them again. The Pilot standing on the poop, seeing this readiness, and the ship going very softly because of the calmness of the wind, he called to them on the South side, where the Viceroy was, and said unto him: Have you wars with us? If you have, it is more than we know; but by your provision it seemeth so: if you have, shoot in God's name and spare not, but they held all fast and shot not. Then the Viceroy himself held up a paper, and said he had a letter for our Captain, and desired us to stay for it. Then we answered and said we would not, but willed him to send it by the Marseillian's boat, and our men also. All this while, our trumpets, drum, and flute sounded, and so we passed out in the face of them all." And the Viceroy gave in, there was an interchange of courtesies and apologies, and "we shot off half a dozen pieces, hoisted our sails, and departed on our voyages." [9]

3

These are samples of the heroic deeds of heroic characters. The heroes of the epic are worthy of their actions, the actions are worthy of the heroes. But the epic is not, like the Iliad, mainly warlike. The struggle of the heroes is not with the malevolence of the gods nor generally of man. There is no such feeble invention of evil in the shape of gods as Camoens devised for his pseudo-epic of Vasco da Gama. The struggle is with reality, with the crushing power of the unknown.

It follows that the epic story is infused by its very nature with the mysterious and the remote. The wonder of the world strikes perpetually across the matter-of-fact pages, the more powerfully because the pages are matter-of-fact. The journey of the English mission to India is replete with such gleams of wonder as follows: "Jamba is an Island among the Javas also, from whence come diamonds. And the king hath a mass of earth which is gold: it groweth in the middle of a river: and when the king doth lack gold, they cut part of the earth and melt it, whereof cometh gold. This mass of earth doth appear but once in a year; which is when the water is low; and this is in the month of April." [10]

Or suddenly, in the midst of a commonplace log, appears this naïve note: "the 4 we were thwart of an Island called Sapientia. There standeth a fair Town and a Castle on the main over against it, called Modon. The same day by reason of contrary winds we put back again to Prodeno, because we could not fetch Sapientia. The ninth we came from thence, and were as far as Sapientia again. The tenth we were as far shot as Cavo Matapan; and that day we entered the Archipelago, and passed through between Cerigo and Cavo Malio. This Cerigo is an Island where one Menelaus did sometimes reign, from whom was stolen by Paris fair Helena, and carried to Troy, as ancient Records do declare." [11]

The drama of exotic customs is frequently played before the armchair of the quiet reader, as another view of the mysterious in human

[9] V 243–249.
[10] V 499.
[11] V 250.

form. This from Burma evokes a pageant: "Within the first gate of the king's house is a great large room, on both sides whereof are houses made for the king's elephants, which be marvelous great and fair, and are brought up to wars and in service of the king. And among the rest he hath four white elephants, which are very strange and rare: for there is none other king which hath them but he: if any other king hath one, he will send unto him for it. When any of these white elephants is brought to the king, all the merchants in the city are commanded to see them, and to give him a present of half a ducat, which doth come to a great sum: for that there are many merchants in the city. After that you have given your present, you may come and see them at your pleasure, although they stand in the king's house. This king in his title is called the king of the white elephants. If any other king have one and will not send it him, he will make war with him for it: for he had rather lose a great part of his kingdom than not to conquer him. They do very great service unto these white elephants; every one of them standeth in an house gilded with gold, and they do feed in vessels of silver and gilt. One of them when he doth go to the river to be washed, as every day they do, goeth under a canopy of cloth of gold or of silk carried over him by six or eight men, and eight or ten men go before him playing on drums, shawms, or other instruments; and when he is washed and cometh out of the river, there is a gentleman which doth wash his feet in a silver basin: which is his office given him by the king. There is no such account made of any black elephant, be he never so great. And surely there be wonderful fair and great, and some be nine cubits in height. And they do report that the king hath above five thousand elephants of war, besides many other which be not taught to fight." [12]

Sacramental customs are also illustrated in a profusion which must have dazzled an age without newspapers to feed it with mysteries. In India, "when they be married, the man and the woman come to the water side, and there is an old man which they call a Bramane, that is a priest, a cow, and a calf, or a cow with calf. Then the man and the woman, cow and calf, and the old man go into the water together, and they give the old man a white cloth of four yards long, and a basket cross bound with divers things in it: the cloth he layeth upon the back of the cow, and then he taketh the cow by the end of the tail and saith certain words: and she hath a copper or a brass pot full of water, and the man doth hold his hand by the old man's hand, and the wife's hand by her husband's, and all have the cow by the tail, and they pour water out of the pot upon the cow's tail, and it runneth through all their hands, and they lade up water with their hands, and then the old man doth tie him and her together by their clothes. Which done, they go round about the cow and calf, and then they give somewhat to the poor which be always there, and to the Bramane or priest they give the cow

[12] V 487.

and calf, and afterward go to divers of their idols and offer money, and lie down flat upon the ground and kiss it divers times, and then go their way." [13] On the margin of this passage Hakluyt noted: "This tying of new-married folks together by the clothes was used by the Mexicans in old time": thus linking the humorous mystery of the East with its counterpart in the West.

Not merely is there record of curious observation. There is curious story for its own sake, which is improved by its remote scene. "They say," wrote the unnamed European who made the pilgrimage to Mecca in 1580, "that when Soldan Guari of Egypt reigned, there was done this miracle following: this good patriarch [of the Greek Church] being envied at by the Jews of the country for none other cause but for his good works, and holy life, it happened (I say) that being in disputation with certain of the Hebrews in presence of the Sultan, and reasoning of their law and faith, it was said unto him by one of these Miscreants: sith thou believest in the faith of Christ, take and drink this potion which I will give thee: and if thy Christ be true Messias and true God, he will (said he) deliver thee from danger. To whom the ancient patriarch answered that he was content: whereupon that cursed Jew brought him a cup of the most venomous and deadly poison that could be found, which the holy Patriarch having perceived, said: In the name of the father, of the son, and of the holy Ghost: and having so said he drank it quite up; which done, he took a drop of pure water, putting it into that very cup, and gave it unto the Jew, saying unto him, I in the name of my Christ have drunk thy poison, and therefore in the name of thy expected Messias, drink this water of mine within thine own cup. Whereupon the Jew took the cup out of the hand of the Patriarch, and having drunk the water, within half an hour burst asunder. And the Patriarch had none other hurt, save that he became somewhat pale in sight, and so remained ever after." Even to the day of the credulous Christian: for "this triumphant Patriarch not long since was alive, and in perfect health, which God continue long time." [14]

Above all else in romantic interest are probably the accounts of the pageantry of exotic peoples: the reception of Drake by the California Indians, the honoring of the first English ambassador to Turkey, and especially the frequent ritual of the reception of English emissaries in Moscow, ritual which speedily merged into the drama of diplomatic intrigue. The romantic note sounds indeed throughout the whole epic. The romance of action runs through even the most pedestrian account of perils and profits, to reach its height in the naval exploits against Spain and in the exploring of the frozen north. The romance of wonder at the marvels of man and of nature illumines the whole fabric of the work which portrays the epic enterprise of England.

[13] V 479–480.
[14] V 339–340.

CHAPTER XVI

The Achievement of Empire

1600–1616

The story of Hakluyt's life reaches its climax with the close of the Tudor century. Nearly fifty years of age, he is a man of achievement, recognized by men of action and by men of learning like van Meteren and Gabriel Harvey.[1] He has felt all along that his achievement has not been sufficiently rewarded. We have seen that his struggle for position and prestige was not really a difficult one, as it was for so many men of letters or of science in his time. But he felt slighted, especially because his most important work, the *English Voyages,* had brought him, on its first appearance, no more than a country living. With his two positions, as canon of Bristol and as parson of Wetheringsett, he was forced to be content throughout all his activities of the nineties.

Yet Hakluyt was comfortably off. He had married at some time before 1595. His first wife died in 1597, and he married again in 1604. He had but one child that we knew of, Edmond, born about 1595. To support his small family he could count on his two church positions and in addition the property which he owned in Hereford and perhaps in London. He had probably fallen heir, on the death of his eldest brother before 1591, to his father's estate, whatever that may have been; and he had benefited by the death of his youngest brother Edmond in 1593. He was not a beneficiary of his cousin Richard the lawyer, who left the bulk of his free property to the fourth brother Oliver the doctor; but between them the two surviving brothers Oliver and Richard seem to have shared the property of the two families, that of the older Richard the lawyer, heir to his father the official, and that of their own father the merchant. I do not imply that the property was large, since there were many Hakluyts in Hereford. But Edmond's will of 1591 disposes of a substantial amount for a youngest son of a younger son; and Richard the clergyman, to whom he left it, managed to acquire by 1612 a house of some size in Hereford, yielding annually some forty pounds a year in modern values, besides the Suffolk manor and the houses in Westminster which he then purchased.[2]

As I do not find any access of wealth in the year 1612 to account for these purchases which Richard mentioned in his will, I suppose

[1] Harvey mentions Hakluyt as promising and as a superior mind in his *Marginalia* (G. C. Moore Smith edit., Stratford on Avon 1913, p. 122 and 233). He speaks of the "importance" of the *Voyages* in *Pierces Supererogation*, A. B. Grosart edit., II 96 (London 1884).

[2] See the beginning of Appendix II for Hakluyt's immediate family.

that he was then for some reason arranging his affairs. He had by that time acquired several sources of income in addition to the living and the Bristol prebend. He had received from time to time such professional fees as those paid him by the East India Company and the Dutch northeastern adventurers. His investment of two shares in the Virginia Company may well have meant a similar fee paid in kind. The living of Gedney in Lincolnshire to which he was presented in 1612 came to him from his brother Oliver the doctor, who had obtained the reversion as far back as 1604; the arrangement between the two brothers probably represented some kind of *quid pro quo.* Most important in the increase of Hakluyt's estate was, however, the patronage of Sir Robert Cecil, first Earl of Salisbury and successor to his father Burleigh as the most influential man in England.

This patronage, Hakluyt wrote, was the first he had received to any purpose. It was noted first in the dedication to Cecil of the 1599 volume of the *Voyages* and was then carried over into the dedication of his next book as well as of Pory's *Africa.* Cecil had indeed been active in his favor. As he succeeded to Walsingham's place as Secretary of State, the second son of Lord Burleigh also took Walsingham's place as Hakluyt's patron.

He first came into known contact with the geographer during the controversy over Raleigh's El Dorado, and he may have begun to smile on him at that time. As early as November of 1599 he bespoke for Hakluyt a post in the Savoy Chapel; and, when that post was not immediately achieved, I fancy it was he who carried the geographer's plight up to the highest authority.[3]

In May of 1600, before the last volume of the *Voyages* had been printed, the Privy Council itself was stirred to action. This exceptional mark of favor is recorded in a letter from the Council to the Archbishop of Canterbury, written in the highly commendatory terms that follow.

18 May. "We are moved to recommend unto your Lordship's good favor Mr. Hackluyt, a learned preacher, that hath not only taken great pains in his calling and served a long time Sir Edward Stafford Knight, being then her Majesty's Ambassador in France in a very dangerous time, but hath bestowed his time and taken great pains in matter of navigation and discoveries, a labor of great desert and use, wherein there may be often occasion to employ him, and therefore our desire is for the good of her Majesty's service that he might be provided of some competent living to reside in these parts. And because we are given to understand that the benefice of Great Allhallows in Thames Street is like to be void, being in your lordship's gift, we do earnestly pray your good Lordship that at our mediation you will be pleased to bestow the same, if by the decease of the incumbent it shall be void, on this learned and painful minister."

The incumbent of Great Allhallows did not, however, die or retire

[3] See the chronology in Appendix II.

as he was expected to. The patrons of the learned and painful minister therefore tried other strings to their bow. With the aid of the Lord Admiral, to whom the first volume of the *Voyages* had just been dedicated, Cecil suggested Hakluyt for the next vacant stall in Westminster Abbey. The Queen refused to do what she had done before for Hakluyt. She would not, she said in her violent way, grant any more prebends in Westminster until there was an actual vacancy. It is likely that the grant of reversions had been overdone, as an easy way for officials to discharge debts by a nearly empty promise.

But the Queen came round. At the end of August 1600 Hakluyt was granted the reversion of a prebend in Westminster, and five days later he dedicated the last of the *Voyages* to Cecil. He had to wait only two years for a vacancy, instead of the seven and seven which he may again have expected, and he was installed in May, 1602.

Still Cecil was not satisfied. I have said that he promised Hakluyt a chaplaincy in the Savoy, which was in his family gift. In 1601 Hakluyt signed himself Cecil's chaplain, a relationship which stands, I fancy, for an interim appointment until the Savoy place should fall in. By 1604 he wrote himself chaplain of the Savoy.

Thus Hakluyt was substantially provided for, after he had turned fifty, and much more substantially than was, for example, John Dee. The preacher was in his last years canon of St. Augustine's Cathedral at Bristol, canon of Westminster Abbey, chaplain of the Savoy, and parson of Wetheringsett in Suffolk and of Gedney in Lincolnshire. He had lodgings at Bristol and in the Savoy and in Westminster. He owned houses in Westminster and the manor of Bridge Place in Suffolk and property in Hereford in addition. For his achievements he had certainly been well rewarded.

The care of his numerous places and properties may well have absorbed his energies in his later years. Not all of the places could have been sinecures. According to a survey made for the Archbishop in 1603 Hakluyt had no curate at Wetheringsett, where he had two hundred communicants. The Westminster chapter called especially for his earnest endeavor. He was for one year, 1603–1604, Archdeacon, a position of certain activity and extra pay. He may have expected to become Dean in 1605; but another of Salisbury's chaplains, described as a man of small note, was instead presented.[4] In 1607–1608 he was steward of the chapter. In 1614–1615 he was treasurer. In two of the years of his incumbency he also received payment for the boarding of scholars.

His clerical duties could not in all have been of the lightest. They may have been enough to interfere with any plans Hakluyt may have made for a still larger geographical work, whether descriptive or even

[4] "The Deanery of Westminster goes to one Dr. Neal, a man of no great note, more than that he is the Earl of Salisbury's chaplain."—Chamberlain to Winwood, 12 October 1605, in *Memorials of Affairs of State*, II 141.

more widely historical. They were not enough to prevent his carrying on as before his major interest, promoting and publishing and keeping up with new geographical records.

2

I hasten to say that Hakluyt by no means retired, at the end of his *Voyages,* to the cloisters. He continued until the end of his life to collect documents of travel and of trade. He remained as alert as ever to the appearance of new works of geography and oversea history, and kept on translating. He reached the climax, before his death in 1616, of his active part in enterprise.

First, and most significantly for his own story, he attained for a moment, after a concern for Virginia which stretched back nearly a quarter of a century, to a high place in the colony. As one of the 1589 directorate he may have continued to agitate throughout the nineties; but we have seen how little was then accomplished. Now the time had come. As the Spanish war drew to its lingering close in 1604, the American prospect emerged from eclipse to focus the attention released from war and privateering.

From the year 1602 a new series of voyages was sent out to the long-abandoned shores. Merchants of the west ports joined with noblemen like the Earl of Southampton and Lord Arundel and with officials like the Lord Chief Justice to rebuild an American trade. Three voyages were made in 1602, two in 1603, and one in 1605. In the last year, trading contracts for more voyages were merged in a plan of settlement from which developed, in 1606, the Virginia Company.[5]

Of these six voyages of preliminary trade and reconnoitering, Hakluyt had a known share in one. The record runs a curious parallel to his first adventure in promoting, which in 1583 had procured a Bristol colonial subscription. Now, twenty years later, "upon many probable and reasonable inducements used unto sundry of the chiefest merchants of Bristol by Master Richard Hakluyt Prebendary of St. Augustines the Cathedral Church of the said City, after divers meetings and due consultations, they resolved to set forth a Voyage for the farther Discovering of the North part of Virginia."

So begins the narrative of the voyage of Martin Pring; and thereupon, the story continues, Hakluyt was commissioned to procure from Raleigh, still the titular patentee, a formal license. With these details the parallel ceases. Whom Hakluyt was representing on this occasion, as he previously represented Walsingham and Carleill, is not made clear. It was probably some one of the many interests that presently coalesced in the Virginia Company. What further share he had in the

[5] The narratives which Hakluyt collected and Purchas published are the authorities here; and Alexander Brown, *The Genesis of the United States* (Boston 1890, 2 vols.), has noted them in his collection of Virginia documents.

enterprise is also obscure. He may have taken a hand in its organizing. He may have invested in it, for he was now comfortably settled in the lap of the church. He may have suggested the special exploring plan of the journey along the New England coast, to settle the question of colonial site, of local commodities, of coast survey. None of these possibilities is vouched for by the record. Only surmise can fill in the picture, whose high light is a meeting of Bristol merchants and fishermen presided over by a persuasive priest.

This is the only record of Hakluyt's activities in the period preceding the company charter. The whole early history of the Virginia Company is obscure. An occasional document, a few voyages, a casual reminiscence, colored by time and partisanship, of many years later, are all that the painstaking historian has been able to line up in tracing the genesis of the project. The reminiscences of the partisans of John Smith stress the credit due to the enterprisers or oversea leaders and so give no hint of such an interest as Hakluyt's. The records of the preliminary voyages contain only what has been mentioned. The documents, in the form of contracts and patents, discover only the achievement, not the preparation; while the memoranda of the organizers can in no case be traced to Hakluyt's writing.[6]

Out of a virtually clear sky Hakluyt then descends to a place in the first Virginia charter. The apparition is little short of amazing. To represent the Plymouth group the charter names four soldiers; to represent the London group, three soldiers and "Richard Hackluit clerk." The amazement persists as one identifies the soldiers and discovers that they are complete strangers to our record. With none of them is Hakluyt known to be connected. With only one of them can a relation be easily inferred. Yet he had apparently joined with the seven soldiers in the petition that led to the patent of 1606.

The one was Raleigh Gilbert, son of Sir Humphrey and nephew of Raleigh; but Raleigh Gilbert has not yet appeared in Hakluyt's history. Others Hakluyt might have known when he was publishing their naval exploits overseas. But all of them were new to colonial enterprise, however famed they were as privateers, and the inclusion of Hakluyt in their company remains a mystery.

The mystery is deepened by the fact that these soldiers were not the real organizers of the scheme. Who these were is not accurately known. The records of the first ten years of the Virginia Company are lost; so also are the Acts of the Privy Council at the time. The principal suspect is the Lord Chief Justice, Sir John Popham, whose nephew and grandson represented the Plymouth group; but there is no link between him and Hakluyt except the dubious one of his member-

[6] The most important early paper, called "Reasons for Raising a Fund" (Brown, I 36–42), can be ruled out at once because of the following sample phrase: "Private purses are cold comforts to adventurers" (p. 37). The alliterative balance is not to be found in Hakluyt, and the general conciseness is certainly not his. The later paper, "The limits of the Spanish Possessions," is State Papers Colonial I 32, printed by Brown, II 669; *vide infra.*

FIG. 29—Empire builders. From Henry Holland, *Herωologia anglica*, 1620.

ship in the Middle Temple, which might reach through the elder Hakluyt to the younger. The Earl of Southampton, who had financed two trial voyages, is also in question; but he was rather Hariot's patron than Hakluyt's.

John Smith's later account of the organizing is too simple to satisfy. "Gosnold," he wrote in his *General History,* referring to the leader of an early voyage, "one of the first movers of this plantation, having many years solicited many of his friends, . . . at last prevailed with some gentlemen, as Wingfield, Smith, Hunt, . . . thence after a year Nobility, Gentry, and Merchants." For Smith the soldier the scheme was organized only by soldiers.

In the view of another soldier, Sir Ferdinando Gorges of Plymouth, the soldiers were also responsible. For with the peace the "men of War by sea and land were left destitute of all hope of employment." The explanation is again too simple. Idle soldiers might prevail upon the Chief Justice to press a colonial plan at court. It was quite another task to prevail upon the merchants who underwrote the voyages. So one assumes that the merchants also moved. One assumes that the soldiers and officials were joined in the course of the promoting by the west-country and London merchants who were later named on the royal council for Virginia and were therefore the real directors of the colony (Fig. 29). Among these merchants was Sir Thomas Smith of the East India Company, later treasurer of Virginia; and, although Smith was in Russia when the patent was granted, his associates doubtless swept Hakluyt into the movement.

At any rate, Hakluyt did appear in the patent, although he was not named on the supervising council, as indeed were none of his fellow patentees. His rôle thenceforth is suggested by a patent of November, 1606, issued four days after the royal council was appointed and seven months after the original Virginia grant. The November patent is a dispensation issued to Hakluyt and to Robert Hunt, a Sussex clergyman. It permitted them "full and free license" to go to Virginia and, without giving up their church positions in England, to hold "one or more benefices, church dignities, or cures in the said parts of Virginia or America."

So Hakluyt was offered this third chance to go to America, not this time as a mere observer but as a beneficed minister of the gospel in the new colony. Again he stayed at home while Hunt went; but he was fifty-four years of age. It is not, of course, clear that he was expected to go himself. That is not the impression given by John Smith in his history. "Jamestown," he noted in his *Advertisements for Planters of New England* in 1631, "was 500 pounds a year, as they say, appointed by the Council here, allowed by the Council there, and confirmed by the Archbishop of Canterbury his Grace . . . An. 1605 to Master Richard Hacluit Prebend of Westminster."

If this item be true, then Hakluyt was to have the living of Jamestown. But the year given by Smith almost invalidates the story, and the figure of five hundred pounds is fantastic. Moreover, there is no record to show that His Grace of Canterbury did confirm the arrangement. There may still be a grain of truth in the Captain's memory. Hakluyt seems to have been destined for the Jamestown living, even before Jamestown was founded, and his clerical name would then add weight to the petition for a patent. The explanation makes him rather a figurehead in the proceedings, but it is probably the true one. He may still have done a good deal in the promoting, known as he was to persons like Smith; but what he did for the achievement cannot be further defined, and he certainly did not receive the living.

In the later history of Virginia Hakluyt's part is also obscure. Only one or two facts may be stated. His name appeared in the second charter of 1609, but only as one on the list of more than seven hundred shareholders. He was not a member of the council; but he apparently took some part in the reorganizing achieved by the second charter, since he mentioned in the preface to his de Soto his presence "at your late solemn meeting in the house of the . . . Earl of Exeter," brother of his patron. The note is reassuring, since it implies that Hakluyt was more or less in the inner councils. He published some propaganda for the company, which was struggling mightily, after its 1609 reorganization, for public support and investment. He may have had some general supervision over the numerous books, pamphlets, and sermons issued in the company's interest; but nothing is assured. With this propaganda, which I shall discuss in the next chapter, his part in Virginia fades. He continued to hold two shares in the company, which he bequeathed to his son and which may represent the equivalent of his benefice. But he was not mentioned in the third charter in 1612, and he seems by that time to have relinquished even his interest in Virginia publicity.

The balance of the account thus falls far short of maintaining that "more than any other man, Hakluyt took upon himself the toil, and earned the credit, of establishing England's first colony." He did much less but still enough. In publicity, in technical advice, in promoting he worked for American colonization from its virtual beginnings. He was named on the first directorate and in the first company patent. He was an ordinary subscriber; and he was perhaps intended to be the head of the church in the colony. No other man of influence in the final foundation had been so long associated with the movement.

3

The last decade of Hakluyt's life found his two major projects at length under way. The trickle of trade with the East meant a slow but persisting expansion of England to India. The painful progress

FIG. 30—Sir Thomas Smith. Reproduced by courtesy of the Houghton Mifflin Company from the plate in Alexander Brown, *The Genesis of the United States*, Boston 1891, vol. II, opp. p. 900.

of Virginia meant the branching out of other American plans to assure the English expansion to America. With these enterprises we have seen Hakluyt's concern; but his further activities in their behalf are lost to the record. Especially in the actions of the Plymouth group, those who founded New England, does he seem to have had no part, despite his west-country connections. Nor was he a member of the Newfoundland Company of 1610; and there is no record of his being consulted by that company, though his books may have been. Nor was he a member of the Virginia offshoot, the profitable Bermuda Company.

He would be expected to appear in the last enterprise, which was also directed by Sir Thomas Smith (Fig. 30); but we cannot be sure how close Hakluyt was to the Pierpont Morgan of his time. Until that great promoter's life is written, and his career disentangled from the records of the Russia Company and the East India Company and the Virginia Company and the many more which he governed, the problem cannot be faced. What can be said now is that he and Hakluyt are constantly to be seen in the same picture. They were both directors of Virginia under the Raleigh assignment. Smith was the first governor of the East India Company when Hakluyt was its consultant. He was a member of the royal council for Virginia when Hakluyt was a Virginia patentee. He was treasurer of Virginia when Hakluyt was an ordinary shareholder. He was director of the Bermuda Company when it split off from Virginia; but he does not seem to have carried Hakluyt into it with him.

The use he made of Hakluyt in these eastern and western ventures is not then completely clear; but his concern for the advancement of learning, which is suggested by the navigation lectures at his house and by his preservation of oversea records, as the East India minutes occasionally mention, opens a door to speculation. One fancies Hakluyt hovering within call and never more so than in the enterprise which was becoming a third on Hakluyt's major list of interests, the Arctic enterprise.

As governor of both the East India and the Russia Companies, Smith was a mainstay of the new searching for the northern passages in the new century. Hakluyt's interest is here unmistakable. In 1600 he was writing, in his notes for the East India Company, "I have also large notes, of twenty years' observation, concerning the Northwest Passage, which your worships shall command if you shall have occasion to use the same." Their worships did have occasion. In 1602 and again in 1606 and the following years they combined with the Russia Company to send out ships to the northern land of Frobisher and Davis. Whether they commanded Hakluyt does not appear; but there is every likelihood that they did.

The likelihood is strengthened by the election of Smith in 1607 to be governor of the Russia Company and hence director in chief not only of the eastern project and the American project but of the new cycle of Arctic projects as well. Between them, the East India and Russia companies monopolized the English actions in the North, the one by virtue of its sole right to trade with the East by whatever route, the other by virtue of its sole right to trade in Russian regions. Both northeastern and northwestern possibilities were being endangered by foreign competitors. In one direction the Dutch had taken the field, having casually competed in Russia since 1565 and having in the three Barents voyages, from 1594 on, begun to threaten the Northeast Passage. In the other direction the Danes were seeking to restore, in the three voyages of 1605 to 1607, their ancient bond with Greenland.[7]

It was to forestall the competition of strangers that the English began the new cycle of Arctic exploring. The name of Henry Hudson is the symbol for this new enterprise. For it was Hudson who in 1607 scoured the Arctic, from Greenland to Spitsbergen, along the ice pack and who forecast a profitable whaling trade for the Russia Company. It was Hudson who in 1609 attempted the Northwest Passage for the Dutch and made the claim to New Netherlands in the valley of the Hudson River. And it was Hudson who in 1610 added Hudson Bay to the English dominion and the story of his own desperate end to the heroic English record.

What Hakluyt had to do with these explorations is conjecture. But one or two facts emerge. On the Northwest Passage he had ready, he said, a large collection of notes; and these notes, or at least those printed in his *Voyages,* like Gilbert's and Davis' treatises or Frobisher's and Davis' records of their exploring, must have been consulted with care by Hudson and Baffin. But Hakluyt was not the only consultant. A manuscript by Thomas Hariot is extant which relates "Three Reasons," founded on the Hudson Bay discovery, to prove a Northwest Passage.[8] These notes were not published; nor were Hakluyt's further notes, so far as one knows; and indeed the treatise on the Passage which was issued as propaganda in 1612 was written by Dudley Digges and not by Hariot or Hakluyt. It is then matter for conjecture if Hakluyt lent his aid as a consultant or a propagandist. He did at least take one substantial part in the action. In 1612 he was named as one of the patentees of the Northwest Passage Company and was thus added to the supporters of Hudson and Baffin, of whom Sir Thomas Smith was the chief.

The event denotes Hakluyt's second directorate. In the case of his other one, in the Virginia matter, we do not know how important he was or how influential in the success of the action. Nor have we

[7] I follow here also the narratives in Purchas; and I have consulted such excellent modern secondary works as Sir Clements R. Markham, *The Lands of Silence* (Cambridge 1921), and the economic history of the explorations in W. R. Scott, *The Constitution and Finance of English, Scottish, and Irish Joint Stock Companies to 1720* (Cambridge 1910–12). The narratives have usually been fully reëdited by the Hakluyt Society.

[8] Additional MSS 8–6789 (Hariot papers).

any further knowledge of him in the Northwest Passage Company, except for a second fact, which shows his distinction. When Baffin made his remarkable voyage of 1616, breaking through the ice on the west coast of Greenland to a point far beyond the 70-degree limit of John Davis, he sowed English names along the bay that is still named after him. He named Lancaster Sound, Wostenholme Sound, Cape Dudley Digges, and the Cary Islands after the merchants and officials who were the directors of the Passage Company. At his farthest north, above 75 degrees, he named Smith Sound after the multifarious governor. And, where Greenland bulges westward to make the narrow strait of Smith Sound, he fell back on a sheltering island which he called Hakluyt Island.[9]

With these two facts ceases our knowledge of Hakluyt's part in the exploring voyages of 1610 to 1620. A further conjecture remains to be spoken of; but first a word must be said of the northeastern ventures. It was Hudson's approach to Spitsbergen instead of the pole that led directly and immediately to the English whaling industry. To that extent, once the island was established as a base, it was needless to call on Hakluyt for advice; and the industry itself was carried on by the Russia Company, in whose membership Hakluyt does not figure. But there was exploring to be done, and he may well have been consulted by the explorers. There is no evidence; but at least he furnished propaganda and some printed information. This took the form of an account of the earlier Dutch voyages, those of 1594 to 1596 to which he had given advice and which had gone over the ground reopened by Hudson, the region of Spitsbergen and Novaya Zemlya. The Barents narratives had been licensed for English publication in 1598 immediately after their original was published in Holland; but for some reason they had not been published then, though two separate translations of them had been made by someone for the state or for the East India Company. At length the English version appeared in print in 1609, the work of William Philip, one of Hakluyt's agents.

The propaganda motive was made clear by the translator in his dedication. He was addressing Sir Thomas Smith " in respect of that particular charge, most worthily recommended to your care, over the Trade of the English in these Northeast Parts "; and he was publishing because " if any of our nation be employed that way in time to come, here they have a great part of their Voyage laid open, and the example of that industrious people . . . for the conquering of all difficulties and dangers: those people (I say) that . . . have first navigated to 81 degrees of northerly latitude, and wintered in 76. . . ."

To this venture Hakluyt then made his customary contribution, an authentic narrative of travel in the parts to be explored. He was again signally honored. In 1608 Henry Hudson led a second voyage north

[9] The authorities for these honors are given in the chronology, Appendix II.

along the fiords and rocky islands that form the west coast of Spitsbergen. At the extreme northwestern stretch of the archipelago the ship Hopewell rounded an island which bore a jutting northern point (Fig. 31). He named the point Hakluyt's Headland. The island is now called Amsterdam Island, and it lies close to the eightieth parallel; but Hakluyt's Headland remains, pointing to the pole, the last bit of Europe seen by the explorer who, like Amundsen and Byrd, follows the Gulf Stream to the limit of open water before daring the ice pack.

Two other Arctic places were named after Hakluyt but less permanently. In 1611 the ship Amity made its exploring way eastward beyond the White Sea to the next large opening, the estuary of the Pechora River. Coasting across the entrance to the White Sea in the track of Stephen Borough's ancient exploration of 1556, the Amity made the island of Kolguyef, halfway to Novaya Zemlya and the narrow strait which had been so vainly hoped, by Borough and Barents, to be the Northeast Passage. The ship followed the shore of the island to the southeast, hoping for a harbor. They found it, as Borough had; but, going previously ashore, the master came to a river, "which we called Hakluyt's River." The terse entry hides the motive. But the pilot was carefully following the course of Borough and following it, without doubt, in the *Voyages*. Hence, it is reasonable to think, the name given the river. The name no longer marks the stream on the west coast of the flat little haunt of sea fowl; but the gratitude of the mariners for the help of the Book is none the less noteworthy.

One need not regret the loss of the river's name. Kolguyef Island has no real part in the English record and has since been frequented only by hunters from the marshy Russian shore. With another island it is different, and there are serious regrets to express.

In the summer of 1615 a Russia Company ship retraced the recent exploring of Hudson for a polar passage. Turned back north of Spitsbergen by the ice pack, Robert Fotherby coasted precariously to the southwest along the line of the pack. Buffeted by frowning winds, "embayed" at times in the ice, he yet persisted halfway to Greenland, ever seeking yet never finding an opening in the pack. At length, in 71 degrees north, "we espied a snowy Hill very high in the clouds . . . but the fog was not yet cleared from the Land, so that we could see no part of it, but only the top of a snowy mountain."

He was fifteen leagues away, he thought, and kept on his course. He passed the land, doubled it, finding it an island about ten leagues long, and turned back to Spitsbergen. The island he named Sir Thomas Smith's Island. "It is high Land," he wrote, "and at the north end of it there is a mountain of a wonderful height and bigness, all covered with snow, which I called Mount Hakluyt."

Fotherby was not the discoverer of the volcanic island which is the

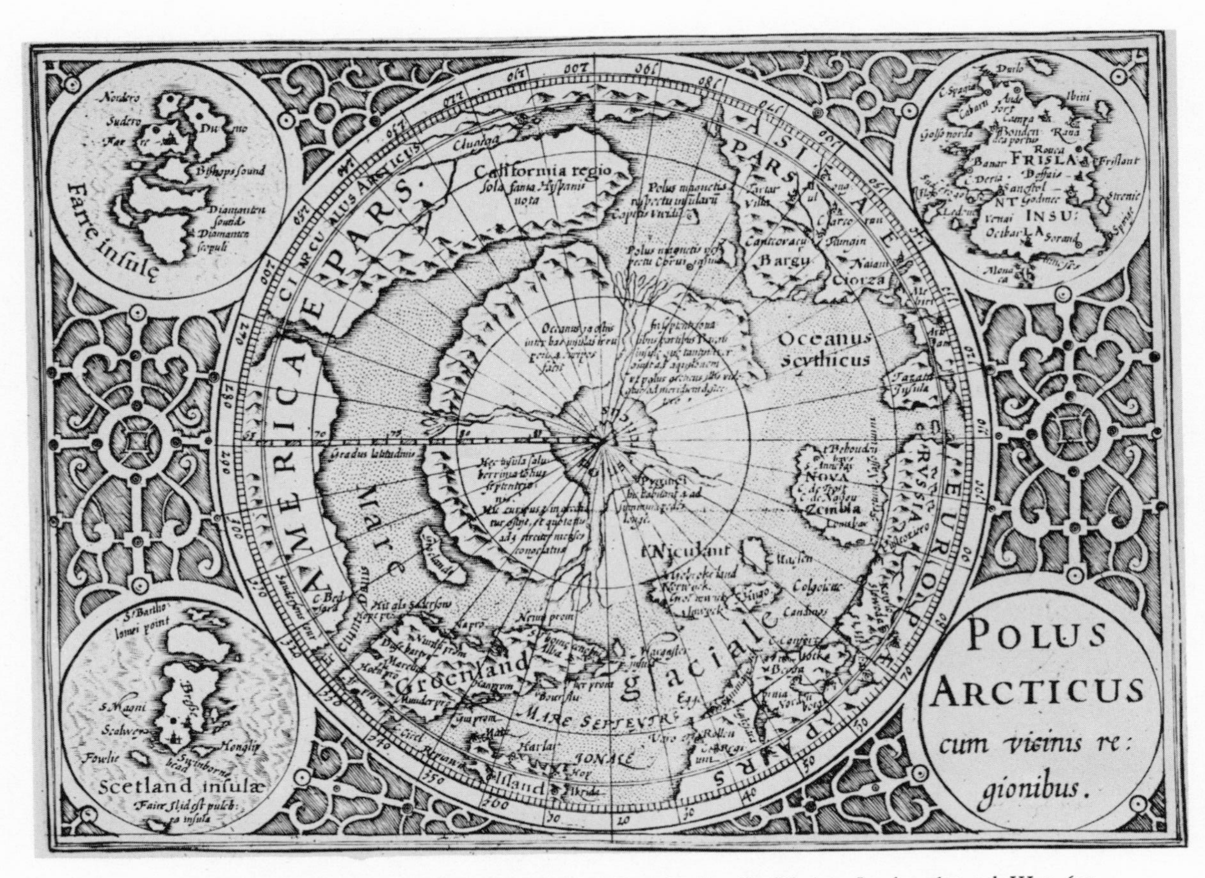

FIG. 31—The north polar regions, according to Hondius. From *Purchas His Pilgrimes*, London 1625, vol. III, p. 625.

only land between Iceland and the pole. The Northmen knew it; the Dutch had been there in 1614; and a Dutch name still remains in Jan Mayen, by which the island is now known. The shining mountain which stood out eight thousand feet above the fog has degenerated into Beerenberg, which is certainly trite enough, and all record of the English discovery has disappeared from the map.

Here is ample record of the esteem which Hakluyt had achieved and which was manifest in his own lifetime. The two names that survive from the four mark the virtual limit of English Arctic enterprise until the nineteenth century: Hakluyt's Headland, in almost eighty degrees north, the last outpost of Spitsbergen; Hakluyt Island in 77° 30′, near the entrance to Smith Sound, the farthest north until the time of Kane, standing on the route of Peary to the pole. Were the insipid name of Beerenberg changed back to Mt. Hakluyt, the great triangle formed by the island, the mountain, and the headland would fittingly record the farthest north of the great Jacobean era of discovery and would inscribe permanently on the map of the world the name of the man whose learning stayed and guided its search and discovery.

4

With one more episode in the culminating years of his life the story of Hakluyt as a man of action is completed. Like so many other episodes of his life, the known fact opens a door to unknown and secret passages. It suggests that there was still another function possible for the geographer than those which we have in turn woven into the record. In addition to promoting, in addition to advising promoters of exploration or of trade or of settlement, in addition to publishing as propaganda the records of travel, the geographer could also become a diplomatic adviser. When national rights were in dispute, rights to trade or to settlement in remote countries, then it would be a matter of course for a foreign office to call for a geographer's brief.

There have already been several instances of the sort in Hakluyt's consultations. Several sections of the *Western Planting* went to declare Virginia open to settlement. The memorial for the East India Company stated the English trading rights in the East. In the new century there were to be many more memoranda of the sort, from one person or another, as the new English companies got more vigorously under way.

One such memorandum may be mentioned for Virginia, a document that has been printed by Alexander Brown, as of 1613, under its title of *The Limits of the Spanish Possessions*. That paper is very probably Hakluyt's, as Brown infers. The sentences carry his cadence; the geographical knowledge is appropriate. There are similar documents in the northeastern records. For the whaling industry of the Russia Company, which was granted a monopoly in 1613, led to extended conflict with the Dutch; and it was this conflict which, as it became a diplomatic matter, produced both Dutch and English arguments on priority of discovery. Two English arguments of 1614 are, for example, preserved in the record; but whether they or any others are of Hakluyt's writing is not certainly known.[10]

One case of his intervention is known, though not the reason for it. In the library of the Inner Temple is now to be found a manuscript translation by Hakluyt of Grotius' first work in international law, the *Mare Liberum* or *Free Sea.* Written in 1604 as a part of a brief for the Dutch rights of trade in the East, the pamphlet was published in Holland late in 1608, probably as a prelude to the peace negotiations with Spain; and I suppose that Hakluyt translated it because it stated the rights of the English East India Company as well as of the Dutch. This seems the simplest explanation and the most appropriate too, especially because the English company was renewing its charter in 1609. That I take to be the date of Hakluyt's translation, immediately after the appearance of the book; and its purpose would be the justifying in law of the company's trade.

That the treatise remained unpublished is, I think, as simply explained. The English policy in making peace with Spain had been to say nothing of national rights in the new worlds ruled by Spain; and the same policy was desirable in the peace making of Spain and Holland, in which England took a hand. A pamphlet supporting the Dutch rights in the East had just, as it happened, been suppressed in England because the Spanish ambassador objected to it.[11] For the same reason it would not be politic to print the Grotius in England.

Once the truce was established between Spain and Holland, there were reasons of a different sort for not publishing. The reasons were that while England maintained the doctrine of the free sea against Spain, it held the doctrine of the closed sea against Holland. The disputes were long and acrid, producing in the end the Anglo-Dutch wars of the later seventeenth century. Essentially they began in 1609 with the closing to the Dutch of the herring fishery off the British coasts and in 1613 with the similar closing of the whaling off Spitsbergen. Throughout they centered on the principle of the closed sea, which John Selden was to justify to the king's satisfaction. With these disputes fairly launched in 1609, when Holland was changed from an ally to a competitor, it was hardly possible to publish Grotius' attack on the English position, particularly because, it is thought, it was Grotius' book which decided the king to answer its argument by deeds, by closing the herring fisheries and therefore the North Sea.

The only fact one has to go on, in the account of Hakluyt's own part in the dispute, is his translation of the *Free Sea;* but that fact

[10] The best account of the controversy is given by George Edmundson, *Anglo-Dutch Rivalry during the First Half of the Seventeenth Century* (Oxford 1911).

[11] *Calendar State Papers Venetian 1607–1610*, par. 203.

proves that it was possible for the geographer to become a diplomatic adviser—adviser to merchant adventurers, be it understood. It would be needless to translate a Latin pamphlet for either diplomats or lawyers. If Hakluyt did draw up a paper on the *Limits of the Spanish Possessions,* he would frame it for the reading of investors in Virginia and therefore in English. If he wrote a paper on the Russia Company rights, he would likewise use English for Sir Thomas Smith and his followers. In fact, one imagines that vigorous promoter turning automatically to the canon of Westminster for such documents; and one further imagines that the supply of diplomatic arguments became a constant function of the geographer who did so much for eastern, western, and northern enterprises.

Who did so much: and here we may finally sum up what he had done. For the approach to India he had regularly given advice: to the first overland mission in 1583; to the organizing merchants, perhaps in 1589 and in the nineties; and formally to the East India Company on its organization and thereafter. For the Northeast Passage experiments he had sought advice for the English attempt of 1580, he had formally advised the Dutch on their attempt of 1595, and he may have been consulted for the Hudson voyages and those following in the new century when his name was planted on northern coasts. With the southwest voyages of Drake and Fenton and Cavendish he seems to have had nothing to do and likewise with the northwest voyages of Frobisher and Davis in the seventies and eighties, which had other advisers. But he had preached the Northwest Passage in his first book of voyages and continued to preach it; and he became a member of the Northwest Passage Company and left his name also on the silent coasts of the North and Northwest. To the northern enterprises and the eastern he added, as of most concern, the western. He worked for Gilbert's Newfoundland and for Raleigh's Virginia. He helped to dispatch a preliminary voyage when, after the war, Virginia again became a possibility; and he was a charter member of the first Virginia Company and remained a shareholder until his death.

The elder Hakluyt remained a lawyer, becoming incidentally a consultant. The younger Hakluyt, becoming a scientist, was not only a consultant but a director of enterprise. His was not the greatest figure in the English expansion. He was not a Gilbert or a Raleigh; he was certainly not a Sir Thomas Smith. But he seems now to have been indispensable.

CHAPTER XVII

The Hakluyt Legacy

If Hakluyt played to a climax in his last years his active part in enterprise overseas, he by no means retired from collecting and editing. It is true that he was to publish nothing more of great importance. He had reached his climax as a man of letters; but in a new era of expansion, when not only the English but the Dutch and the French as well were taking to the seas in unexampled numbers, when there was building a host of new records for the historian, his zeal for collecting remained undismayed.

He continued to collect the records; and, had he lived longer, there would have been a third edition of the *Voyages* to bring the epic story down to its triumph. He did not live long enough; or, if he did, no further edition appeared. But the collections were made and came at length to publication in an unexpected form. The several volumes issued by him in the meantime were either fragments of the new collection or supplements to the old.

The *English Voyages* of 1600 brought the history of English enterprise down to date. In its additions and in the volumes of others for which he was responsible in the nineties Hakluyt brought down to date as well the knowledge of the new discoveries as a whole. It is perhaps important that his interests remained modern, that in his publications there is no trace of the humanist impulse. I cannot find that he had anything to do with the appearance of various geographical classics during his lifetime. With the abstract of Pliny which was translated during his school days and with the translation in 1572 of Dionysius of Alexandria he had of course no concern. Arthur Golding's versions of Solinus and Pomponius Mela, in 1585 and 1587, seem to have owed nothing to him; and there is no record of his concern with Holland's Pliny in 1601. With the gradually growing library of the classical geographers, which was completed in English except for Ptolemy by the end of the Tudor century, he seems to have had nothing to do.[1]

It was otherwise with modern knowledge. As Hakluyt continued to collect the narratives of English voyagers, he became a virtually official historian and was so regarded, as is shown by more than one instance I have mentioned. These narratives were building up the new collection. Hakluyt also continued to collect the printed records of foreign travelers; and there is not a single important narrative or geo-

[1] English translations from the classics are listed in Henrietta R. Palmer, *List of English Editions and Translations of Greek and Latin Classics Printed before 1641*, published by the Bibliographical Society of London (1911).

graphical work in his time that did not find its way among his papers, there to be done into English.

He continued also to make inquiries, as an occasional note suggests. The notes were made by Purchas, Hakluyt's literary legatee, in his *Pilgrims*. It appears in one that as late as 1605 Hakluyt was still in touch with Simon Fernandez the navigator—if it be the same man—and that he had learned from him of the Spanish discovery of the New Hebrides Islands in the Pacific. It appears from another that Hakluyt was still interested in news of foreign colonies and that he therefore approached a member of the Spanish peace mission which came to King James's court to end the long war. Apparently the learned delegate was willing to find out for Hakluyt all he wanted to know about the Spanish colonial system. After returning to Spain the delegate, who was the Licentiate Luis Tribaldo Toleto, obligingly called on his friends for their knowledge. He reported to Hakluyt in the one letter that has been kept, in which he was able to give an account of the recent Spanish exploration in New Mexico and also to enclose the official regulations for reports from the colonies. But he could not send any information from the reports themselves, since a friend's book about them was not allowed publication. I suppose that Hakluyt wanted these facts for the Virginia enterprise; but, being denied them, he was obliged to fall back on the new official history of the West Indies which was just being published.[2]

Hakluyt was still keeping abreast of the times. Though he was undertaking no new plans on a large scale, though he was not for example drawing up an independent work on geography, he was still finding material to publish. Immediately after the *Voyages* he issued a kind of supplement. "While I went about to publish our English Voyages and Discoveries," he wrote, explaining, "I was advised by Master Walter Cope, a gentleman of rare and excellent parts, to draw them into a short sum. . . . Although in that work then under the press I could not conveniently alter my course, . . . I here present unto your Honor a brief Treatise most agreeable to the same." Accordingly he made use of a book which, "though small in bulk, containeth so much rare and profitable matter as I know not where to seek the like within so narrow and strait a compass."

The book was a chronology of discovery, compiled by Antonio Galvano, a distinguished Portuguese colonial official, and published in Lisbon in 1563 as the *Discoveries of the World*. The translation into English had been made by an unknown hand—an astonishing fact in an age in which translators were not so numerous as to be easily lost sight of. Hakluyt had discovered the manuscript in 1589. It was represented to him as the work of a London merchant, perhaps one of those traders in Spain who had done so much translating during the

[2] See the chronology, 1605, in Appendix II.

Frobisher period; and I conjecture that, since Hakluyt could not learn his identity, the manuscript had somehow reached a City counting-room and lodged there. At any rate it was turned over to Hakluyt, perhaps for good riddance. The editor had tried for years to get sight of the original Portuguese and, not succeeding, at length published the English as it stood.

The annals thus oddly come by covered the discoveries from ancient times to the year 1555; and in so far as they summed up the travels of all nations, their publication announced Hakluyt's interest in universal history as distinct from English history. The step to the larger interest again raises the question why Hakluyt did not compile the discoveries of all nations. Again we are compelled to infer the same answer, that he had done enough and still had enough to do. To compile even the annals of universal travel went beyond his plans.

He did not even augment the Galvano from his own *English Voyages,* promising only that the "travels of our men, because as yet they be not come to ripeness and have been made for the most part to places first discovered by others, when they shall come to more perfection and become more profitable to the adventurers, will then become more fit to be reduced into brief epitomes by myself or some other." The result is that the *Discoveries of the World* represents none of Hakluyt's toil except that of seeing it through the press; and for an English reader it represents only an introduction to the discoveries of his nation.

For this and other reasons the book is Hakluyt's least important production; and the fact that he was not able to obtain the original suggests the question of whether his research, as well as his publishing, was not slackening pace. In other words, why did he not at length proceed to Spain for research as he had once proceeded to France? The question is suggested, not raised, by the Galvano: for peace had not yet been made, in 1601, between England and Spain. If, however, the original Galvano could not be had outside of Portugal or Spain, why did not Hakluyt go to Spain after the peace to find it as well as to make other inquiries such as he had made in Paris?

I think the answer is that he did think of doing so. The evidence is in the overtures made by him to the Spanish peace commissioner, of whom I have just spoken. If there were possibilities in Spain, he was planning in 1605 to investigate. The letter from the Licentiate must have quashed the intentions, as insisting that Spanish secrecy was still rigid and especially so, we infer, against a man who was compromised by his part in Virginia.

To keep abreast of Spanish books at least, Hakluyt did not need to go to Spain. He had amply proved that thesis by his prompt acquiring of Mendoza's *China* in the year of its publication; by his acquiring of Acosta's *Indies* at the height of the naval war; and by his finding in the period of peace the new official history of Herrera, published in 1601 and 1605, which he translated. If he were to be denied facilities for research in Spain and if he could obtain the important new Spanish books without going there for them, he might as well stay at home.

He had enough to do there in any case, what with his family, his church dignities and duties, his collecting, and his work for Virginia, whatever that might be. Some of the last was publicity; and indeed most of Hakluyt's remaining books concerned Virginia. There are six books with which he probably or certainly had still to do: I shall consider them in chronological order.[3]

2

The first two can be imputed to Hakluyt on only the vaguest grounds, and I do not really impute them. I may say simply that it is possible that Hakluyt guided the publication of Brereton's *True Relation* in 1602 and of the English Acosta in 1604. Of the latter I have already spoken. Hakluyt had seen the new descriptive work on the West Indies soon after its issue in 1590 and had made abstracts from it for the government. According to precedent, he should then have proceeded to translate and publish it, either directly or through an agent. That the Edward Grimstone who in 1604 did translate and publish it on his own account had no connection with Hakluyt it is difficult to believe. Not that I mean to imply that Hakluyt was the only man in England who published geographical works: but merely that, since he had the habit of reissuing such works as came into his hands and since Acosta did come into his hands, it would be odd if he relinquished it.

The case is not proved; and it is even less proved for the Brereton book. This is mainly a narrative of Gosnold's "discovery of the north part of Virginia," the reconnaissance voyage of 1602 which opens the second chapter of Virginia's history. The book constituted the most substantial piece of American propaganda published since the *Divers Voyages* of twenty years before: for in addition to the account of Gosnold's voyage it included a note on the relief expedition that had just been sent out by Raleigh in the forlorn hope of finding the lost colony; a lengthy discourse on colonization by one of the Gilbert colonizers; and, in a second edition in the same year, the elder Hakluyt's *Inducements to the liking of Virginia.*

Brereton's book, like the voyages it commemorates, is a sign of the reawakening of the colonial idea; and it would be surprising if Hakluyt, director of Virginia and an acknowledged director of publicity, had had no share in it. The two treatises do not perhaps prove such a connection. Edward Hayes, once a captain in the Gilbert col-

[3] For these books, see the bibliography, Appendix III.

ony and the author of one of the Brereton discourses, must indeed have been known to Hakluyt; but I do not doubt that the author of the official account of Gilbert's last voyage was quite able to publish a treatise on his own account. At any rate, he left no reference to Hakluyt's part in the plan; and, as we know so little of the latter's relation with the various new colonizing groups, we can trace no positive connection.

The elder Hakluyt's essay is even less indicative. The proper place in which to publish it had been the *Voyages,* since the paper of 1585 was a part of the history of the Roanoke colony, exactly as Peckham's discourse of 1583, which Hakluyt did reprint, was a part of the history of the Gilbert colony. Perhaps Hakluyt suppressed it in 1600, as he suppressed his own *Western Planting,* because of the pending negotiations with Spain. But it seems more likely that he did not have the paper. If it turned up in print only two years after the final *Voyages,* I conclude that it was put into print by someone else.

At any rate, there is nothing in the two pamphlets now printed with Brereton's relation to connect Hakluyt with the publishing. It is quite possible that the Hayes and Hakluyt papers had been urged upon the printer by Raleigh or another of the older colonial party, by Arundel or another of the newer Court group, by the Lord Chief Justice and his Plymouth adventurers, or by the Russia Company group in the City, without, except in the last case, the younger Hakluyt's participation.

The evidence may be otherwise interpreted, however, when the Brereton narrative itself is considered. It was Hakluyt's habit, sustained over a long period of years, to gather narratives of new voyages: nay more, to persuade voyagers to write down their records for his use. Now Brereton was one of those who had had to be persuaded by somebody; for he wrote in the dedication to Raleigh: "Honorable sir, being earnestly requested by a dear friend to put down in writing some true relation of our late performed voyage to the north Parts of Virginia: at length I resolved to satisfy his request, who also imboldened me to direct the same to your honorable consideration."

Now the dear friend may not have been Hakluyt; but persuasion of the sort is so characteristic of his whole lifetime of activity that he is almost certainly the one who kept after Brereton until "at length" he yielded. It is certain that Hakluyt would have procured the narrative sooner or later, had not someone else got it into print previously; and he would as certainly have been quick to follow up a voyage so significant to him as this of Gosnold's. With that statement the question must be left unresolved. Someone had urged Brereton to write and publish his story and had probably helped with both. That someone was most likely Hakluyt, who had the habit of such persuasion. But there were others who had the same special interest in this new Virginia voyage and who may have taken the job out of his hands.

A certain weight is lent to this alternative by Hakluyt's apparent indifference, during all his life, to the publication of individual English narratives. I say apparent because of the absence of evidence, as in the Brereton sample; and I point to the Gilbert colony record, to Hariot's Virginia, to the two books published by Raleigh on Guiana, to the Drake narratives, and to many others, which Hakluyt had nothing to do with. What did concern him was the eventual collective publication of all English narratives. For that purpose he made sure that the narratives were written out and handed to him. But, while he was prompt to publish the accounts of foreign voyages, there is no authentic case of his agency in the printing of individual English accounts.

Hakluyt the propagandist and Hakluyt the historian followed quite different methods. The historian made sure of his English records and eventually published them. The propagandist found outside material and published it separately and soon. The distinction is emphasized by Hakluyt's future concern with Virginia publicity. There was to be a large quantity of it, for the venture was even more substantially financed than had been the Russia Company ventures of a half century past or the Frobisher ventures of a generation past; and the habit of publicity had undeniably been acquired and strengthened. So the five preliminary voyages were to be recorded in print. The yearly expeditions to Jamestown and the colony's own history were to be set down at length; and in the especially critical years from 1609 to 1611, when enthusiasm waned as the colony did not take hold and when there was serious question of its continuance, there was a variety of propaganda to be issued, ranging from sermons at Paul's Cross to the printing of lottery tickets. Presses worked with vigor. Prospectuses and appeals were lavishly issued. Complete histories of the colony were published from 1610 on.[4]

How great a part Hakluyt took in these activities it is again impossible to say, since the company records are lost. As in the actual organizing of the company and the colony, he may have had much or he may have had little to do. He may have felt it distinctly unwise to lend either his name or his funds to works of uneven quality and so refrained. Or he may on the other hand have flung all his energies into encouraging new publicity. It is not possible to say; and certainly there is no positive evidence of his concern with more than two enterprises of the sort. The two books are both of the critical year 1609. They are both essays in publicity for the desperate colony. They both represent the knowledge acquired by "strangers." In the one case the "strangers" were Spanish, and their knowledge was not

[4] The authority on Virginia is still Alexander Brown, *The Genesis of the United States.*

new. In the other they were French, and their knowledge was of the most recent.

The first one bore the catch title of *Virginia Richly Valued by the description of the main land of Florida her next neighbor.* It was in fact, as the title page then stated, an account of de Soto's exploration, seventy years before, of southeastern North America. Hakluyt was himself the translator. His source was the only separately printed account of the striking and pathetic expedition, that published in 1557 by a surviving Portuguese, the unknown Gentleman of Elvas. The other account was imbedded in the official and accessible history of Oviedo.

The book had taken a long time to reach its English form, and it is odd that Hakluyt had not hitherto noticed it. For the expedition was perhaps the most useful episode in the history of American overland exploration, as it had covered in its futile course the whole territory between Florida and the Mississippi. Thus it notably supplemented the French account of the Florida coast—the Laudonnière—on the one hand and the Spanish journeyings north from Mexico—the Espejo—on the other. It should therefore have been brought to press with the Espejo and the Laudonnière or at least included with them and the other Spanish narratives in the *Voyages*. If Hakluyt had delayed so long in publishing it, I conclude that he did not have it and that the peace with Spain had at length allowed him to unearth the volume.

The translation was dedicated to the Council and Company of Virginia, for the reason that the work "doth yield much light to our enterprise now on foot: whether you desire to know the present and future commodities of our country; or the qualities and conditions of the inhabitants, or what course is best to be taken with them." Captain John Smith perhaps needed only his native wits to tell him how to deal with such inhabitants as Powhatan; but investors might find much comfort in the commodities. For it was manifest that the pompous march of the Spanish soldiery had discovered, if they had not profited by gold and copper, pearls, oxen or buffalo, mulberry trees which promised silk, dyes of all colors, grapes for wine, and salt. Surely no more could be desired by the "cheerful adventurers" to whom the book was dedicated and who were justifiably worried by their investment.

What Hakluyt privately thought of the value of these commodities it is of course not possible to say. At least they had been observed to be there and by more than one observer. Surely no economic geographer could do less than present the observations. Their value could be determined, after all, only by experiment; and, I suppose, the unpredicted wealth of Mexico, of the Antilles, and of Peru was still a dazzling memory. Hakluyt was not above making the most of its power. The second edition of de Soto, in 1611, while bearing the more apt title of *The Discovery and Conquest of Terra Florida,* promised on the same page "excellent and rich mines of gold, silver, and other metals, etc., which cannot but give us a great and exceeding hope of our Virginia, being so near of one continent."

The historical value of the narrative is at any rate unquestioned. Next to French Florida, the de Soto expedition ranks as the most dramatic episode in the early history of the mainland. It is the most important piece of continental exploring before the French discoveries of the next century; and its malign fate conveyed a singularly pointed lesson to future travelers.

With the de Soto narrative Hakluyt virtually completed the printing of such records of the Spaniards in North America as were accessible to him. In the same year he brought to publication the new chapter of New France. French colonization had recommenced in earnest with the new century. Champlain had begun his Canadian career with his exploring voyages of 1603 down the coast; Acadia had been settled in 1604; and Champlain had founded Quebec in 1608. Of this movement, which was parallel to Virginia, there was already a substantial record. Champlain's first voyage had been accounted for in his book *Des Sauvages,* which Hakluyt had translated but had not for some unexpected reason published. The Port Royal colony in Acadia had given rise to a more elaborate eyewitness work, the *History of New France.* Of this history Hakluyt immediately published a portion as *Nova Francia, or the description of that part of New France which is one Continent with Virginia.*

It was Pierre Erondelle, or Arundel, a popular French teacher of London, who did the translating and who wrote in the preface as follows: "Gentle reader, the whole volume of the navigations of the French nation into the West Indies . . . was brought to me to be translated by M. Richard Hakluyt, a man who for his worthy and profitable labors is well known to most men of worth, . . . and by him this part was selected and chosen."

The motives are obvious. The translation was made, Erondelle wrote, "for the particular use of this nation, to the end that comparing the goodness of the lands of the northern parts herein mentioned with that of Virginia, which . . . must be far better by reason it stands more southerly nearer to the Sun; greater encouragement may be given to prosecute that generous and goodly action."

The parts of the book of the spirited lawyer Lescarbot which Hakluyt picked out were descriptive, not historical. The aim was not to record French history or even travel history; it was to set down from the French history what had been observed of the northern lands and notably what had been observed by settlers not by travelers. Cartier had wintered in Canada nearly a century before. Lescarbot lived through the seasons of the year in Acadia, and his record was therefore the more valuable.

These books complete Hakluyt's known contributions to Virginia publicity. The printed volumes on the English colony itself seem to have owed nothing to him; but he brought to press the best observations on Florida to the south and on New France to the north, and he continued to collect with customary care the individual narratives of Virginia, which came at length to print.

He was, we suppose in other words, holding his fire while he stacked his ammunition. The new works of "strangers" he translated, like Champlain's *Sauvages* and Herrera's new history of New Spain; but he did not publish them at the time. Only two more books remain to be mentioned which acknowledge Hakluyt as their sponsor. One related the Dutch voyages to Novaya Zemlya, as I have already told. Licensed for publication in 1598 on the appearance of the original in Holland, it did not reach print until 1609. Published then as de Veer's *Three Voyages to the Northeast,* its purpose was to spread interest in the new trade of the Russia Company; but the delay is a mystery. In any case, the story was distinctly worth the telling. It was not the first story of a Dutch voyage to the north; but it was the first such story in English. More significantly, it gave the first account of a winter spent under the Arctic circle, and it was a worthy record of fortitude.

With these three books of 1609, the de Soto and the de Veer and the Lescarbot, Hakluyt seems to have ceased to publish. I except of course the two translations I have already mentioned, the *Mare Liberum* of Grotius, which never came to publication, and the Malay-English dialogues, which in 1614 did. Neither of them was exactly in Hakluyt's line; neither of them could be properly counted as more than routine labor. Only one further publication during Hakluyt's last years recalls the broad and scholarly interest of the earlier period.

Rightly it belongs to that earlier period, for it was the English version of Peter Martyr, of which Hakluyt had published the second complete Latin edition in Paris in 1587. It was fitting that Hakluyt's last publication should look back to the first history of the discoveries. It was fitting that it should look back as well to the first history of the discoveries in English: for it will be recalled that Eden had translated three of the *Decades* in the year of the founding of the Russia Company and that twenty years later, at the beginning of the second cycle of expansion with the Frobisher experiments, Willis had published four of the *Decades.* The complete Latin reëdition had been perhaps Hakluyt's most substantial editorial achievement apart from the *Voyages.* Now in the third period of the expansion, in the period in which expansion had become a fact, the complete English *Decades* at length appeared.

FIG. 32—Samuel Purchas. From *Purchas His Pilgrimes*, London 1625, title page (dated 1624).

The translation of the venerable volume was the work of Michael Lok, who has appeared before as one of Hakluyt's earliest merchant friends. It will be recalled that Lok was the treasurer of the Frobisher undertaking, from which he reaped only immense debts. Obliged thereby to give up the idea of becoming a merchant prince, he had resumed for a time his former quality of commercial agent *in partibus infidelium.* I do not know whether he had been originally designed by Hakluyt to translate the *Decades;* but I think it likely that he had spent the long years of his exile at Aleppo and Venice in working on the Spanish history. I am supposing that it is the same Michael Lok, now of an advanced age, and not a descendant: though it has been noted that the translator called himself "gentleman," and addressed the book in rather distant tone to Sir Julius Caesar, the old man's stepson.[5]

After twenty-five years, at any rate, the book was completed and published in 1612 with due acknowledgment to the *vir eruditissimus* who had sponsored it. A mild success attended the work; for, although neither Hakluyt nor the older Lok lived to see it, the book was twice reprinted.

With this late return to the earliest history of the discoveries the record of Hakluyt's publications comes to an end. After the great roll of the *Voyages* had been closed the collector had seen six further books through to publication. Only one of them, the de Soto, did he issue as his own, having himself translated and edited it. The Galvano he had edited but not translated. The Lescarbot, the de Veer, and the Peter Martyr he had commissioned and perhaps also other books like the Brereton and the Acosta. Of these works, again, all but two were issued as direct propaganda; and those two exceptions, the *Decades* and the *Annals,* were of general rather than national historical interest. Three of the books have a distinct historical and scientific value. The de Soto and the de Veer were each the record of outstanding achievements. The *Decades* was and is a classic.

3

Of Hakluyt's collections during these final years before his death in 1616 it is at length time to speak. By an arrangement which has not been fully recorded they passed to another clergyman of somewhat similar interests and were by him, though with what completeness we cannot say, included in the fourth great collection of the records of travel, *Purchas His Pilgrims* (Fig. 32). This book is Hakluyt's literary legacy. Published in 1625, it continued Hakluyt's career in the catch title of *Hakluytus Posthumus.*[6]

[5] The objections are those of J. A. Williamson, in "Michael Lock," *Blackwood's,* 196, 58–72 (1914).

[6] What is known of Purchas is contained in his prefaces and marginal notes and his will, as summed up in the *Dictionary of National Biography.* The name was pronounced Purkas, as is shown by the spelling of it in the East India Company minutes (Sir William Foster, in *Geographical Journal,* 68, 193–200, 1926).

One's first impression of the Reverend Samuel Purchas, chaplain to the Archbishop of Canterbury, is that he distinctly lacked dignity. The tone of his prefaces is a mixture of naïve parade with fawning humility. The style is a vapid and tasteless euphuism of a sophomoric sort. By contrast Hakluyt immediately increases in moral stature; his lapses, as they seem now, from self-respect become insignificant, his manner of address to men of rank a model of dignity. To dwell on the contrast is to discover a growing dislike to Purchas, whose features gradually and irresistibly resolve into the features of Pecksniff.

Following out the contrast in less unfriendly mood, one discovers that Purchas was a self-made man, as Hakluyt unmistakably was not. Instead of being a gentleman born, Purchas was the son of an Essex farmer or tradesman. Instead of finding a swift road to preferment, leveled by family prestige and official favor, Purchas made his way through St. John's College, Cambridge, and on leaving became a poor curate and household servant of an Essex rector. He married a fellow servant and by the time he was thirty had managed to become the vicar of a neighboring parish. To lift himself from rural obscurity Purchas then devoted his talents to history and, by dint of what must have been a long and labored process of compilation, produced in 1613, when he was forty years old, the folio volume he called *Purchas His Pilgrimage.*

The volume brought its author instant recognition. Within a year he was made chaplain to the Archbishop, to whom it was dedicated and who had himself written a brief textbook on geography. The King read the bulky volume seven times, though he seems to have given the author no more than the breath of his approbation. But the Bishop of London obtained for Purchas the living of St. Martin's, Ludgate, and subsequently he was able to bring out three successively enlarged editions.

The death of Hakluyt in 1616 gave him new opportunity. Seeking out, it is likely, Hakluyt's son or widow, he obtained Hakluyt's papers. The manuscripts became the nucleus of a new work. He added to them a vast amount of compiling of the records of universal travel; he brought the English travel records down to date; and with the help of "charitable friends" he published in 1625, with a dedication to the new King, the four immense folios of the *Pilgrims.*

It follows from this personal history that, again in contrast with his predecessor, Purchas was in no intelligible way concerned with the history and development of science or of enterprise. "Being," he wrote in the preface to his first book, the *Pilgrimage,* "I know not by what natural inclination, addicted to the study of history, . . . I here bring Religion from Paradise to the Ark, and thence follow her round about the World, and (for her sake) observe the World itself, with the several Countries and Peoples therein." At the beginning he was then primarily an anthropologist; and, though his interests may have developed as he took over Hakluyt's heritage, they remained, as far as we know, essentially academic. With him is then reached the final and perhaps decadent stage in specialization which, I have said, conditions the advancement of learning. Hakluyt was the historian and the scientist by profession; but by virtue of that profession he was the man of action as well. Purchas was exclusively the antiquarian. Hakluyt met on nearly equal terms the captains of enterprise. Purchas, except for some possible dealings with Captain John Smith and except for a late acquired membership in the Virginia Company, was an outsider, a bookish clergyman who came hat in hand to copy the records of trade.

So at least the picture composes. Instead of the gentleman, the poor man; instead of the churchman of rank, the holder of a single living; instead of the professional scientist, the self-made historian; instead of the adviser of privy councillors and merchant princes, the obscure penman. Whatever our impression of Purchas' manners, the picture compels admiration for the persistence of his long struggle.

Our feelings toward him thus improved, we may consider his relations with Hakluyt in order to understand his achievement. Purchas' first work, the *Pilgrimage,* being a sort of religious geography, was dependent for its information on the historians and political geographers of all ages and, for modern times, especially on Ramusio and on Hakluyt, whose works, Purchas acknowledged, "have been two libraries unto me." The appearance of his immense history of religion, already in its first edition larger than Hakluyt's first *English Voyages,* apparently brought its author to the geographer's notice. There was an exchange of courtesies, and for his enlarged second edition, printed in 1614, Purchas wrote that "now in this edition I have been much beholden to Mr. Hakluyt for many written treatises in this kind." Hakluyt had sent him manuscripts; and, in return Purchas launched upon his easy flow of praise. The veteran, he wrote in the same edition, "though known at this time only by those portraitures [the *Voyages*] hath been an Admiral, holding out the light unto me in these Seas, and as diligent a guide . . . and now his helps in this second edition have much more obliged me." And his praise rose to his usual hyperbole when he called Hakluyt "Neptune's Secretary and the Ocean's Protonotary." [7]

Then followed a coolness. Perhaps Neptune's Secretary took offense: one is only too willing to believe that Purchas could be offensive; and the third edition of the *Pilgrimage,* in 1617, presents its author in a nobly forgiving pose. "Although in this third edition," he wrote, "I could not obtain like kindness from him, I know not how affected or infected with emulation or jealousy: yet shall his

[7]Page 782. See item 1 on Page 269 below for an article in defense of Purchas as editor.

name live while my writings endure. . . . And this [book] is my epitaph in his memory, who hath yet a better, his own large volumes being the best and truest Titles of his House; and if some Juno Lucina would help to bring forth the Posthumus issue of his Voyages not yet published, the World should enjoy a more full testimony of his pains in that kind." [8]

One cannot go behind this version of *de mortuis nil nisi bonum.* One cannot discover from it Hakluyt's dying attitude toward Purchas. It is likewise difficult to be sure of the transactions between Purchas and the Hakluyt heirs. Purchas had probably planned to take on at once, on Hakluyt's death in November 1616, the functions of Juno Lucina; and he did obtain the Hakluyt legacy on "hard conditions," as he said later. Meantime he set to work on another immense book. In 1619 he published the eight hundred pages of *Purchas His Pilgrim.* This was subtitled *Microcosmus, or The Historie of Man,* and related the "Wonders of his Generation, the Vanities in his Degeneration, the Necessity of his Regeneration." A sermon to work off the grief of family losses, this book has no relation to Hakluyt's works.

By August of 1621 the *Hakluytus Posthumus* started piecemeal through the press. By 1622 Purchas was given official access to the East India Company records, a date that would have allowed him time to prepare Hakluyt's papers before he went on to supplement them. In the summers he secluded himself by royal permission in the Chelsea Hospital to prepare the copy, unassisted except by his son. In 1625 the complete four volumes of the *Pilgrims* were at length released by the printer, thanks to "charitable friends" and to Purchas' own "extraordinary Labors of Lecturing." They were followed in the next year by a fourth edition of the *Pilgrimage;* by a gift of £100 from the East India Company; and by the speedy death of the cringing, unctuous, and indefatigable parson.[9]

Whatever the grudge he bore Hakluyt for the coldness which he called jealousy, and Hakluyt's son for the hard conditions, be they what they might, Purchas was full and honest in his acknowledgments. "As for Master Hakluyt's many years' Collections," he explained in the preface to the *Pilgrims,* "and what stock I received from him in written papers, in the Table of Authors you shall find: whom I will thus far honor, that though it be but Materials, and that many Books have not one chapter in that kind, yet that stock encouraged me to use my endeavors in and for the rest. I was therein a Laborer also," he added in necessary candor, "both to get them (not without hard conditions) and to form and frame those Materials to their due place and order in the Edifice, the whole Artifice (such as it is) being mine own."

[8] Page 972.

[9] Purchas' dealings with the Company are represented in the minute books by the following entries: *Calendar 1622–1624,* par. 38; *ibid.,* par. 639; *Calendar 1625–1628,* par. 10, 21, 23.

He was scrupulous in labeling Hakluyt's items; and much of the offensiveness of his manner is eclipsed by that honesty.

And, one is suddenly surprised to discover, by a certain modesty as well. This unexpected quality emerges when we reckon the additions made by Purchas to his stock. On a rough count it appears that Hakluyt supplied something like two-fifths of the *Pilgrims,* that Purchas more than doubled what he had received. At the same time, as I judge, he intended at the start to make of the *Pilgrims* a thoroughly amplified third edition of the *Voyages.* The first volume of the four was so arranged; but then the intention seems to have failed and been succeeded by the simpler one of making the *Pilgrims* a supplement to the *Voyages.* Except on this theory I cannot understand why Purchas on the one hand reprinted so much and on the other gave mere abstracts of so much important material from Hakluyt's volumes. The reason for the change, if there really was a change, is fairly obvious. As it stands, the *Pilgrims* is more than twice as long as the final *Voyages.* A third edition of the *Voyages* would have run to at least six or seven volumes instead of Purchas' four, to some six million words instead of Purchas' four million.[10]

What Purchas did was done with a flourish and with the ingenuity which one discovers in his style. It was ingenuity which produced the elaborate new numbering of the *Pilgrims.* In the *Voyages* the narratives had been geographically arranged, the three parts covering successively the northern and northeastern, the southern and southeastern, and the western voyages; and only consecutive voyages to a given region were numbered. In the *Pilgrims* the arrangement became highly formal. The work was divided into two parts, one covering generally the world known to Ptolemy, the other the worlds discovered in modern times. Each part was further divided into ten books to deal with separate countries, and each voyage or other separate item was further numbered as a separate chapter. The systematizing was rather overdone, since the word chapter supposes a continuity which frequently does not exist; but on the whole the Purchas system is an improvement.

Fundamentally, if not on the surface or perhaps even in Purchas' intention, the plan of the *Pilgrims* is still the plan of the *Voyages.* The English voyages of trade and discovery and war are still the mainstay of the collection; the voyages and treatises of "strangers" are still admitted when they deal with countries not known to the English. Hakluyt's accumulations since 1600 are the nucleus. On them have

[10] A rough summary of the *Pilgrims* gives a total of 3,900,000 words. Hakluyt's material amounts to 1,625,000, or somewhat more than 40 per cent; of this amount, 1,350,000 was new, nearly as much as was in the complete *Voyages,* while the rest was selected or abstracted from what Hakluyt had already published. Of the 200 new items additional to those in the *Voyages,* 75 were Hakluyt's, 125 were Purchas'; but of Purchas' 125, only 64 were from manuscripts he had collected, the rest being printed material. The translations which Purchas found in Hakluyt's manuscripts and which Hakluyt had supposedly translated himself, amount to 400,000 words, or more than the amount of translation in the *Voyages.*

been piled the English voyages since 1615 as well as the voyages printed by others in the first quarter of the century; and introductory chapters have then been written to summarize the earlier voyages, as in the account given, for example, of Raleigh's Virginia or of the northern voyages before 1600.

Substantially this is the plan of the *Pilgrims,* and there is no need to exaggerate Purchas' departures from it. Departures there are and in number. The first book is thus a summary of ancient travel; the second book presents the six circumnavigations from Magellan to Schouten; the fifth book of Part II contains descriptions of the West Indies and Mexico from four Spanish historians rather than from one. Purchas was serving fuller measure than Hakluyt. The reason is doubtless that his purpose was naturally modeled by his interest; and that interest I have already said was not the interest of the recorder and promoter of English enterprise. It was geographical and historical, to be sure; but the geography and the history were of an amateurish, or one may say of a literary, sort. His preface speaks of the work as natural history, or rather as bricks for the house of natural history; its purpose was to record "varieties of nature." Such a purpose may be carried out with the scientific spirit, with the spirit of Solomon's House in the New Atlantis. Unrestrained by such a spirit, it may become sheer journalism.

Fortunately Purchas was restrained by the nature of his legacy from Hakluyt, and the *Pilgrims* is not journalism. Forty per cent of the work is, as I have said, Hakluyt's; and an examination of his material proves that he continued to the last to be an ardent collector. He had gathered all the East India narratives down to 1615; they fill the third book, and Purchas was to bring them down to date in the fourth. The fifth book, on Africa, is Hakluyt's, being made up from Pory's *Africa* and Pigafetta's *Congo* and from much new material on Abyssinia which Hakluyt had translated from Ramusio. Book eight, on the Levant, is curiously meager, being mainly an account of the crusades: one wonders what had happened to Hakluyt's ties with the Levant Company. Books nine and ten, on the overland route to India, are mainly Purchas and distinctly miscellaneous; but Caesar Frederick and Fitch and Linschoten are reprinted in large portions, and Hakluyt also contributes a large translation from the Portuguese.

The first two books of Part II, on northern Asia and China, are distinctly a triumph for Purchas, since they contain many international discoveries of his own. Yet Hakluyt contributes Mandeville, his contemporary Haiton the Armenian, and the groundwork for Purchas' summary of the English in Russia. Books three and four, on the northeast and northwest voyages, are almost all Hakluyt; the remaining five books, on the Americas, are also in large part Hakluyt's, down to the recent history of Virginia and the northern colonies. From the survey one must conclude that Purchas added nothing of importance of his own initiative, even though he made some valuable finds. The plan was Hakluyt's, and Purchas is to be praised for carrying it out almost in spite of himself.

Or so one supposes. For to present varieties of nature was one thing; to bring mankind to the full discovery of the world was quite another. The difference is fundamental, as one may judge from Purchas' excessive editing. To represent Hakluyt's own volumes he wrote in their appropriate places the summaries of English enterprise up to 1600; and, though the summaries do no harm, they are of small good. What he added in this way was unimportant; but what he later subtracted was disastrous. "Tedious" was a favorite editorial word of Purchas; and, when a manuscript was tedious, he abridged it or even omitted it entirely. When a voyage dwindled to the pattern of a mere log book, Purchas was quite likely to abridge; and dates and positions and sailing distances went by the board. When one observer seemed to Purchas to repeat another, one was omitted; and the perspective of two witnesses gave way to the possible bias of one. The fear of the tedious was thus as intense in Purchas as in any journalist; and it is amusing that his feeling was approved by the eighteenth-century editor we have mentioned before, who found Purchas far more interesting as an historian of travel than the Hakluyt whom he condemned for excesses.

In revenge, the complaints of modern and more scientific times have been loudly raised over the shears of Purchas. When he threw out, for example, the log of Baffin in the epochal 1616 voyage to Baffin Bay and Smith Sound, he allowed a doubt to rest for three centuries on the achievements of that stout explorer. When he cut down the narrative of the voyage which first rounded the north end of Spitsbergen and incidentally named Hakluyt's Headland, he seriously curtailed the history of exploration. His marginal notes, explaining that he has a map or a supplementary narrative which he finds too tedious to publish, leer maliciously at the desperate student of the record. It is only fair to say that the omissions were often due to the heavy expense of additions; but, all allowances made, the tedium which Purchas spared his readers has been replaced by a frequently acute irritation, which is not lessened by his unctuous style.

Purchas was not the man to continue Hakluyt's great work. One may acknowledge his piety and his industry and his honesty, which saved the last collections of his master: but one declines to admit his capacity. He was not a scientist and, like a well-meaning servant, did not know what to do with the treasures he intended faithfully to guard. When he enlarged, however extensively, the great edifice of Hakluyt, he enlarged it like an unskilled laborer.

4

The story of Hakluyt's legacy thus runs to anticlimax; and the ruins to which Purchas reduced it are a symbol of our fragmentary knowledge of Hakluyt's last years. The dignity of directorates is indeed his during these years, and we have supposed that the promoter here came to his most fruitful and active period. All that we have really known, however, is that he was a patentee and a shareholder of the Virginia Company and a member of the Northwest Passage Company. We have at the same time suggested that these honors were a sign of much vigorous activity. We have even drawn a picture of a Hakluyt at the elbow of Sir Thomas Smith, potent in advice and continuing up to his last years to be an instigator of expansion. But the picture is uncertain; and, though we may certainly say that he was venerated, it is unwise to say more.

If we are wary of exaggerating his part in promoting, we are likewise dissatisfied with our account of his consultant activities. The story of Hakluyt's earlier relations with Raleigh, with the Dutch, and with the East India Company can be matched by no like story of the Virginia Company, of the Northwest Passage Company, or of the Russia Company in its revived enterprises. I have brought forth conjectures merely, supposed that documents of advice might be his, inferred even a new rôle of diplomatic adviser. Again the picture is faint; and one can scarcely decide whether the last years find Hakluyt withdrawn from advising as from promoting, from the advancement of learning as from advising. Again one ascribes to him rather more than less, blaming our unsure knowledge rather than his inertia.

Even in our last picture, which is less faint, we admit a serious weakness. The collector of records is unmistakably as vigorous as ever. At the same time he is not publishing with anything like his former vivacity. There is only one book of the period that we can be sure is new, and that is the *Nova Francia.* The others date back, possibly or surely, to a really earlier period, and only happen—like the de Veer, the de Soto, and the *Decades*—to be delayed in their publication. He is not moreover starting new ventures, like going to Spain to steal from the Seville archives, or beginning a new edition of the *Voyages.* For all that we can see—and I repeat that we cannot see clearly—Hakluyt is, even as an archivist, marking time. As far only as publishing is concerned, of course: for he is collecting voluminously, translating, keeping close contact with French and Spanish and Danish enterprise, preparing probably the great collection that would add to his original epic the climax of the expansion to East and to West.

That story cannot be suitably told. We have no idea when Hakluyt would have brought out his third *Voyages.* The year 1612 and the age of sixty find him buying property and making a will. The year

1616 finds him drawing to his death, which may have come stealthily or openly, slowly or suddenly. Before the 23rd of November he is dead. On the 26th he is buried in Westminster Abbey. His son Edmund, rising to be a fellow of Trinity College, Cambridge, and to be ordained in his turn, inherits. His brother Oliver, doctor and father of a family in Eyton, survives seven years longer. Nine years later, the last collections appear in the often grotesque disguise of the *Pilgrims.* Hakluyt grows in esteem. Scientists continue to consult his volumes; explorers fall back upon them in their search and discovery of the world; the historian finds his record indispensable; the mere reader continues to thrill to the epic story of the English nation in search of the unknown; and, two centuries and a quarter after his death, a Hakluyt Society is founded to perpetuate and to carry on his toil.

So the name has become one to conjure with; but the man remains as obscure as ever in his living and breathing actuality. This is the final and regretful conclusion of the biographer. I think I have told the story of the scientist and something of the story of the zealous laborer for empire. Professionally, the man stands out with distinctness and distinction among the picturesque pioneers of the expansion, much like the inevitable central figure that focuses the light and color of a Brangwyn naval picture of Hakluyt's own time. There we leave his career; but the story of the man cannot be told.

Of his intellectual temperament I have indeed ventured to infer certain qualities. Hakluyt seems to have been industrious and painstaking; quick of apprehension if one considers the extent of his reading; probably of an orderly habit; wide-ranging in mental interest; ably imaginative, since he planned and carried through his collections of voyages; and possessed of a considerable literary skill, as is witnessed by the passages I have quoted from both his formal and his informal writing.

His personal and social qualities can be much less definitely judged. But one revealing remark has been made of Hakluyt by a contemporary, that of the ambassador whom he served as chaplain and who twice called him "honest": at the same time entrusting to him an oral dispatch of the highest consequence. The tribute is considerable in the age of Elizabeth; but, aside from the one bit of evidence, one must deal in inferences. From his writings one might judge the man at times naïve, at times pedantic, at times self-seeking; but these are the qualities of an age or rather of the manner of speech of an age. By comparison with his contemporaries, by especial comparison with Purchas, Hakluyt reveals an easy dignity.

What remains is uncertain. Whether he was stolid or vivacious of discourse, cheerful or malcontent of disposition; whether, being of a large family, twice married, and a father, he was affectionate, merely dutiful, or remote; whether, being a clergyman, he was capable or ineffective, straightforward or intriguing, conscientious or lax; whether, attaching himself as he did to men of importance in the state, he was aggressive, congenial, plausible, or merely useful: on none of these questions is there evidence. One thing can be said of him. He was never spoken of but with respect. It is only fair to hold him an upright man and an honorable, as he was a man of great ability and lasting achievement.

APPENDIX I. RICHARD HAKLUYT, LAWYER

The immediate family of Richard Hakluyt of the Middle Temple is given below. The fact that his father was Esquire proves that he was of the gentry and not one of the yeomen or tradesmen who are mentioned in the Leominster corporation records or who are known by their wills. He was moreover closely related to the Hakluyts of Eaton, as is proved by the settlement of 1564 (given below); and his arms, "azure three battle-axes gules" (Dugdale, below), are a variant of the arms of Hakluyt of Eaton, "gules three hatchets or," and of similar arms borne by earlier members of the family (Hereford Visitation).

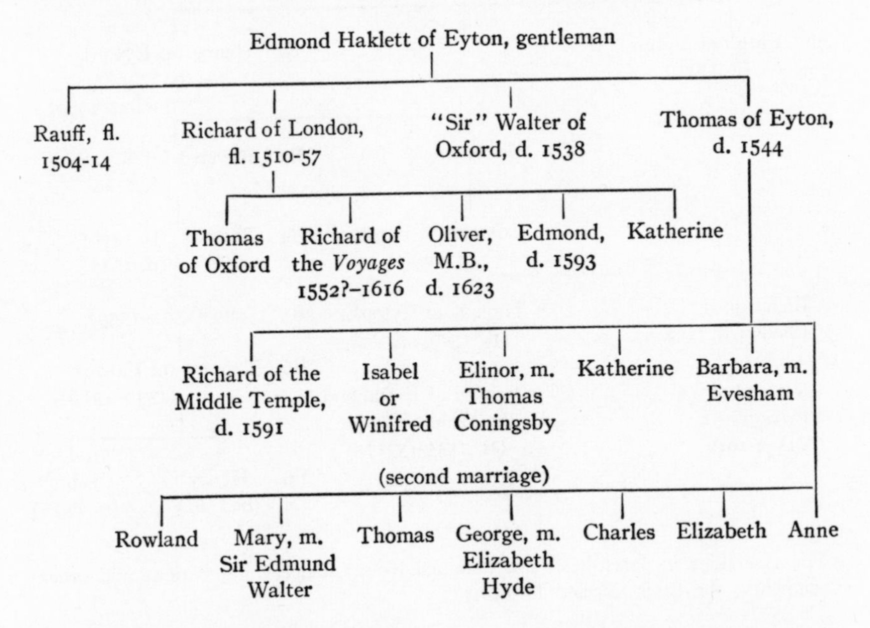

The table results from much fitting together of evidence. The lawyer was the son of the Thomas of Eyton who died in 1544 rather than of the Thomas who died in 1561 (Hereford wills): so much is proved by comparing the wills of Richard and the earlier Thomas (Canterbury wills, 7 Pynning). Thomas mentions the four daughters of his first wife—Isabel, Elinor, Katherine, Barbara; Richard mentions Winifred (as eldest and "best beloved" sister), Barbara (as the youngest), and Elinor. Moreover, the probate of Richard's will (see below) names Rowland as next of kin; and Rowland heads the second family of Thomas in the list given in the Shropshire Visitation (Fox family, into which Thomas' second wife remarried).

The immediate family of Richard the lawyer is then as follows. That Thomas of Eyton had two brothers Richard and Walter is proved by the will of William Martin, gent., of Hereford, their uncle (Canterbury wills, 4 Dyngeley, 1537), which mentions them. This relationship once established, there are many corroborating facts. The will of Richard of London (Canterbury wills, 16 Wrastley, 1557), mentions a deceased brother, "Sir Walter of Oxford"; it also mentions a "cousin," which in Tudor times also meant nephew, Richard, who was to be overseer of the will and who therefore, it is likely, was resident in London. Professor Taylor has found a fourth brother, Rauff, who was apprenticed skinner in 1502, and died in 1514. The fact that Edmond Haklett was the father of the brothers is proved by the apprenticeship record of Richard of London, who was also apprenticed, in 1510, to a member of the Skinners' Company.

The main Hakluyt lines A and B are taken from the Hereford Visitation of 1569; the C line is added by Professor Taylor's discovery of Edmond Haklett's place in the family.

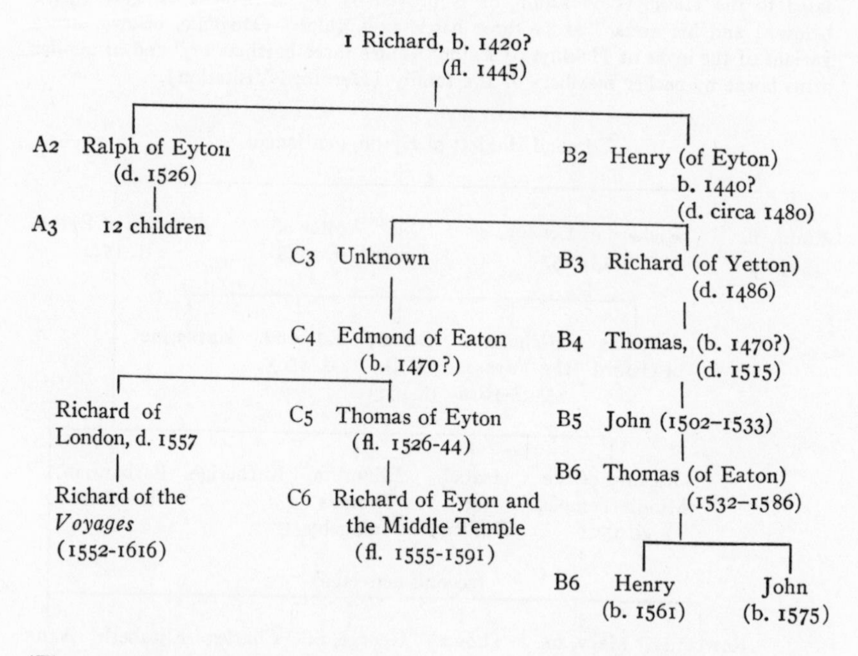

(The assertions in parenthesis are obtained from Chancery inquisitions and other documents; the dates queried I infer.)

Ralph Hakluyt of Eyton was a leading member of the family—Sheriff, M. P., J. P., and so on, being mentioned officially from 1476 to 1490 and again (if it is the same one) in 1507 and 1518. He had no son named Edmond. Henry, whose line the Herald was specially following, was possessed of the manors of Eton Lemster called Oldcourt, Eton Bedford, Eton Gamage, and Eyton; of 70 acres in Luston, 32 in Bradford; and of 13 messuages in Leominster (*Calendar of Patent Rolls,* 20 Edward IV, p. 228). This was Crown property and yielded, during the minority of Richard of Yetton, £55 14s. 4d. to the Crown (*ibid.*) All these Etons are almost certainly in Eyton, northwest of Leominster (Canon Bannister, in private letter, for which I am indebted to Miss Lilian Redstone).

Now in 1564 Richard the lawyer was next of kin to Thomas B6 or at least close enough to be chosen first contingent heir (see section 3 below). In summary, Richard the lawyer was descended from a younger son, but remained closely related to the head of the house Thomas (B6). The home manors are much too complicated to be distinguished. The lawyer's property was probably scattered about Leominster, especially near Eyton, two miles northwest of the borough.

(I am much indebted here to Miss Redstone for research at Hereford as well as in London.)

The family of Richard of the *Voyages* is considered in Appendix II.

2

The name Hakluyt was thought in Tudor times to be Welsh in origin. When Leland stopped at Eaton Manor in Herefordshire, on the Welsh border, he was told by the head of the Hakluyt house that "the chief and ancientest of the Hackluits have been Gentlemen in times out of memory, and they took their names of the Forest of Cluid in Radnorshire, and they had a Castle and Habitation not far from Radnor."

If the name did in fact go back to any such Welsh form as ap Cluid, I find no record of it. I find the first entry of the name in 1260, when it is written Haklutel. If the family had been Welsh, its name had been drastically anglicized, like the family itself, which was consistently on the English side during the conquest of Wales.

The name can be traced back in numerous state documents to some three centuries before Leland. In the thirteenth century it is usually Haklutel or Hakelutel or even Hacklitel. These forms appear in 13 out of 20 entries. Five times it is Hakelut; and once each Hacclut and Hakeluyt. I hesitate to dogmatize, especially because the last form is nearly as old as the normal; but the presence of the "l" in so many spellings makes the name almost inevitably Germanic, at least after 1260, and derived, as Bardsley's *Dictionary of Surnames* gives it, from "hack little."

In the fourteenth century the form Hakelut or Hakelute predominates. Out of 59 items, it takes up 35, all but one in the first half of the century. Haklutel survives once, Hakelutel twice: neither after 1317. Haclut appears six times, once as Hauclut; Haukelet once, Hacluyt once. In the second half of the century, Hakeluyt is, with one exception, the rule, appearing twelve times. The variations do not seem to come from personal whims, since the same man's name may be spelled in nearly all the different fashions.

So far the case seems to be fairly plain. The name was Hak-lu-tel, accented on the first syllable. The first "l" became syllabic like the second, and the name developed into Ha-ke-lu-tel. In the course of time the final "l," remaining remote from the accent, was unvoiced and then dropped. The name is now Ha-ke-lut and remains so. The later spelling of the fourteenth century, Hakeluyt, adds the "y" merely to mark the "u" as long. So I suppose now; but I gather that the sixteenth century did not think so. The "ui" or "uy" combination seemed then to point to a Welsh origin, since a Tudor king had made Welsh origins fashionable.

At any rate the fifteenth century items follow the fourteenth in preserving Hakeluyt, 13 times out of 19; two of the 13 are spelled Hakluyt, one Hakiluyt. That the final vowel is weakening, however, I infer from the appearance, along with one Hakelut, of three spellings Hakelet, one Haklet, and one Hakelyt. Though the spelling remains fairly constant, the name is moving toward Ha-ke-let, replacing the unaccented "u" with the obscure vowel or "mute e." This becomes, I submit, the regular pronounciation; but the sixteenth century brings in confusion, which still persists.

Leland spelled the name Hackluit, as we have seen, and in reporting a Welsh origin seems to suggest an accented "u." Yet the name of the preceding head of the family, John, is written Hakelut in 1526, Hakeluyt in 1533, and Hackluit in 1535. These spellings are in Chancery documents. The name of Ralph, the outstanding member of the family at an earlier date, under Henry VII, is written Hakelet, Hakluyt, Haklet, Hackluyt, and Hakeluyt. In the drawing up of wills, where one would expect to find the nearest to a family standard spelling, the form Hackluit predominates in this century. This is usually the spelling of the name of Richard the lawyer; and Richard the geographer standardized his own spelling to Hakluyt. Spelling of course is not decisive; but at least one may decide that the original Hacklutel has come to be spelled Hackluit. How has it come to be pronounced?

The Oxford Registers record the following spellings of the name of the geographer from 1570 on: Hacklette, Haklette, Haclette, Hakluette, Hakluit, Hackluitt, Hacklewit, Hacklewight. The intrusion of the "w" in the last two forms upsets our hitherto simple theory of a progression from Ha-ke-lut to Ha-ke-let, which would be upheld by the other Oxford forms. The "w" forms suggest another progression, from Ha-ke-lut to Ha-ke-lu-wit and thence perhaps to Ha-kel-e-wit and Ha-kel-wit. The first step might be explained as an attempt to pronounce the "ui" in the traditional spelling as a Welsh rather than an English combination, to make a new and artificial spelling pronunciation replace the usual one. Or it might be explained as a western variant of the "u" vowel.

So I infer, for it seems difficult to argue that the "ui" had meant a Welsh form in the days of Hacklutel. I infer also that the pronunciation did not altogether succeed. On the contrary, the natural pronunciation, as we may call it, is still represented in the Tudor century, especially in entries which seem plainly phonetic. The Skinners' Company admitted Richard Haklett to apprenticeship in 1510. The geographer himself, however he pronounced his name at Oxford, was addressed as Haklete in his Oxford friend Gager's Latin epigram of 1583. The foreign dispatches write Haklit and Hackett. He was written down Haclette when he spoke before the East India Company in 1600. His burial record at Westminster Abbey spelled his name Hackler, a mistake which could certainly not have been made if the artificial pronunciation was generally used. I conclude that people continued to pronounce Ha-ke-let or Hak-let; that they spelled Hackluit or Hakeluyt whenever they were not spelling by ear, in which case they wrote Haclette; and that some members of the family pronounced Ha-kel-wit or something like it.

(I am grateful to Professors P. G. Thomas and Allen Mawer for their judgments on this matter of phonology.)

3

The facts known about the lawyer's father, Thomas of Eyton, are as follows:

1526. Named clerk of the Council for Wales and the Border Counties (Patent 18 Henry VIII, I 30).

1529. As clerk of the Council for Wales, he drew for Council charges £100 from the King's Treasury of the Chamber (Trevelyan Papers 156: in *Camden Society Publications* 67, 1856).

1529. Was clerk of the Princess' (Mary's) Council (Brewer, *Letters and Papers of Henry the Eighth,* V 314).

1530. Drew as before £62 3s. 9d. (Trevelyan Papers 166: *ibid.*).

1538. Referred to as of Eyton (Brewer, *op. cit.,* XIII, part II, 128).

1539. Steward in Wales of the Countess of Salisbury (*ibid.,* XIV, part I, 64).

1541. Granted by Queen Katherine "all the fishing of her water of Eydon, co. Hereford" "for 21 years at 5s. a year" (Public Record Office, Ancient Deed B 6852, 33 Henry VIII).

1544, 15 May. His will was probated (Canterbury wills, 7 Pynning).

1546, January. Succeeded by Julian Evans in the clerkship of the Council for Wales (Brewer, *op. cit.*, XXI 71).

Thomas' brother Walter is the "Sir Walter" of the will of Richard the Skinner, the third brother. To Walter is there ascribed a bequest to the poor in Oxford. The Oxford Registers note a degree of B.Can.L. awarded to him in 1530. According to the Parish Records of Shotley, Suffolk (edited by Rev. S. H. A. Hervey), Walter Haklet was presented to the rectory in 1522 by Thomas Felton, Esq., being replaced "upon his death 1538." Shotley is opposite Trimley St. Martin, the seat of the Cavendishes; both Felton, patron of the living, and Richard Hakluyt the geographer married into the Cavendish family. Walter's will does not seem to be extant.

There is no record of the birth of Richard Hakluyt the lawyer. The table shows that he was the only son of his parents, though one of five children; that his mother, whose name is unknown, must have died in the fifteen-thirties; and that his father married again and had seven children before his death in 1544. It is likely that Richard was born in the earlier thirties. There is no record of his marrying.

Of his private life the following facts are known:

1557. It was probably he who was made "overseer" of the will of Richard Hakluyt of London, whom we believe to be his father's brother (see Appendix II for the will). If the latter was the father of Richard Hakluyt of the *Voyages*, it is likely that the lawyer later acted as guardian of his infant cousins.

1564. In a deed of settlement drawn up by Thomas Hakluyt of Eaton to provide for his succession, Richard Hakluyt was named contingent heir after the "heirs of the body of Thomas." The other contingent heirs are, in order: Charles (half brother of Richard), Miles (unplaced), George (also half brother of Richard), Charles Leyghton (unplaced), Richard Acton (nephew of Thomas' wife: Inquisition of Thomas of Eaton 1587, Chancery Inquisitions, series 2, vol. 215, no. 260, Hereford). Rowland, the eldest half brother of Richard, was omitted.

1583?. Harleian MS 7369, fols. 1 to 28, contains an undated survey of Richard Hakluyt's lands, entitled: "This is my Boke of Survey for Eyton taken by Richard Hackluitt as fowellth," signed "Jo: Walle." The survey distinguished "my lands" and those of others; and, though there are no totals taken, there are certain figures. In fol. 6, for example, is written: "Soe that it wold seme that there is of errable not belonging to me R.H. 224 acres And of myne of Acres 556." In fol. 7 "the sum of Mr. Hakluyt's oxen is 23," under the year 1583. Various dates scattered through the survey suggest this as the approximate date of its making.

1586. Richard was named one of the commissioners in the Chancery inquisition post mortem of Thomas Hakluyt of Eaton. The writ was issued 20 October; the inquiry was held on the following 3 March. (Inquisitions, ser. 2, vol. 215, no. 260.)

1589. Lansdowne MS 58 (Burleigh Papers), no. 56, is a letter from Richard Hakluyt of Eyton and the Middle Temple to Lord Burleigh, complaining, under date of 20 March 1588–9, of an unfair bargain made by the treasurer of the royal household for some of his oxen two years before. The treasurer's answer is no. 57 following. *

1591, 4 March. Richard Hakluyt's will was proved at Hereford: I print it at the end of this appendix. In it he bequeathed his "lands," all apparently in the neighborhood of Eyton, to his cousins Oliver, Edmond, and Richard in that order, and in default of their issue to his sister Winifred. *

1591, 6 March. Richard Hakluyt was buried in Leominster Church (Burial Register).

4

Richard Hakluyt's connection with the Middle Temple is set down as follows (*Middle Temple Records,* edited by C. H. Hopwood, vol. 1, 1904).

1555, 4 June. Richard, son and heir of Thomas Hakluyt of Eyton, Herefordshire, Esq., generally, to Clerks' Commons, at the instance of Mr. Carus. Pledge,—Bell. (This is the regular form of admission as a student, clerks' commons being the table assigned to juniors of less than two years' standing. Mr. Carus was a bencher; Mr. Bell shortly became one.) p. 100.

1555, 18 October. (Hakluyt was one of the sureties for John Hall, admitted from Henwick, Worcester.) p. 102.

1555, 22 November. Hackluyt and More to the chamber late Mr. Ynglers. (A regular room assignment. More was Thomas More, gent., who had been admitted on 20 October preceding.) p. 104.

1564, 27 October. Mr. Phillips to a chamber with Messrs. Hackluyt and Atkyns near the Church, in expectancy of their ancients. (Atkyns was Thomas Atkyns, of Ashelhow, Gloucester, who had been admitted in 1558. Phillips was Fabian Phillips of Leominster, who was admitted in 1560; he was M.P. in 1572 and became an associate Bencher in 1590. The final phrase is difficult to interpret, for the term "ancient" was used in the Middle Temple to mean barristers who had passed beyond the age of summons to the Readers' table. But in nine years Hakluyt would barely have been called to the bar; he would not even be eligible to plead, under the rules of 1559, until 1567. The term must not be a technical one then and can hardly be interpreted.) p. 144.

1567. (A room survey of this year finds Hakluyt and Phillips living on Inner Temple Lane, in an "upper chamber" at one remove from the northwest corner of the Temple Church. Together they paid 6s. 8d. yearly and as much more for a bedchamber below.) p. 433.

1571, 10 February. (Hakluyt and Phillips were sureties for George Detton of Detton, Shropshire.) p. 176.

1575, 16 March. Mr. John Delaber, gent., to Mr. Hackluyt's chamber in expectancy of Mr. Fabian Phillips. (Delaber had been admitted on the preceding 10 February from Southam, Gloucester, by way of the preparatory New Inn. His was a Parliamentary family. The "expectancy," I take it, means simply that Phillips was planning to move.) p. 209.

1582, 17 February. (Hakluyt and David Williams were sureties for Charles Bethell of Northoppe, Flint, who came from the New Inn.) p. 258.

1584, 13 July. Mr. Thomas Stevens to the chamber of Messrs. Hacluit and De Labeare in place of Hacluit, who forfeited for discontinuance. p. 270.

1585, 12 May. Thomas Morgan and Richard Hackluit shall be associate with this bench for their commons. None shall henceforth be so associate unless he give £10, or plate, or some provision for the table, unless he be a Reader. p. 277.

1591, 4 June. Mr. Walter Pye to the chamber of Messrs. Hackluyt and Delabere on the death of the former. p. 321.

Sir William Dugdale lists Hakluyt's arms as among those emblazoned "in the first window of the south wall of the Hall" of the Middle Temple. They are described as "azure three battle-axes gules." (*Origines juridiciales,* 1666, p. 226.)

5

The following facts show the relations of Hakluyt to the state and to trade.

1557. A Richard Hackluyt, gent., was M.P. for Leominster in the last Marian Parliament (*Members of Parliament 1213–1874: Parliament Accounts and Papers,* vol. 62, 1878).

1567. Henry Lane of the Skinners' Company, who had been English agent in Russia, is said to have written Hakluyt a letter on the fur trade (Alexander Brown, *The Genesis of the United States,* II 908). I have not found the letter; and I am inclined to think that it is the one written much later to the younger Hakluyt and published by him (*Voyages,* III 98) on the Russian mission to England in 1567.

1570–71, 28 February. Hakluyt wrote to Burleigh on the naval preparations of Spain (State Papers Domestic Elizabeth 77,18), enclosing the testimony he had taken down (State Papers Foreign 112,183). The letter about Stukeley is registered in *Calendar State Papers Foreign 1569–71* as par. 1560; the Queen's letter to Walsingham as par. 1601; the quieting letters of the envoy as pars. 1683, 1684.

1571, 7 November. Hakluyt wrote to Burleigh in behalf of Oliver Dawbeny (State Papers Domestic 83,7). The career of that merchant as Surveyor of Customs and Duties on all beer exported may be followed in State Papers Domestic Elizabeth Addenda 14,16, which is the draft of his patent; State Papers Domestic 46,66—46,71—54,51—57,51—58,50, which is his report of 1571—83,6—83,7—83,12—85,39—85,40, which is a further report—85,41—85,53—and in the *Acts of the Privy Council 1575,* p. 370, the canceling of Dawbeny's commission. The iniquities of Thomas Smith, "Customer," were exposed after his death by a memorandum listed as State Papers Domestic 239,67.

1572. Hakluyt asked for information on Mexico from Henry Hawks. The latter's letter, addressed to Eyton, was later printed in the *Voyages,* IX 378.

1578, 30 June. Hakluyt visited John Dee at Mortlake (Dee's *Diary, Camden Society Publications* 19, 1842).

1578, 13 November. Hakluyt received from Anthony Parkhurst of Bristol, of whom he had asked information on Newfoundland, a letter of this date (*Voyages,* VIII 9).

1579. Hakluyt drew up the instructions for Morgan Hubblethorne, Dyer, who was sent with a Russia Company mission to Persia. The memorandum, which extends to less than a thousand words, was printed in the *Voyages,* III 249; the order of the Privy Council to the Dyers' Company is given in *Acts of the Privy Council 1578–1580,* p. 147, under date of May 31.

1580. Hakluyt drew up one of the memoranda for the northeast expedition, which was printed in the *Divers Voyages* and in the *English Voyages,* III 264.

1581, 14 June. Hakluyt was named by the Privy Council to a committee on repairs to Dover Harbor (*Acts of the Privy Council 1580–1581,* p. 80). In many of the State Papers Domestic of the time are references to subscriptions to that work.

1582, 12 May. Hakluyt may have been the author of a "Note for all such English wares as are good and most necessary for the parts of Brazil, for Mr. Fenton and Luke Warde's voyage" (State Papers Domestic 153,43). The paper is not in Hakluyt's handwriting.

1582. Hakluyt drew up two memoranda on the new Levant Company trade. One, for the use of "a friend that was sent into Turkey" was printed in the *Voyages,* V 229; the other and longer one, for "a principal English factor at Constantinople," was printed *ibid.,* V 231.

1585. Governor Ralph Lane wrote to Hakluyt from Virginia, his newsletter being printed in the *Voyages,* VIII 319.

1585. Hakluyt wrote a prospectus entitled *Inducements to the liking of a Voyage intended towards Virginia.* It does not seem to have been printed until 1602, when it was added to the second edition of John Brereton, *Discovery of the*

North Part of Virginia. The whole book has been reprinted in 3 *Collections Massachusetts Historical Society,* VIII 69 ff., 1843.

* 1590?. Hakluyt wrote to Abraham Ortelius to suggest a world-map on rollers. The letter is printed under this conjectural date in J. H. Hessels, *Abrahami Ortelii epistulae,* Cambridge 1887, pp. 415–418.

now dated 1567-8

* Will of Richard Hackluyt of Eyton, 1591
(Hereford Probate Registry)

In the name of God Amen I Richard Hackluyt of Eyton in the Countie of He . . . hole of bodie and sownde of mynde, yet consideringe the mortall state of man and the . . . pestilent fevers soe co͞monly Raigneinge, make this my last will and Testament in maner (following)

Firste I bequeathe my Sowle redeemed by the mearitts & passions and death of Jesus Christ . . . Worlde, to the same Christe that is deyd buried, risen and ascended and that shall be the Judge of all Nations under heaven, My body I bequeath to the earthe till the generall resurr(ection) bodie and sowle shall ioyne to everlastinge Salvacion.

My funeralls wthowt pompe discharged and my debtes duely paied, my Plate, Corne C . . . stuffe wth all my goods and Chattells whatsoever I bequeathe according to a Schedule of . . . hereafter to this my laste will to be annexed.

My lands that bee in my disposicion to bequeathe, late leased to Edmond Burrop and to Thomas Goolde . . . of Thomas Golde called commonly Burropps fearme lying in Eyton and in the fyeldes of the same . . . of Luston in the County of Hereford I bequeathe and geve to Olyver Hackluyt of Christchurch Oxf(ord my) uncles sonne and to the heyres males of his bodie lawefully begotten and for lacke of suche yssue I give bequeathe the same to Edmond Hackeluytt his brother and to the heires males of his body lawfully begotten for lacke of such yssue male to Richard Hackeluyt theire elder brother and to the heires males of (his body) lawfully begotten, and for lacke of such issue to Wynifride my Sister wief to Roger Bruton of Hal . . . County of Salopp esquire and to her heires to dispose at her will and pleasure to any of my name that shall possesse the reste of my lands in Eyton if any such shalbe founde thriftie, or otherwise to bestow them at her good will and pleasure. The rest of my landes unbequeathed lyinge in quilletts and . . . and heereafter that shall be purchased, I bequeathe to Olyver Hackluyte, Edmond Hackeluyt and to R . . . Hackeluyt and to Wynifreid Bruton and to the heyres males of their bodies in manner and forme as is lymytted in the guyfte of Burropps fearme.

In wittnes whereof I have sette my hande and seale this xiijth of September 1587 and ordeigne (and) make sole executor of this my laste will and testament Olyver Hackeluyt of Christchurch Oxeford aforesaid.

The Schedule that I appointe to bee annexed to my last will and Testament.

Firste I bequeathe to Barbera Evisham my yongeste Sister the so͞me of v li in money.

Item to my eldest and beste beloved Sister Wynifried Bruton if she Chaunce to overlyve her husband (a) goblett of Sylver remayneinge at my sister Elnor Conesbies.

Item to Elnor Conesbie my Sister one dosen of Silver Spones.

Item to Thomas Conesbie her sonne one other dosen of Silver Spones.

Item I also gyve and bequeathe to Barbera my said Sister my smaler Salteseller of Silver.

Item to Olyver Hackeluyt of Christchurch in Oxeford my greater salteseller of Sylver

Item I bequeath to Richard Fenmor suche waiges as I owe him wth fortie shillinges in money over and besides.

Item I gyve to Ellnor Burrope my servaunte alsoe other fortie shillinges wth all her waiges due at (my) deathe wth a course paier of sheetes, a Corse peyer of Blancketts A Canvas and one of the Couer(lets) made by Benettes wief of Leompster.

(No signature—no witnesses)

(Proved at Hereford 4 March 1590–91 by the executor, upon renunciation and revocation of the administration to the next of kin Rowland Hackluitt.)

*An asterisk in these appendices indicates that the item marked is printed in E. G. R. Taylor, *The Original Writings and Correspondence of the Two Richard Hakluyts* (2 Hakluyt Society 76, 77, 1935).

APPENDIX II. RICHARD HAKLUYT, PREACHER

The preacher's immediate family is charted as follows:

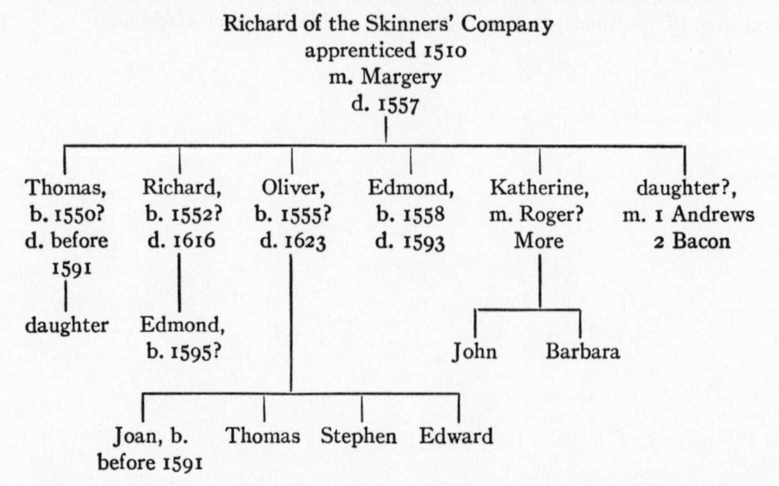

There is no record of the birth or parentage of the preacher or of his brothers and sisters. Since the four brothers were educated at Westminster School, it may be inferred that the parents lived in London. This inference is confirmed by the matriculation entry of the youngest brother, who was written down "of London, gentleman." This brother Edmond was born in 1558; and in his will occurs the only reference to the parents: "my father and mother forsook me and were taken from me by death even in my infancy" (Prerogative Court of Canterbury, 18 Nevell, 1593).

Parents

Of London Hakluyts who might have been the father of Richard and the rest, there is but one discoverable. This is Richard Hakluyt, Skinner, of the parish of St. Augustines, Old Change, who died in 1557. That he was actually one of the Hereford Hakluyts is attested by his apprenticeship record, for which I am indebted to the present clerk to the Skinners' Company:

"Md. that Richard Haklett the son of Edmond Haklett of Eyton of Hereford Gentylman, hath put hymselff apprntyce unto peter Myddylton from the ffest of seynt Michell Tharcangell in the second yere of the reigne of Kyng Henry the 8th (1510) unto the ende of sevyn yeres."

There is no record of his admission to the Company.

To prove that the Skinner was actually the father of the preacher and the others, I present the following inferences. He died at the right time to suit the statement of Edmond above; and, since there is no record of the burial of his wife after 1559, when the church registers begin, it is likely that his wife died before that date and thus also forsook the children in their infancy. In his will the Skinner spoke often of his "cousin Richard," which in Tudor English might mean "nephew"; and I have shown above, in Appendix I, that the Skinner was the brother of the Clerk of the Council for Wales and therefore the uncle of the lawyer. Now Edmond's will also speaks of his "uncle's son" Richard; and both Edmond and his brother the preacher frequently mention the lawyer in affectionate terms, as if he had been, as was suggested in the Skinner's will, a kind of guardian to them. Unless then there was still another uncle of the lawyer who also lived in London and who also died between 1557 and 1560, there can be no question that Richard the Skinner was the father of the family given above.

The Skinner's will is abstracted as follows: *

Prerogative Court of Canterbury, 16 Wrastley.

Richard Hackelett, citizen & skinner of London, dwelling within the parish of St. Augustines, at the Lower end of the Old Change, Pauls gate, within the City of London: "sick in body with the visitation of Almighty God": 31 March 1557.

To be buried in said church of St. Augustine, so near the "little pulpit" as conveniently may be: to the high altar there for tithes and oblations forgotten, 3s. 4d.

To my cousin Richard Hackelett 40s. in money.

Residue of estate to be equally divided into three parts according to the laudable custom of the City of London: one part to myself, one part to Margerie Hackelett my well-beloved wife, one third to be divided among my children.

Wife Margerie executrix.

Cousin Richard Hackelett overseer: to be aiding, assisting, and comforting my said executrix, he to have the above 40s. for his pains taken.

I will that according to my brother Sir Walter Hackelett's will such money be bestowed upon the poor and otherwise at Oxeford as his will purporteth, amounting to £7, viz. &c.

Proved 27 May 1557 by the widow Margerie.

I find no other record of Margerie Hakluyt.

The Preacher's Brothers

Thomas Hakluyt was educated at Westminster School. In 1567 he was elected to a Westminster studentship at Trinity College, Cambridge, proceeded Bachelor of Arts in 1572 and Master of Arts in 1575 and was incorporated in 1576 at Oxford, though in what capacity is not known (Foster, *Alumni Oxon*). He died before 1591 and was buried at Oxford (will of Edmond: "praying him [the executor] to bury me near my cousin Richard Hakluyt or by my brother Thomas in Oxford"). He left female issue (*ibid.*).

Oliver Hakluyt was elected from Westminster to a studentship at Christchurch, Oxford in 1573, from which event his birth may be dated about 1555. He took the degree of Bachelor of Arts in 1577, Master of Arts in 1580, and Bachelor of Medicine, with license to practice, in 1588 (Foster, *op. cit.*). Two Latin poems were written to him, as to other members of Christchurch, by William Gager in 1583: one an insignificant epigram on his profession (Additional MSS 22,583, fol. 63); the other a trivial apology (*ibid.*, 67). Of him Anthony à Wood wrote (1691) that "being graduated in physic (he) had a happy hand in the practice of it," which Foster paraphrases (1891) "an eminent physician."

At the time of Richard's will (1612), Oliver was living in a house owned by the preacher in Leominster Oare, Hereford, paying a rent of sixteen nobles, or five to eight pounds, and therefore enjoyed a comfortable living. At the same time Oliver presented Richard to the living of Gedney, Lincolnshire, of which he had been made patron, apparently "for one turn," by grant of Queen Anne in 1604 (record of presentation). The royal grant may have been made for medical services, and it may have been passed on to Richard as a *quid pro quo* of some kind. Oliver was not a beneficiary of the will of either Richard or Edmond, though he was of Richard the lawyer, his uncle. His children received sufficient legacies from Richard the preacher: £20 to the daughter, £10 each to the sons.

Oliver's own will was dated 1621. He there wrote himself of Eyton. His property, "in Eyton, Luston, and Eye," north and northwest of Leominster, was arranged to yield 20 marks and five bushels of wheat, annual rent, to his wife Rose. His children were listed as (1) Thomas, cut off with 20 shillings because of "his unbridled and abhominable life"; (2) Stephen, principal legatee; (3) Edward; (4) Johane (the eldest, since she was living in 1591 and was mentioned in Edmond's will), who, not being "so dutiful and loving a child unto me as I expected," was given "only £ 50" (Prerogative Court of Canterbury, 94 Swann).

Oliver's dutiful son Stephen had added to the family by 1634. The Leominster records note a lease to him in that year of plow land, to run for ninety-nine years "if Frances Hackluitt, Anne, and Mary, daughters of Stephen, so long live" (Chamber Leases, fol. 15).

Edmond Hakluyt was born in 1557 or 1558, matriculated at Oxford in 1575, when he was recorded as seventeen years old, of London, a gentleman, and was admitted to St. John's College. It is not certain that it was the same Edmond who, in 1582, being described as "clerk of New College," applied for the Bachelor's degree (Foster, *op. cit.*). There is no record of his taking the degree. At some time before 1591 he was for four years tutor to Lord William Howard, son of the Lord Admiral of England and nephew of the Ambassador whom Richard served in France (Edmond's will: "unto whom I was tutor four years together"). From his will it appears that he had studied the civil law, borrowing books for the purpose from "my cousin Norwood."

Edmond died in 1593, possessed of considerable property which he bequeathed as follows: to Richard, "my free Land in Eaton and elsewhere"; to Richard and Katherine jointly, "my lease of five years to come of eight pounds yearly bought of Richard Coox of Dorking"; to Katherine and her children, to "my sister Andrews children," and to "my cousin Dorothy Davies," "my Stocke in Ireland between forty and fifty pounds"; to "my gentle cousin Vernon" and to Lord William Howard, sums of money for rings; for the erection of a tombstone for himself and "for my dear cousin Richard Hakluyt Esquire," the value of his clothing. Richard Hakluyt, as executor, took out letters of administration on the 1st of February 1593 (Prerogative Court of Canterbury, 18 Nevell).

Two sisters are mentioned in the wills of both Richard and Edmond. Katherine More or Morer was a chief beneficiary of both; it was doubtless her husband, Roger Moer, who witnessed Edmond's will. In 1612 she was living in Holborn, the mother of John and Barbara (Richard's will). It may have been the son, John Moore, who bought in 1621 the Hakluyt shares in Virginia.

The other sister's name is not given. She is mentioned by Edmond as "my sister Andrews," by Richard as "my sister Bacon." She received only minor bequests from both. She may have been a half sister or a sister-in-law, wife of the deceased Thomas.

Richard's Family

Richard's first wife is called "Duglasse Hackluytt" in her burial entry (Wetheringsett Register), for a record of which I am indebted to the Rev. V. B. Redstone, F.S.A. Davy's eighteenth-century "Suffolk Collections" identifies her as Douglas Cavendish, daughter of Richard Cavendish of Hornsey. Richard Cavendish was of the Trimley St. Martin family (Suffolk), an author and politician, uncle of Thomas Cavendish the circumnavigator (*Dictionary of National Biography*). By this marriage Hakluyt became allied to Thomas Cavendish, his wife's cousin; to Sir Robert Dudley, son of Leicester and of the Countess of Sheffield, Hakluyt's patroness, since Dudley married Thomas Cavendish's sister; and remotely enough to Stafford the Ambassador, husband of the Countess.

I find no record of the marriage. Presumably it took place between 1587, when Hakluyt resigned his studentship at Christchurch, and 1594, in time for the birth of a son about 1595. Douglas Hakluyt died in 1597 and was buried on

August 8. In 1604 Hakluyt married again, his second wife being Frances, widow of William Smith of London. I cannot identify her further. (See under 1604, in the chronology following.)

Only one child is mentioned in Hakluyt's will. Born probably about 1595, Edmond was admitted as a pensioner to Trinity College, Cambridge in 1611; took the degree of A.B. in 1616, A.M. in 1619, and was elected a Fellow of the College in 1618 (J. and J. A. Venn, *Alumni Cantab.*, part I, vol. II, 1922). He was ordained in 1626 (*ibid.*). Edmond was chief heir and executor of his father's will, which he probated in 1616. In 1621 he transferred his father's two shares in Virginia to John Moore (Alexander Brown, *The First Republic in America,* 1898, p. 423: citing the court minutes of the Company). Moore may have been, as I surmised above, his cousin. Fuller (1662) called him "an unthrift son, who embezzled (a fair estate) on this token, that he cheated the covetous usurer, who had given him spick and span new money for the old land of his great great grandfather." As this neat story is also credited to the Henry Hakluyt who sold Eaton manor, it has not a great deal of value. I find no further record of Edmond.

A cousin Dorothy is mentioned in both Edmond's and Richard's wills. By Edmond twenty shillings were bequeathed to "my cousin Dorothy Davies as a token for my thankful mind." By Richard five pounds were bequeathed to "my loving cousin Dorothy Patrickson." To her son, John Davies, who was made "supervisor" of Richard's will, were left five pounds; and mention was made of his "counsel I have had hitherto in my two late purchases"—of real estate in Westminster and in Suffolk. Dorothy may have been the daughter of Thomas and niece of the clergyman.

To "my gentle cousin Vernon at her house" Edmond left money for a ring; he had borrowed law books from a "cousin Norwood." To a cousin Thomas Hackluit Richard bequeathed twenty shillings and some clothes. This may be the Thomas of Hereford who matriculated at Oxford in 1601, though I cannot place him in the family. "My cousin Wigmore" is mentioned in Richard's letter to Burleigh in 1588: possibly the Wigmore who was M.P. in 1585.

Richard's will is abstracted under the year 1612, below.

The Preacher's Annals

1551 or 1552

Richard Hakluyt was born. (His application for a marriage license, 30 March 1604, gives his age as "about 52."—J. L. Chester, *Allegations for Marriage Licenses*, p. 286: *Harleian Society Publications* 25, 1887.)

1557

May. Death of his father (see above).

1560–1570

For some years during this period Hakluyt was a student at the newly refounded Westminster School (dedication of the 1589 *Voyages:* "one of her Majesty's Scholars at Westminster").

At some time in these years he paid the famous visit to his cousin Richard's rooms, which determined his life work (*ibid.*). The year was probably 1568, since in 1594 Hakluyt reckoned his devotion to geography as dating back twenty-six years (Hakluyt to van Meteren, 6 December 1594).

1570

Hakluyt was elected to Christchurch, Oxford, as one of the two Westminster Students of that year (Foster, *Alumni Oxon.;* Sargeaunt, *Annals of Westminster School,* p. 57). He held the studentship until at least 1587 (dedication of the

Decades, 1 May 1587); he probably relinquished it before 1589 (title page of the 1589 *Voyages:* "Student sometime of Christchurch, &c.").

1574

Hakluyt took the degree of Bachelor of Arts (*Register of Oxford University Degrees,* vol. II, part III, p. 39: "Hacklette—Haklette, Haclette, Hakluette, Hakluit, Hackluitt, Hacklewit, Hacklewight,—Richard; suppl. B. A. Oct. 1573, and again 16 Jan. 1573/4, adm. 19 Feb. 1573/4, det. 1573.4; suppl. M. A. 14 May, lic. 27 June 1577, inc. 1577").

1575

Hakluyt was the recipient of the sum of ten shillings from the Nowell educational bequest, which was supplemented by two shillings sixpence on June 4. Robert Nowell, Attorney-General of the Court of Wards and steward of the Chapter of St. Paul's Cathedral in London, who died in 1569, provided in his will for payments to needy scholars, among whom were to be Edmund Spenser and Richard Hooker. The entries in the executors' book of disbursements are as follows:

"To one Mr. Hakeluite Bachelor of Arts of Christe College in Oxforde the xiith of Maye (1575) by Dr. Humfrey x s."

"To one Mr. Hackeluett the iiijth of June 1575 of Christe Church in Oxforde ij s. vj d."

—Towneley MSS: in *Historical Manuscripts Commission, Fourth Report,* Appendix, p. 614.

Dr. Humfrey was vice-chancellor of Oxford.

1577

Hakluyt proceeded Master of Arts, as above.

At some time in this year he met the Flemish geographer Ortelius on the latter's visit to England (statement in the *Discourse on the Western Planting,* p. 102). It has been seen above that Richard Hakluyt the lawyer was acquainted with Daniel Rogers, relative of the Fleming.

1578

At some time between the beginning of this year and 1583, Hakluyt was ordained. (Presentation deed to the living of Gedney, 1612: "ordained deacon and priest by Bishop Piers of Salisbury." Bishop Pierce, formerly Dean of Christchurch, Oxford, was installed at Salisbury December 23, 1577, and was translated from Salisbury in 1583—John Le Neve, *Fasti Ecclesiae Anglicanae.* The Salisbury registers contain no record of the ordination.)

1580

Hakluyt procured the publication of Cartier's first two voyages to America, translated by John Florio of Oxford from the Italian of Ramusio. The book was licensed June 7 by the Stationers; the dedication was dated June 25. (The authority for Hakluyt's share in this venture, which is not noted in the book itself, is his own statement in the dedication of the *Divers Voyages:* "the last yeere, at my charges and other of my friends, by my exhortation, I caused Jaques Cartier's two voyages . . . to be translated out of my volumes." Florio himself speaks only of "the requests and earnest solicitations of divers my good friends here in Oxford"; while the dedication, to the sheriff of Oxford, was suggested by "Master H. Leigh.")

Hakluyt wrote to Mercator, the Flemish geographer, for advice on the expedition which the Russia Company was sending to explore the Northeast Passage. The letter is not extant. Mercator's reply, dated July 28, which arrived only after the expedition had sailed, was printed in the *Voyages* (III 275). It does not appear that Hakluyt was personally acquainted with the foremost geographer of his time; but he knew Mercator's son Rumold at the time of the printing of the *Divers Voyages,* 1582 (dedication), and he later printed a letter written in 1581 to the geographer on Arctic projects of the Dutch (*Voyages,* III 450). *

1581

Hakluyt held conversation with the Portuguese Ambassador, Don Antonio de Castillio (dedication of *French Florida,* 1587). It was probably in this year that he also approached Sir Francis Drake with a plan for subsidizing a chair of navigation (dedication of *Divers Voyages,* 1582).

1582

Hakluyt published his first work, the *Divers Voyages:* licensed by the Stationers 21 May, dedicated to Philip Sidney. That the book was the work of the younger and not the elder R. H. ("R. H." is the signature of the dedication) it might be difficult to prove. I assemble these evidences: *

1. It was done by the same person who paid for Florio's Cartier, and all the named participants in that work are of Oxford, with which the elder Hakluyt seems to have been unconnected.
2. The author was a young man: for the Portuguese with whom he had talked had said that "if he were now as young as I (for at this present he is threescore years of age) he would sell all he had" and take up oversea exploring (Epistle Dedicatory).
3. Savile wrote to Camden from Merton College, Oxford, 27 June (1582?): "It is rumored among us that something of Hakluyt's is now in press" (Thomas Smith, *Vita Camdeni et epistolae,* 1691).

During the summer of this year, when plans were being made for Gilbert's American colony, Hakluyt seems to have been consulted by at least two of those interested—Sir George Peckham and Mayor Thomas Aldworth of Bristol (Walsingham to Hakluyt, 11 March 1583: see below).

1583

11 March. Walsingham wrote to Hakluyt commending his interest in geography. On the same day he commissioned Hakluyt and another to proceed to Bristol, there to obtain the support of the Corporation for Gilbert's colony. Hakluyt left Bristol, having accomplished his mission, on 25 March (Walsingham to Hakluyt, Walsingham to Aldworth, Aldworth to Walsingham: *Voyages,* VIII 131–134. The index of the 1589 edition proves that this episode concerns the younger, not the elder, Hakluyt). * *

Early in this year Hakluyt conferred with John Newbery on the latter's mission to India. He gave Newbery a copy of the letter of Thomas Stevens from Goa (printed in *Voyages,* VI 377) and a note, presumably on India, by "Francis Fernandes the Portugal" (Newbery to Hakluyt, from Aleppo the 28 May: *Voyages,* V 452). *

Hakluyt had some idea of following Gilbert to America, probably in a ship to be commanded by Carleill or Frobisher. Gilbert sailed June 11 (Parmenius to Hakluyt, from St. John's, N.F., 6 August: "You thought in June last to have followed us yourself": *Voyages,* VIII 81). *

If Hakluyt did not accompany the expedition, he introduced Parmenius to Gilbert, probably in the spring of 1583. Parmenius was a Hungarian of Buda, whom Hakluyt described (*Discourse of the Western Planting,* 31) as "lately my bedfellow of Oxford." The learned foreigner composed a Latin *Carmen* in Gilbert's honor, which was published; he was taken on board and went down with Gilbert's flagship. (*Carmen Stephani Parmenii Budaeii,* 1582, prefatory letter to Sir Humphrey Gilbert: "It happened that when I was paying my respects to and making acquaintance with excellent Londoners, I was brought to you by my worshipful and learned friend Richard Hakluyt, who had explained to me your noble plan": *Voyages,* VIII 24, reprinting the poem. A verse translation of the ode, by Abiel Holmes, was published in I *Collections Massachusetts Historical Society,* IX, 1804; a translation in prose by W. G. Gosling in his *Life of Sir Humphrey Gilbert,* London 1911.)

Hakluyt was attached as chaplain to the English ambassador to France ("I passed at length the narrow seas into France with Sir Edward Stafford, her Majesty's careful and discreet Ligier, where during my five years abroad with him . . .": dedication of the 1589 *Voyages.*—"Master Hakluyt, then Chaplain to the English Embassador in France": *Purchas His Pilgrims,* XV 413. Hakluyt is called "secretary" to the ambassador in the Index to *Calendar State Papers Foreign 1584–1585*). Stafford arrived at Boulogne September 28, at Paris October 7 (*Calendar State Papers Foreign 1583–1584,* pp. 117, 128).

In this year William Gager of Christchurch wrote to Hakluyt the epigram printed at the beginning of this volume (Additional MSS 22,583, fol. 63).

1584

Hakluyt wrote to Walsingham from Paris January 7 and April 1 (State Papers Domestic Elizabeth 167,7 and 170,1 respectively). * *

Hakluyt seems to have been in England before July 21 (Philip Sidney to Stafford, 21 July: "We are half persuaded to enter the journey of Sir Humfrey Gilbert very eagerly, whereunto your Mr. Hakluyt hath served for a very good trumpet."—*Complete Works of Sir Philip Sidney,* III 145, edited by Albert Feuillerat, Cambridge 1923).

He had returned to Paris by October 15 (*Calendar State Papers Foreign 1584–1585,* p. 106). "Two days before his dispatch" he presented to the Queen the *Discourse on the Western Planting,* together with a Latin essay on the *Politics* of Aristotle. At this interview the Queen granted him a mandate for the next vacant prebend in the Bristol Cathedral Chapter (Hakluyt to Walsingham, 7 April 1585). The mandate is abstracted as follows: *

Patent Roll (No. 1249) 26 Elizabeth, part 13, m.4

5 October (A.D. 1584). The Queen grants to Richard Hackluyt master of arts and professor of theology that canonry or prebend within the cathedral church of the Holy Trinity Bristol which shall the first become vacant, with all its appertaining emoluments, To hold for life provided always that if the same grant cannot take effect by reason of any prior grant that then the present grant shall extend to the second or third vacancy of any canonry or prebend within the said Cathedral Church. By writ of Privy Seal.

1585

7 April. Hakluyt wrote to Walsingham, mainly with regard to his prospective prebend (State Papers Domestic Addenda 1580–1625, 29,9: calendared p. 141. The letter is printed in the edition of the *Western Planting,* introduction). *

4 May. Hakluyt left Paris for England, carrying dispatches (*Calendar State Papers Foreign 1584–1585,* p. 461).

24 May. Hakluyt presented the Queen's mandate to the Bristol Chapter (Le Neve, *Fasti Ecclesiae Anglicanae,* I 226–227: "prebendaries of the first stall—Arthur Sawle 1559–1585?—Richard Hackluyt, A.M. and theological professor. So he is styled in the Queen's mandate for the next vacant prebend, which he exhibited 24 May 1585. The exact date of his admission is not known, but it was before 1587").

Hakluyt had some influence in the publishing of Marc-Antonio Pigafetta's *Itinerario* (preface: the author would have destroyed or left unpublished his manuscript, had it not been that he was "exhorted, principally by Mr. Richard Hakluyt, a young man endowed with a kind and noble mind, and not only learned in the knowledge of his calling, but also both learned in and devoted to matters of geography"—cited by Foster Watson, "Hakluyt and Mulcaster," in *Geographical Journal,* XLIX 52, 1917). The book was published in London in Italian. Pigafetta wrote a sonnet in Italian as one of the prefatory poems to the *Voyages,* 1589 and 1598.

1586

February. Hakluyt was again apparently in England (Examination of Spanish Pilots, "written by me Pedro Dias . . . upon the request and gratification of M. Richard Hakluyt, in February 1586"—*Voyages,* XI 458. Dias was captured by Sir Richard Grenville on the latter's return from landing the first Raleigh colony in Virginia. Grenville arrived in England in October 1585).

1 March. Hakluyt is spoken of as on his way to England, though he had probably arrived earlier, in time for the above event (State Papers France, 15, 42: in *Calendar 1585–1586,* pp. 85, 86). He was apparently expected to return in May with the Ambassador's son (*ibid.,* 15, 123); but he had not yet returned by July 15, when Stafford wrote to Walsingham: "I desire to have Shapwith and Hacklytt when you shall see cause" (*Calendar 1586–1588,* p. 53). He was in England then when Drake returned, in July, from the naval raid on the West Indies, bringing back the first Virginia colony ("The relation of Pedro Morales a Spaniard, which Sir Francis Drake brought from Saint Augustines in Florida . . . taken from his mouth by Master Richard Hakluyt 1586."—"The relation of Nicholas Burgoignon . . . in mine and Master Heriot's hearing."—*Voyages,* IX 112).

1 March. Date of the dedication of *L'histoire notable de la Floride,* edited by Martin Basanier and published at Hakluyt's expense. The date of the *privilége* is 4 January 1586; the dedication is to Raleigh. (Dedication: "je l' ai tirée [the manuscript] avec la diligence de Monsieur Hakluyt, comme du tombeau."—Hakluyt, dedication of *Voyages,* II, 1599: "I had caused the four voyages of Ribaut Laudonniere and Gorgues to Florida, at mine own charges, to be printed in Paris.") *

Hakluyt also sponsored the publication, with the same editor, of a French translation of Espejo's voyage to New Mexico (dedication of *Voyages,* II, 1599: the riches of Virginia acknowledged by the Spaniards "in their own writings, printed in Madrid 1586, and within few months afterward reprinted by me in Paris"). Basanier's dedication, to the Admiral of France, is dated 12 November. No mention is made therein of Hakluyt, acknowledgement being assigned instead to François de Carle for his experience of "the language and customs of foreign sailors."

30 December. Hakluyt wrote to Raleigh from Paris (letter calendared in *Clarendon State Papers,* I 500, Oxford 1872).

1587

22 February. Date of dedication of Hakluyt's edition of the *Decades* of Peter Martyr. The *privilége* is dated 4 February. The map, by F. G., is dedicated to Hakluyt under date of 1 May. *

13 April. Date of dedication of the English *New Mexico, otherwise the Voyage of Anthony of Espeio.* The book was licensed by the Stationers on 2 May. Both the Spanish and French editions are mentioned on the title page, but the translator, A. F., makes no mention of Hakluyt. Indeed, he got the original from a Master Boldley, and he dedicated the book to Master Henry Anderson, Merchant, for his "Christian and loving care unto the common weal of your country

in wishing unto our nation the knowledge that belongeth unto all good Christian people, that nothing be hidden whereas some profit may be reaped." I cannot relate any of these persons to Hakluyt; and I note further that the version of Espejo which Hakluyt printed in the *Voyages,* 1600 (IX 186), is another and better rendering, in something like Hakluyt's own style. The English edition may not therefore be Hakluyt's doing.

* 1 May. Date of dedication of Hakluyt's English version of the *French Florida.* As the date line is headed London, it is likely that Hakluyt had crossed to England in the spring. The second Virginia colony sailed in this month.

19 June. Hakluyt received a letter of this date from a descendant of Jacques Cartier, which led to his recovery of the manuscripts of the last Cartier voyage and colony (Jacques Noel of St.-Malo to John Grout, law student in Paris: *Voyages,* VIII 272). Noel had just been shown the *Decades* map of America, which he was criticizing: he asked to be sent a copy of the map and also a copy of the New Mexico relation. "I will not fail," he added, "to inform myself if there be any mean to find out those descriptions which Captain Cartier made after his two last voyages into Canada." The second letter, undated, which apparently enclosed the fragment of Cartier's third narrative, added: "I can write nothing else unto you of anything that I can recover of the writings of Captain Jaques Cartier."

1588

8 January. Hakluyt delivered to Burleigh a letter from Stafford. The latter wrote therein of him: "I know this bearer is faithful, and will deliver this into your hands" (*Calendar 1586–1588,* pp. 486, 508). He returned to Paris about March 21 (Stafford to Walsingham: *ibid.,* p. 550).

* 11 April. Hakluyt wrote to Burleigh from Paris, to transmit the petition of the Earl of Westmoreland (State Papers Domestic Addenda 1580–1625, 30, 96: in *Calendar,* p. 248). The Earl's business was then taken over by the Ambassador (Stafford to Walsingham, 25 April: Harleian MSS 288, fol. 187, no. 98).

29 May. Hakluyt was again dispatched to England on a special mission (Stafford to Burleigh: "The not returning of Lilly maketh that I am fain to send Haklit, not being possible that Lile being absent I can let Grimston go at this time. If lack of experience maketh that he cannot deliver so well matter of so great weight, necessity hath no law. I have taken his oath upon a book for secrecy: for his honesty I will answer"—*Calendar,* p. 627. Probably enclosed in this letter was a passage in cipher: "Pinart is the man that hath delivered unto me [as from the King] that matter of weight that Haklit shall deliver to you, though he know not who it is, but only a friend of one near the French King, that sent it me from the court; for fear lest he should suspect anything, for he knoweth Pinart is here"—*ibid.,* p. 628).

* The message which Hakluyt thus carried was summarized for Burleigh as "secretly brought . . . by Hackett" (p. 630); Hakluyt wrote it down for Walsingham under the belated date of July, 1588 (it is Harleian MSS 288, fol. 212, no. 111). It concerned the military support which the King desired from England in his war with the League. It may have been as a result of Hakluyt's message that Sir Thomas Leighton was sent to Rouen in early June, to offer forces to Henry III, returning to England by June 18 (*Letters of Philip Gowdy,* in *Roxburghe Club Publications* 148, 1906, p. 38).

Hakluyt may also have brought a letter to Walsingham from a Portuguese refugee, Joam de Castro (*Calendar,* pp. 601–603).

27 July. Hakluyt returned to Paris (Stafford to Walsingham, State Papers France, 18, 135).

1 August. Hakluyt may have been the author of a letter from Paris, signed R. H., to Sir Thomas Heneage, Vice Chamberlain, and the rest of Her Majesty's

Council. The letter concerns French political news as well as Spanish rumors about the Armada (it is printed from the Rutland MSS in *Historical Manuscripts Commission, Twelfth Report,* Appendix, part IV: vol. I, 256–258). Hakluyt may have sent it in case the Ambassador was absent, attending the King at Chartres. But one suspects that there was another R. H. in France, if one credits to another the letter of "R. H. to Mr. Jacquelin," Paris, 16 June 1588 (Harleian MSS 288, fol. 202, no. 106), which seems rather better informed than Hakluyt usually was.

25 November. "From Emanuel (van Meteren's) letters I learn that Master Hakluyt is very hopeful of an edition of Abulfeda's Geography. He thinks it may be published within a year. I hope so" (Ortelius to Camden, in Thomas Smith, *Vita Camdeni et epistolae,* 1691). I find no other mention of this edition.

Toward the end of this year or the beginning of the next, Hakluyt finally returned to England (dedication of the 1589 *Voyages,* dated 17 November 1589: "myself being the last winter returned from France . . .").

1589

1 January. Date of dedication of the English translation, by Robert Parke, of Mendoza's *China,* undertaken at Hakluyt's suggestion (preface: "which labors I have undertaken at the earnest request and encouragement of my worshipful friend Master Richard Hakluyt, late of Oxford. . . . And also for the zeal he beareth to his country and countrymen brought the same (Mendoza) first above two years since into this court"). The work was licensed by the Stationers, "both in Italian and English," 13 September 1587; the dedication is 1 January 1589; the title page bears date of 1588, probably old style.

Parke refers to Hakluyt as "late of Oxford." As the latter had signed himself "Oxoniensis" in the *Decades,* it is to be inferred that he gave up his studentship at Christchurch between May 1, 1587, and January 1, 1589.

7 March. Hakluyt was one of the nineteen, described as "merchants of London," to whom Raleigh assigned his rights in the Virginia colony. (The assignment is printed in the 1589 *Voyages,* reprinted in Ebenezer Hazard, *Historical Collections,* I, Philadelphia 1792.)

15 May. The geographer Ortelius on this date wrote to his nephew Jacob Cole in London: "In the Frankfort fair catalogue I read that your Hakluyt has edited Peter Martyr's Decades of the new found isles. Is there nothing else in the work? or has he added something of his own? or why has Hakluyt edited it? —I am glad you are discussing fossils (with Hakluyt). I should like to know what I ought to think about them . . ." (J. H. Hessels, *Abrahami Ortelii epistulae,* p. 394).

1 September. Entry at the Stationers "by warrant of a letter under Sir Francis Walsingham's hand" of "the voyages and Discoveries of the English nation." Hakluyt was working on the book at the beginning of the year (Parke's Mendoza, dedication 1 January 1589: Hakluyt "at this present hath in hand a most excellent and ample collection . . . a matter long intended by him." Hakluyt had spoken of the idea in the *Decades,* dedication). The date of the dedication, to Walsingham, is 17 November. The title page is dated 1589, but the book had not appeared by January 24, 1589–90 (dedication of Philip Jones's translation of Meierus) and should therefore be dated 1589–90. *

1590

20 April. Hakluyt was installed as rector of Wetheringsett and Blockford, Suffolk, holding the living until his death ("Ricardus Hakluyte, M.A., institutus ad Wetheringsett cum Blockford dioc. Norwic. 20 April 1590."—Anthony à Wood, *Athenae Oxon.,* II 186). The patron of the living was the Countess of Sheffield,

wife of Stafford (Norwich Diocese Registry); later (1603) he was Sir Stephen Soame, member of the Levant Company and Lord Mayor of London in 1598. The number of communicants was in 1603 two hundred; in that year the parish had no curate or vicar (Archbishop's Return, in Harleian MSS 595: printed in *Proceedings Suffolk Institute of Archaeology and Natural History,* XI 26 (1901–03).

25 August. At some time before this date Hakluyt urged on Ortelius the making of a map of the northern portions of Mexico, probably to supplement the excellent map of Central Mexico which had appeared in the *Theatrum* (Ortelius to his nephew Jacob Cole in London, dated 25 August: "Greet Hakluyt from me when you happen to see him. Of his edition of *Florida* I have heard from others. You say that he wants me to publish something on the coast which lies north of the city of Mexico. I wish I might. . . . If he will furnish the means, I will gladly do it, and not forget to mention Master Hakluyt in honorable fashion."—J. H. Hessels, *Abrahami Ortelii epistulae,* p. 443).

To this year is assigned a paper labeled "Notes concerning Sir Walter Raleigh's discovery of Dorado, translated from Acosta, Sevila, 1590, by Richard Hackluyt" (State Papers Domestic Elizabeth 235,43, the paper printed in the *Voyages,* XI 16–19). The date of the paper should probably be given as several years later.

De Bry's *Peregrinationes* began to appear in this year, starting with Hariot's *Virginia* and continuing in the following year with De Morgues' *Florida.* Hakluyt's share in the first is thus acknowledged by De Bry. (1) Preface: "I was very willing to offer unto you the true pictures of those people which by the help of M. Richard Hakluyt of Oxford . . . who first encouraged me to publish the work, I craved out of the very original of M. Jhon White, an English painter." (2) Preface to French version: "(Hackluit) qui a été au dit pays, et est cause de l'advancement de ce présent Traicté." (3) Title page of English version of the text for White's drawings: "Translated out of Latin into English by Richard Hackluit."—Henry Stevens (in *Thomas Hariot,* 59–60) suggests that Hakluyt also wrote the White text and modified the maps.

1591

Richard Hakluyt of the Middle Temple died before June 4 (see Appendix I).

1593

* Edmond Hakluyt died before February 1, when Richard probated his will (see above). Richard inherited his brother's property in Eyton and also four pounds a year, the proceeds of a lease in Dorking.

Gabriel Harvey refers to the *Voyages* as "a work of importance" in showing a great literary subject for a Spartan age, the age of Gilbert, Drake, Frobisher, Raleigh, and "other famous discoveries and adventures" (*Pierce's Supererogation,* Grosart edit., II 96).

1594

Winter Jones supposed that Hakluyt was first married in this year, perhaps by reckoning back from his son's matriculation in 1611 to a probable birth date of 1595. It is as reasonable to suppose that Hakluyt was married in any earlier year back to 1587 or 1588, when he resigned his studentship. His wife is identified below (1597) as Duglasse Hakluyt and by Davy's *Suffolk Collections* as Douglas Cavendish, daughter of Richard Cavendish of Hornsey, uncle of the circumnavigator.

November 1594 to February 1595. Hakluyt was engaged to draw up geographical notes for the Dutch Northeast expedition of 1595. The following letters trace the consultation:

15–25 November. The Treasurer of Zeeland to Emanuel van Meteren (not extant).
27 November–7 December. Van Meteren to Hakluyt (not extant).
6–16 December. Hakluyt to van Meteren (extant only in Dutch). *
15–25 December. Van Meteren to the Treasurer, enclosing Hakluyt's letter, translated. *
6–16 January. The Treasurer to van Meteren, authorizing the consultation (not extant).
18–28 January. Van Meteren to the Treasurer, announcing the engaging of Hakluyt.
8–18 February. Van Meteren to the Treasurer, announcing the end of the work.
14–24 February. Van Meteren to the Treasurer, announcing that he has paid Hakluyt.

(Van Meteren's letters are given in *Linschoten-Vereeniging Werken,* XV, Vol. II, 1917, pp. 201–210, with editorial comment by S. P. L'Honoré Naber, Introduction, p. xv. The letters are in the Holland archives, Recueil Commercie, Algemeen Ryks Archief, fol. 1–68.)

1597

"Duglasse Hackluytt the wieff of Mr. Richard Hackluytt parson of Wetheringsett was buryed the 8 day of August 1597" (Wetheringsett Register. I am indebted to the Rev. V. B. Redstone, F.S.A., for this item).

Sir Robert Cecil, Secretary of State, consulted Hakluyt "touching the state of the country of Guiana, and whether it were fit to be planted by the English" (dedication, *Voyages,* II, 1599).

1598

Hakluyt was responsible for the translation of Pigafetta's *Relatione del Reame di Congo,* Rome 1591, by Abraham Hartwell, secretary to the Archbishop of Canterbury (Address to Reader: Hakluyt "intreating me very earnestly that I would take him with me and make him English"). The dedication is dated 1 January 1597(–98).

17 February. In the Stationers' Register was entered the English translation of Linschoten's *Voyages into the East and West Indies,* by William Philip (Printer's dedication to Julius Caesar: "About a twelvemonth ago a learned Gentleman brought unto me the . . . Linschoten written in the Dutch tongue, which he wished might be translated into our Language. . . . Upon this commendation and opinion, I procured the translation thereof accordingly." The identity of the "learned Gentleman" is made clear in the Address to the Reader: "which book being commended, by Master Richard Hackluyt, a man that laboreth greatly to advance our English Name and Nation, the Printer thought good to cause the same to be translated into the English tongue").

The account of the first Dutch voyage to India was translated by the same man, and perhaps also at Hakluyt's suggestion (Houtman's *Voyage,* 1598), since Hakluyt is mentioned in the dedication (16 January 1597–98), and since the Linschoten is promised there.

13 June. In the Stationers' Register was entered the English translation of De Veer, also by William Philip. The book was not published until 1609, q.v.

7 October. Date of dedication, to Lord Charles Howard, Lord Admiral, of the first volume of the *Voyages.* This second edition is of course not reëntered in the Stationers' Register. *

Gabriel Harvey wrote on the margin of his 1598 Chaucer: "I looke for much, as well in verse, as in prose, from mie two Oxford friends, Doctor Gager, and

M. Hackluit: both rarely furnished for the purpose" (fol. 394 verso, cited by Moore Smith, *Gabriel Harvey's Marginalia*, p. 233). He also listed Hakluyt among the exceptional minds of England, along with Smith, Ascham, Wilson, and Digges and Blundeville (Quintilian, *ibid.* 122).

1599

16 October. Hakluyt was present at a meeting of the organizers of the East India Company, which considered the application for a patent (Henry Stevens, *The Dawn of British Trade to the East Indies*, p. 10).

* 24 October. Date of dedication, to Sir Robert Cecil, of the second volume of the *Voyages*.

23 November. Hakluyt was granted a reversion to the next vacancy in the Savoy Chapel (William Mount to Sir Robert Cecil: "Whereas it is your pleasure to have the next place in the Savoy, being a chaplain's, by death or otherwise void, to be stayed for the preferment of Mr. Hackluyt, one of good note and merit: if any shall chance to be void in my time, the same shall be at your commandment for him."—*Historical Manuscripts Commission Reports, Salisbury Papers* 74,97: part IX, p. 397).

1600

* Early in this year Hakluyt probably wrote the paper C.O. 77, vol. I, 17: "Reasons why English merchants may trade into the East Indies" (printed in John Bruce, *Annals of the East India Company*, 1815, I 115–121).

18 May. Hakluyt was recommended by the Privy Council to the living of Great Allhallows, Thames Street (letter from the Council to the Archbishop of Canterbury, in *Acts of the Privy Council 1599–1600*, pp. 330–331). I have reprinted the letter in Chapter XVI above. The Lord Admiral and Sir Robert Cecil were present at the meeting, as was also the Lord Chief Justice, Sir John Popham.

27 August. Hakluyt was granted the reversion of the next vacant prebend in Westminster Abbey (Patent Rolls, 42 Elizabeth, part 13). This in spite of an earlier refusal by the Queen (Thomas Windebank to Sir Robert Cecil: ". . . I attempted the signing of the bill for Mr. Hackluit, recommended by my Lord Admiral and yourself, but had the repulse, with answer that she would not grant any prebend in Westminster till they fall void."—*Historical Manuscripts Commission Reports, Salisbury Papers* 83,48: part X, p. 436. The letter is not dated).

* 1 September. Date of dedication, to Sir Robert Cecil, of the third volume of the *Voyages*.

17 November. Date of dedication, to Sir Robert Cecil, of John Pory's translation of Leo Africanus (dedication: "my reverend friend Mr. Richard Hakluyt: who out of his mature judgment in these studies, knowing the excellency of this story above all others in the same kind, was the only man that moved me to translate it"). For the translation Hakluyt wrote a commendatory foreword to the same effect. *

1601

29 January. Hakluyt read before the East India Company his geographical notes of advice (Henry Stevens, *The Dawn of British Trade to the East Indies*, p. 123: the excerpt from the Minutes is given in Chapter XII, section 3, above).

16 February. Hakluyt was ordered paid for his notes of advice and maps (*ibid.*, p. 143). The notes are in the Bodleian, MS Arch. Selden B 8. They were listed by Anthony à Wood, *Athenae Oxon.*, in the "MS among those given by Selden's executors to the public library at Oxon.," and were first printed by Winter Jones as an appendix to *Hakluyt Society Publications* 7 (1850). *

29 October. Date of dedication, to Sir Robert Cecil, of Hakluyt's English edition of Galvano's *Discoveries of the World*. The dedication is dated "from London" and is signed "Your Honor's Chaplain." *

During this year was published the translation of the account of the second Dutch voyage to India, translated by William Walker. The translation was commissioned by Hakluyt (dedication to Thomas Smith: "These considerations being seconded by the persuasion of M. Richard Hakluyt, a man for his matchless industry in collecting the English Voyages most incomparably deserving of this state, prevailed so much with me that . . . I could not do (less) than cast into your East India treasury this poor myte").

1602

4 May. Hakluyt was installed as prebendary of Westminster (Le Neve, *Fasti Ecclesiae Anglicanae,* III 353: "Prebendaries, Fourth Stall. Richard Hackluyt installed 4th May 1602. Died possessed of this stall 23d November 1616, and was buried in the Abbey."—J. L. Chester, in *Registers of Westminster Abbey,* p. 113, notes in this connection that Hakluyt "signed the records of the chapter meetings from that date until 3 May 1616").

5 May. Hakluyt joined with the Dean and Prebends in signing a letter, on a choir appointment, to Sir Robert Cecil (*Historical Manuscripts Commission Reports, Salisbury Papers,* 93,23: part X, p. 142).

The Treasurer's Account in the Westminster Abbey records shows Hakluyt receiving, during 1602, eight pounds sterling for scholars, as well as his "corn money" as prebendary.

It is possible that Hakluyt was responsible in this year for the publication of John Brereton's *Discovery of the North Parts of Virginia,* including his cousin's *Inducements* (see Chapter XVII, section 2, above).

1603

Hakluyt was Archdeacon of Westminster 1603–1604 (Abbey Records). A later entry (1615) shows that the Archdeacon received twenty pounds for the year.

In the early part of this year Hakluyt induced the merchants of Bristol to send the reconnaissance voyage of Martin Pring to New England and obtained from Raleigh the necessary license (*Purchas His Pilgrims,* XVIII 322: excerpt from the Pring narrative, which I have quoted in Chapter XVI, section 2). The expedition sailed on March 29.

1604

30 March. Hakluyt applied for a license for a second marriage ("Richard Hakluyt [same signature as in Westminster Chapter Books] one of the chaplains of the Savoy, who hath been a widower about 7 years, aged about 52, and Frances Smithe, of St. Lawrence, Old Jury, about 50, widow of William Smithe, while he lived at St. Botolph, Bishopsgate, gent., dec'd about 8 months since; at St. Michael's, Wood Street, London."—J. L. Chester and G. J. Armytage, *Allegations for Marriage Licenses Issued by the Bishop of London 1530–1610, Harleian Society Publications* 25, 1887, p. 603). The marriage itself is not recorded at St. Michael's.

The above item is the first evidence of Hakluyt's year of birth and of his chaplaincy in the Savoy.

1605

18 March. Hakluyt heard from Simon Fernandez, Portuguese mariner, of the discovery of the New Hebrides Islands (Purchas, XVII 246). *

Hakluyt received a letter from the Licentiate Luis Tribaldo Toleto, late of the Spanish peace mission to England, on the new Spanish movements in New Mexico and on the Spanish colonial system (letter from Valladolid, dated July, printed by Purchas, XVIII 76). *

According to John Smith, Hakluyt was appointed to the living of Jamestown in Virginia, sending Robert Hunt as a curate (*Advertisements for Planters of New England,* 1631: excerpt quoted in Chapter XVI, section 2, above). The item probably refers to the dispensation below, 1606.

Hakluyt moved unaware in Gunpowder Plot circles, as the following report of an agent testifies: On the Thursday "sennett" before the 5 November there met at dinner at the Mighter in Bread Street the Lord Mordaunt, Sir Jocelyn Percy, Sir William Monsonn, Sir Mark Ive, Mr. Robert Catsby, Dr. Tailor belonging to the Archduke's Ambassador, Mr. Pickering Esq. of Northants, Mr. Hackelett, and Spero Pettingarre: & there amonst other discourses Taylor said that all princes' ambassadors were but honourable spies. Dinner being ended, Mordaunt, Percy, and Catesby with Pickering went away together, and coming up the hill Sir William Mounsonn and Taylor took a blind way in by a church; they two alone, for Hackelett and Pettingarre went together to Pettingarre's chamber to peruse a rutter of Sir Francis Drake's works of navigation and so parted. (Cecil Papers, Transcripts. Gunpowder Plot. 1605 (Nov.) Hatfield Ref. 112/160. Advertisements concerning the plot, unsigned.)

1606

Hakluyt was named one of the four London patentees in the first Virginia Company charter (Col. Entry Book 79, printed in full in Alexander Brown, *The Genesis of the United States,* I 52). The petition for a patent is not extant.

24 November. Hakluyt was granted a dispensation to hold a living in Jamestown without relinquishing his English preferments (Patent Rolls, 4 James I, part 18: abstract from the Latin, as follows:

Dispensation for Richard Hackluit and Another

The King to Richard Hackluit clerk prebendary both in the Collegiate Church of St. Peter Westminster and in the cathedral church of Holy Trinity Bristol and rector of the parish church of Wetheringsett co. Suff. dioc. Norwich and one of the chaplains of the Savoy Hospital co. Middlesex, and to Robert Hunt clerk M. A. vicar of the parish church of Heathfield co. Suss. dioc. Chichester—

Whereas Richard and Robert, together with Thomas Gates and George Somers knts., Edward Maria Wingfeilde, Thomas Hannam, Rawleigh Gilbert Esq., William Parker, George Popham, and others had the king's authority to make a habitation and plantation and lead forth a colony to those parts of America commonly called Virginia and other territories of America either belonging to the King or not belonging in fact to any other Christian prince, and are about to set forth shortly for these parts; and whereas the King has heard by trustworthy information of the great ignorance in those parts; now the King grants to Richard and Robert full and free licence to go thither with Thomas Gates and the rest and make a plantation and lead forth a colony. "And that you may the more freely and better watch and perform the ministry and preaching of God's word in those parts, you and both of you may leave whatever parish churches benefices prebends and ecclesiastical dignities and cures and hospital Chaplaincies now held by you and both of you within our kingdom of England. . . ." And they may continue to take the profits of their said incumbencies in England; and the King grants them dispensation to take and to hold, together with the said incumbencies in England, "one or more benefices, church dignities, or cures in the said parts of Virginia or America."

The warrant is dated 21 November and has nothing to denote at whose instance the grant was made.)

Drayton's "Ode to the Virginian Voyage" contained this last stanza:

Thy Voyages attend,
Industrious HACKLUIT,
Whose reading shall inflame
Men to seek fame,
And much commend
To after-times thy wit.

(Ode 11 in *Poems Lyric and Pastoral,* 1606: licensed by the Stationers 19 April 1606.)

1607

Hakluyt was steward of Westminster Abbey from Michaelmas 1607 to Michaelmas 1608 (Abbey Records). The steward accounted for "salt, drink, fish, ale, wheat, candles, wood, charcoal, seacoal, liveries to scholars of the choir."

1608

Hakluyt's Headland, Spitsbergen, was named by William Hudson on a Russia Company exploration (Purchas, XIII 10).

29 September. A survey of the Lordship of Leominster lists as a free tenant of the Manor of Stoke (to the south): "Eaton—Richard Hackluyt for a messuage, 2s.8d." (Misc. Book, Land Revenue, 217, fol. 183). This may be the location of the house rented to Oliver Hakluyt (see 1612 below).

1609

15 April. Date of dedication, to the Virginia Company, of the de Soto narrative, translated from the Portuguese by Richard Hakluyt under the title of *Virginia Richly Valued.* The dedication was written from "my lodging in the college of Westminster." *

23 May. Hakluyt was named as one of the numerous patentees in the second Virginia Charter. According to Alexander Brown (*The Genesis of the United States,* II 908), his total investment in the Company was twenty-one pounds. This investment seems to have been prorated to two shares (value twenty-five pounds), which were sold by Edmond Hakluyt in 1621 (Court Minutes, cited by Alexander Brown, *The First Republic in America,* 1898, p. 423).

12 June. Entered at the Stationers "a booke called Nova Ffrancia," a translation by Pierre Erondelle, at Hakluyt's suggestion, of parts of Lescarbot's *Nova Francia.* I have quoted from the preface, in Chapter XVII above, the passage testifying to Hakluyt's share in the book. (The preface is reprinted in Brown, *The Genesis of the United States,* I 321.)

At some time in this year finally appeared the translation by William Philip of Gerrit de Veer's *True and Perfect Description of Three Voyages,* originally licensed in 1598. It was reëntered at the Stationers 15 May 1609. The translator had been "intreated by some of my friends, and principally by M. Richard Hakluyt (a diligent observer of all Proceedings in this nature) to Translate and publish."

It was probably in this year that Hakluyt translated Grotius, *Mare liberum* (1608) as *The Free Sea* (Inner Temple MSS 529, in 25 folios). The fact that the Grotius original was not published until 1608, November (introduction by James Brown Scott to the translation, *The Freedom of the Seas,* Carnegie Endowment, New York 1916), obviates the possibility that it was Hakluyt's translation which was suppressed at the request of the Spanish Ambassador in March 1608 (*Calendar State Papers Venetian 1607–1610,* par. 203). * (part)

1611

Second edition of de Soto narrative, under the title *The Discovery and Conquest of Terra Florida.*

Hakluyt's son Edmond was admitted to Trinity College, Cambridge (*Trinity College Admissions,* I, Index).

* Hakluyt's River, in the island of Kolguyef, off the north Russian coast, was so named by a Russia Company expedition (Purchas, XIII 197). Two letters to Hakluyt from Josias Logan, one of the leaders of the expedition, are printed in part in Purchas (XIII 236–238).

1612

In the early part of this year Hakluyt bought, jointly with his son, the manor of Bridge Place, in Coddenham, Suffolk, and also certain houses in Tothill Street, Westminster (mentioned in his will and in the Bridge Place Court Rolls).

19 July. Richard Hakluyt, M.A., was presented by Oliver Hakluyt, gent., patron for this turn (by reason of a grant made to him by Queen Anne, dated 1 August 1604), to the rectory of Gedney, Lincolnshire. He was admitted at Buckden 24 July 1612 (abstract of Presentation Deed, 1612, no. 34, Registry of Bishop of Lincoln). The deed is endorsed as follows: "Richard Hackluit, M.A., of Christ's College Oxford, ordained deacon and priest by Bishop Piers of Salisbury; aged 60; Beneficed at Wetheringsett, co. Suffolk." As "Richard Hakluyt, clerk, M.A.," he was instituted 24 July (Bishops' Certificates, Public Record Office). The value of the living was assessed at £23 12d. or £23 11s. ½d.; the number of communicants was 240; there was a vicar (Lincoln Liber Cleri 1603, printed in *Lincoln Record Society* 23, part I, p. 312, 1926).

26 July. Hakluyt was named a charter member of the Northwest Passage Company (*State Papers Colonial, East Indies,* par. 616: printed in *Hakluyt Society Publications* 88).

* 20 August. Hakluyt made at Wetheringsett his last will and testament. It appears that he possessed not only the property just mentioned above but also a house in Leominster Oare, Hereford (see 1608 above), and that he retained lodgings in the Savoy and in the Westminster and Bristol chapters. The real property was left to the testator's son, with an allowance in either cash or real property for the maintenance of the widow. To the widow were to go the plate, jewels, and household stuff; £55 10s. to near relatives—sisters, nieces, and nephews; some £6 and clothes in small bequests to dependents; £5 for repairs in Westminster Abbey; the furnishings in his Savoy and Bristol chambers to those institutions; and finally £5 to the poor in his parish. (The will was printed in *Hakluyt Society Publications* 7, 1850).

Hakluyt's name does not appear in the third Virginia charter of this year.

In this year was published the translation into English by Michael Lok, of Hakluyt's edition of Peter Martyr's *Decades* (1587).

1613

* (dated 1598) The paper in State Papers Colonial, I 32, entitled "The limits of the Spanish possessions," is attributed to Hakluyt by Alexander Brown (*The Genesis of the United States,* II 669–675, where the paper is printed).

1614

22 January. "A book of dialogues, heretofore translated into Latin by the Hollanders, and printed with the Malacca tongue, Mr. Hakluyt having now turned the Latin into English, and supposed very fit for the factors to learn, ordered to be printed before the departure of the ships" (East India Company minutes, in *State Papers Colonial, East Indies,* par. 682). The translation was actually done,

according to the dedication, by Augustine Spalding, company factor. It was presented to the Company by Hakluyt, and, dedicated by the translator to Sir Thomas Smith, was published 1614.

The Account of the Treasurer of Westminster Abbey, for the year from Michaelmas 1614 to Michaelmas 1615, shows payments to Hakluyt of £4, his fee as Treasurer for the year; of £10 for boarding scholars; of one-twelfth of £339 (£28 5s.) "corn money" as prebendary (Abbey Records).

1615

Mount Hakluyt, on the island first called Hudson's Touches, now called Jan Mayen, was so named by Robert Fotherby (Purchas, XIV 86).

1616

5 July. Hakluyt Island, off the northwest coast of Greenland, was named by William Baffin (Purchas, XIV 408).

23 November. Hakluyt died (William Camden, *Annals,* 1623 edit.).

23 November. The will was probated by Edmond Hakluyt (Prerogative Court of Canterbury, 109 Cope).

26 November. Hakluyt was buried in Westminster Abbey (J. L. Chester, *Registers of Westminster Abbey,* under Burials: "1626. Richard Hackler, Prebendary of this Church."—The editor notes that the year and the name were thus wrongly transcribed in the register). The exact place of the burial is not known. According to Dean Stanley, he was buried "in an unmarked and unknown grave" (7 *Notes and Queries,* VIII 215, 1889).

1620

John Smith, writing of the slowness of investment in colonies, remarks: "which makes me remember and say with Mr. Hackluit; oh incredulitie the wit of fools, that slovingly do spit at all things fair, a sluggard's cradle a coward's castle, how easy it is to be an Infidel" (*New England's Trials,* p. 267 of Arber reprint; repeated in the *General History of Virginia,* 1624, p. 772 *ibid.*). The phrases are, of course, popular ones of the time, and can only vaguely be connected with Hakluyt.

1626

Bridge Place in Coddenham, Suffolk, passed to Simon Bloomfield, gent. (Court Rolls).

APPENDIX III. HAKLUYT'S WRITINGS

Letters

1580. Hakluyt to Mercator (not extant): asking advice for the Northeast Passage expedition. Mercator's answer, dated 28 July, is printed in the *Voyages,* III 275. *

* † 1583, 11 March. Walsingham to Hakluyt, commending Hakluyt's interest in geography (*Voyages,* VIII 131).

* † 1583, 28 May. John Newbery to Hakluyt, from Aleppo, concerning Hakluyt's notes of advice (*Voyages,* V 452).

* † 1583, 6 August. Parmenius to Hakluyt, from Newfoundland (*Voyages,* VIII 81).

* 1584, 7 January. Hakluyt to Walsingham, from Paris, on his researches (State Papers Domestic Elizabeth 167,7, in the *Calendar 1581–1590,* p. 150: printed in *Archaeologia,* vol. 33, and in *Hakluyt Society Publications* 7, introduction).

* 1584, 1 April. Hakluyt to Walsingham, from Paris, on a lectureship in navigation (State Papers Domestic Elizabeth 170,1, in the *Calendar 1581–1590,* p. 169: printed with the preceding. Reproduced in facsimile in the 1903–05 edition of the *Voyages,* XII 80).

* 1585, 7 April. Hakluyt to Walsingham, from Paris, mainly on his grant of a prebend at Bristol (State Papers Domestic Addenda 1580–1625, 29,9, in the *Calendar,* p. 141: printed in 2 *Collections Maine Historical Society* II, introduction).

* 1586, 30 December. Hakluyt to Raleigh, from Paris, on his publications (Clarendon MSS: calendared in *Clarendon State Papers,* I 500).

* 1588, 11 April. Hakluyt to Burleigh, from Paris, on the petition of the Earl of Westmoreland (State Papers Domestic Addenda 1580–1625, 30,96, in the *Calendar,* p. 248).

1588, July. Hakluyt to Walsingham, a writing down of the oral dispatch from the Ambassador (Harleian MSS 288, fol. 212, no. 111).

1588, 1 August. R. H. to Sir Thomas Heneage, a diplomatic report, of which Hakluyt's authorship is doubtful (Rutland MSS, calendared in *Historical Manuscripts Commission, Twelfth Report,* Appendix, part IV, I 256).

† 1594, 27 November. Emanuel van Meteren to Hakluyt, proposing Northeast-Passage consultation (not extant).

* 1594, 6 December. Hakluyt to van Meteren, on the same (Dutch version only, printed from the Holland archives, Recueil Commercie, Algemeen Ryks Archief, fol. 63, in *Linschoten-Vereeniging Werken* XV, vol. II, 1917, p. 201).

† 1595, January. Van Meteren to Hakluyt, on the same subject (not extant).

1602, 5 May. The Dean and Prebendaries of Westminster, including Hakluyt, to Sir Robert Cecil, on a choir appointment (*Historical Manuscripts Commission Reports, Salisbury Papers* 93,23: part X, p. 142).

* 1605, July. The Licentiate Luis Tribaldo Toleto to Hakluyt, from Valladolid, on Spanish colonial enterprises (*Purchas His Pilgrims,* XVIII 76).

* 1611, summer. Two letters to Hakluyt from Josias Logan, of the Russia Company expedition to northeast Russia, the letters printed in part in Purchas, XIII 236–238.

MANUSCRIPTS

1583. A commentary in Latin on Aristotle's *Politics* (Ms Royal 12.G.xiii, also Sloane, 1982), presented to the Queen with the following item. * (dedication)

1584. The Discourse on the Western Planting, presented in October to the Queen. The full title is: A Particular Discourse, concerning the great necessity and manifold commodities that are likely to grow to this Realm of England by the Western Discoveries lately attempted, written in the year 1584 by Richard Hakluyt of Oxford.

The modern editor supposes at least five copies:

1. Kept by Hakluyt (not extant).
2. Presented to the Queen (not extant).
3. Presented to Walsingham after Easter 1585 (Hakluyt's letter of 7 April) (not extant).
4. Presented to an unknown "Your Worship" and now in the State Papers (Domestic Elizabeth 195,127, calendared in *Calendar 1581–1590*, p. 377, and in the *Calendar State Papers Colonial, East Indies, 1513–1616*, par. 237, as follows: "Copy, probably in handwriting of James Lancaster, of 20 Heads of Chapters contained in book of Sir Walter Raleigh's voyage to the West Indies, which is offered for the rareness of the matter, and for that few or more (Her Majesty excepted) hath seen the same. The bearer and author, Mr. Hakluyt, will present the book to the Secretary . . . who hath very earnestly often times writ for it, and so hath the Earl of Leicester."
5. A copy with an additional twenty-first chapter, containing a list of American commodities. This copy was sold from the Sir Thomas Phillipps collection in 1913 and is now in the New York Public Library. *

The Discourse was edited from copy 5 by Leonard Woods and Charles Deane for the Maine Historical Society, 2 *Collections*, vol. II, Cambridge, Mass., 1877.

1594–95. Translation into Dutch of the account of the Pet-Jackman voyage to the Northeast in 1580 (*Voyages*, III 282–303). The translation was found by Captain Gundersen in 1875 at the Barents winter quarters in Novaya Zemlya and is now at Oslo.

1596?. "Notes concerning Sir Walter Raleigh's discovery of Dorado, translated from Acosta, Sevila, 1590, by Richard Hackluyt" (State Papers Domestic Elizabeth 235,43; printed in the *Voyages*, XI 16–19).

1600. Hakluyt is possibly the author of the paper "Reasons why English merchants may trade into the East Indies" (Colonial Office 77, vol. I, 171). The paper is printed in John Bruce, *Annals of the East India Company*, 1815, I 115–121. *

1601. Notes of advice to the East India Company, now in the Bodleian Library, Oxford, listed as MS Arch. Selden B 8. They were printed in *Hakluyt Society Publications* 7, 1850, pp. 151–171. *

1601?. A discourse on the Northwest Passage, mentioned in the preceding notes and in the dedication of the de Soto, 1609, but not extant.

1609?. "The Free Sea": a translation of Grotius' *Mare liberum* (1608). The manuscript is numbered 529 in the Inner Temple collection and contains 25 folios (*Historical Manuscripts Commission, Eleventh Report*, Appendix, part VII, p. 234). * (part)

1612. Last will and testament, written at Wetheringsett 20 August. It was probated by Edmond Hakluyt, executor, 23 November 1616 (Prerogative Court of Canterbury, 109 Cope). *

1613?. A note on "The limits of the Spanish possessions" (State Papers Co- * (as of 1598) lonial, I 32) is possibly in part by Hakluyt. It is printed in Alexander Brown, *The Genesis of the United States,* II 669–675.

A large number of documents printed by Hakluyt in the *English Voyages* are to be found in the State Papers. Notable is volume 196 of the State Papers Domestic Elizabeth, made up of "Copies and extracts of treatises . . . relating to trade and voyages of discovery." A number of letters, or copies of letters, to Hakluyt for publication are extant in the Carew MSS (*Historical Manuscripts Commission, Fourth Report,* Appendix, pp. 372 ff.). A MS containing official documents and returns of Duart de Meneses, Portuguese Viceroy of the Indies 1521–1524, now listed as Additional MSS 28,433, has Hakluyt's name on the first leaf (v. Henry Thomas in 4 *Library,* VII 11, 1926). It was used by Purchas in the *Pilgrims,* VII 172–184. Many more such manuscripts are doubtless extant.

Publications

Note.—In describing size of volumes I follow the classifying system (according to height) of the American Library Association.

† 1580. Jacques Cartier. *A shorte and briefe narration of the two Nauigations and Discoueries to the Northweast partes called Newe Fravnce: First translated out of French into Italian, by . . . Ramutius, and now turned into English by John Florio. . . . London, H. Bynneman, 1580.* 12mo, 78 pp. Licensed by the Stationers 7 June 1580. Dedicated to Edmond Bray, Esq., High Sheriff of Oxford, 25 June 1580.

(Narratives of Cartier's voyages of 1534 and 1535, the translation and publication arranged by Hakluyt from his copy of Ramusio's *Navigationi,* vol. III, 1556 or later.

Reprinted, with a fragmentary account of Cartier's last voyage, in Hakluyt's *Voyages,* 1600, VIII 183 ff.)

1582. R. H. *Divers voyages, touching the discoucrie of America, and the Ilands adjacent unto the same, made first of all by our Englishmen, and afterward by the Frenchmen and Britons: And certaine notes of advertisements for observations, necessarie for such as shall heereafter make the like attempt. . . . London, Thomas Woodcocke, 1582.* 16mo, 60 leaves.

Licensed by the Stationers 21 May 1582. Dedicated to Philip Sidney by "Your worship's humble always to command, R. H."

(The contents noted in Chapter V above. Of the two maps, one was drawn by Michael Lok for this volume; the other was drawn by or for Robert Thorne to accompany his *Book,* printed in this volume.

All the items of the *Divers Voyages,* except the last, the list of American commodities, were reprinted separately in the final *Voyages.* The last item, with additions, was incorporated in the *Discourse on the Western Planting,* 1584.

The *Divers Voyages* was reprinted complete as *Hakluyt Society Publications* 7, 1850, with introduction by J. Winter Jones, and appendices containing Hakluyt's will and the East India Company notes.)

† 1585. Marc-Antonio Pigafetta. *Itinerario, o viaggio da Vienna a Constantinopoli 1567. Londra, appresso Giov. Vuolfio.* 24mo, 141 pp.

Not entered on the Stationers' Register. Dedicated "all' illustriss. Sign. Edw. Seymer, conte d'Hertford." (The book was published at Hakluyt's instance: see the chronology, Appendix II, above.)

† 1586. Antonio de Espejo. *Histoire des terres nouvellement descouvertes . . . par Antoine de Espeio, et nommées le Nouveau Mexico. traduit de l'Espagnol en langue françoise par M. Basanier, gentilhomme françois. A Paris, veuve Nicolas Roffet, 1586.* 24mo, 48 pp. See p. 269 below.

The *privilége* is undated. The dedication, to the Amiral de France, is dated 12 November 1586.

(Translated for Hakluyt from the Madrid original of the same year.)

† 1586. René de Laudonnière. *L'histoire notable de la Floride . . . mise en lumière par M. Basanier . . . Paris, Guillaume Auuray, 1586.* 24mo, 132 leaves. *

Privilége dated 4 January 1586. Dedication, to Sir Walter Raleigh, dated 1 March 1586. *

(Manuscript discovered by Hakluyt and published at his expense. Reprinted, Paris 1853.)

1587. *De Orbe novo Petri Martyris Anglerii Mediolanensis . . . Decades octo, . . . labore & industria Richardi Hakluyti Oxoniensis Angli. Paris, Guillaume Auuray, 1587.* 16mo, 605 pp. *

Privilége dated 4 February 1587. Dedication, to Sir Walter Raleigh, dated 22 February 1587. *

(Reprint of the original complete edition, Complutensis 1530. The map drawn by "F. G." was dedicated to Hakluyt under date of 1 May 1587. Hakluyt added an "Index Rerum Memorabilium."

The book was translated into English in 1612; see that date.)

† 1587. *New Mexico, otherwise the voiage of Anthony of Espeio . . . London, Thomas Cadman.* 16mo, 16 pp.

Translated from the Spanish by A. F., perhaps on Hakluyt's initiative. Licensed by the Stationers 2 May 1587. Dedicated to Henry Anderson, merchant, 13 April 1587.

(An improved translation, seeming to be Hakluyt's, was printed in the *Voyages,* IX 156 ff. A retranslation from Espejo's manuscript is given by H. E. Bolton in *Spanish Exploration in the Southwest,* New York 1916, pp. 168–195. The volume was republished in photostat in the Massachusetts Historical Society Americana Series, no. 50, 1921.)

1587. René de Laudonnière. *A Notable Historie Containing foure voyages made by Certayne French Captaynes unto Florida: . . . Newly translated out of French into English, by R. H. . . . London, T. Dawson, 1587.* 12mo, 64 leaves. *

Not entered at the Stationers. Dedicated to Sir Walter Raleigh 1 May 1587. *

(Reprinted, with Basanier's dedication of the original, in the *Voyages,* VIII 439 ff.)

† 1588–89. Juan Gonzalez de Mendoza. *The Historie of the great and mightie kingdome of China, . . . Translated out of Spanish by R. Parke. London, J. Wolfe, for E. White, 1588.* 16mo, 410 pp.

Licensed by the Stationers 6 February 1588. Dedicated to Thomas Candish 1 January 1589.

(Translated from the 1586 Madrid original at Hakluyt's suggestion. Reprinted by the Hakluyt Society, *Publications,* 14, 15, 1853–54, edited by Sir George T. Staunton, introduction by R. H. Major.)

1589–90. *The principall Navigations, Voiages and Discoveries of the English nation, made by Sea or over Land, to the most remote and farthest distant Quarters of the earth at any time within the compasse of these 1500 yeeres: . . . By Richard Hakluyt Master of Artes, and Student sometime of Christchurch in Oxford.* London, G. Bishop and R. Newberie, Deputies to C. Barker, 1589.* 4to, 825 pp. *

Licensed by the Stationers 1 September 1589. Dedicated to Sir Francis Walsingham 17 November 1589. *

(The map taken from Ortelius, *Typus orbis terrarum.* Reprinted, with the exception of some items, in the augmented final *Voyages,* 1598–1600.)

† 1589–90. *Certain briefe, and speciall Instructions for Gentlemen, merchants, . . . employed in services abrode . . . London, J. Woolfe, 1589.* 12 mo, 30 pp.

Dedicated to Sir Francis Drake 24 January 1589(–90).

(Translated from the Latin of Albertus Meierus, *Methodus describendi regiones,* Helmstadt 1587, by Philip Jones, to whom Hakluyt suggested the patronage of Drake and perhaps the translation itself.)

† 1590. Theodore de Bry. *De commodis et incolarum ritibus Virginiae.* Frankfort 1590, 1608, 1634. Folio. Also in English, French, and German.

(Published at Hakluyt's suggestion as a translation of Thomas Hariot, *A briefe and true report of the New found land of Virginia,* London, 1588, with illustrations by John White. Hakluyt also translated, for the English edition, the legends of White's pictures.

The English version has been reprinted by Joseph Sabin and Sons, New York 1871. The illustrations were reproduced in the *Century Magazine,* November 1882 and May 1883.)

† 1591. Theodore de Bry. *Brevis narratio eorum quae in Florida Americae Provincia Gallis acciderunt.* Frankfort 1591, 1609. Folio. Also in German 1591, 1603.

(Text and illustrations by Jacques Le Moyne de Morgues, protégé of Raleigh: the publication possibly arranged by Hakluyt.

English translation, with the illustrations, published Boston 1875.)

† 1597–98. Filippo Pigafetta. *A Report of the Kingdom of Congo . . . Drawen out of the writinges and discourses of Odoardo Lopes, a Portingall* [1578] *by Philippo Pigafetta* [1591]. *Translated out of Italian by Abraham Hartwell. London, J. Wolfe, 1597.* 12mo, 217 pp.

Licensed by the Stationers 26 August 1595. Dedicated to Archbishop Whitgift 1 January 1597(–8).

(Translation suggested by Hakluyt. Two maps engraved by William Rogers.

Reprinted in *Purchas His Pilgrims,* VI. A German translation published by Theodore de Bry, Frankfort 1597. An English retranslation by Margerete Hutchinson, London 1881. The narrative was used by Defoe in *Captain Singleton.*)

† 1598. Cornelis Houtman. *The Description of a voyage made by certaine Ships of Holland into the East Indies . . . Translated out of Dutch into English by W. P(hillip). London, J. Wolfe, 1598.* 16mo, 86 pp.

Licensed by the Stationers 12 November 1597 and 17 February 1598. Dedicated to Sir James Scudamore 16 January 1598.

(Catalogued by the British Museum under the name of the Dutch publisher Langhenes.

Possibly translated at Hakluyt's suggestion. Reprinted in vol. V of Hakluyt's *Voyages,* edition of 1809–1812.)

† 1598. *John Huighen van Linschoten his Discours of Voyages into ye Easte and West Indies . . . London, J. Wolfe, 1598.* 4to, 462 pp.

Licensed 12 November 1595 and 21 June 1597. Dedicated to Julius Caesar, Master of the Court of Requests.

(Translated from the Dutch original of 1596, at Hakluyt's request, by William Philip. Twelve maps.

Reprinted as *Hakluyt Society Publications* 70,71, 1885.)

1598. *The principal Navigations, Voiages, Traffiques and Discoveries of the English Nation, made by Sea or over-land, to the remote and farthest distant Quarters of the Earth, at any time within the compasse of these 1500 yeeres . . . By Richard Hakluyt Master of Artes, and sometime Stu-*

dent of Christ-Church in Oxford. London, G. Bishop, R. Newberie, and R. Barker, 1598. Folio, 619 pp.

Not entered at the Stationers. Dedicated to Lord Howard of Effingham, Lord Admiral, 7 October 1598. *

(The first volume, containing voyages to the north and northeast. What has been considered a second edition, omitting the account of the Cadiz expedition of 1596, is dated 1599, the phrase "1500 yeeres" in the title being changed to "1600." The change was simply a rebinding, with a new title page—see J. T. Lee in New York *Nation*, 99, 628–629, 1914.)

1599. *The Second Volume of the Principal Navigations, Voyages, Traffiques and Discoveries of the English Nation, made by Sea or overland, to the South and South-east parts of the World, at any time within the compasse of these 1600 yeres. . . . By Richard Hackluyt Preacher . . . London,* the same, *1599.* Folio, 516 pages.

Dedicated to Sir Robert Cecil 24 October 1599. Map made from Molineux's globe, 1592. *

1600. *The Third and Last Volume of the Voyages, Navigations, Traffiques, and Discoveries of the English Nation, and in some few places, where they have not been, of strangers, performed within and before the time of these hundred yeeres, to all parts of the Newfound World of America . . . Collected by Richard Hakluyt Preacher . . . London,* the same, *1600.* Folio, 868 pages.

Dedicated to Sir Robert Cecil 1 September 1600. *

The *Voyages* have been reprinted as follows:

1809–12. *Hakluyt's Collection of the Early Voyages, Travels, and Discoveries of the English Nation.* London, R. H. Evans. 4 vols. folio, plus a fifth volume of supplementary items, such as the Galvano, the de Soto, and the *Decades.*

1884–90. *Principal Navigations of the English Nation.* Edited by Edmund Goldsmid. Edinburgh. 16 vols. 8vo.

1903–05. *The Principal Navigations,* etc. Reprint as *Hakluyt Society Publications, Extra Series,* by Maclehose and Sons, Glasgow. 11 vols. 8vo, plus a twelfth volume containing an index and an essay on "The English Voyages of the Sixteenth Century" by Professor Sir Walter Raleigh.

Among the partial reprints are:

1880. *Voyages of the Elizabethan Seamen to America.* Edited by E. J. Payne. Reëdited Oxford 1893–1900, 2 vols.

1903. *Voyages and Travels* (in *An English Garner*). Edited by C. R. Beazley, London. 2 vols. 8vo.

1908. *Hakluyt's Voyages.* Everyman edition, with introduction by John Masefield. 8 vols. 12mo. Reprinted, 8vo, illustrated, 1927.

1926. *A Selection of the Principal Voyages,* etc. Preface by Laurence Irving, illustrations. London. 318 pp.

Many individual items have been edited in Hakluyt Society Publications, 1846—, and also in Original Narratives of American History, New York.

† 1600–01. Leo Africanus. *A geographical Historie of Africa, Written in Arabicke and Italian by John Leo a More . . . Translated and collected by John Pory . . . London, G. Bishop, 1600.* 4to, 420 pp.

Licensed by the Stationers 1 September 1600. Dedicated to Sir Robert Cecil on "Coronation Day (15 January) 1600(-1)."

(The work started and supervised by Hakluyt. Map by Hondius.

Reprinted in the 1809–12 edition of the *Voyages,* vol. V, and as *Hakluyt Society Publications* 92, 93, 94, 1896, edited by Robert Brown.)

1601. Antonio Galvano. *The Discoveries of the World from their first originall unto the yeere . 1555. Briefly written in the Portugall tongue by Antonie Galvano, . . . Corrected, quoted, and now published in English by Richard Hakluyt . . . London, G. Bishop, 1601.* 16mo, 97 pp.

* Licensed by the Stationers 30 September 1601. Dedicated to Sir Robert Cecil 29 October 1601.

(Translated by an unknown hand from the original published at Lisbon in 1563.

Reprinted, with the original, as *Hakluyt Society Publications* 30, 1862, edited by C. R. D. Bethune.)

† 1601. Jacob van Neck. *The Journall, or Dayly Register . . . of the Voyage . . . by eight Shippes of Amsterdam . . . London, printed for C. Burby and J. Flasket, 1601.* 12mo, 126 pp.

Licensed by the Stationers 16 January 1601. Dedicated to Thomas Smith and the East India Company.

(Translated on Hakluyt's persuasion by William Walker from the Dutch account of the voyage of van Neck to the East, 1598.

Reprinted in vol. V of the 1809–12 edition of the *Voyages.*)

† 1602. John Brereton. *A Briefe and true Relation of the Discoverie of the North part of Virginia . . . London, George Bishop, 1602.* 16mo, 22 pp. 2d edit., 1602, 16mo, 46 pp.

Licensed by the Stationers 29 October 1602. Dedicated to Sir Walter Raleigh.

(Perhaps published at the instance of Hakluyt. The second edition adds the *Inducements* of the elder Hakluyt.

Reprinted in 3 *Collections Massachusetts Historical Society,* VIII, 69 ff., 1843; also, facsimile, New York 1903.)

1609. Hernando de Soto. *Virginia richly valued, By the description of the maine land of Florida, her next neighbour: out of the foure yeeres continuall travell and discoverie . . . of Don Ferdinando de Soto . . . Written by a Portugall gentleman of Elvas . . . and translated . . . by Richard Hakluyt. London, F. Kyngston for M. Lownes, 1609.* 16mo, 180 pp.

* Not entered at the Stationers. Dedicated 15 April 1609 to "The Right Honorable, the Right worshipful Counsellors and others the cheerful adventurers, for the advancement of that Christian and noble plantation in Virginia."

(Translated from the original of 1557. Reprinted in 1611 as *The worthye and famous History, of the travailes, discovery, and conquest . . . of Terra Florida. London, printed for M. Lownes, 1611.* Several times reprinted in the nineteenth century, notably as *Hakluyt Society Publications* 9, 1851, edited by William B. Rye. Retranslation by Buckingham Smith 1866, edited by E. G. Bourne, *Narratives of de Soto,* I, 1904, 1922.)

1609. Gerrit de Veer. *The True and perfect Description of three Voyages . . . performed . . . by the Ships of Holland and Zeland . . . London, Imprinted for T. Pauier, 1609.* 16mo, 81 leaves.

Licensed by the Stationers 13 June 1598 and 15 May 1609. Dedicated to Sir Thomas Smith.

(Translated at Hakluyt's instance by William Philip from the original Dutch account, 1598, of the Barents voyages.

Reprinted as *Hakluyt Society Publications* 54, 1876.)

1609. Marc Lescarbot. *Nova Francia Or the Description of that Part of New France, which is one Continent with Virginia . . . Translated . . . into English by P. E(rondelle). London, George Bishop, 1609.* 12mo, 307 pp.

Licensed by the Stationers 12 June 1609. Dedicated to Prince Henry.

(Translated, on Hakluyt's motion, from Books IV and VI of the original, of the same year. Another issue of the same, undated, was published by another printer, Andrew Hebb, after 1624.

The complete Lescarbot is translated in *Champlain Society Publications* 1, 7, and 11, 1907–14. The preface of Erondelle is reprinted in Alexander Brown, *The Genesis of the United States,* I 321.)

† 1612. Peter Martyr. *De Novo Orbe, or the Historie of the west Indies . . . newly added by the Industrie, and painefull Travaile of M. Lok, gent. London, Thomas Adams, 1612.* 16mo, 323 leaves.

Licensed by the Stationers 9 April 1612. Dedicated to Sir Julius Caesar.

(Translated at Hakluyt's instance from his Paris edition, adding the last five decades to the three translated by Richard Eden in 1555.

Other editions were issued in 1625?, 1628, and a reprint made in vol. V of the 1809 Hakluyt. A retranslation was published by F. A. McNutt, 1912, 2 vols.)

† 1614. Gothard Arthus. *Dialogues in the English and Malaiane Languages . . . First written in Latin, Malaian, and Madagascar tongues, by . . . Gotardus Arthusius . . . translated into the English tongue by Augustine Spalding, merchant . . . London, Felix Kyngston for W. Welby, 1614.* 12mo, 78 pp.

Licensed by the Stationers 9 March 1614. Dedicated to Sir Thomas Smith. *

(Brought to the attention of the East India Company by Hakluyt and perhaps translated under his supervision from the Dutch of Frederick de Houtman, 1603, or the Latin of Arthus, 1608. Published for the Company.)

† 1625. Samuel Purchas. *Purchas his Pilgrimes. London, W. Stansby for H. Fetherstone, 1625.* 5 vols., fol.

(Part I has a special title page, *Haklytus Posthumus, or Purchas his Pilgrimes.*

Reprinted as *Hakluyt Society Publications, Extra Series,* 1905–07, 20 vols.)

Hakluyt Studies

1662. Thomas Fuller. *History of the Worthies of England.* (Brief biography, under Herefordshire, vol. II, 78, 1840 edit.)

1691. Anthony à Wood. *Athenae Oxonienses.* (Brief biography, vol. II, 186, 1813 edit.)

1757. William Oldys. Article "Hakluyt," in *Biographia Britannica,* vol. IV. (The author of the article is identified by J. Bolton Corney in the pamphlet, *Facts Relative to William Oldys, Esq.,* 1837.)

1850. John Payne Collier. "On Richard Hakluyt and the American Discoveries," in *Archaeologia,* 33, 283–292.

1850. J. Winter Jones. Introduction to *Hakluyt Society Publications* 7, an edition of the *Divers Voyages.*

(Biographical introduction, with reprint of Hakluyt letters from the preceding item.)

1852. J. A. Froude. "England's Forgotten Worthies," in *Westminster Review* (July 1852), reprinted in *Short Studies on Great Subjects,* London 1867 (I 358–405, 1905 edit.).

(The article mainly concerns Hakluyt's naval records, coining incidentally the phrase "the prose epic of the modern English nation.")

1857. J. G. Kohl. *Descriptive Catalogue of Maps . . . in Hakluyt,* Washington, D. C.

1877. Charles Deane. Biographical introduction to *The Discourse on the Western Planting,* Cambridge, Mass.

1889. Note on Hakluyt's grave, in 7 *Notes and Queries,* VIII 215.

1890. J. K. Laughton. Article "Hakluyt" in *Dictionary of National Biography.*

1897. "The Jubilee of the Hakluyt Society," in *Geographical Journal,* IX 169–178.
(Mainly an address by Sir Clements Markham on Hakluyt's life and work; also printed separately.)

1901. C. W. Moulton. *Library of Literary Criticism,* Buffalo, N. Y. (excerpts from Hakluyt criticisms, I 445–446.)

1905. Walter Raleigh. *English Voyages of the Sixteenth Century,* in vol. XII of the Hakluyt Society reprint of the *Voyages;* also published separately, 1906.

1910. C. N. Robinson and John Leyland. "The Literature of the Sea," in *Cambridge History of English Literature,* vol. IV, Chapter 4.

1910. C. H. Coote and C. R. Beazley. Article "Hakluyt" in *Encyclopaedia Britannica,* 11th edition.

1911. Reproduction of photograph of tablet erected in Bristol Cathedral (Hakluyt Society pamphlet).

1916. W. P. M. Kennedy. "Richard Hakluyt, the Spirit of our Race," in *Canadian Magazine,* 46, 491–495.

1916. E. H. Morehouse. "The Tercentenary of Richard Hakluyt," in *Cornhill Magazine,* 41, 560–568.

1916. Foster Watson. "Richard Hakluyt and His Debt to Spain," in *Fortnightly Review,* 106, 827–840.

1916. "The Tercentenary of Richard Hakluyt," in *Geographical Journal,* 48, 449–456 (excerpts from Raleigh, 1906, and from the Leominster Guide, 1908, on the Eaton manors).

1917. Albert Gray. An address on the occasion of the tercentenary of the death of Richard Hakluyt (printed for the Hakluyt Society, 19 pp.).

1917. Foster Watson. "Hakluyt and Mulcaster," in *Geographical Journal,* 49, 48–53.

1921. Robert R. Cawley. *The Influence of the Voyagers in Non-Dramatic English Literature 1550–1650.* (A Harvard doctoral dissertation, printed in part as follows:
1922. "Warner and the Voyagers," in *Modern Philology,* 20, 113–147.
1923. "Drayton and the Voyagers," in *Publications Modern Language Association of America,* 38, 530–556.)

1921. Lois Whitney. "The Literature of Travel in the Faery Queene," in *Modern Philology,* 19, 143–162.

1922. George B. Parks. "Hakluyt's Mission in France 1583–1588," in *Washington University Studies,* 9, 165–184.

1924. George B. Parks. "The Ancestry of Richard Hakluyt," in 13 *Notes and Queries,* II, 235–237.

1924. Arthur W. Secord. *The Narrative Method of Defoe, University of Illinois Studies,* vol. 9, no. 1.
(On Defoe's use of Hakluyt in *Captain Singleton.*)

1924. Foster Watson. *Richard Hakluyt.* (A popular life of Hakluyt, 99 pages, in the Pioneers of Progress Series, issued by the Sheldon Press. Professor Watson has also written articles on Hakluyt in *United Empire* and the *Birmingham Daily Post.*)

1926. Robert R. Cawley. "Shakespeare's Use of the Voyagers in *The Tempest,*" in *Publications Modern Language Association of America,* 41, 688–726.

1926. Sir William Foster. "Purchas and His 'Pilgrimes,'" in *Geographical Journal,* 68, 193–200.

1926. George B. Parks. "The Forerunners of Hakluyt," in *Washington University Studies,* 13, 335–370.

1930. E. G. R. Taylor. "Samuel Purchas," in *Geographical Journal* 75, 536-539.
——*Tudor Geography.*
1934. ——*Late Tudor and Early Stuart Geography.*
1935-49. Ernest Godfrey Cox. *A Reference Guide to the Literature of Travel.* Seattle, 3 vols. (A descriptive bibliography of all travel records before 1800 which have been published in English: vol. I, The Old World; II, The New World; III, Britain.)
1936. E. G. R. Taylor, ed. *The Original Writings and Correspondence of the Two Richard Hakluyts.* 2 Hakluyt Society 76, 77.
1938. Robert R. Cawley. *The Voyagers and Elizabethan Drama.* Boston.
1940. ——*Unpathed Waters: Studies in the Influence of the Voyagers on Elizabethan Literature.* Princeton.
1940. Willis Holmes Kerr. "The Treatment of Drake's Circumnavigation in Hakluyt's *Voyages,* 1589," in *Publications Bibliographical Society of America,* 34, 281-302.
1943. Louis B. Wright. *Religion and Empire.* Chapel Hill.
1945. Howard Mumford Jones. "The Image of the New World," in *Elizabethan Studies in Honor of George Fullmer Reynolds.* Boulder, Colorado.
1946. ——"The Colonial Impulse: An Analysis of the 'Promotion' Literature of Colonization," in *Proceedings of American Philosophical Society,* 90, 131-161.
1946. James A. Williamson. "Richard Hakluyt," in *Hakluyt and His Successors,* 2 Hakluyt Society 93, 11-46.
1947. E. G. R. Taylor. "Richard Hakluyt," in *Geographical Journal* 109, 165-171.
1948. J. Hamard. "Richard Hakluyt, historien," in *Les langues modernes,* année 42, 249-259.
1955. Charles E. Armstrong. "The 'Voyage to Cadiz' in the Second Edition of Hakluyt's 'Voyages'," in *Papers of Bibliographical Society of America,* 49, 254-262.
1955. William Beckler White. *The Narrative Technique of Elizabethan Voyage and Travel Literature from 1550 to 1603.* Ph.D. dissertation, Lehigh University.
1958. Janet Hampden, ed. *Voyages and Documents.* World's Classics, Oxford University Press. (Selections from the *Voyages.*)

†1586. Antonio de Espejo. *El Viaie Qve Hizo Antonio De Espeio en el Anno de ochenta y tres . . . Impressa en Madrid anno de 1586. Y de nueuo en Paris el mesmo anno, a la costa de Richardo Hakluyt, 1586, 24mo, 16 ll.*
(A reprint of chs. 7 to 10 of part 2 of Mendoza's *China, q.v.*)

APPENDIX IV. A LIST OF ENGLISH BOOKS OF TRAVEL OVERSEAS AND GEOGRAPHICAL DESCRIPTION TO 1600

1496. *The boke of John Maundvyle* . . . (1356). Many reprints before its inclusion in *Purchas his Pilgrimes* (1625). Latin version in Hakluyt, 1589 only. Many modern eds.

[1498] *Informacon for pylgrymes vnto the holy londe,* Reprinted 1524; facsimile ed., 1893.

[1509?] Balthasar Springer. *Of the newe landes and of ye people founde by the messengers of the Kynge of portyngale named Emanuel.* Antwerp? translated from the German or Flemish version, 1598. Ed. Edward Arber in *The First Three English Books on America,* Birmingham, 1885.

1511. *The Pylgrymage of Sir Richarde Guylforde* [1506] *towardes Jherusalem.* Ed. Sir Henry Ellis, Camden Society 51, 1851.

[1518] *The Pylgrymage of Sir Richard Torkyngton Person of Mulberton in Norffolke. And how he went towardys Jherusalem.* Ed from Ms., BM Addit. 28561-62, by W. J. Loftie, 1884.

1522. Robert Langton. *The pylgrimage of Robert Langton clerke to saynt James in Compostell.* Ed. E. M. Blackie, Cambridge, Mass., 1924.

[1528?] Pierre Garcie. *The Rutter of the Sea, . . . with the Havens, Rodes, Soundings,* . . . Translated by Robert Copland from the *Routier de la Mer,* Rouen, n.d. Reprinted [1550?], [1553?], [1587?], the last adding "A newe Rutter of the Sea, for the North parties."

1533. Damião de Góis. *The legacye or embassate of prester John* [of Abyssinia) *vnto Emanuell, Kynge of Portyngale.* Translated by John More from the *Legatio . . . Presbyteri Johannis,* Antwerp [1532?]

1541. Roger Barlow. *A Brief Summe of Geographie.* [A world pilot, based on Martín Fernández de Enciso, *Suma de geographia,* Seville 1519, 1530, 1546.] Ed. from Ms., BM Royal 18. B. xxviii, by E. G. R. Taylor, 2 Hakluyt Society 69, 1932.

1541. Benedetto Ramberti. *The order of the Great Turckes courte* . . . Translated via the French from *Libri tre delle Cose de Turchi,* Venice 1539.

1541. John Rotz. *The Boke of Idrography.* [An atlas]. Ms., BM Royal 20.E.ix. (See figs. 3, 9, 24 above.)

1542. Nicolas Durand de Villegagnon. *A lamentable and piteous Treatise . . . the high Enterprise and Valiauntness of th'emperour Charles the V . . . to the Towne of Argier in Affrique* . . . Translated from *Caroli V. Imperatoris Expeditio in Africam* . . ., Paris, 1542. Reprinted *Harleian Miscellany,* vol. IV.

1546. Paolo Giovio. *A shorte treatise vpon the Turckes Chronicles.* Translated by Peter Ashton from the Latin version of *Commentarii delle cose de Turchi,* Venice 1531.

1549. William Thomas. *The historie of Italie.* Repr. 1561.

[1550?] Giosafatte Barbaro. [Travels to Tana and Persia, 1436-52 and 1471]. Translated by William Thomas from the *Viaggi fatti in Tana, in Persia* . . ., Venice 1543; his Ms., BM Royal 17.C.x, ed. Lord Stanley, Hakluyt Society 49, 1873.

1553. Richard Eden. *A treatyse of the Newe India.* Translated from Book v of Sebastian Münster. *Cosmographia unversalis,* Basel 1550. Repr. Edward Arber in *The First Three English Books on America,* Birmingham, 1885.

1554. William Prat. *The Discription of the Contrey of Aphrique.* Translated from a French version of Johannes Boemus, *De omnium Gentium ritibus,* Augsburg 1520, later *Omnium Gentium Mores.*

1555. William Watreman. *The Fardle of facions . . . of the peoples . . . of Affrike and Asie.* Translated from books i and ii of the same. Repr. in vol. V of the 1812 edition of Hakluyt.

[1555] Thomas Hoby. *A Booke of the Travaile and Lief of Me Thomas Hoby.* [diary of travels in Europe 1547-55]. Ms., BM Egerton 2148, ed. Edgar Powell in Camden Society *Miscellany* X, 1902.

[1555] *The Journey of the Queen's Ambassadors unto Rome, anno 1555.* Ms. BM Harleian 252, ff. 49-73, part ed. in [Philip Lord Hardwicke], *Miscellaneous State Papers,* I, 62-102, 1778.

1555. Pietro Martire d'Anghiera. *The Decades of the newe worlde or west India.* Translated by Richard Eden from the *De Orbe novo Decades,* Alcalá 1516, and the *De nuper repertis insulis,* Basel 1521, with many additions (see p. 22 above). Repr. Edward Arber, *The First Three English Books on America,* Birmingham 1885.

——A second edition, adding among others a translation by Eden of Ludovico Varthema's *Itinerario* (1510) to the East Indies, was completed by Richard Willes as *The History of Travayle in the West and East Indies,* 1577.

1559. William Cunningham. *The Cosmographical Glasse.*

1561. George North. *The Description of Swedland, Gotland, and Finland . . . Collected and gathered chieflye out of Sebastian Mounster.* Translated from the Cosmographia, Basel 1550. Repr. Scholars' Facsimiles, 1946.

1562. Andrea Cambini. *Two very notable Commentaries, The One of the Originall of the Turcks . . . and thother of the warres of the Turcke against George Scanderbeg.* Translated by John Shute from the *Libro della origine de Turchi,* Florence 1529, etc.

1562. Anthony Jenkinson. *Russiae Moscoviae et Tartariae Descriptio.* [A map, published London]. Repr. Abraham Ortelius, *Theatrum orbis terrarum* [an atlas], Antwerp 1570 *et seq.,* no. 46. (See fig. 6 above).

1563. Jean Ribaut. *The whole and true discoverye of Terra Florida.* Translated from the French. Repr. Hakluyt, *Divers Voyages,* 1582, and *Principal Navigations,* 1600. The Ms., BM Sloane 3644, ff. 112-121, ed. with variants from the book by H. P. Biggar, *English Historical Review* 32, 253-270, 1917.

[1563] Richard Smith. *The Jorney of Sir Edward Unton . . . into Italy.* Ms., BM Sloane 1813, ff. 4-55; part. ed. A. H. S. Yeames in *Papers of the British School at Rome,* 7, 92-113, 1914.

[1566] William Hack. [Ms. maps of Newfoundland: BM Addit. 13,972, and King's Drawings 119, 9].

1566. Nicholas LeChalleux. *A True and perfect . . . description, of the last voyage . . . by Capitaine John Rybaut . . . into Terra Florida . . .* Translated from the *Discours et Histoire de la Floride,* Dieppe 1566. Repr. Stephen Lorant, *The New World,* New York 1946.

1568. André Thevet. *The New founde worlde, or Antarctike.* Translated by Thomas Hackit from *Les Singularitez de la France antarctique,* Paris 1558.

1569. John Hawkins. *A true Declaration of the troublesome voyadge . . . to Guynea and the West Indies.* Repr. Hakluyt 1589, 1600.

[1570?] Bartholomaeus Georgievitz. *The ofspring of the house of Ottomano, and officers pertaining to the greate Turkes Court.* Translated by Hugh Gough from the *De Origine Imperii Turcorum,* Wittenberg 1562.

1572. Sebastian Münster. *A Briefe Collection and compendious extract of straunge and memorable thinges.* Anon. translator. Repr. 1574.

1575. Hieronymus Turler. *The Traveiler.* Translated from *De Peregrinatione, et Agro Neapolitano,* Strasbourg 1574. Repr. Scholars' *Facsimiles,* 1951.

1576. Sir Humfrey Gilbert. *A Discourse of a Discoverie for a new Passage to Cataia.* Repr. Hakluyt, 1589, 1600. Ed. D. B. Quinn in 2 Hakluyt Society 83, 1940.

1576. Richard Rowlands. *The Post of the World. Wherein is contayned the antiquities and originall of the most famous Cities in Europe.* Translated from an unidentified German source.

1577. Nicolás Monardes. *Joyfull Newes out of the newe founde worlde.* Part translated by John Frampton from *Historia Medicinal de . . . nuestras Indias Occidentales,* Seville 1574. Repr. 1580; complete translation, 1596. Repr. Tudor Translations, 1925, 2 vols.

[1577?] *The strange and marveilous newes lately come from the great Kingdome of Chyna. Translated out of the Castlyn tongue by T. N*[icholas?].

1577. Dionyse Settle. *A true report of the laste voyage into the West and Northwest regions . . . 1577, . . . by Capteine Frobisher.* Repr. Hakluyt 1589, 1600. Translated French, Geneva 1578; German, Nuremberg 1580; Latin, *ibid.,* 1580; Italian, Naples, 1582. Ed. V. Stefansson in *Three Voyages of Martin Frobisher,* 1938.

1578. George Best. *A true Discourse of the late voyages of discoverie, for the finding of a passage to Cathaya, by the Northweast.* Repr. Hakluyt, 1600. Ed. V. Stefansson, *ibid.*

1578. Thomas Ellis. *A true report of the third and last voyage into Meta Incognita: atchieved by . . . Frobisher.* Repr. Hakluyt, 1589, 1600. Ed. V. Stefansson, *ibid.*

1578. Martin Fernández de Enciso. *A Briefe Description of the Portes, Creekes, Bayes and Havens, of the Weast India.* Translated by John Frampton from the *Suma de geographia,* Seville 1519 *et seq.*

1578. Francisco López de Gómara. *The Pleasant Historie of the Conquest of the Weast India . . . by . . . Hernando Cortes.* Translated by Thomas Nicholas from *La Istoria de las Indias, y Conquista de Mexico,* Saragossa 1552, etc. Repr. Scholars' Facsimiles, 1940.

1579. Bernardino de Escalante. *A discourse of the navigation which the Portugales doe make to . . . the East partes of the world.* Translated by John Frampton from the *Discurso de la navigacion,* Seville 1577.

1579. *An excellent Discourse of Jhon Fox an inglishman who Delivered 266 Christians* [*from the galleys at Alexandria*]. Repr. Hakluyt 1589, 1600. Expanded as *The Admirable Deliverance of 266 Christians by John Reynard Englishman,* 1608.

1579. Marco Polo. *The most noble and famous travels of Marcus Paulus . . . into the East partes of the world.* Translated by John Frampton from the Spanish version, *Cosmographia breve,* Seville 1503, etc. Ed. N. M. Penzer, 1929.

[c. 1580] William Borough. [Chart of the Northern Ocean, above Russia]. Ms., pr. in Hakluyt, vol. III (1905 ed.)

1580. Jacques Cartier. *A shorte and briefe narration,* etc. See p. 262 above.

1580. John Dee. [A map of North America]. Ms., BM Cotton Augustus I i 1, pr. in Hakluyt, vol. VIII (1905 ed.)

[1580] Francis Fletcher. *The First part of the second voiage about the world . . . by Mr Ffrancis Drake.* Ms., BM Sloane 61, ed. Sir R. C. Temple, *The World Encompassed,* 1926.

1580. Johannes Boemus. *A Discoverie of the countries of Tartaria, Scithia, & Cathaya.* Translated by John Frampton from the Spanish version of Francisco Thamara, Antwerp 1556.

1581. Gregory Martin. *Roma Sancta.* Ms., owned by Lord Clifford of Chudleigh, describing (in English) the religious and charitable institutions of the city of Rome.

1581. Augustín de Zárate. *The . . . History of the discoverie and Conquest of the Provinces of Peru.* Translated by Thomas Nicholas from the *Historia del descubrimiento y conquista del Peru,* Antwerp 1555, etc. Ed. D. B. Thomas, 1933.

1582. Richard Hakluyt. *Divers voyages . . .* See p. 262 above.

1582. Fernão Lopes de Castanheda. *The first Booke of the Historie of the Discoverie and Conquest of the East Indias . . .* Translated by Nicholas Lichfeild from the *Historia do descobrimento,* book i, Coimbra 1551.

1582. Anthony Munday. *The English Romayne Life. Discovering: The lives of the Englishmen at Roome.* Repr. 1590. Ed. G. B. Harrison, 1925.

[1583] Christopher Carleill. *A discourse upon the extended Voyage to the hethermost partes of America.* Repr. Hakluyt 1589, 1600.

1583. [Sir] G[eorge] P[eckham]. *A true Reporte, Of the late discoveries, and possession . . . of the New-found Landes: By Sir Humfrey Gilbert.* Repr. Hakluyt 1589, 1600. Ed. D. B. Quinn, 2 Hakluyt Society 84, 1940.

1583. Bartolomé de las Casas. *The Spanish Colonie, or Briefe Chronicle of the Acts and gestes of the Spaniardes in the West Indies.* Translated by M. M. S. from the French version, Antwerp 1579, of the *Brevissima relacion de la destruycion de las Indias,* Seville, 1552.

1583. [Thomas Nichols]. *A Pleasant description of the fortunate Ilandes, called the Ilands of Canaria.* Repr. Hakluyt, 1599.

1584. Richard Hakluyt. *A Particular Discourse,* etc. See p. 261 above.

1584. Robert Norman. *The Safegard of Sailers, or great Rutter* [for northern Europe]. Translated from the Dutch. Repr. 1587, 1590, 1600; augmented by Edward Wright, 1605, 1612, 1640, 1671.

1585. Humphrey Mote. *The Primrose of London with her valiant adventure on the Spanish coast.* Repr. Hakluyt, 1599.

1585. Nicolas de Nicolay, Seigneur d'Arfeuille. *The Navigations, peregrinations and voyages, made into Turkie.* Translated by Thomas Washington the younger from *Les quatre premiers livres des navigations et peregrinations orientales,* Lyon 1568, etc.

1585. Marc'Antonio Pigafetta. *Itinerario,* etc. See p. 262 above.

1586, 1587. Antonio de Espejo. *El Viaje,* etc. See pp. 262, 269 above.

1586, 1587. René de Laudonnière. *L'Histoire notable de la Floride,* etc. See p. 263 above.

1587. Henry Haslop. *Newes out of the Coast of Spain* [of Drake's raid on Cadiz].

1587. Robert Leng. *The True Discripcion of the last voiage . . . of Sir Frauncis Drake . . .* Ms., ed. Clarence Hopper, Camden Society *Miscellany* V, 1863.

1587. Pietro Martire d'Anghiera. *De orbe novo.* See p. 263 above.

1587. Thomas Saunders. *A true Discription . . . Of a most lamentable Voiage, made lately* [1584-85] *to Tripolie in Barbarie, in a Ship named the Jesus. Set foorth by Thomas Saunders, one of those Captives.* Repr. Hakluyt 1589, 1599.

1587. John White. [Map of Virginia and Florida]. Ms., BM Prints Department, pr. in Hakluyt, vol. III (1905 ed.), in 2 Hakluyt Society 77, 1935.

1588. Cesare Federici. *The Voyage and Travaile of Caesar Frederick . . . into the East India.* Translated by Thomas Hickok from the *Viaggio nell'India Orientale,* Venice 1587. Repr. Hakluyt, 1599.

1588. Thomas Hariot. *A briefe and True Report of the new found Land of Virginia.* Repr. Hakluyt 1589, 1600; ed. D. B. Quinn in 2 Hakluyt Society 105, 1955. Translated into Latin, French, German, in the Grands Voyages of Theodor de Bry, Frankfort 1590, together with engravings of the watercolors of John White. Repr., with the watercolors, in Stephen Lorant, *The New World,* 1946.

1588. Lucas Wagenaer. *The Mariners Mirrour . . . in divers exact Sea-charts.* Translated and adapted by Anthony Ashley from *Spieghel der Zeevaert,* Amsterdam 1584, or the Latin, Leyden 1586.

1589. Thomas Cates. *A Summarie and True Discourse of Sir Frances Drakes West Indian Voyage* [1585]. Repr. 1589; by Hakluyt, 1600. Translated into Latin, Leyden 1588, and Nuremberg 1590; into French, Leyden 1588; into German, Nuremberg 1589.

1589. Richard Hakluyt. *The Principall Navigations,* etc. See p. 263 above.

1589. Juan Gonzalez de Mendoza. *The Historie of the great and mightie kingdome of China.* Translated by Robert Parke from the *Historia del gran reyno de la China,* Madrid 1586. Ed. Sir G. T. Staunton in Hakluyt Society 14, 15, 1854.

1589. Petruccio Ubaldini. *A Discourse concerninge the Spanish fleete invading Englande in the yeare 1588.* Translated for Augustine Ryther from the Italian. Repr. *Harleian Miscellany,* I; Roxburghe Club, 1919. Retranslation from a more complete Ms. ed. G. P. B. Naish, Navy Records Society, 1952.

1589. [Anthony Wingfield]. *A True Coppie of a Discourse . . .* [on] *the late Voyage of Spaine and Portingale.* Repr. Hakluyt, 1599; Purchas, 1625. Translated into Latin, Frankfort 1590, and Nuremberg, 1590; into German, Munich [1590].

1590. Edward Webbe. *The Rare and most wonderful thinges which Edward Webbe . . . hath seen and passed in his troublesome travailes, in the Landes of Jewrie, Egipt, Gtecia, Russia, and the Land of Prester John.* 3 eds. 1590; repr. 1600; ed. Edward Arber, 1868.

1591. Giles Fletcher. *Of the Russe Common Wealth.* Repr. Purchas, 1625. Ed. E. A. Bond, Hakluyt Society 20, 1856.

1591. Sir Jerome Horsey. *A Relacion or Memoriall abstracted owt of . . . his Travells, Imploiments, Services and Negociacions* [in Russia, 1573-91]. Ms. Harleian 1813, ed. E. A. Bond in Hakluyt Society 20, 1856.

1591. Job Hortop. *The Rare Travailes of Job Hortop, an Englishman* [left by Hawkins in Mexico, 1569]. Repr. 1591; by Hakluyt, 1600.

1591. [Sir Walter Ralegh.] *A report of the Truth of the fight about the Iles of Açores . . . Betwixt The Revenge . . . and an Armada.* Repr. Hakluyt, 1599.

1592. [John Eliot] *The Survey or Topographical Description of France.* Repr. 1593.

1592. Thomas Hood. [Sailing Chart of Atlantic coast of Europe and Africa from the Orkneys to the Cape Verde islands.] Repr. in Hakluyt, vol. VI (1905 ed.)

1592. Emery Molineux. [A terrestrial globe.] See fig. 26 above.

1593. Ludovico Guicciardini. *The Description of the Low countreys.* Translated by Thomas Danett from the *Descrittione di tutti i Paesi Bassi,* Antwerp 1567, *et seq.*

1594. H[enry] R[oberts]. *Newes from the Levane Seas. Discribing the many perilous events of Edward Glemham, Esquire* [in a privateering voyage of 1593].

1594. William Smith. *Breef Description of the famous Cittie of Norenberg.* Ms., Lambeth 508.

1595. Christian Adrichomius. *A briefe Description of Hierusalem and of the Suburbs therof.* Translated by Thomas Tymme from the *Jerusalem et suburbarum descriptio,* Cologne 1584.

1595. John Davis. *The Worldes Hydrographicall Discription.* Repr. Hakluyt Society 59, 1880.

1595. Richard Hasleton. *Strange and Wonderfull Things happened . . . in his*

Ten yeares Travailes [1582-93, in slavery to the Moors and in the prisons of the Spanish Inquisition]. Repr. C. R. Beazley in *Voyages and Travels,* 1903.

[1595] Thomas Maynarde. *Sir Francis Drake his Voyages,* 1595. Ms., BM Addit. 5209, ed. W. D. Cooley, Hakluyt Society 4, 1849.

1595. Giovanni Tommaso Minadoi. *The History of the Warres betweene the Turkes and the Persians.* Translated by Abraham Hartwell from the *Historia della guerra fra Turchi e Persiani,* Venice 1588.

1595. Henry Roberts. *Lancaster his Allarums, honorable Assaultes, and supprising of block-houses in Brasill.* Ed. Sir William Foster in 2 Hakluyt Society 85, 1940.

1596. Sir Walter Ralegh. *The Discoverie of the Large Rich, and Bewtifull Empyre of Guiana.* 4 eds. 1596; repr. Hakluyt, 1600. Numerous reprints, ed. V. T. Harlow, 1928. Translated into German, Nuremberg 1598, etc., Dutch, Amsterdam 1598, etc., Latin, Nuremberg 1599, etc.

[1596] Sir Walter Ralegh. [Map of Guiana]. Ms., BM Map Room, printed in Hakluyt, vol. X (1905 ed.)

1596. Lawrence Keymis. *A Relation of the second Voyage to Guiana.* Repr. Hakluyt, 1600. Translated into Latin, Frankfort 1599; Dutch, Amsterdam 1605.

[1596]. Sir William Slingsby. *The voyadge to Calis in Andaluzia.* Ms. Alnwick, ed. J. S. Corbett, Navy Records Society, 1902.

1597. Jean DuBec-Crispin. *The Historie of the Great Emperour Tamerlan.* Translated by H. M. from the *Histoire du grand Empereur Tamerlanes,* Rouen 1595.

1597. Philippus Lonicerus. *The Policy of the Turkish Empire.* Translated anon. from *Chronicorum Turcicorum Tomus Primus,* Frankfort 1578.

1597. Filippo Pigafetta. *A Report of the Kingdom of Congo.* See p. 264.

1598-1600. Richard Hakluyt. *The principal Navigations . . .* See pp. 264-65.

1598. *The Description of a Voyage . . .* See p. 264.

1598. Cornelis Geritszoon. *An Addition to the Sea Journal . . . of the Hollanders unto Java.* Translated from the *Appendix ofte Byvoechsel . . .,* Middelburg 1598.

1598. *John Huighen van Linschoten . . . his Discours of Voyages . . .* See p. 264.

1599. *The Theatre of the Earth. Containing very short and compendious descriptions of all countries . . . in alphabeticall order.* Repr. 1601.

1599. [George Abbot] *A Briefe Description of the whole worlde, Wherein Is Particularly described, all the Monarchies, Empires, and kingdomes of the same.* Repr. 1600, 1605, 1608, 1617, 1620, 1624, 1636, 1664.

1599. Gasparo Contarini. *The Common-wealth and Government of Venice.* Translated by Lewis Lewknor from the Italian version, 1544, etc., of the *De Magistratibus et Republica Venetorum,* Paris 1543.

1599. *The Conquest of the Grand Canaries, made . . . by threescore and thirteene saile of* [Dutch] *shippes.*

1599. *A True Report of the gainefull, prosperous and speedy voiage* [1598-99] *to Java . . . by . . . eight ships of Amsterdam.* Translated from the Dutch. Reprin. in 1812 Hakluyt, vol. V.

1599. Edward Wright. "The Voyage of the Right Ho. George Earle of Cumberland to the Azores": in *Certaine Errors in Navigation.* Repr. Hakluyt, 1599.

1600. Leo Africanus. *A geographical Historie of Africa . . .* See p. 265 above.

1600. Girolamo Conestaggio. "The description of Portugall . . . Of the East Indies . . ." in *The Historie of the uniting of the Kingdom of Portugall to the Crowne of Castill.* Translated for Edward Blunt from *Dell' Unione del Regno di Portogallo,* Genoa 1585.

[1600]. Thomas Dallam. [The Diary of a voyage to Constantinople 1599-1600] Ms., ed. J. T. Bent, Hakluyt Society 87, 1893.

1600. *The Mahumetane or Turkish Historie.* Translated Raffe Carr [from various sources].

1600. *A True Report of Sir Anthony Shierlies Journey . . . to Persia.* Repr. Sir E. D. Ross in *Sir Anthony Shirley and his Persian Adventure,* 1933.

1600. *A true Report of a great Fight at sea between certaine Ships . . . of England and five . . . ships of warre of the King of Spaines.*

1600. Ellert de Jonghe. *The True and perfect declaration of the mighty army by sea under . . . Peter Vander Does.* Translated from the *Waerachtigh verhael vande machtighe Scheeps-Armade,* Amsterdam 1600.

1600. *A true Report and description of the taking of the Iland of St. Maries 1599.* Translated from the Dutch.

INDEX